Prophetic Interruptions

Prophetic Interruptions

Critical Theory, Emancipation, and Religion in Paul Tillich, Theodor Adorno, and Max Horkheimer (1929-1944)

Bryan L. Wagoner

MERCER UNIVERSITY PRESS
Macon, Georgia
2017

MUP/ H944

Published by Mercer University Press
1501 Mercer University Drive
Macon, Georgia 31207

9 8 7 6 5 4 3 2 1

Books published by Mercer University Press are printed on acid-free paper that meets the requirements of the American National Standard for Information Sciences—Permanence of Paper for Printed Library Materials.

ISBN 978-0-88146-634-8
Cataloging-in-Publication Data is available from the Library of Congress

To Corin and Tobias,
in hopes for their courage to interrupt injustice

Contents

Commonly Used Abbreviations

AP: "The Actuality of Philosophy" (Adorno)
ATR: *Against the Third Reich* (Tillich)
BPSS: *Between Philosophy and Social Science* (Horkheimer)
CT: *Critical Theory* (Horkheimer)
DA: *Dialektik der Aufklärung* (Adorno and Horkheimer)
DE: *Dialectic of Enlightenment* (Adorno and Horkheimer)
DD: *Dawn and Decline* (Horkheimer)
Entwurf: *Entwurf Contra Paulum* (Adorno)
ER: *Eclipse of Reason* (Horkheimer)
GS: *Gesammelte Schriften* (Horkheimer OR Adorno)
GW: *Gesammelte Werke* (Tillich)
INH: "The Idea of Natural History" (Adorno)
KT: *Kritische Theorie* (Horkheimer)
MSRS: "Man and Society in Religious Socialism" (Tillich)
MW/HW: *Main Works / Haupt Werke* (Tillich)
PCCP: "Protestantism as a Critical and Cultural Principle," in *Political Expectation* (Tillich)
PE: *Political Expectation* (Tillich)
SD: *Socialist Decision* (Tillich)
SE: *Sozialistische Entscheidung* (Tillich)
TCT: "Traditional and Critical Theory," in *Critical Theory* (Horkheimer)
ZfS: *Zeitschrift für Sozialforschung* (Journal of the Institute of Social Research)

Preface

The two most obvious and seemingly compelling paths for articulating a connection between the German-American philosopher of religion Paul Tillich, and the critical social philosophers Max Horkheimer and Theodor Adorno, are precluded from the start. First, textual evidence does not support the claim that there is any definitive 'mutual influence,' as several colleagues and early readers urged me to argue. It would have been far easier, and in some senses preferable, to shape this book if the research substantiated a central theme of a mutual influence, but I am convinced it warrants neither, as chapter one demonstrates.

Secondly, some scholars have made arguments for treating Adorno as a type of political theologian, and if the arguments were compelling, a relatively easy connection with Tillich could be articulated. Yet it is not 'theology' of any sort that ultimately unites Adorno, Horkheimer, and Tillich. The few scholarly attempts to make such an argument have been entirely unpersuasive and represent conceptual leaps which the textual evidence does not substantiate outside of very narrow parameters. Clearly, Tillich offers a critical and political theology through his religious socialism, and at points, the early Adorno and (particularly the late) Horkheimer, to varying extents, gesture toward a critical or inverse theology. Nevertheless, the textual evidence does not support the broader thematic claim that there is any 'theology' (political, critical, etc.) that binds the three thinkers, nor that what binds them can or should be characterized as 'theology.' Furthermore, the word 'theology' is contested in multiple realms of academic discourse; I believe this appellation, particularly if claimed as a definitive linkage among the three thinkers, is also unsupported by textual evidence and its use would merely allow critical theory and Frankfurt School scholars to continue ignoring Tillich, and for theologians to continue to marginalize the constructive role of critical theory.

Acknowledgments

I am profoundly grateful for the support and feedback I have received from wise mentors and professors at Harvard, including Francis Schüssler Fiorenza, Peter E. Gordon, Harvey Cox, Gordon D. Kaufman, Sarah Coakley, and Ronald Thiemann, among many others, and David Kelsey, Serene Jones, and Seyla Benhabib at Yale. Their collective wisdom laid the foundations for this work. Many colleagues, including Derek Nelson, Philip Francis, Rebekka King, Curtis Thompson, Kevin Starcher, Frederick Parrella, Jill Peterfeso, Nikolaus Wandinger, Eva Pascal, Matthew Freeman, Peter Slater, Laura Brekke, Robert McCutcheon, Marty DeNicolo, and Brent Saindon have strengthened this book through feedback and advice, both specific and general. Julia Ritter was a great help in the initial translation of Adorno's complex *Entwurf*, here an Appendix. Three exceptional students at Davis & Elkins College, Kaïa Kater-Hurst, Emily Coffman, and Sabrina Pößl, have provided invaluable perspective and they have each significantly helped me with the many necessary revisions. My gratitude extends first and foremost to my parents, George and Susan Wagoner, for their years of support, to my sister Anne Wagoner-Ford, and particularly to my wonderful sons, Corin and Tobias. Any and all errors are mine, and mine alone.

Introduction

This work commences by demonstrating several substantial yet little-known personal and contextual connections shared by Paul Tillich and members of the 'Frankfurt School' of critical social theory, with primary and central focus on Max Horkheimer and Theodor W. Adorno. The study specifically focuses on the period between 1929 and 1944, with some attention to texts and conversations until 1950, representing the fruitfully collaborative years in Frankfurt (1929-33), and their interactions during the exilic years in the United States (1933-50).[1] In 1929, Paul Tillich, a Protestant theologian and philosopher, was called to fill the chair of philosophy and sociology at the young University of Frankfurt where Horkheimer was a colleague and Adorno his advisee. It was during these years (1929-33) that the most regular direct contact and collaboration between Tillich, Horkheimer, and Adorno took place, under the growing shadow of National Socialism. All three were exiled for their anti-Nazi viewpoints (and the Jewish heritage shared by Adorno and Horkheimer), emigrating to New York City, where they continued to be in close personal conversation.

The limited extant scholarship engaging Tillich's critical social philosophy in the context of, or in conversation with, the critical theory tradition commonly referred to as the Frankfurt School[2] comes primarily from religious studies

---

[1] This choice of period and limiting dates is somewhat arbitrary, but it is relatively common, particularly among Adorno and Horkheimer scholars, to distinguish the exilic and post-exilic periods in their thought. Among Tillich scholars, a more common distinction is drawn between Tillich's 'German period,' through 1933, and his 'American period,' from 1933 until his death in 1965, although this has severe limitations when interpreting Tillich. I have chosen to limit the scope to 1944, with limited attention continuing until 1950, not only because this fits most easily with Frankfurt School scholarship, but also because this general period in the late 1940s marks a transition in Tillich's writings toward systematic and explicitly theological reflection, with the first volume of his *Systematic Theology* being published in 1951. It is in 1943 and 44 that we see Adorno's critique of Tillich, explored in chapter three and translated here as an appendix, and from the publication of *Dialectic of Enlightenment*, Adorno and Horkheimer generally reflect a bleaker outlook on society than Tillich was willing to do.

[2] The term 'Frankfurt School' is itself misleading, as will be explored in subsequent chapters. For the immediate purposes of the introduction, this phrase refers to members, affiliates and associates of the Institute for Social Research/*Institut für Sozialforschung* in

scholars rather than critical theorists or intellectual historians. Nearly all of the scholars who have noted any connection have rather narrowly focused on the question of the presence of any definitive 'mutual influence' between Tillich and the Frankfurt School, with scant attention given to significant points of historical and intellectual confluence between Tillich and individual Frankfurt theorists,[3] especially Adorno and Horkheimer, on specific issues of common importance and their frequent dialogues.

This study pursues this overlooked intellectual matrix further, engaging in a work of intellectual history leading to contemporary questions of philosophical and political import. Although Tillich on the one hand, and Horkheimer and Adorno on the other, do not directly refer to one another in their published writings during their lifetimes,[4] there are numerous compelling reasons to suggest that Tillich's thought can be profitably illuminated in light of his personal relationships with Horkheimer and Adorno, along with their similar scholarly orientations, interests, concerns, and goals. And the same must be said for Horkheimer and Adorno: by reference to their life-long personal and intellectual engagements with Tillich, certain aspects of their work can be seen anew. It is hoped that in this light, renewed possibilities for constructive dialogue between critical theory and religious studies might emerge, just as Tillich, Adorno, and Horkheimer pursued.[5]

Frankfurt, Germany, during the 1920s until 1933. The term will be challenged and nuanced below.

[3] The most obvious sources for understanding the relation between these figures would seem to be the numerous essays by Adorno, Horkheimer, and other members of the Frankfurt School, written about Tillich and his friendships with and influence on them after Tillich's death; these are collected in various *Festschriften*. However, since these are occasionally elegiac in tone and style and far removed temporally from the period in question, most of them will be omitted from this study.

[4] In their lecture notes, many of which have been published in the past decade, we do see Tillich quoting Horkheimer in 1935, for example: *Frühe Vorlesungen im Exil* (1934-1935) in *Ergänzungs-und Nachlassbände zu den Gesammelten Werken von Paul Tillich,* hrsg. von Erdmann Sturm (Berlin: Walter de Gruyter, 2012) Bd. 17, 316. Likewise, there are mentions of Tillich's ideas (and recollections of him as an individual) in the lecture notes of both Horkheimer and Adorno, but all of these reflect *Nachlassen*, remainder texts based on lecture notes, etc., which were not published in their lifetimes.

[5] Some contemporary social, political, and economic critiques, from thinkers like Terry Eagleton, David Harvey, and Thomas Piketty have very recently drawn attention to the nexus of concerns raised by Tillich, Horkheimer, and Adorno and examined in detail here, but the parameters of this book do not allow pursuit of these contemporary iterations of similar themes.

English-language Paul Tillich scholarship exhibits, and continues to reveal, an unwarranted bias toward the later 'American' (and explicitly theological) Tillich as a more 'mature' expression of his thought, often overlooking the riches of Tillich's philosophical work in Germany. Similarly, much of the scholarship engaging the core members of the Frankfurt School, especially Adorno and Horkheimer, both in Frankfurt and in exile in the United States, engages their work in isolation from a hermeneutically significant contextual dimension: the personal and intellectual confluences of Tillich's 'religious socialism' and early independent formulations of critical theory by Horkheimer, and, to a lesser extent, Adorno.

One orienting claim of this study *vis-à-vis* much of the extant scholarship is that the numerous historical connections outlined in chapter one do not amount to evidence of traceable 'mutual influence,' much less interdependence. Instead, the argument is that the similarities and differences among these three thinkers are best approached contextually and through thematic 'dialogue.' Seeking to avoid the trap of 'influence,' this work identifies and exposes new avenues of comparative critical analysis and engages these three thinkers through an examination of four themes: emancipatory rationality, anthropology, metaphysics, and religion. Centrally, the argument is that that the projects of critical theory and religious socialism are complementary emancipatory solutions to a common view of instrumental rationality and threats to subjectivity like alienation, domination, and reification. The ongoing direct personal and professional contact among these thinkers, along with their shared intellectual milieu and social goals warrants such an endeavor and vivifies the comparison. This is an important moment of intellectual history to reevaluate and examine as a point of reference for potential dialogue between critical theory, religious studies, and public philosophy.

I. Central Argument

This book centers on the claim that the central commonality shared by Adorno, Horkheimer, and Tillich is illumined by the category of 'prophetic interruptions.' There are both common critiques and parallel methodologies of 'prophetic interruptions,' together questioning a bankrupt modernity violating human agency. These shared interruptions simultaneously reflect the sources of the key differences revealed among Tillich, Adorno, and Horkheimer. The collective 'prophetic interruptions' among the three thinkers have a common goal of naming and remediating injustices, and of interrupting forms that inhibit individual and collective agency. The word 'prophetic' is used throughout to connote a combined power and will both to *denounce* and *announce*. While there are in-eliminable echoes of religious language in the word prophetic, the book problematizes any facile equation of 'prophetic' and 'religious.' The prophetic is here clearly rooted in the Jewish prophets who inspired all three, but it is increasingly a productive secular category, for Adorno in particular. After delineating what is meant by 'prophetic interruptions' more clearly, I will show that Tillich prophetically interrupts both theology (including his own Lutheran tradition) and social philosophy, while Adorno and Horkheimer prophetically interrupt what they see as the cancer of a modernity that violates human subjectivity. Tillich's distinction between rational and prophetic criticism attempts an unmediated interruption; he seeks to re-instill a prophetic, religious element in socialism via the humanism of the early Marx. Adorno's secular messianism, influenced by Benjamin, demands a prophetic denunciation of injustice shared by Horkheimer. Prophetic power empowers emancipatory agency, and I argue that Tillich's grounded approach provides distinct supplemental resources.

Thus, herein I make the deceptively straightforward claim that there are substantial historical, personal, and ideological connections shared among Adorno, Horkheimer, and Tillich, and that these commonalities, when situated around the category of 'prophetic interruptions' serve as a fruitful basis for the comparison of their differences in four central areas: emancipatory rationality, anthropology, metaphysics, and religion. It is my contention that through such comparison, we are better enabled not only to understand these thinkers in relationship to one another, but that such inquiry also yields important insights into the depth and breadth of each thinker and their shared milieu. By placing key writings of these three thinkers in conversation, precisely during the period in which they were most actively involved in personal conversation and debate with one another, this work reveals new avenues for productive inquiry, both normative and in intellectual history. No substantial extant scholarship has attempted this, and the 'exilic' period from the mid-1930s into the late-1940s has been roundly ignored in this respect.[6] Some of the relevant materials examined in this

[6] Gary Simpson (*Critical Social Theory*) and Christopher Brittain (*Adorno and Theology*) are among the few recent scholars who make even brief references to points of comparison between Tillich and the Frankfurt School. John Abromeit's work, *Max Horkheimer and the Foundations of the Frankfurt School*, is helpful in this regard, but it almost entirely ignores Tillich, with only 3 superficial references in a substantial work of intellectual history.

work were not available until the 1990s when later volumes of the unpublished works (*Nachlassbände)* of each author's complete works, drawing upon archival materials, including discussion protocols and the *Entwurf Contra Paulum,* became available.

This work demonstrates that, despite significant differences, the ideas of Adorno, Horkheimer, and Tillich intersect, align, and are interwoven within a shared personal and intellectual context and an unyielding demand for justice. Moreover, it argues that the thought and writings of each individual evoke deep resonances in the others when placed in conversation, to a degree that has not yet been satisfactorily acknowledged or explored. This work is an initial attempt to bridge this chasm in religious and intellectual historical scholarship by engaging Tillich, Horkheimer, and Adorno in conversation, focused on the specific themes of emancipatory rationality, anthropology, metaphysics, and religion; the subject of chapters two through five, respectively.

Furthermore, when the writings of Adorno, Horkheimer, and Tillich are placed along side of one another, something greater than demonstrable intellectual influence is revealed. Namely, despite important differences in methodology and some key assumptions, there are remarkable consonances between the *types* of critical social theory developed by Tillich and by Horkheimer and Adorno. When read in conversation with one another—as we know these writings were formed amidst such conversation—new insights into each scholar's thought become increasingly clear in some cases, while increasingly complex in others. Each of the chapters incrementally reveals a unique consonance which can no longer be dismissed as mere coincidental timing, *i.e.* the idea that the historical overlaps while superficially interesting, amount to nothing more than friendly respect for scholars working in completely separate fields with incommensurable presuppositions and methods.

Tillich, Horkheimer, and Adorno (along with many of the other Frankfurt theorists) shared several fundamental intellectual presuppositions, dialectical commitments, notions of justice and common views of socialism, all of which contributed to their common critique of and challenge to the perils facing Germany, even before the ascent of Hitler. Methodologically, they shared interests in the quest for a 'mediating' socialism, seen through the lenses of neo-Marxism, Weber, Freud, and Lukács. It is, in part, the distinctive combination of seeking to reclaim reason within the Enlightenment legacy from empiricists and Comtean positivists, along with shared socialist convictions and a critical social conscience exemplified in all three thinkers, which functions as critical buffer against the destabilizing forces of 'unreason' and political romanticism reflected in National Socialism.

One of the central purposes of this work is to identify the underlying assumptions and guiding norms used by Adorno, Horkheimer, and Tillich; in exposing the often profoundly different articulations of and rationale for these shared concerns, I illuminate central areas of productive disagreement among the three thinkers. Based upon a general agreement with the Marxian-Weberian-Lukácsian diagnoses of alienation and reification, Adorno, Horkheimer, and Tillich are in general agreement toward a common emancipatory goal. While their respective prognoses share some key commonalities, Adorno and Horkheimer advocate determinate negation leading to autonomy in decidedly secular social critique, while Tillich advocates an *Aufhebung* leading to theonomy in the guise of religious socialism. Finally, this work offers the first in-depth discussion of Adorno's *Entwurf contra Paulum*; this document is translated as an appendix and analyzed in chapter three, and is of interest to both Adorno and Tillich scholars.

Utilizing a detailed examination of the ways in which four key themes (emancipatory rationality, anthropology, metaphysics, and religion) generate constructive paths for discourse, the argument demonstrates clearly that with similar orientations and goals, yet different emphases, Tillich, Horkheimer, and Adorno uniquely structure what are largely complementary critical interpretations of a modernity which they see to be pathological, and whose subjects are unable to realize the promises of enlightenment. They shine similar light on the 'steel-hard casing'[7] of a modernity which they hope to overcome, and possibly to redeem, in largely compatible ways. In demonstrating this, the study unearths some striking similarities shared by the three thinkers, while also simultaneously revealing clear lines of distinction between them in other key areas and seeking to maintain the tension between the two. This includes important differences between Adorno and Horkheimer—particularly concerning anthropology in chapter three, not only in the 1930s but also in the 1940s—by which time they claimed to be writing with a single mind and purpose.

Key similarities include an initial reliance on Hegel's dialectical structure, Marx's emancipatory social vision and trenchant critique of the dehumanizing

[7] This is a phrase from Max Weber that has long been somewhat deceptively translated as 'iron cage.' The debate about the translation and its implications for Weber, and for Tillich, Horkheimer, and Adorno is explored in chapter 2.

forces of capitalism, and engagement with Lukács' analysis of reification. The modern subject imagines itself free but cannot achieve the liberation promised by enlightenment; instead, the subject experiences alienation and estrangement. Common goals include a demand for justice and hope, not only to end barbarism and the suffering it causes, but to also to hold alive the memory of those who have died without justice. In a similar manner, major differences arise from common sources and hopes. The drive for transcendence takes a very different form in Tillich's Protestant theological system than it does in the secular-Jewish longing for a hypothetical messianic moment found in the work of Adorno and Horkheimer; this will be addressed in chapters four and five.

Emancipatory social critique is *not* inherently secular, as Tillich tirelessly argues. In fact, using Tillich, I claim that critical social theory could productively be challenged to refine some of its core assumptions and values through dialogue with religion; Habermas and others in the critical theory tradition have realized this. While I by no means seek to read Adorno or Horkheimer as 'religious' thinkers in any conventional sense (although some scholars have attempted this with the 'later Horkheimer' in particular), it is suggested that the religious or transcendent dimension of human existence is fundamentally social, and despite the history of and potential for abuse in religion, its transformative power can be profitably used in pursuit of a common emancipatory praxis and goal. Critical theory and social emancipation can be *both* secular *and* religious, in a nuanced sense of the term. The demand that injustice not be given the last word is the key prophetic interruption that serves as origin and goal of the shared critique seen in the works of Adorno, Horkheimer, and Tillich.

II. Chapter Roadmap

Chapter one is historical, examining the Weimar Republic context vis-à-vis the three thinkers, focusing primarily on the years of 1929-33 during which Adorno, Horkheimer, and Tillich worked together at the University of Frankfurt. Adorno's early relationship to Tillich, as advisee and teaching assistant, is explored. Through an analysis of correspondence between Adorno and Horkheimer in 1935-6, one can clearly discern tension between Adorno, who felt trapped in Oxford as an 'Advanced Student,' and Horkheimer, who had a more comfortable academic position at Columbia University in New York and steady financial support through the *Institut*. This tension seems to be resolved by each party blaming miscommunication regarding Adorno's position and possible future with the *Institut* on Tillich, who was their intermediary in many cases between 1933 and 1937.

There is a significant common intellectual and philosophical genesis shared among Adorno, Horkheimer, and Tillich, explored briefly at the beginning of chapter two. Crucially, they share a conception of reason as both critical and emancipatory, rooted in a largely common reading of Hegel, Marx, Nietzsche, Weber, Lukács, and Freud. In particular, Hegel's views of dialectic and pure insight as a disease or pathology profoundly influence all three thinkers, in complementary ways. Marx's exhortation to social transformation is an early impetus as all three thinkers shared the Weberian diagnosis of the disenchantment endemic to modernity. Lukács' theory of reification is a critical hermeneutical lens for all three, but one begins to see a rift regarding the interpretation and extent of reification *vis-à-vis* human persons between Tillich on the one hand, and Adorno and Horkheimer on the other. Chapter two explores the similarities and distinctions in their respective conceptions of reason and its critical capacity in modernity.

The second chapter continues with an analysis of a gradual shift in Horkheimer's work from an initial hope for emancipatory social theory and praxis to an increasing *angst* concerning the all-pervasive effects of instrumental reason. For Adorno, as for Horkheimer, determinate negation was to prove a critically formative theme. Horkheimer starts out with a relatively hopeful notion of reason and its emancipatory possibilities, but he ends by the 1940s with a rather bleak picture of reason's inability to liberate the subject. Tillich operates with a more hopeful conception of reason and he is more optimistic about reason's capacities than Adorno or Horkheimer. Tillich's 'religious socialism' contains a core social critique that has many of the same features of Horkheimer's more famous 'critical theory,' although Tillich and others in the religious socialist movement posited similar views a decade before Horkheimer and other members of the Frankfurt School. The question of whether critical social critique can or should be seen as inherently secular is raised in this chapter and again in the conclusion.

The shared concern for emancipation, directed specifically toward the (human) subject of modernity, is the focus of chapter three, along with the differences among the three thinkers in terms of their specific characterization of philosophical anthropology. In Horkheimer, one sees the most transition; in the early 1930s, he acknowledged the importance of anthropological reflection for critical social thought, while consistently claiming that the idea of an unchangeable human nature was patently false. Even in the early 1940s, Horkheimer was willing to engage the language of a 'nature of humanity' but by the time of his collaborative work with Adorno, this largely disappeared. Tillich's position is remarkably similar to that of the early Horkheimer, arguing against an 'eternal, unchanging' human essence or nature, while insisting that a basic 'nature of humanity' was both knowable and necessary for social transformation. Adorno is largely consistent in his critique of any philosophical engagement with anthropology, but this rarely surfaces, with two notable exceptions. The first is Adorno's initial *Habilitation,* which engages psychoanalysis and subjectivity, and second is his substantial critique of Tillich in 1943-44. Adorno does not critique Horkheimer in any published writings or known letters, although Horkheimer's views on the 'nature of humanity' socially transformative agency are strikingly similar to the aforementioned views of Tillich which Adorno attacks. While Adorno may have been right to reject the universalizing, corruptive manifestations of any supposed 'human nature,' he retained no illusions about the barbarity of human history.

Chapter four explores the role of metaphysics and norms in critical social theory and in religious socialism against the background of a debate with the 'Vienna School' of logical positivism. The anti-utilitarian, non-instrumental emphasis reflects a common focus on transcendence that orients the fourth chapter's reflections on the metaphysical commonalities and differences evident among Adorno, Horkheimer, and Tillich. Here, the similarities between Tillich and Horkheimer are more pronounced. The shared concern for the transcendent—while substantially different in each thinker—leads to the reflections of each on the role of religion in modern society in the fifth and final chapter.

Chapter five specifically examines the function and scope of religion in the work of each thinker and more broadly examines the role of religion in critical social theory. Several scholars have claimed an underlying 'Jewishness' to the thought of the members of the Frankfurt School, and while evaluations of objections to this claim are explored, the chapter is in general agreement with this assessment. What is retained is a distinctly secular, messianic Judaism which holds out the possibility—while tacitly denying any actuality—of a hypothetical moment of redemption. Another central Jewish moment in the work of Adorno and Horkheimer, reflected in Tillich, who was unusually sympathetic to and a powerful advocate of Judaism in a period of general Christian anti-Semitism (whether overt or implicit), is the *Bilderverbot,* or prohibition of images—rooted in Exodus 20 and Deuteronomy 5—that pervades Jewish literature. Adorno in particular uses the *Bilderverbot* to connote not only visual images, but verbal images as well, causing some to misread Adorno as advocating a 'negative theology,' wherein only *apophatic* statements may offer cautious articulation of what (God) is *not*. Horkheimer simultaneously critiques organized religion as a force of oppression, while acknowledging its uniquely inherent emancipatory potentialities. He advocates a doctrine-free and content-less future 'religion' which could serve as the repository of human hopes and the recorded memory of those who have been victims of instrumental reason and the barbarism of the 20th Century. The influence of Walter Benjamin on Adorno is explored, and in this context, Adorno's cryptic conception of an 'inverse theology' is examined.

Each chapter increasingly reveals a unique consonance which can no longer be dismissed as mere coincidental timing. The general scholarly consensus thus far has been based on dubious assumptions that the historical overlaps between the three thinkers, while superficially interesting, amount to nothing more than friendly respect among scholars who happened to overlap in an interesting place and time. This common theory suggests that these historical idiosyncrasies are simply that; the three thinkers worked in completely separate fields with incommensurable presuppositions and methods. This work demonstrates the myopia of such theories.

I.

Historical Convergence and Personal Relationships

> A rich old man, the grain speculator Weil, dies, disturbed by the miseries on earth. In his will he leaves a large sum for the establishment of an institute to investigate the sources of that misery, which is, of course, he himself. —Bertolt Brecht, *Arbeits journal*[1]

Introduction and Context

The power vacuum in post-World War I Germany and dissatisfaction with the punitive treaty signed at Versailles led to the establishment of the Weimar Republic in 1919. The German intelligentsia and artists of the 1920s flourished in the hopes and expectation of a new era, seemingly engulfed by an awareness that an older order was passing away. Yet the average German worker almost certainly did not share this nascent optimism. Dissatisfied with aspects of the Weimar Republic and culture, Paul Tillich, along with other Christian and Jewish thinkers, advocated 'religious socialism,' born of the pregnant possibilities posited by Tillich's concept of *Kairos*, or the 'fullness of time in the present moment.' Most members and affiliates of the 'Frankfurt School'[2] advocated a socialist turn as well, yet nearly all (including Tillich and other religious socialists) rejected the extremes of the Leninist experiment in Russia. Among many shared concerns explored in this and the following chapters, the foundation of their common

---

[1] Bertolt Brecht, *Arbeits journal 1938-1942, vol. 1*, ed. by Werner Hecht (Frankfurt: Suhrkamp Verlag, 1973) 443; cited by Zoltán Tar, in *Foundations of the Frankfurt School of Social Research*, ed. by Judith Marcus and Zoltán Tar (New Brunswick: Transaction Books, 1984) 5.

[2] The *Institut für Sozialforschung* was not referred to as the 'Frankfurt School' until after their return to Germany from the U.S. in 1950, and then, as now, is an informal and imprecise reference. At least Adorno seems to have enjoyed the reference later in life. Warrant for the appellation 'school' is explained by Agnes Heller in "The Frankfurt School," by Agnes Heller, in *Rethinking the Frankfurt School: Alternative Legacies of Cultural Critique*, ed. by Jeffrey T. Nealon and Caren Irr (Albany: State University of New York, 2002) 207-22.

prophetic interruptions, the three evince a shared desire for a mediating socialism and emancipatory reason throughout this period.

The context of the early Frankfurt years is crucial for understanding the interconnections among Tillich, Adorno, and Horkheimer. The personal and political spheres will be explored, but a brief reminder of some of the challenges Germany was facing in the late 1920s and early 1930s is necessary. During the height of the global economic depression, and under the weight of the harsh reparations agreed to at Versailles, the German *Reichsmark* reached astronomical levels of inflation. There was record unemployment among the massive urban working classes. Among the many sources of *angst* in Weimar Germany, tensions between the competing ideologies of nationalism and militarism led to polarization across the political spectrum. The weakened democratic ideals of Weimar (1919-1933) competed with fascism and communism; this resulted in limited unity or commonality of purpose even within the democratic system of Weimar. Christian churches often blindly followed the dictates of the existing powers and easily fell prey to anti-Semitism. The arts in general, however, flourished during the Weimar period.

This chapter begins with an exploration of the historical and intellectual connections and the interrelation of ideas between critical theory, exemplified by the work of Max Horkheimer (1895-1973), Theodor Wiesengrund Adorno (1903-1969), and the thought of philosopher and Protestant theologian Paul Tillich (1886-1965), particularly between the years 1929-44. Numerous similarities between Horkheimer and Adorno, on the one hand, and Tillich on the other, which justify a fruitful comparison of constructive intellectual history with contemporary resonances, are demonstrated throughout. While profound, and in some cases irreconcilable, differences remain, the shared prophetic interruptions ultimately require interpreters to reconsider the numerous parallels which have been far too easily dismissed in previous scholarship.

Tillich's personal and professional life overlapped with those of many Frankfurt School members, first in Frankfurt from 1929-33, and again in New York during the darkest years of the Third Reich.[3] Beginning with Tillich's Frankfurt appointment as chair of the philosophy faculty in 1929, a unique "in-

[3] The continuing intellectual and personal connections between these thinkers during and after the war are even less well known and researched, though it lies outside the time frame on which I focus.

tellectual matrix"[4] was forged which included Herbert Marcuse, Friedrich Pollock, Leo Lowenthal, Adolf Löwe,[5] Eduard Heimann, and in a more peripheral sense, Walter Benjamin, Gershom Scholem, and Erich Fromm, in addition to the three figures that are the focal point of this study. Tillich, Heimann, and Löwe had been friends since at least 1919 when they participated in a group in Berlin known as the *Kairos* Circle.[6] Heimann and Löwe were both economists who were also interested in religious socialism.

Many of these scholars regularly participated in intellectual salons in Frankfurt, and many continued their debates and discussions later upon relocation to New York City. Martin Jay notes: "Tillich was a close friend of Horkheimer, Lowenthal and Pollock, belonging with them to a regular discussion group" or *Kränzchen* in Frankfurt, a group which "was to continue in New York for several years, after most of its members were forced to emigrate."[7] Upon his return from studying music and composition with Alban Berg in Vienna, Theodor Adorno was "welcomed into its company."[8]

I. Brief Biographical Sketches

I.1 Paul Johannes Tillich (1886-1965)[9]

Paul Johannes Tillich was born August 20, 1886 in Starzeddel, in territory which today belongs to Poland. The son of a Lutheran pastor, Tillich lived in Berlin for part of his youth and attended *Gymnasium* in Königsberg. He studied theology at the University of Berlin, followed by the University of Halle, where

---

[4] The phrase 'intellectual matrix' is used to include both Tillich and the Frankfurt School members.

[5] The spelling of his first and last names vary; Adolph or Adolf and Löwe or Lowe. Similarly, Leo Lowenthal is often referred to as Leo Löwenthal. I have generally followed the primary sources and alter the spelling according to the individual source.

[6] *Kairos* is the Greek term for and philosophical concept meaning "right time" or "fullness of time," describing the sense many had of the great opportunity and challenge following Germany's defeat in World War I.

[7] Martin Jay, *The Dialectical Imagination: A History of the Frankfurt School and the Institute of Social Research 1923–1950* (Berkeley: University of California Press, 1996) 24.

[8] Jay, *The Dialectical Imagination*, 24..

[9] The definitive source for Paul Tillich is the excellent biography of Wilhelm Pauck and Marion Pauck, *Paul Tillich: His Life and Thought*, vol. 1: Life (New York: Harper & Row, 1976). Renate Albrecht and Werner Schüssler have also written an important biography of Tillich in German, *Paul Tillich: sein Leben* (Frankfurt am Main: Peter Lang, 1993).

Martin Kähler and Fritz Medicus profoundly influenced him. Both of his dissertations were written on Friedrich Schelling; the second was accepted by the University of Breslau. Tillich was ordained in the Lutheran Church, like his father, and for a short time served as a pastor outside of Berlin. He voluntarily joined the German army as a chaplain in 1914, a grueling position in which he would serve until 1919. In 1915-16, the young patriotic Lutheran chaplain began to experience serious doubts as a massive number of his friends and fellow soldiers died in the trenches on the western front. Reading Nietzsche and the Bible in the trenches, Tillich's own perspectives began to change; it was a time he regarded as his "personal *kairos*."[10]

Tillich's academic teaching career began in Berlin in 1919. He later moved to Marburg, followed by Dresden, where he taught religious studies, as opposed to theology. He finally moved to the University of Frankfurt, where he was appointed chair of philosophy and sociology in 1929. Upon his dismissal by the Nazis in 1933, Tillich moved to New York City, where he taught philosophy of religion and later Protestant theology at Union Theological Seminary. Tillich later taught at Harvard University as a distinguished University Professor, and finally at the University of Chicago, until his death in 1965.

I.2 Max Horkheimer (1895-1973)[11]

Max Horkheimer was born in Stuttgart on February 14, 1895; his father was the owner and director of an industrial company. Horkheimer noted that he was raised "in a certain strict—I wouldn't say orthodox, but at least conservative, Jewish manner."[12] Horkheimer was groomed to run his father's factories and he served as an apprentice for a time. Conscripted into military service in 1917, Horkheimer was ultimately found 'unfit for service.'[13] He began his studies in philosophy, psychology, and economics in Munich but transferred, along with his close friend Friedrich Pollock, to the University of Frankfurt, where he

---

[10] Pauck and Pauck, 51.

[11] Among the many excellent sources are and Zvi Rosen's *Max Horkheimer,* Martin Jay's *Dialectical Imagination,* and Rolf Wiggershaus' *The Frankfurt School: Its History, Theories and Political Significance.*

[12] "Das Schlimme erwarten und doch das Gute versuchen. Ein Gespräch mit Prof. Dr. Max Horkheimer," in *Dienstagsgespräche mit Zeitgenossen*, hrsg. von Gerhard Rein (Stuttgart: Kreuz Verlag, 1976) 151. This interview was conducted sometime in 1972, according to Rein, 149.

[13] Rolf Wiggershaus, *The Frankfurt School: Its History, Theories and Political Significance* (Cambridge: MIT Press, 1994) 44.

worked with Hans Cornelius.[14] Horkheimer's dissertation was on teleological judgment and his *Habilitation* was on Kant's *Critique of Judgment*. Serving first as a *Privatdozent*, Horkheimer was eventually appointed, with the backing of Tillich, to a position in social philosophy at the University of Frankfurt concurrent with his directorship of the *Institut für Sozialforschung* in late 1930. Upon his emigration to the United States in 1933, he taught at Columbia University and spent time writing in Pacific Palisades, California, before returning to Frankfurt in 1950.

I.3 Theodor Wiesengrund-Adorno (1903-1969)[15]

Although commonly known as Theodor W. Adorno, he was born Theodor Ludwig Adorno-Wiesengrund, in Frankfurt[16] on September 11, 1903. A gifted musician as well as a philosopher, Adorno was profoundly influenced by Siegfried Kracauer, Walter Benjamin, Georg Lukács, and Ernst Bloch, among others. His dissertation, also written under Hans Cornelius at Frankfurt, was on Husserl's phenomenology. After receiving his doctorate in philosophy, Adorno went to Vienna to study music composition with Alban Berg; he wrote dozens of articles on music and criticism during the 1920s. By contrast, his first philosophical publication was his *Habilitation*,[17] which was written under Tillich upon Adorno's return to Frankfurt, focusing on Søren Kierkegaard's aesthetics. After serving as a *Privatdozent* and Tillich's assistant, Adorno went to England when the National Socialists came to power in 1933. For four years at Oxford University, Adorno continued his study of Husserl as a reluctant advanced student. It was not until 1938 that Adorno came to New York, and only then did he officially become a member of the *Institut* and an affiliate of Columbia University. Adorno joined Horkheimer in California in the mid-1940s, during their

---

[14] Horkheimer also studied in Freiburg for one year, where he met and was deeply impressed by Husserl's assistant, Martin Heidegger. See Wiggershaus, 46.

[15] The best sources are Stefan Müller-Doohm's *Adorno: A Biography*, Jäger Lorenz's *Adorno: A Political Biography*, Detlev Claussen's *Theodor W. Adorno: One Last Genius*, Jay, and Wiggershaus.

[16] Adorno grew up in Frankfurt, which according to Buck-Morss was a secular city, and she claims that "an openness and lack of dogma were characteristic of its large Jewish population," the "second largest Jewish community in Germany at the time." Susan Buck-Morss, *The Origin of Negative Dialectics: Theodor W. Adorno, Walter Benjamin and the Frankfurt Institute* (Hassocks: Harvester Press, 1977) 2; also 192, note 14.

[17] Adorno's first attempted *Habilitation* was on the concept of the unconscious and was rejected by Hans Cornelius.

most fruitful period of collaboration, before returning to New York and eventually to Frankfurt in 1949.

Adorno's familial religious lineage arguably points as much to Christianity as it does to Judaism, with which Adorno was ultimately to feel a greater, if guarded, affinity. While Adorno's father, Oscar Wiesengrund, had been raised Jewish, he seems to have converted to Protestantism around the time Adorno was born,[18] although scholars do not agree on this point.[19] Adorno's mother, Maria Calvelli-Adorno, was an Italian Catholic and the young Adorno was baptized as a Catholic.[20] He later dropped the patronymic Wiesengrund to the middle initial W., taking the matronymic Adorno as his surname in the late 1930s, partially in response to a curious request from Friedrich Pollock. Martin Jay notes that Pollock had asked Adorno in 1938, when he came to New York, "to drop the Wiesengrund from his name, because there were too many Jewish-sounding names on the Institut's roster."[21] Most scholars agree that Adorno had always personally identified much more strongly with his Catholic mother and her sister, Agathe, who Adorno regarded as a second mother. Later in life, Adorno was to show his affinity with Judaism obliquely as he defended his name change.[22]

---

[18] Wiggershaus, 66-7. Buck-Morss notes that Adorno had been confirmed in the Protestant church "as a matter of expediency." Buck-Morss, 2.

[19] According to Jay, Oscar Wiesengrund was an "assimilated Jewish wine merchant." Jay makes no mention of Oscar's Protestant conversion. Jay, 22.

[20] Buck-Morss, 2. Adorno had been confirmed as a Protestant like his father (c.f. Wiggershaus, 66-7) and had a brief period in the 20s when he was again interested in Christianity and Catholicism. In a letter written October 7, 1934, Adorno acknowledged having strongly considered conversion to Catholicism a decade earlier while studying with Berg in Vienna, but "just short of conversion," Adorno realized he could not accept the metaphysics and romanticism he saw in it. Theodor W. Adorno und Ernst Krenek, *Briefwechsel*, hrsg. von Wolfgang Rogge (Frankfurt am Main: Suhrkamp Verlag, 1974) 46.

[21] Jay, 34.

[22] "The idea that Jews should show more pride by sticking to their names is but a thin rationalization of the desire that they should come into the open so that one might recognize and persecute them the more easily." Adorno, in a 1944 memorandum of the *Institut* on anti-Semitism. Cited in Jay, 308, note 100.

II. Origins of the 'Institute for Social Research'

Founded officially in 1923 in conjunction with the young University of Frankfurt by an initial donation from Hermann and Felix Weil,[23] the *Institut für Sozialforschung* was led by Carl Grünberg from 1923-1929. The initial financial donation and yearly income provided by Weil's endowment allowed the *Institut* and its members relative independence. Since it was only loosely tied to the University of Frankfurt, Weil's endowment allowed a crucial degree of mobility. Horkheimer was able to move the Institute with relative ease from Frankfurt to Geneva in 1933, then to New York in 1935 through an arrangement with Columbia University, and finally back to Frankfurt in 1950. Hermann Weil's initial endowment and subsequent gifts to the *Institut* allowed the "creation and maintenance of an institution whose financial independence proved a great advantage,"[24] as Jay and others have noted. In fact, Jay claims as a central contention of his study *The Dialectical Imagination* that "the relative autonomy of the men who comprised the so-called Frankfurt School...was one of the primary reasons for the theoretical achievements produced by their collaboration."[25]

The *Institut* was the conceptual brainchild of Felix Weil[26] (and his friend Friedrich Pollock to an extent), whose goal was the creation of a Marxist-oriented "interdisciplinary institute dedicated to a radical dissection of bourgeois society."[27] The son of a wealthy Jewish grain merchant and capitalist, Felix Weil quickly became an admirer of Marxism and a patron of radical causes, including support for the *Institut's* independence. Although a vague commitment to Marxism was one key defining factor of the *Institut*, some scholars have suggested that the *Institut's* central defining characteristic might be its indescribability and

---

[23] Zoltán Tar claims that Hermann Weil had tried to found such an institute as early as 1920. Tar, 5.

[24] Jay, 8.

[25] Jay, 4.

[26] Felix Weil received his doctorate in political science from the University of Frankfurt, but he 'refused' to continue his academic career or assume a position of leadership in the *Institut* out of concern for the appearance of nepotism. Jay, 8.

[27] Jay, 10. The original idea was to name it the *Institut für Marxismus*. This was rejected, and the Education Ministry's proposal to name it after Felix Weil was rejected by Weil himself. Jay, 8.

its freedom from any one point of view or narrowly-circumscribed political persuasion.[28]

In line with the acerbic irony of Brecht's view, cited as the epigraph of this chapter, one of the early and ongoing concerns of the *Institut* was an interdisciplinary analysis of the origins and ongoing causes of human misery. This would be a central concern for Max Horkheimer and nearly all of those affiliated in some way with the 'Frankfurt School.' Rolf Wiggershaus describes Weil as a "patron of the left...and a part-time scholar."[29] Weil and other supporters, as well as early members of the *Institut,* hoped to bring Marxism and other neglected or taboo subjects[30] such as anti-Semitism and labor history into academic discourse in German universities, and it is important to note that the Marxian movements represented by Rosa Luxembourg and Antonio Gramsci are in the background. Gramsci's method of moving from materialism to an analysis of cultural hegemony was important in the waning years of World War I, and he was profoundly influential on many young Marxists.

The *Institut für Sozialforschung* was officially founded in conjunction with the German Education Ministry on February 3, 1923. Carl Grünberg, a professor of law and political science in Vienna, and an established Marxist[31] scholar assumed leadership[32] of the *Institut* with an Inaugural address on June 22, 1924.[33] Jay notes that the *Institut's* selection of Grünberg brought the "first avowed Marxist to hold a chair at a German university;"[34] something aided by the financial independence of the *Institut.* Weil wanted to minimize political problems with the university and thus steered clear of the often-rigid KPD (German Communist Party). Although he had initially hoped to model the *Institut* on the Marx-Engels Institute in Moscow, with a communist like Karl

[28] David Held thus begins his characterization of the *Institut* by negation. David Held, *Introduction to Critical Theory: Horkheimer to Habermas* (Berkeley: University of California Press, 1980) 24-6.

[29] Wiggershaus, 13.

[30] Jay, 8

[31] Grünberg was known for his work in editing the *Archiv für die Geschichte des Sozialismus und der Arbeitsbewegung* in Vienna, dating back to 1909.

[32] The initially chosen director of the *Institut* was not Grünberg but the economist and social scientist Kurt Gerlach, who died in October 1922 before delivering his inaugural lecture.

[33] Darrow Schecter, *Instrumental Reason from Weber to Habermas* (New York: Continuum, 2010) 85.

[34] Jay, 10.

Korsch or Georg Lukács as director, Weil came to understand that this was too risky.

Karl Korsch's *Marxism and Philosophy* and Georg Lukács' immensely influential *History and Class Consciousness* were both published in 1923, and the latter in particular made a deep impression on the early *Institut* as it sought to re-imagine socialism and re-interpret Marx's diagnosis and prognosis for society during the tempestuous years of the Weimar Republic.[35] October 1923 saw a communist insurrection in Hamburg, and Hitler's 'Beer Hall' *Putsch* in Munich took place in November. This happened against the background of the staggering hyperinflation of the German *Reichsmark*, alleviated by the parity of 1 trillion *Reichsmark* to 1 *Rentenmark*. A realignment with the gold standard in October 1923 began to stabilize the economy.

Under Grünberg's leadership, the *Institut* was relatively 'orthodox' in its interpretation and application of Marxian theory. Comparatively little research has been done on the early years of the *Institut* under Grünberg, and it is outside the scope of this study to engage this material.[36] Pollock and Lowenthal had been affiliated with and active in the *Institut* since the 1920s,[37] and Pollock's close friend Max Horkheimer was in Frankfurt as a student of Hans Cornelius at the time. Horkheimer and the younger Adorno had both studied with Cornelius, having met in one of Cornelius' seminars on Husserl in 1922, before Adorno went to study music in Vienna.[38] Horkheimer studied with and wrote both his dissertation and his *Habilitation* (both on aspects of Kant's thought) under Cornelius and then served as the latter's assistant. Cornelius had hoped Horkheimer would replace him as chair of philosophy,[39] but it was the philosophical theologian Paul Tillich who ultimately assumed the chair of philosophy and sociology at the University of Frankfurt, replacing Cornelius (and very briefly Max Scheler) in 1929. Whether this caused any overt tension between Horkheimer and Tillich is unknown, but is quite plausible.

Although he was not appointed philosophy chair, Max Horkheimer was appointed director of the *Institut* in October 1930, following Grünberg, despite

---

[35] Lukács' *History and Class Consciousness* will be explored further in chapter 2.

[36] See however Ulrike Migdal, *Die Frühgeschichte des Frankfurter Instituts für Sozialforschung* (Frankfurt a. M.: Campus, 1981).

[37] Held, 31.

[38] Jay, 23. Although Adorno had also studied with Cornelius, it was Cornelius who rejected Adorno's first *Habilitation*, discussed further below.

[39] Wiggershaus, 47.

his limited engagement with the *Institut* in the previous years. With the directorship came a university appointment in social philosophy secured, in part, with the help of Tillich.[40] Wiggershaus notes that this appointment was somewhat unexpected as Horkheimer was not among the 'inner circle' of the *Institut*, nor had he published widely.[41] Since Horkheimer had received his *Habilitation* at Frankfurt, an exception had to be made for him to receive a professorship at the same university; Tillich was instrumental in securing this exemption, as Horkheimer himself recalled.[42] Horkheimer's inaugural lecture was delivered January 24, 1931.[43] Under the new leadership, the *Institut's* goal was nothing less than "the reconstruction of society based on nonexploitative relations between persons; and the restoration of man to center place in the evolution of human society as a self-conscious, self-managing subject of social reality,"[44] in Stanley Aronowitz's formulation. Such renegotiation of the social contract with respect to power dynamics and social agency is a key source of the prophetic interruptions which were to come.

III. A Theologian Called to the Chair of Philosophy in Frankfurt

Kurt Riezler had been selected as the curator (highest administrative officer) of the University of Frankfurt in 1928, which itself had only been founded in 1914. When Cornelius retired, Max Scheler was appointed philosophy chair, but Scheler died before he assumed the position. It thus fell to Riezler to find an acceptable successor. The Prussian Minister of Education, Carl Becker,[45] nomi-

---

[40] See Wiggershaus, 36-7.

[41] Wiggershaus, 37. Pollock was the more likely choice, and Horkheimer, "who until then had taken almost no part in the Institute, probably succeeded in becoming a candidate mainly because Pollock was prepared to withdraw in favour of his friend. With no hope of attaining a professorship in the normal way, Horkheimer was pushing for the post of director, which brought with it the prospect of an accelerated academic career." Wiggershaus, 37-8.

[42] See Horkheimer's recollections of this in *Gesammelte Schriften*, bd. 7, hrsg. von Alfred Smith und Gunzelin Schmid Noerr (Frankfurt a. M.: S. Fischer Verlag, 1985–1996) 277.

[43] Wiggershaus, 38.

[44] Max Horkheimer, 'Introduction,' in *Critical Theory: Selected Essays.* trans Matthew O'Connell, et.al. (New York: Herder and Herder, 1968) xiv.

[45] Becker encouraged Tillich's move from Berlin to Marburg in 1923, and Becker may have had some influence in Tillich's transfer from Marburg to his new position as a professor of humanities and religious studies at the Dresden Institute of Technology in 1925. Pauck, 95, 99. The Paucks also note Becker had a "great liking" for Tillich and they cite an exemplary letter from Becker to Tillich in 1930 in which Becker describes his

nated Paul Tillich, and with the approval of Riezler and the director of the Prussian Ministry of Education, Tillich was appointed and assumed the chair of the philosophy faculty as Professor of Philosophy and Sociology[46] in Frankfurt on March 1, 1929.[47] Although Scheler filled the position only temporarily—largely on paper—and although Tillich was realistically the successor to Cornelius, the Paucks note that "Tillich always wrote and spoke of being the successor of Scheler in Frankfort [sic] rather than of Cornelius...." By this, Tillich "meant was that he was Scheler's spiritual successor in a way he could not have been to Cornelius."[48] The feeling, as far as Cornelius was concerned, seems to have been mutual, and Werner Schüssler reports that Cornelius was somewhat displeased Tillich was his replacement.[49]

Having been trained as a philosopher of religion and a Lutheran theologian, Tillich may have initially appeared a curious choice for a university chair in philosophy. On the other hand, his training was quite broad and both his dissertation and *Habilitation* engaged German Idealism and explored several dimensions of the thought of Friedrich Schelling. For Tillich, throughout his life, philosophy and theology were always understood as mutually informing and reinforcing. Wiggershaus, among others, notes the unique breadth of Tillich's background and interests which allowed him to thrive in his new position. Wiggershaus writes: "What was distinctive about Tillich," in comparison to other 'dialectical theologians' of the time, "was his interests beyond the field of theology, in German Idealism and Marxism, in social philosophy, psychology and politics."[50] In his new position in Frankfurt, Tillich was expected "to teach social education, and in his lectures and seminars between the years 1929 and 1933 he thus emphasized the aspects of social ethics, historical action and political direc-

---

acquaintance with Tillich among the most positive experiences and interactions he had in recent years. See Pauck and Pauck, 304-5, note 34.

[46] Pauck and Pauck, 112-3; also Werner Schüssler, "Als protestantischer Theologe in philosophischem Material," *in Spurensuche: Lebens- und Denkwege Paul Tillichs*, hrsg. von Ilona Nord und Yorick Spiegel (Münster: Lit, 2001) 142. In most other scholarship, Tillich is referred to as the chair and Professor of Philosophy, with no mention of sociology.

[47] Pauck and Pauck, 111; also 305, note 37.

[48] Pauck and Pauck, 113.

[49] Werner Schüssler, "Als protestantischer Theologe in philosophischem Material," in *Spurensuche: Lebens- und Denkwege Paul Tillichs*, 145.

[50] Wiggershaus, 91.

tion..."[51] according to Pauck and Pauck. Cornelius' reservations notwithstanding, scholars in other fields, including economics, sociology, linguistics, and psychology welcomed Tillich in Frankfurt.

In the early 1930s in Frankfurt, according to Wiggershaus, "The intellectual left consisted of the Sociology Department, headed by Karl Mannheim, the Institute of Social Research, headed by Horkheimer, and a group around Paul Tillich.... Mannheim, Horkheimer and Adorno all belonged to the 'circle' and were always ready to cooperate with the group around Tillich."[52] The Paucks' biography recounts much the same, noting Tillich's regular and active participation in two discussion groups in Frankfurt. One was a discussion group led by Kurt Riezler known as the *Weisheitsseminar*, although "Tillich referred to this group as 'classical-pagan.'" Tillich claimed to have been a "peripheral figure" in this group, but he strongly identified with another group "which he described as 'religious, philosophical, prophetic'"[53] and included Horkheimer, Adorno, Pollock, Mannheim,[54] Mennicke, and Löwe. These were lively discussions with little agreement—Adorno recalls "We often attacked one another like wild animals,"[55] but above all else, it was a place for candid exchange of ideas among friends. Adorno recalled Tillich being open, reasoned and logical—a "pacific arguer"[56] among a heated conversation group.

Despite being an 'outsider' in some sense as a philosophical theologian in a philosophy chair, Tillich "won the ear of his colleagues as easily as the attention of his students,"[57] and his relatively short years in Frankfurt were marked by an impressive amount of collaboration with fellow scholars approaching philosophy from different perspectives, as well as with colleagues in widely disparate fields.

---

[51] Pauck and Pauck, 113. "More than ever he felt obliged to make philosophical questions existential for the numerous students for whom philosophical courses were mandatory." Wiggershaus, 91.

[52] Wiggershaus, 111.

[53] Pauck and Pauck, 119.

[54] Mannheim does not seem to have been as actively or regularly involved, and the disagreements between Mannheim on the one hand and Tillich and Horkheimer (who both wrote critiques of Mannheim's 1929 book on ideology) seem to have been more deeply entrenched.

[55] Theodor W. Adorno, in *Werk und Wirken Paul Tillichs: Ein Gedenkbuch* (Stuttgart: Evangelisches Verlagswerk, 1967) 29. Author's translation, "Wir sind oft wie die wilden Tiere übereinander hergefallen."

[56] Pauck and Pauck, 119. Adorno is reported to have given Tillich the nickname "Pacidius."

[57] Pauck and Pauck, 118.

Tillich's colleagues were impressed by his integrity and openness, and "some even become indebted to his political integrity."[58] Most of his Frankfurt colleagues were Jewish, and Tillich relished being referred to as "Paul among the Jews,"[59] according to the Paucks and reminisces from Horkheimer, Adorno, and others.

Erich Fromm, Herbert Marcuse, and others who sought to synthesize the insights of Marx and Freud found in Tillich a helpful interlocutor. Tillich collaborated with the nearby Frankfurt Institute of Psychoanalysis, delivering several lectures and participating in colloquia.[60] Horkheimer also collaborated to an extent with the Institute of Psychoanalysis, which was founded in 1929,[61] and Horkheimer "had been instrumental in securing university approval for the new 'guest institute'.... Freud himself wrote two letters to Horkheimer to express his gratitude."[62] The parallel attempts at a synthesis of Marx and Freud by members of the Frankfurt School and by Tillich reflect a notable characteristic of their respective and collective thought in this period, and yet another foundation of their prophetic interruptions.[63]

During the years in Frankfurt, Tillich taught seminars on, among other thinkers, Kant, Hegel, Schelling, Locke, and Aquinas. His lecture courses included "'Being and Action,' 'The Masses and the Spirit,' 'Philosophy of Religion,' and 'The History of Philosophy.'"[64] The Paucks note that although he was primarily trained as a theologian, Tillich only offered one informal course dealing directly with theology during his time in Frankfurt, and this was during his

[58] Pauck and Pauck, 118. Tillich was suspended from his teaching position soon after the Nazis came to power not only for his direct criticism of the party in *The Socialist Decision* and other writings, but also for his personal support and identification with Jewish students and colleagues.

[59] Pauck and Pauck, 118.

[60] Wiggershaus, 55.

[61] Like the *Institut für Sozialforschung*, the Frankfurt Institute of Psychoanalysis was largely independent from, though affiliated with, the University of Frankfurt.

[62] Jay, 88. Jay also notes that Horkheimer underwent psychoanalysis himself, although more for educational than therapeutic purposes, in Jay's estimation.

[63] For Adorno, this influence is manifest early in his first *Habilitation*, *Der Begriff des Unbewussten in der transzendentalen Seelenlehre*, which was rejected by Hans Cornelius. Horkheimer himself underwent psychoanalysis and employed several of Freud's concepts and theories in his early work. Tillich found Freud a helpful interlocutor for his developing theology. In the writings of all three thinkers, one can see commonalities with Freud's social critique, for example, *Civilization and its Discontents*.

[64] Pauck and Pauck, 113-4.

final semester.[65] Tillich was "in the unique position of being the only theologian on the faculty of the university, a Christian scholar teaching philosophy in a secular setting,"[66] according to the Paucks. Years later, he would reflect on the relationship between philosophy and theology thusly: "No theologian should be taken seriously as a theologian, even if he is a great Christian and a great scholar, if his work shows that he does not take philosophy seriously."[67] This was a concern Tillich took seriously throughout his life, always proud of his life 'on the boundary;' the phrase became the title of his autobiographical reflections.

Although Tillich missed some of the theological debates of the era and "frequently traveled to Marburg in an effort to remain in touch with the discussion of theological ideas"[68] missing in Frankfurt, he quickly turned down an offer to serve as the chair of systematic theology at the University of Halle, from which he had received an honorary doctorate in 1925. While in Frankfurt, Tillich helped organize a conversation between leading theologians and philosophers on the topic of "The Function of Protestantism in Secular Civilization," which took place on June 27, 1931. Beyond Tillich, Emil Brunner, Heinrich Frick, Hans von Soden, and Martin Dibelius were among the theologians present. The philosophers—broadly construed—who participated in this discussion (beyond Tillich) were Horkheimer, Adorno, Pollock, Mannheim, Mennicke, and Riezler.[69]

The years in Frankfurt were perhaps "the richest and most successful of Tillich's German career."[70] As a teacher, according to his biographers and students and echoed by Adorno's comments soon after Tillich's death,[71] he excelled. Many former colleagues and students recalled Tillich's unusual "openness" as a teacher.[72] Unlike some theologians, he taught in a "nonauthoritarian way," and the Paucks write that Tillich's colleagues were impressed that he "had

---

[65] Pauck and Pauck, 114.

[66] Pauck and Pauck, 118.

[67] Paul Tillich, *Biblical Religion and the Search for Ultimate Reality* (Chicago: University of Chicago Press, 1955) 7-8.

[68] Pauck and Pauck, 120-1.

[69] See "Gespräche: Paul Tillich in Frankfurt," in *Spurensuche: Lebens-und Denkwege Paul Tillichs*, 163 ff. Also in Max Horkheimer, *Gesammelte Schriften*, bd. 11, 345-405.

[70] Pauck and Pauck, 114.

[71] Adorno comments particularly on Tillich's pedagogical skill in his remarks on Tillich during his November 9, 1965 lecture. See *Lectures on Negative Dialectics*, cited below.

[72] Pauck and Pauck, 114. Adorno, *Lectures on Negative Dialectics*, cited below.

somehow freed himself from the stuffy moralism of his Protestant background."[73] The Paucks note that Paul and his wife Hannah were consummate entertainers, hosting elaborate parties, including a memorable 'dialectical costume party' to which Adorno came dressed as Napoleon and Kurt Riezler as a fascist brown shirt.[74]

IV. The Intellectual Matrix in Frankfurt

Wiggershaus and others describe Frankfurt in the early 1930s as the epicenter of the German left. The wider context of Germany's political climate in the waning years of Weimar are vital for context: by September 1930, in the midst of rampant unemployment, a major global economic depression, and the growth of the communist party in Germany, the National Socialist Party had 107 members in the Reichstag, making them the second largest party.[75] It took another three years before the Nazis were able to control the *Reichstag*, and much of the most fascinating research, teaching, collaboration, and conversation took place during this uneasy interim. The faculty in Frankfurt in 1930 included Tillich, Adolph Löwe, and Carl Mennicke (all three were 'religious socialists,' which will be explained in the following chapters), Karl Mannheim, Martin Buber, and Hendrik de Man, among others.[76] Horkheimer joined them later that year as director of the *Institut* and professor of social philosophy.

As noted, Tillich had been influential in hiring Horkheimer as the Director of the *Institut für Sozialforschung* and he was instrumental in helping Horkheimer secure the necessary accompanying professorship in social philosophy in 1929. While Susan Buck-Morss claims Friedrich Pollock "was largely responsible for Horkheimer's assuming the directorship [of the Institute] in 1931,"[77] other scholars like Martin Jay note that "with the support of Tillich and other members of the philosophy department, a new chair of 'social philosophy' was established for Horkheimer."[78] Since Pollock was a professor of economics and the position created for Horkheimer was in philosophy, it makes far more sense

[73] Pauck and Pauck, 114.

[74] Pauck and Pauck, 122; original invitation in Harvard Paul Tillich Archive.

[75] Wiggershaus, 109. See also Buck-Morss, 29. "In the September election of 1930, with more than 4 million German workers unemployed, 6.4 million votes were cast for the National Socialists, while the Communists received 4.6 million." By the July 1932 elections, a majority of the votes went to non-democratic parties.

[76] Wiggershaus, 111.

[77] Buck-Morss, 10.

[78] Jay, 25.

that Tillich, as the chair of philosophy, would have had greater influence in this matter. Indeed, Horkheimer himself would later credit Tillich with helping him secure the academic position.[79] Tillich co-taught with Horkheimer beginning in 1930 with a seminar on 'Reading Philosophical Texts,' followed by a seminar on Locke and another in the summer semester of 1931 on an unknown topic.[80] Although Tillich and Adorno co-taught several courses, Horkheimer and Adorno never taught together before their exile in 1933. A seminar with Horkheimer and Adorno jointly teaching Hobbes' constitutional theory was planned for 1933, but never happened.[81]

Tillich's relationship with Adorno during this period in Frankfurt requires careful consideration. Susan Buck-Morss is among the few Frankfurt School scholars who explicitly mention Tillich among "others who as members, journal contributors, friends or enemies played a role in the Institute's history."[82] Tillich is regarded by Buck-Morss as a friend of the Frankfurt School theorists, and she describes Tillich as a theologian and "antiauthoritarian teacher with prosocialist leanings."[83] Yet in describing Tillich as Adorno's *Habilitation* supervisor, Buck-Morss uses the passive voice, mentioning, almost in an aside, that Tillich "accepted" Adorno's study of Kierkegaard.[84] In two footnotes—the only other references to Tillich in *The Origin of Negative Dialectics*—Buck-Morss seems to be at pains to characterize Tillich as an outsider, perhaps a friend, but not a true colleague. She claims: "Tillich's intellectual position was quite different, and he

[79] Horkheimer, *GS* 7, 277. As a close friend of both Horkheimer and Tillich, and more importantly, as a friend of Felix Weil, Friedrich Pollock almost certainly was influential in some sense, but not "largely responsible" as Buck-Morss claims. Jay, 24, *inter al.*

[80] Wiggershaus, 111.

[81] Wiggershaus, 111. Perhaps *the* major influence on Adorno's early thought was Walter Benjamin, an independent scholar who was loosely supported by the *Institut für Sozialforschung*, but who remained on its periphery, as did Adorno until 1938. Buck-Morss makes the common claim, "The really formative influence on Adorno occurred before 1931, and it came from Walter Benjamin." Buck-Morss, xii. The influence of Benjamin on Adorno is not a central concern of this study, although it is briefly addressed in chapter 5, and it has been well documented elsewhere.

[82] Buck-Morss, xi. This is implied, but not stated directly, by Jay and Wiggershaus. Held and numerous others completely ignore Tillich.

[83] Wiggershaus, 23.

[84] Stefan Müller-Doohm, in his biography of Adorno, notes that Tillich had offered to supervise Adorno, while also hinting that Adorno had no choice and was stuck with Tillich. *Adorno: A Biography*, trans. Rodney Livingston (Cambridge: Polity Press, 2005) 109, 122.

cannot be said to have influenced Adorno. Their relationship was a personal one,"[85] almost implying Tillich's supervision of Adorno's *Habilitation* was a favor, accommodating a formality in Adorno's professional career.[86] While there may be superficial truth to this, Buck-Morss ignores the fact that it was Tillich who, in addition to supervising Adorno's *Habilitation* on Kierkegaard's aesthetics, also supported Adorno and helped him secure a position as *Privatdozent*.[87] John Abromeit is similarly dismissive in his otherwise impressive intellectual history of the early Horkheimer, mentioning Tillich only in passing, and only in connection to Adorno's 'theological' *Habilitation*.[88] Although Adorno himself freely acknowledged his indebtedness to Tillich, Martin Jay and Rolf Wiggershaus are among the few Frankfurt School scholars who have granted basic facts about the relationship between these thinkers, and the latter scholars at least acknowledge that Adorno's academic position was secured with Tillich's help.[89]

Tillich's biographers, Wilhelm and Marion Pauck offer a more nuanced and sympathetic account of the interactions between Adorno and Tillich. Adorno was still a student and Tillich's predecessor, Hans Cornelius, had rejected Adorno's first *Habilitation*. Adorno's first impressions of Tillich[90] came during one of Tillich's early lectures on Plato in the summer semester of 1929. Quoting the Paucks, who drew on an interview with Adorno:

> Adorno listened intently, unaware that he was being observed. On the following day, he and Tillich were introduced...[at a salon]. Tillich immediately seized Adorno, saying that he had seen him in class the day before, and describing in the greatest detail precisely how Adorno had reacted to every statement he had made. Adorno, amazed at Til-

---

[85] Buck-Morss, 211, note 237.

[86] In German universities, a second thesis is required after the doctoral dissertation. A *Habilitation* is this second thesis, and it should be on a different subject or employ a different methodology, and it is only after writing and having the *Habilitation* approved that one can be called Professor and assume a more permanent position in a German university.

[87] This is analogous to an assistant professor in the United States, although *Privatdozenten* did not receive a state salary like full professors, but rather shared in the (modest) income from student fees. Additionally serving as Tillich's assistant, however, Adorno would have had even greater responsibility and greater income as well.

[88] John Abromeit, *Max Horkheimer and the Foundations of the Frankfurt School* (Cambridge: Cambridge University Press, 2011) 351-2.

[89] Jay, 24.

[90] Theodor W. Adorno, "Erinnerungen an Paul Tillich," in *Werk und Wirken*, 24-26, 29-30.

> lich's power of observation, was immediately captivated. He came to know intimately what he then only sensed, namely, that he was in the presence of someone who had enormous intuition and an extraordinary capacity to register other people's reactions to him.... [Adorno also noticed] how [Tillich] concentrated exclusively and absolutely on the person to whom he was talking, and what a powerful magnetic effect such concentration had on the object of this intense attention.[91]

Such remarks about Tillich are almost completely absent from major Adorno scholars.

Impressed by Tillich, Adorno asked Tillich to supervise his second attempt at a *Habilitation*, a study of Kierkegaard's aesthetics.[92] With Horkheimer as a second examiner, Adorno's second *Habilitation* was accepted, and "Tillich did not agree with Adorno's conclusions, but he defended him in the oral examination and gave him an A."[93] In his official report for university records, Tillich "praised the difficult, 'textured' nature of the thesis," noting that Wiesengrund, as Adorno was known at the time, "had pointed, with his 'rescuing of the aesthetic' in Kierkegaard, to the course of his future philosophy—a philosophy 'whose truth lies in the interpretation of the tiniest facts of each historical moment.'"[94] Tillich's comments concerning the future shape of Adorno's thought

---

[91] Pauck and Pauck, 115-6. See Adorno's own, slightly distinct account of this first encounter with Tillich, in *Werk und Wirken*, 24-5.

[92] Wiggershaus claims that "Tillich's arrival [in Frankfurt] was the opportunity for Adorno to bring the theologically inspired materialism of his friends [Benjamin above all] to bear, not just on music, but on philosophy as well, and to make the academic world accessible to it." Wiggershaus, 91.

[93] Pauck and Pauck, 116. There is an anecdotal and humorous story that Tillich claimed of Adorno's work on Kierkegaard, "I can't understand a word of it, but it's wonderful." See Pauck and Pauck, 116. Although a "charming tale," as the Paucks put it, the statement is merely tongue-in-cheek hyperbole given Tillich's incisive review of the *Habilitation* for the official Frankfurt philosophy faculty review and a review of the published work a few years later. Indeed, Adorno claims that Tillich understood his Kierkegaard book quite well in a letter to Kracauer dated January 2, 1931. *Theodor Adorno—Siegfried Kracauer Briefwechsel 1923–1966*, bd. 7, hrsg. von Wolfgang Schopf (Frankfurt am Main: Suhrkamp Verlag, 2008) 258.

[94] Paul Tillich, "Gutachten über die Arbeit von Dr. Wiesengrund: *Die Konstruktion des Aesthetischen [sic] bei Kierkegaard*," in the Theodor Adorno file of the philosophy faculty of the University of Frankfurt am Main. "Die Rettung der äesthetische Sphäre fasst Wiesengrund in seinem Schlusssatz zusammen: 'Denn der Schritt aus Trauer in Trost ist nicht der größte, sondern der kleinste.' Wiesengrund will sich mit diesem Satz und das heißt mit seinem ganzen Buch die Bahn frei machten für eine Philosophie, deren Wahrheit die Interpretation der kleinsten Gegebenheit eines geschichtlichen Augenblicks ist.

were prescient. For his part, Adorno described Tillich as a demanding supervisor.[95]

Horkheimer's comments were in basic agreement with Tillich, but offer an insightful point of distinction and critique. Horkheimer pointedly noted of Adorno's thesis that the philosophical interests, method and linguistic form

> are not related to my own philosophical aspirations. If Wiesengrund considers that he has recovered hope and reconciliation, of all things, from Kierkegaard's thought, he has thereby expressed a basic theological conviction which points to philosophical intentions radically different from my own, and this is noticeable in every single sentence.[96]

This is an intriguing statement for Horkheimer to make concerning Adorno's work. It should be recalled that a decade later, Horkheimer and Adorno both professed such commonality of thought and purpose that they claimed it would not be feasible to determine who wrote what in their collaborative efforts.[97] Perhaps Horkheimer's remarks were reacting against Tillich, or simply against the "theological" element that he perceived in Adorno's *Habilitation*, perhaps as a result of Tillich's guidance. This dynamic and possible tension will be discussed more fully in later chapters.

Tillich supported Adorno's thesis despite intellectual differences and disagreement with the conclusions and hired Adorno as his assistant. With an ap-

---

Er deutet damit den Weg an, der er selbst als Philosoph gehen will." *Ergänzungs- und Nachlassbände zu den Gesammelten Werken von Paul Tillich*, bd. 11, 346.

[95] In a letter dated May 12, 1930 to Kracauer, Adorno wrote: "...dann unter dem Übermaß der Arbeit, zu der mich Tillich sehr drängt, der mich noch in diesem Semester habilitieren will, damit ich als sein offizieller Assistent nächstes Semester bereits lesen kann." *Adorno-Kracauer Briefwechsel*, bd. 7, 206.

[96] Max Horkheimer, "Bemerkungen in Sachen der Habilitation Dr. Wiesengrund,' February 1931, in Theodor Adorno file of the philosophy faculty of the University of Frankfurt am Main. Cited in Wiggershaus, 93. Horkheimer's *Gutachten* concerning Adorno's *Habilitation* does not appear in the *Gesammelte Schriften* of Horkheimer or Adorno. Wiggershaus does not adequately cite his source. Adorno himself acknowledged that he "went into theological categories more deeply than I wanted to...." Letter, Adorno to Kracauer, August 6, 1930. "...dass mir beim Kierkegaard oft gar nicht wohl zumute ist—ich bin tiefer in theologische Kategorien gekommen, als ich gewünscht hatte und habe Angst, dass ich bei Rettung und vor allem natürlich Versöhnung zu viel gewiehert habe." *Adorno-Kracauer Briefwechsel*, bd. 7, 244.

[97] The extent of this connection will be discussed subsequently. For the claims of profound interconnection of thought between Adorno and Horkheimer, see the Prefaces to *Dialectic of Enlightenment* and *Eclipse of Reason*.

proved *Habilitation* and Tillich's support, Adorno was able to assume an official position as *Privatdozent*. As Adorno remarked shortly after Tillich's death, the elder's support in approving a thesis with which he disagreed and hiring the younger scholar as his assistant gave Adorno an official university position (though he had no affiliation with the *Institut* until he arrived in New York), which allowed him greater mobility and ultimately to flee fascist Germany. Adorno claims that in this, Tillich may have saved his life. Adorno recalls assisting Tillich unofficially with seminars prior to his promotion,[98] and following his promotion, he assisted and co-taught courses with Tillich, including seminars on Hegel's philosophy of history, Lessing, and one on Simmel.[99] During the summer of 1931, Tillich co-led a philosophy seminar with three other professors, a course with which Adorno, as Tillich's assistant, almost certainly helped. Adorno also wrote a brief piece for the *Neue Blätter für den Sozialismus*, of which Tillich was an editor, in 1931.[100]

While it may be accurate to say that the relationship between Tillich and Adorno was primarily personal, the dismissal of Tillich characteristic of most scholars risks overlooking an important figure in Adorno's life and intellectual development. In his published work after Tillich's death, including his public lectures, Adorno himself regarded the relationship with more significance than many scholars have been willing to acknowledge, perhaps attempting to downplay any possible significance a Protestant theologian could have played in Adorno's life, whether personal or professional. Soon after Tillich's death in 1965, Adorno began his November 9th lecture with homage to Tillich, which many Adorno scholars may have missed, or perhaps have deliberately overlooked as hyperbole, ignoring Adorno's own words. Describing Tillich not only as a teacher and friend, but as "one of the most extraordinary people I have met in my life,"[101] Adorno declared his indebtedness to Tillich personally, professional and pedagogically. He continues:

> I owe [Paul Tillich] the most profound debt of gratitude for having approved of my Habilitation thesis in 1931, in other words, at a time

---

[98] Theodor W. Adorno, *Lectures on Negative Dialectics: Fragments of a Lecture Course 1965/1966*, ed. by Rolf Tiedemann (Cambridge: Polity, 2008) 3. *Vorlesung über Negative Dialektik*, 11.

[99] Wiggershaus, 111.

[100] "Was lieben Sie eigentlich an Ihrem Mann?," by T. W.-A. [Theodor W. Adorno] in *Neue Blätter für den Sozialismus* (2:1) 1931, 42-4.

[101] *Lectures on Negative Dialectics*, 2. *Vorlesung über Negative Dialektik*, 10.

> when fascism with all that this meant was on the rise. It is a debt such as I owe to few others. Had he not exerted himself on my behalf, something he did despite the differences in our respective theoretical points of view, differences that we frankly declared to one another from the very outset, it is very questionable whether I would be able to speak to you today; it is even questionable whether I would have survived.[102]

Horkheimer expresses a very similar sentiment, crediting Tillich with going well above and beyond the call of academic duty in exerting himself on behalf of both himself and Adorno. In a 1966 memorial event for Tillich, Horkheimer also suggested that Tillich had perhaps also saved his life.[103]

Although eulogies are common and overstatement often characterizes reflection on departed friends and colleagues, Adorno was not known to regularly employ hyperbole. His claim was that Tillich's support, despite their differences, allowed him to attain the position of *Privatdozent* at the University of Frankfurt, and this helped him secure the stability and academic position which ultimately enabled him to leave Nazi Germany. Indeed, Adorno continues by immediately denying exaggeration in his remarks:

> This is no mere private reminiscence but something integral to Tillich's unprecedented and truly unique qualities of character: an openness and open-mindedness such as I have never encountered in anyone else.... Tillich's liberal-mindedness set an example of enduring worth.... I should like to add that whatever I have myself acquired in the way of pedagogic expertise and whatever may have encouraged you to place some confidence in me, namely this ability to encourage the growth of objectivity in other people's minds, as far as that is possible, and to achieve a meeting of minds; that whatever of this I have learned—even though I am very aware how far I lag behind Paul Tillich in this respect—I owe to him and the years of our seminars and junior seminars together.[104]

Going further, Adorno concludes his comments following Tillich's death (recorded in *Lectures in Negative Dialectics*): "You may take my word for it that not only are there very few people who have meant so much to me but that I attribute an *influence* to them that far surpasses anything that is contained in

[102] *Lectures on Negative Dialectics*, 3. *Vorlesung über Negative Dialektik*, 10-11.
[103] Horkheimer, in *Werk und Wirken*, 116, 125-6.
[104] *Lectures on Negative Dialectics*, 3-4. *Vorlesung über Negative Dialektik*, 11-2.

their writings."[105] With all due respect to Löwenthal and Löwe's reminisces recorded by Terrence O'Keefe, which deny any intellectual influence between Tillich and Adorno (or Horkheimer), it behooves interpreters to respect and acknowledge Adorno's own language. While claims of mutual intellectual influence are indeed too far reaching, there remains a profound level of connection between these thinkers, connections which had important effects on the life and thought of each. Horkheimer's published comments concerning Tillich are similar in quality and tone to those of Adorno.[106]

V. Adorno's 1930s Letters as Critiques of Tillich

In his private letters Adorno was, in some cases, much less kind concerning Tillich, although his private letters are rarely elegiac of anyone.[107] At the heart of some of these critiques lies something which had little to do with Tillich himself. Poor communication between Adorno and Horkheimer while Adorno was in Oxford as an 'Advanced Student' built up deep resentment, and Adorno seems to have felt abandoned by the *Institut.* Tillich, as the frequent intermediary and messenger between the two, may have unnecessarily taken some of the brunt of Adorno's frustration. Tillich was Adorno's primary connection to Horkheimer and the other Frankfurt School thinkers in New York during his time in Geneva and Oxford. Adorno seems to have felt Tillich was not being frank with him about his relationship with the *Institut.* In fact, Adorno had no official relationship with the *Institut* until he came to New York in 1938, and Tillich likely did not know the full details of the situation and contingencies (including funding, travel visas, etc.) as Europe and the US slowly emerged from economic downturn. There is of course the possibility that Tillich unintentionally mixed messages on some occasions in his role as intermediary, but Adorno's frustration seems to have found a scapegoat in Tillich in this period. Wiggershaus suggests that Adorno—mistakenly—thought Tillich was confusing mes-

---

105 *Lectures on Negative Dialectics*, 4; emphasis added. *Vorlesung über Negative Dialektik,* 12-3.

106 See, inter al., "Letzte Spur von Theologie—Paul Tillichs Vermächtnis," von Max Horkheimer, in *Werk und Wirken Paul Tillichs: Ein Gedenkbuch*, 125-32.

107 This is true not only of Tillich but many others in Adorno's letters as well. Adorno's comments about Marcuse in a May 13, 1935 letter to Horkheimer are much more extreme than anything Adorno wrote in private correspondence about Tillich. Adorno implied that it was largely Marcuse's Judaism which kept him from functionally being a fascist. *Adorno-Horkheimer Briefwechsel, 1927-1969,* hrsg. von Christoph Gödde und Henri Lonitz (Frankfurt am Main: Suhrkamp Verlag, 2003) bd. 1, 65.

sages between the *Institut* and himself in the months and early years following March 1933.[108]

For a year and a half, there was no direct contact between Adorno and Horkheimer, and it was finally Horkheimer who contacted Adorno by letter, wondering if future collaboration with the *Institut* would be possible.[109] Adorno's almost immediate response was to accuse Horkheimer of having abandoned him when Horkheimer and the others left for New York. In a flurry of letters between the two, the resolution of this impasse appears to have been Adorno's assigning blame for miscommunication on Tillich, with whom he had more regular contact. A surprising amount of time—particularly on Adorno's part—was devoted in letters exchanged with Horkheimer to blaming Tillich. From November 1934 thru May of 1935, Adorno returned to this theme in his rather formal letters to Horkheimer, revealing a high degree of insecurity with regard to his relationship to the *Institut*. He was understandably disappointed to find himself an 'Advanced Student' at Oxford, having two doctoral degrees in hand, and he undoubtedly had hoped to be invited—and funded—by the *Institut* in coming to the United States much earlier. Horkheimer's letters respond largely by equivocation and thus passively and unintentionally treat Tillich as a scapegoat to diffuse Adorno's palpable irritation.[110]

It is in this context of recrimination that one finds a relatively harsh critique of Tillich from Adorno to Horkheimer in a letter in January 1936. Adorno had received a letter from Hannah Tillich, asking him to contribute to a *Festgabe* for Tillich's 50th birthday. Adorno writes, ostensibly to ask Horkheimer's advice on contributing to this (among a number of other subjects in the letter):

> One cannot escape, but still less identify. It strikes me as a solution to contribute something about Tillich as an educator. I know him most closely as such and here I see his real talent. But I cannot yet celebrate

[108] Wiggershaus, 159. Wiggershaus notes that Adorno also blamed Pollock for his perception that "there was a policy of secretiveness towards him at the Institute...." See also 157.

[109] 25 Oktober 1934. *Adorno–Horkheimer Briefwechsel,* bd. I, 18.

[110] Wiggershaus hints at this, noting a certain craftiness with which Horkheimer engaged while resisting Adorno's zeal and desire to join the *Institut* formally, with funding, and physically in New York. See Wiggershaus, 158-60.

the 'rings.' Please advise me what to do. Were you also asked or did she not trust you?[111]

The praise of Tillich as a teacher has already been noted, but those were public remarks in Adorno's lectures shortly after Tillich's death. This private letter was written thirty years earlier and in the context of understandable but misplaced frustration. Particularly perplexing is how to understand the sentence: "Aber ich kann doch nicht das 'Ringen' feiern." Adorno is clearly wrestling with whether to contribute to the honorary essay collection, and so perhaps he cannot 'celebrate' that he has been given this offer or task; he notes he cannot say no. He is possibly wary of celebrating the 'struggle' of religious socialism in a *Festgabe* for Tillich, but '*Ringen*' could also be an athletic metaphor, perhaps suggesting that he does not want to participate in the 'sport' of celebration typical of *Festgaben*. There is no context within the letter, and the fact that Horkheimer does not reply to this part of the letter (while responding in detail to other portions) only complicates the matter of interpretation.

Several months later, in May of 1936, a distinctly negative description of Tillich arose in two further letters from Adorno to Horkheimer, one of which will be discussed in the context of anthropology in the third chapter. The first letter recounts a few days which Adorno and Tillich spent together in Oxford, presumably in early May 1936. Here, Adorno writes (to Horkheimer concerning Tillich), notably using the first person plural:

> We need to be clear that, no matter how 'nice' he is, there is in truth no common conviction that unites us with him. I was particularly displeased that he tried to construct theoretical differences between us (you and me), by opposing your greater 'flexibility' with my preferred 'rigid radicalism.' It is hard to say whether praise or attack is the greater insolence.[112]

---

[111] *Adorno-Horkheimer Briefwechsel*, bd. I, 105. Author's translation, "Man kann sich schlecht entziehen, noch weniger aber doch sich identifizieren. Mir schwebt als Lösung vor, etwas über Tillich als Pädagogen beizutragen. Als solchen kenne ich ihm am genauesten und hier sehe ich seine wirkliche Begabung. Aber ich kann doch nicht das 'Ringen' feiern. Bitte raten Sie mir, was tun. Sind Sie auch aufgefordert oder hat sie sich nicht getraut?"

[112] *Theodor W. Adorno und Max Horkheimer Briefwechsel*, bd. I, 144-5. Author's translation, "Wir müssen uns darüber klar sein, dass, so 'nett' er auch ist, uns mit ihm in Wahrheit keine gemeinsame Überzeugung verbindet. Besonders missfiel mir, dass er zwischen uns (Ihnen und mir) theoretische Differenzen zu konstruieren suchte, indem er Ihre größere 'Beweglichkeit' als Vorzug meinem 'starren Radikalismus' entgegenstelle.

Adorno's language here stands in stark contrast to his public comments concerning Tillich. Is this simply a matter of Adorno's private views, reflecting a private rejection of any commonly binding convictions, versus eulogistic public statements after Tillich's death, where he attributes some influence?[113] The criticism in this May 1936 letter likely refers to Adorno's conviction that his (and Horkheimer's position) is *quite specific*, as much as, or even more than as a direct critique of Tillich. Indeed, since Adorno had neither official affiliation with the *Institut* nor regular and direct communication with Horkheimer, it is understandable that he sought to clearly align himself with Horkheimer. There is an obvious desire to reassure Horkheimer that their views remain similar—if not identical—despite what Adorno characterizes as Tillich's attempt to distinguish their respective views.[114]

The letters, from November 1934 through 1936, wherein Adorno criticizes Tillich should be read through the lens of his concerns *vis-à-vis* his own position with the *Institut* and his perception of Tillich as having complicated that position[115] along with his insecurity over remaining in Oxford as an 'Advanced Student.' In this final letter blaming Tillich, Adorno raises concerns about his ability to legally and financially remain in Oxford much longer,[116] suggesting the larger issues for which Tillich may have functioned as a scapegoat. By contrast, a letter the following year, written from Paris, has a different, entirely positive, depiction of Tillich,[117] further suggesting that Adorno's critique, if it is a cri-

---

Schwer zu sagen, ob Lob oder Angriff die größere Unverschämtheit sind." Adorno began with a more personal, albeit equally negative account of Tillich during that particular meeting: "Obwohl sie äußerlich so harmonisch verliefen wie es mit einem solchen Harmonisten nur sein kann, war mein Eindruck ungemein negativ. Ich fand ihn zerfahren, geschäftig, theoretisch stehen geblieben und voll der ärgsten reaktionären Instinkte."

[113] Taken with Adorno's critique of Tillich's anthropology in the third chapter, this could be seen as decisive, but neither is definitive in my view. This does, however, imperil any claim concerning 'mutual intellectual influence' in the stronger sense of the claim.

[114] Wiggershaus notes this dynamic, which is mentioned below in footnote 118. Cf. Wiggershaus, 160.

[115] 25 June 1935, Adorno to Horkheimer. *Adorno-Horkheimer Briefwechsel*, bd. I, 163. Adorno writes: "Ich habe Tillichs Argument, dass ich, weil ich selber in verhältnismäßig guten Umständen, auf materiellen Lohn zu verzichten habe, so wenig anerkannt wie Sie es anerkannten." In a marginal note to this letter, Adorno makes the intriguing claim that "Tillich gehört im Grunde zu den Heideggers, fühlt sich aber durch uns erwischt und sucht nach einem Loch, in das er schlüpfen kann." Wiggershaus, 165.

[116] Wiggershaus, 163.

[117] 7 August 1937, Adorno to Horkheimer. "Mit Tillich war ich öfters [in Paris] zusammen, durchaus angenehm." Wiggershaus, 393.

tique, should be read in large part in light of his tenuous situation at the time. Furthermore, Adorno was not an easy person to get along with, and even Horkheimer is clear about this as early as a December 26, 1935 letter to Pollock, in which Horkheimer notes "a number of disturbing aspects, the source of which lies in [Adorno's] personality...."[118] Given that the only interaction between Adorno and Horkheimer during this time period was in the form of letters, in many of which Adorno continued to blame Tillich, Horkheimer's caution concerning Adorno's personality was almost certainly reinforced by Adorno's attacks on his own *Doktorvater*. While in Frankfurt, and later again in New York, Adorno displayed much greater respect for Tillich as a thinker, both publicly and privately, despite ongoing intellectual disagreement with Tillich's metaphysical and ontological orientation. Adorno's respect for Tillich as a person and a teacher is never called into question.

Horkheimer equivocates somewhat in his single, brief response to Adorno concerning Tillich in June 1936. According to Wiggershaus, there is a curious, symbiotic pattern of long letters from Adorno followed by short, often cryptic replies by Horkheimer.[119] This dynamic is evident here, where Horkheimer ambiguously writes: "What you write about Paulus is absolutely right. There is hardly anyone outside our circle who shares common views with him in the decisive philosophical matters."[120] Did Horkheimer mean to imply that those within their circle agreed with Tillich on key philosophical issues? The most obvious

---

[118] Horkheimer to Pollock, cited in Wiggershaus, 159-60. This letter does not appear in Horkheimer's *Gesammelte Schriften*, bd. 15, which includes his letters for 1935. Wiggershaus does not adequately cite his source. Two online sources indicate that this letter is solely archival. Both cite the following: "Trotz einer Reihe störender Momente, die in seiner [Adornos] Persönlichkeit begründet sind, scheint es mir notwendig zu sein, dass ich mit ihm zusammenarbeite." See http://www.welt.de/print-welt/article236607/Buch_der_Woche_Wissenschaftsmanager_und_Prinzenkind.html, ac cessed on 11/5/11, and http://marcuse.org/herbert/people/adorno/AdornoToHorkheimer1935.htm, accessed on 11/5/11.

[119] "The long letters from Adorno, and Horkheimer's short replies, up to the time of Adorno's emigration to New York in February 1938, are evidence of a strange mixture of continuing mutual reserve on some basic points and psychological and theoretical symbiosis, a lasting interaction between Adorno's mental fireworks and Horkheimer's measured and selective application of them." Wiggershaus, 160.

[120] Horkheimer to Adorno, 6 June 1936. *Adorno-Horkheimer Briefwechsel*, bd., I, 156. Author's translation, "Was Sie über Paulus schreiben, ist durchaus richtig. Es gibt außerhalb unseres Kreises kaum jemand, mit dem in entschiedenen philosophischen Dingen wirkliche Gemeinsamkeit besteht."

interpretation is to see Horkheimer 'thoroughly' agreeing with Adorno's critiques, further criticizing Tillich as a philosopher, and one may quite plausibly interpret Horkheimer in this light. One could also read the "außerhalb unseres Kreises" as a slight rebuff of Adorno, suggesting that within their circle (later called the Frankfurt School) there was at least some commonality of purpose and philosophical perspective shared with Tillich, despite the latter's increasing role as a theologian at Union Theological Seminary. Horkheimer's opinions of Tillich, at least during Tillich's life, as a philosopher are unknown; in the final chapter, it is suggested that Horkheimer was critical of Tillich as a theologian, although this is largely implicit. To the point, in a 1947 letter from Horkheimer to Tillich, in response to the latter's comments concerning *Eclipse of Reason*, Horkheimer wrote: "During the last weeks [Adorno and I] have been writing on the concept of Truth, but we are still in the beginning. Even though it is clear that your own viewpoint [is] represented in our discussions as distinctly as it can be without your being present, I miss our regular meetings, particularly during this part of our work." [121] Despite Horkheimer's equivocations in response to Adorno, and even despite his own critiques of Tillich's theological position, Horkheimer still highly valued the relationship with Tillich as a catalyst for his own thought. It apparently remained important for his collaborative thought with Adorno, particularly when thinking about the possibilities of a second volume of the *Dialectic of Enlightenment*.

VI. Political In/Action

An important locus of constructive similarity and difference among Adorno, Horkheimer, and Tillich lies in their respective understandings of the intersection of theory and praxis, specifically regarding the relative importance of political action. This will be fleshed out more thoroughly in the following chapters' analyses of distinctions in the respective thinkers' theories of rationality and subjectivity, but it is instructive to mention it briefly at this point. Neither Horkheimer nor Adorno was ever politically active in any robust sense,[122] despite their

---

[121] Horkheimer to Tillich, 29 August 1947. MH, *GS* 17, 884. In this letter, Horkheimer mentions plans for the second part of the *Dialectic of Enlightenment*, which never appeared. He specifically asks Tillich for sources of "competent theoretical interpretations of the words of Jesus 'I am the Truth.'" *Adorno-Horkheimer Briefwechsel*, bd., I, 156.

[122] "From time to time the question of Horkheimer's possible membership in the KPD has been raised. But hard evidence to support this view seems unavailable, and there is much in his writings and actions that makes his current denial of membership entirely plausible.... Horkheimer's earliest political sympathies were with Rosa Luxem-

early and reasonably consistent insistence upon the unity of theory and praxis. Neither was actively involved in political causes, and they did not speak out publicly, even with respect to the increasingly anti-Semitic tenor of German politics in the early 1930s. This was reflective of the semi-official position of the *Institut*, whose founders wanted to remain independent of any political party.[123] Adorno's later indifference to radical students in the 1960s may be seen as continuation of this lethargic praxis.

Tillich was not initially engaged in political matters either, but increasingly, and to a greater extent than Horkheimer and Adorno, he came to realize the significance of political theorizing coming to fruition in political action. His upbringing in a conservative home, raised in a Lutheran tradition left him initially uneasy with direct political engagement. Following his ministry in Berlin's Moabit district and his distress following service as a chaplain in the First World War, Tillich gradually became more involved in political theory and activity, first as a pastor, later as a philosopher and public intellectual. Although Tillich had been committed to the ideals and principles of religious socialism since the early 1920s, he was reticent to become overtly involved in political action. He acknowledged to the Paucks that he had "only with great difficulty transcended his father's sentimental and romantic adherence to what he considered a false application of Lutheran theology to political affairs."[124] It was not until 1929 that Tillich officially joined the Social Democratic Party largely in opposition to the encroachment of National Socialism. Ultimately expelled from Germany, in part for the political views expressed in his "Ten Theses Against the Nazis," and detailed in *The Socialist Decision*, Tillich's political engagement gradually waned in the United States, whose political system he never fully understood.

Despite being actively involved in two socialist journal publications during the 1920s and 30s (*Blätter für den Religiösen Sozialismus* from 1919-1926 and the *Neue Blätter für den Sozialismus* from 1930-33), Tillich, like many German intellectuals, was slow to see the diabolical reality of National Socialism. He "deluded

burg, especially because of her critique of Bolshevik centralism. After her murder in 1919, he never found another socialist leader to follow." Jay, 14.

[123] Martin Jay writes: "Political activism as such was...not in itself a reason for rejection by the group. It could, however, prove a hindrance, as in the case of Karl Korsch... [who] was never offered a full membership." Jay, 13. Jay continues: "When the Institute did accept members who were politically committed, it was solely because of their nonpolitical work." Jay, 15.

[124] Pauck and Pauck, 124.

himself" into thinking that Hitler and the romanticized nationalism he manipulated would never overcome Germany. Wilhelm and Marion Pauck write: "The extremism of Nazi views and the propensity for wild propaganda of the party's leaders misled many German citizens into supposing it unimaginable that such ideas and such men could ever come into power."[125] This was perhaps particularly true of the intelligentsia. Throughout the Weimar years, Tillich "remained preoccupied with the theoretical and philosophical elaboration of the principles of religious socialism."[126] Tillich did not take an overtly active role in condemning and working against National Socialism—either as a political movement or its increasing presence in Christian churches—until 1932. Adorno had pressured Tillich to respond earlier,[127] although Adorno himself did not engage in any political response.

Tillich's 1932 "Ten Theses Against the Nazis"[128] called upon fellow German Protestants to prove their "prophetic-Christian character by setting the Christianity of the cross against the paganism of the swastika. Protestantism," Tillich continued, "must testify that the cross has broken and judged the 'holiness' of nation, race, blood, and power."[129] In April 1932, Tillich co-wrote a 'remarkably bold' letter to his beloved Wingolf fraternity, condemning their exclusion of socialists and Jews from among their ranks, and he later resigned with great regret.

Perhaps to some degree in response to the challenges and encouragement of friends and colleagues, Tillich wrote *The Socialist Decision* in 1932. The book was not published until 1933, however, making it too late to reach its intended audience or have any real effect. During 1933, Tillich toured Germany trying to decide what to do next, holding onto some hope that the Nazi experiment would soon collapse. Horkheimer warned Tillich that his own writings made him an enemy of the Nazi state[130] but it took Tillich some time to realize this and then decide to leave Germany. Adorno recalled discussions he had with Tillich on the island of Rügen in the Baltic Sea during the summer of 1933. In those conversations, Tillich related some of the "overtures" the Nazis had made

---

[125] Pauck and Pauck, 123.

[126] Pauck and Pauck, 123.

[127] Adorno, in *Werk und Wirken*, 30-1.

[128] For the English translation of Tillich's "Ten Theses," see *Paul Tillich: Theologian of the Boundaries*, ed. Mark Kline Taylor (San Francisco: Collins, 1987) 116-8.

[129] *Paul Tillich: Theologian of the Boundaries*, ed. Mark Kline Taylor, 117.

[130] Horkheimer, in *Werk und Wirken*, 16-7.

to him, trying to win over what Adorno describes as Tillich's "extraordinary charisma."[131]

Even more than Horkheimer, and in many ways quite different from the 'early' Tillich, Adorno rejected any political theory leaning towards praxis. For Adorno, theory itself became a kind of praxis.[132] Susan Buck-Morss writes, "Although he continued to insist on the necessity for revolutionary social change, such statements remained intentionally abstract insofar as Adorno's theory contained no concept of a collective revolutionary subject which might accomplish that change."[133] This would prove to be a major source of tension with his more radical students in Frankfurt in the 1960s.

VII. Exile and Diaspora

Hitler's ascension to power in 1933 interrupted the collaboration of these scholars. The astonishing group of intellectuals in Frankfurt, the majority of whom were Jewish, was scattered when suspended from their teaching positions, and almost all chose to leave Germany for the duration of the war. Tillich, Horkheimer, and Mannheim were among the first faculty dismissed, described as "enemies of the state" in lists printed in newspapers on April 13, 1933.[134] Within the year, 1,684 scholars were dismissed from German universities for being politically suspect (Socialist, Communist) or 'racially' suspect (Jewish).[135] The *Institut* in Frankfurt officially closed in the late spring of 1933, but Horkheimer and Löwe had already fled in March to Geneva, where the *Institut* had set up a branch for an eventuality like this, showing impressive foresight.[136]

---

[131] Adorno, *Lectures on Negative Dialectics*, 3. *Vorlesung über Negative Dialektik,* 11-2.

[132] "After 1951, Horkheimer and Adorno appeared to lose the connection to a concrete struggle for the future, and thus by implication lost the basis for the construction of the appropriate theory and practice that emerges from that struggle." Jeffrey Paris, "Obstinate Critique and the Possibility of the Future," in *New Critical Theory: Essays on Liberation*, ed. William S. Wilkerson and Jeffrey Paris (Lanham: Rowman & Littlefield, 2001) 26.

[133] Buck-Morss, 24.

[134] Of the twelve faulty suspended from teaching posts at Frankfurt in April 1933, eleven were Jewish; Tillich was the twelfth. Pauck and Pauck, 130.

[135] "National Sozialismus—Hochschule Politik" von Hans Meier, in *Die Deutschen Universität im Dritten Reich*, hrsg. von Helmut Kuhn (München: R. Piper, 1966) 82; cited in Pauck and Pauck, 130.

[136] The *Institut* moved to Geneva, where it was renamed the *Société Internationale des Recherches Sociales.* Paul Tillich was listed among the board members at that time. Jay, 307, n. 87.

While many prepared to leave Europe, Adorno left for Geneva, even though he was not officially dismissed from his post in Frankfurt until later in 1933.[137] Adorno's politics were not particularly radical at this point, and he was likely dismissed more for his partial Jewish ancestry. Following the initial political coup of National Socialism, Adorno, like many intellectuals including Tillich, was "convinced that the whole charade would soon be over," according to Wiggershaus. He even tried to gain employment as a music critic in Berlin.[138] Curiously, Adorno went so far as to write a positive, albeit ironic, review of a Nazi-influenced musical composition of Herbert Munzel. This was likely an attempt to remain in Germany and keep his teaching position in Frankfurt, despite his Jewish ancestry and the Marxian influences in his thought.[139] Since he was reticent to leave Germany and he had no official status with the *Institut*, he did not immigrate to New York until 1938, after time spent as an 'Advanced Student' studying Husserl at Oxford.

Tillich took the news of his dismissal from Frankfurt very hard and briefly retained "the vain hope that the Nazi regime would last only a short time and that he and his friends might be reinstated."[140] Tillich and his wife travelled, spending the summer of 1933 on the Baltic island of Rügen trying to figure out what to do next. Adorno, among others, visited the Tillichs on Rügen and tried to convince Tillich to leave. After a close call with the Nazi secret police near Dresden and a disappointing meeting with the culture ministry late in the summer of 1933,[141] Tillich became resigned to the fact that he would need to leave Germany. While *The Socialist Decision* was being burned by the Nazis in Germany, officials at Columbia University and Union Theological Seminary in New York City agreed to offer Tillich a joint position as a visiting professor, despite the fact that Tillich spoke no English and was largely unknown in the United States. More astonishing was the fact that the faculty of Union agreed to a 5% pay cut, at the height of the Great Depression, to bring the 47-year old Tillich and his family to the U.S. Union provided them with a large apartment at the seminary furnished with donated furniture.[142] Tillich began studying English

[137] Jay, *Dialectical Imagination*, 29-30.
[138] Wiggershaus, 157.
[139] Wiggershaus, 157.
[140] Pauck and Pauck, 131.
[141] Pauck and Pauck, 136-7.
[142] Pauck and Pauck, 133-4, 140. Union Theological Seminary President Henry Sloane Coffin and Professor Reinhold Niebuhr knew Tillich's work and they were in-

and saying his goodbyes in the summer and fall, finally arriving with his family in New York in November 1933.

Tillich came to love New York and settled into life in a new country quickly though he spent a great deal of his time with fellow refugees, particularly friends and colleagues from Frankfurt. The Paucks note that "[b]y the end of 1934 an increasing number of [Tillich's] friends had arrived in [New York], where they reassembled with regularity, mostly in Tillich's home...."[143] Tillich's Frankfurt friends and colleagues Eduard Heimann and Adolf Löwe taught at the New School for Social Research, while Horkheimer and Max Wertheimer taught at Columbia with Tillich, in his initial joint appointment at Columbia and Union Theological Seminary. Adorno did not join them until 1938, but the Paucks report that Adorno was at the Tillich's apartment in Harlem within a few hours of his arrival in the United States. From 1938-1941, Adorno worked with Paul Lazarsfeld on the Princeton Radio Project. Adorno remained in New York, in contact with Tillich and others, until joining Horkheimer in California in 1941, when they began collaborative work in earnest on what would become *Dialectic of Enlightenment*.

It was in large part the sizable endowment of the *Institut* which allowed Horkheimer to establish an informal link with Columbia University. While the Columbia sociology department was in favor of the *Institut's* move and granting a limited affiliation, Columbia's president was a staunch conservative and in hindsight, it is remarkable that the affiliation was effected.[144] With an independent endowment and support from the sociology department, Horkheimer was able to maintain loose ties with Columbia through the 1930s. Tillich's joint affiliation with Columbia eventually ended and he shifted to philosophical theology at Union full-time, where he began to write and teach in English, although his accent was notoriously hard to understand. Tillich's shift away from pure philosophy, and particularly into English marks a shift from other Frankfurt scholars who continued to work primarily in German.[145] Although Adorno

strumental in securing the initial visiting professorship for Tillich. Union was and remains independent but loosely affiliated with Columbia University. It lies on Broadway in Morningside Heights/Harlem, surrounded by Columbia, Barnard, Teacher's College, and the former location of the Julliard School of Music.

[143] Pauck and Pauck, 155.

[144] Lewis S. Feuer, "The Frankfurt Marxists and the Columbia Liberals," *Survey* 25 (1980) 156-76; cited in Tar, 8.

[145] The *Institut's* journal, *Zeitschrift für Sozialforschung*, published two volumes primarily in English beginning in 1940.

wrote some articles in English, he rather pompously claimed that German philosophical ideas were not translatable into English and, combined with his disdain for American culture, it is not overly surprising that he never found a teaching position in the United States.[146]

Throughout the 1930s and 40s (and beyond), the friendships and correspondences among these Frankfurt scholars continued in exile in New York. It is well known that these 'salon' style discussions of philosophical and theological topics which had begun in Frankfurt continued in New York[147] with many of the same participants. The Tillich Archive in Germany has what appears to be detailed discussion notes from twelve of these conversations between 1941 and 1945 in which Tillich, Horkheimer, Pollock, and Löwe, among others, were participants. In these conversations, which began in Berlin and Frankfurt in the 1920s, continuing into exile in New York, these thinkers developed and honed the prophetic interruptions which guided their respective works.

Conclusions

This study focuses on the critical Frankfurt years of Tillich, Horkheimer, and Adorno (1929-1933) and the years of exile in the United States until Horkheimer and Adorno returned to Germany, and Tillich definitively shifted to philosophical and systematic theology (1950). This chapter has begun to show that not only was there a substantial historical and personal overlap and connection, both during the Frankfurt years, and during the exilic period in New York, there was a substantial level of intellectual engagement between Tillich, Horkheimer, and Adorno which has been heretofore neglected. These thinkers were actively involved with each other, teaching seminars together, engaged and embroiled in common official and unofficial discussion groups, and relaxing together as friends. Throughout this exilic period, and until (and even beyond) the return of the *Institut* to Frankfurt in 1950, Tillich remained an important inter-

---

146 "Adorno…had always been anxious to return to Germany, in large measure because of his belief that his native tongue was the most appropriate medium in which to express dialectical thought." Martin Jay, *Adorno* (Cambridge: Harvard University Press, 1984) 45.

147 Horkheimer wrote, "Wir sind sogleich miteinander zusammengekommen, als er in Amerika eintraf. Und die Diskussion, die wir in Frankfurt begonnen hatten, über philosophische und theologische Gegenstände, ist fortgesetzt worden, fortgesetzt in New York, später in Chikago und schließlich dann wieder, als er mich in Deutschland aufgesucht hat." Horkheimer, in *Werk und Wirken*, 17-8.

locutor and friend to Adorno and Horkheimer, despite some of the negative characterizations one finds in some of Adorno's letters.

In addition to the contextual, historical, and important personal connections and overlaps explored in this chapter, there are a number of conceptual similarities shared among Adorno, Horkheimer, and Tillich, which will be explored in detail in the following chapters. As a foundation for what I have termed 'prophetic interruptions,' all three thinkers offer a clear critique of capitalism combined with socialist sympathies to varying degrees and with varying practical and political import. Each wrote articles for the Journal of the *Institut.*[148] All three were critical of the Nazis (to differing extents) and each stood against fascism. Beyond Nietzsche's work, Freud's development of psychoanalysis and his social critique of structural repression, particularly in *Civilization and its Discontents,* further influenced all three. Adorno, Horkheimer, and Tillich each spent much of their life's work seeking to articulate an emancipatory social critique—a prophetic interruption of an unjust status quo. The function and limitations of rationality as a primary vehicle for emancipatory theory and practice is the subject of the next chapter.

[148] Tillich's contributions to the *Zeitschrift für Sozialforschung* were in the form of reviews, of Kurt Goldstein in 1936 and of Herbert Marcuse in 1941.

2.

Critical Reason with an Emancipatory Goal

> When we criticize, we are not doing something arbitrary and impersonal; it is, at least very often, proof that there are living, active forces within us shedding skin. We negate, and we have to negate, because something in us wants to live and affirm itself, something we might not yet know or see! -- This in favor of criticism. —Friedrich Nietzsche, *The Gay Science*[1]

Introduction

This chapter demonstrates that the prophetic interruptions—shared among Adorno, Horkheimer, and Tillich—are evinced in common diagnoses of modernity and mutual concerns with institutional rationality and domination. These can be seen through three primary loci: modern alienation (or estrangement), domination inscribed through instrumental reason, and social reification. Most importantly, their common diagnoses were seen through a shared lens of emancipation as a primary individual and social goal. This chapter will focus on the 1930s up through the composition of *Dialectic of Enlightenment* in 1944. These diagnostic loci and the emancipatory goal help reveal the dangers of modernity and challenges to subjectivity, and each points toward what Adorno, Horkheimer, and Tillich commonly believed to be the primary and most accessible social remedy: critical emancipatory reason. Each thought that because of the alienation, domination, and reification experienced by the subject, it was necessary for critical social thought to explore and indeed reimagine ways in which the subject could be liberated.[2] Among their greatest commonalities is this sense of critical reason standing as a dialectical gesture in thought against the forces of domination and oppression. This crucial common nexus of presuppositions orients

---

[1] Friedrich Nietzsche, *The Gay Science: With a Prelude in German Rhymes and an Appendix of Songs*, 307, trans. Josefine Nauckhoff (Cambridge University Press, 2003) 175.

[2] Subjectivity and agency are explored in detail in the following chapter on anthropology.

much of their writings, and it demonstrates their shared focus on the emancipatory capacities of reason.

Through a brief historical survey of the ways in which Hegel, Marx, Weber, and Lukács collectively influenced Adorno, Hegel, and Tillich, the chapter examines the ways each of these thinkers focused their attention on issues of alienation, domination, and reification as pressing problems facing modern human subjects. I will then transition to the ways in which the three thinkers came to see that reason has, and can be refocused on, profound emancipatory possibilities. In so doing, this chapter analyzes the changing conception of critical reason's capacities as evidenced by each thinker's prognosis for the possibilities of change. As Nietzsche notes in the epigraph to this chapter, criticism is a living thing, and there are several important shifts in the conceptualization of reason and its emancipatory potentialities in each thinker which are traced and explicated in this chapter.

While all three thinkers started from a premise of seeking social transformation and emancipatory praxis, Adorno and Horkheimer ultimately came to despair of any collective emancipation by the 1940s. They argue that the individual, through use of critical reason, may be able to obtain a limited degree of freedom *through* the social realm, but importantly not *from* the social realm. By the 1940s, both see the promise of enlightenment[3] (as a historical movement in philosophy *and* as a process of human development) finally negating itself as reason falls into the service of fascism and the culture industry. In *Dialectic of Enlightenment*, there is limited hope remaining in the bleak philosophy of history proffered. Understood in the context of increasing knowledge about the extent of the Holocaust, this pessimism is by no means surprising. This chapter argues that the movement in the thought of Adorno and Horkheimer during this period is not best characterized as a move from an early optimism to an increasing pessimism in light of the encroachment of fascism. Rather, it is argued that the transition in Adorno and Horkheimer's thought should be seen as reflecting an increasingly nuanced, *dialectical tension between emancipation and domination*. They diagnose, in a Marxian vein, a dialectical tension between the hope for social change and an increasing realization of the pervasive extent of instrumental rationality. Tillich, by contrast, maintains some hope for social

---

[3] Enlightenment, for Adorno and Horkheimer, refers both to a human process of development and to a historical movement in the 18th Century. They typically capitalize the historical movement, which they see as a manifestation of the overall process of enlightenment which is coterminous with human beings. This is further explicated below.

transformation through a reimagined socialism in touch with its 'depth dimension' even as he became increasingly aware of the limitations of religious socialism's capacity to affect change. This chapter demonstrates that what unites these three thinkers, their common focus on critical emancipatory reason, is ultimately stronger than what divides them.

I. The Genesis of Modern Critique

The first chapter began to elucidate the deeply shared personal connections and hinted at the common intellectual milieu shared by Adorno, Horkheimer, and Tillich. Here I will expand on the analysis of the shared philosophical combination of German Idealism through Marx, along with the distinct Nietzsche-Weber-Freud lineage of influence clearly identifiable in all three thinkers.[4] This chapter nuances this question of how the shared and respectively distinct notions of reason and its critical capacities in modern society influence and arguably determine how Adorno, Horkheimer, and Tillich thematize reason as both the primary possibility for emancipation, but also inevitably doomed. How do their respective notions of critical rationality inform their respective diagnoses and prescriptions for any emancipatory efforts within the individual or society? We must keep in mind the context of the collapse of the Weimar Republic, the rise of Fascism, and the outbreak of war. Likewise, we must recall that the debates and conversations about rationality were discussed among the three thinkers (and others) in an ongoing dialogue with mutual respect within this broader historical context.

Here I begin to expound upon some of the compelling resonances and ideological similarities between the intellectual projects of Adorno and Horkheimer on the one hand, and Tillich on the other, during the 1930s and 1940s, building on the common personal and professional ties demonstrated previously. What would become the hallmark of the 'Frankfurt School,' a critical social theory, came to be seen as the vehicle of emancipatory reason. Yet with Adorno and Horkheimer's resistance to normative accounts of emancipation, it is not immediately clear that there even *could* be such a thing as emancipatory critical social theory, given their emphasis on determinate negation. In Tillich's case, critical social theory is seen largely through the lens of religious socialism and the pro-

[4] For several reasons, space being primary, this chapter reluctantly focuses on Weber to the general exclusion of Nietzsche and Freud.

phetic Protestant principle, which will be dealt with most fully in the concluding chapter on religion.

The individual and social limitations identified above (alienation, domination, and reification) are thought to be rooted in reason itself, both in terms of problem and solution. Tillich's prognosis begins with reason, and is rooted therein, but his diagnosis for and explanation of these social limitations is sin—separation from God (as 'ground of being,' not *a* Being), complicated by socio-psychological structures. Careful examination of the role of alienation, domination, and reification reveals ways in which critical reason is thematized by Adorno, Horkheimer, and Tillich to be a central, if not the only, hope for humanity in the face of barbarism. It is suggested here that the projects of critical theory and religious socialism are two parallel and complementary emancipatory solutions to a common view of instrumental rationality and threats to subjectivity like alienation, domination, and reification. Instead of attempting a comprehensive account of the scope of reason within any of these three thinkers (a multi-volume project), I instead focus on selective moments pointing towards the development of critical social theories, roughly from 1925–45.

It is clear that Adorno, Horkheimer, and Tillich were each profoundly influenced by the philosophical tradition of German Idealism, even as they each rejected or refined substantial portions of this tradition. Kant's critical philosophy is marked by the attempt to reground philosophy in reason, as opposed to empiricism, tradition, authority, and faith, and his unwavering commitment to the maxim of the Enlightenment—"*Sapere audi*! Dare to know!" The focus on critique as the goal of philosophy marks the central Kantian theme which most influences Adorno, Horkheimer, and Tillich. The German idealist tradition, very broadly construed, thought progress could be attained by subjecting everything to rational analysis and through it, reason, maturation, justice, stability, peace, etc. would (it was thought) gradually increase. In his "Postscript" to *Critical Theory*, Horkheimer acknowledges his indebtedness to German Idealism, despite his frequent critiques of the movement.[5] Pushing back against neo-Kantian transcendental idealism, Adorno, Horkheimer, and to a lesser extent Tillich,[6] all felt that "reason was grounded neither primarily in the transcenden-

[5] *CT*, 245.

[6] Tillich was much more indebted to Schelling than to Kant, although Tillich shares this view unequivocally with respect to rational criticism. Prophetic criticism, on the other hand, is based in a more transcendental and metaphysical order for Tillich.

tal realm nor in universal laws but in *human history*,"[7] according to Yvonne Sherratt.

A brief background into Hegel, Marx, Weber, and Lukács in particular is necessary to demonstrate the shared context of Adorno, Horkheimer, and Tillich, particularly their shared assumptions arising from these thinkers, as Adorno, Horkheimer, and Tillich examined and sought to employ critical emancipatory reason in the face of societal domination and the shadow of Fascistic unreason. Naturally, any account of the intellectual genesis of the Frankfurt School will inevitably be incomplete, but should begin with Hegel (if not Bacon and Vico).[8] At the same time, there is a competing set of themes and sphere of influence from Nietzsche and Freud, working at times perpendicularly to the Kant-Hegel-Marx trajectory from German idealism. Here it is the latter trajectory from German idealism which is of greater import, so while it reflects a significant lacuna, an analysis of the importance influence of Nietzsche and Freud must be omitted for the sake of brevity and cogency,[9] and several excellent studies of this line of influence exist.

---

[7] Yvonne Sherratt, *Adorno's Positive Dialectic* (New York: Cambridge University Press, 2002) 27.

[8] Indeed, a thorough analysis should begin with Bacon and Vico, but Hegel is more crucial for the shared project of the three thinkers in question in this study and in the interest of keeping this section on intellectual genesis as brief as possible, I begin with Hegel. Any complete discussion of Tillich's intellectual legacy would have to include Friedrich Schelling, on whom Tillich wrote both of his academic theses, but Schelling is also omitted here since he was of minimal importance for Adorno and Horkheimer. Other scholars have traced the role of Schelling in Tillich's development. Perhaps the most thorough treatments of the intellectual genesis of the Frankfurt School come from Wiggershaus, Jay, and Held.

[9] Nietzsche's analysis of power (*inter al.*) and Freud's dichotomy between the 'pleasure principle' and the 'reality' principle, as well as his analysis of social repression in *Civilization and its Discontents*, are admittedly very important for all three thinkers. All three were influenced by psychoanalysis, Adorno's first (rejected) *Habilitation* drew heavily from Freudian theories, and Tillich increasingly drew on psychoanalysis for his own existential theology. Horkheimer's comments to Leo Lowenthal concerning Freud in an October 1942 letter are instructive here: Freud's "thought is one of the *Bildungsmächte* [foundation stones] without which our own philosophy would not be what it is." Cited in Jay, 102. Where germane in the text, I have noted the influence of Freud and in some cases Nietzsche as well. Although I have excluded an introductory summary and analysis of Nietzsche and Freud from the 'Genesis of Modern Critique' with respect to critical theory in this chapter, this is by no means intended to downplay the immense significance of either thinker on Adorno, Horkheimer, or Tillich. Where relevant in the indi-

I.1 The Influence of G. F. W. Hegel

G. F. W. Hegel's importance for Adorno, Horkheimer, and Tillich, separately and jointly, is hard to overstate.[10] Four loci are suggested here in and through which one can discern the insight and influence of Hegel along with the application of Hegel to their own individual and joint purposes in articulating a critical social theory. The first locus of Hegel's thought employed and adapted by Adorno, Horkheimer, and Tillich can best be exemplified by Hegel's own words from *Phenomenology of Spirit* where he analyzes *negativity as the power of critical development*. Hegel writes:

> ...the life of Spirit is not the life that shrinks from death and keeps itself untouched by devastation, but rather the life that endures it and maintains itself in it. It wins its truth only when, in utter dismemberment, it finds itself. It is this power, not as something positive, which closes its eyes to the negative, as when we say of something that it is nothing or is false, and then, having done with it, turn away and pass on to something else; on the contrary, *Spirit is this power only by looking the negative in the face, and tarrying with it. This tarrying with the negative is the magical power that converts it into being.*[11]

This focus on negation, along with the dialectical structure, is arguably the most crucial aspect of the Hegelian structure adopted and adapted by Horkheimer, and especially by Adorno. Hegel's conception of 'determinate negation' always affects something specific, precise and imperfect.[12] 'Determinate negation' is part of the dialectical process and despite negating something, Hegel sees a new affirmation arising, a renewing, positive union.[13] Moving from affirmation

---

vidual chapters, I have tried to note and analyze the influence of Nietzsche and Freud on the three thinkers.

[10] This is not to suggest, however, that the influence of Kant (or neo-Kantianism) and Hegel are mutually exclusive by any means.

[11] Georg Friedrich Hegel, *Phenomenology of Spirit*, trans. A. V. Miller (New York: Oxford University Press, 1977) Preface, section 32, 19; emphasis added. Georg Friedrich Hegel, *Phänomenologie des Geistes* (Stuttgart: Philipp Relam, 1987) Vorrede, 32-3.

[12] In his *Science of Logic*, Hegel writes: "Determinateness is negation posited as an affirmative and is the proposition of Spinoza: *omnis determinatio est negatio*.... Of this proposition that determinateness is negation, the unity of Spinoza's substance—or that there is only one substance—is the necessary consequence." Hegel, *Science of Logic*, 113.

[13] Singer describes it thusly: "A determinate negation...is the result of the discovery that a form of consciousness is inadequate, is itself a new form of consciousness, namely, consciousness aware of the inadequacies of the previous form and forced to adopt a dif-

to negation to a negation of that negation leads to an *Aufhebung*, a reconciliation which Hegel presupposed but which Horkheimer and especially Adorno could not accept. Negation is also important for Tillich, and he accepts parts of Hegel's metaphysics, even as he reframes them. Importantly for Tillich, negation is not the end of the journey or a goal unto itself, as it arguably became for Adorno, but a crucial step along the way to an anticipated reconciliation.

The second central area in which Hegel profoundly influenced Adorno, Horkheimer, and Tillich concerns 'pure insight,' that which leads to enlightenment; here Hegel uses the metaphor of *disease* which became so important for Horkheimer and Adorno's analysis of reason under the conditions of modernity. Although Hegel ultimately denies that there can be pure insight, he writes:

> ...the struggle against [pure insight, i.e. enlightenment] betrays the fact that the infection has occurred. The struggle is too late, and every remedy adopted only aggravates the disease, for it has laid hold of the marrow of spiritual life... there is thus no power in which it could overcome the disease.[14]

Horkheimer explicitly claimed this image of disease, and it served as a general epigraph for both Adorno and Horkheimer in the 1940s. In *Eclipse of Reason*, Horkheimer wrote: "The disease of reason is that reason was born from man's urge to dominate nature, and the 'recovery' depends on insight into the nature of the original disease, not on a cure of the latest symptoms."[15] This is the project and goal of *Dialectic of Enlightenment* and of critical theory generally. Even more than Hegel, *Adorno and Horkheimer understand enlightenment as a human process*—not (just) a historical moment in modernity—*to be infected with the seeds of its own demise.* For Tillich, the image of enlightenment (or reason broadly) as infected and diseased is far less common, but perhaps reflects a rough analogue for the Christian teaching of sin as estrangement from God (as ground of being). In the Edenic myth, the first 'choice' against God's will has ontological effects, literally infecting all of humankind with the desire to put the self first and to distort human choices against the good and the just, and against God.

ferent approach in order to surmount them." Peter Singer, *Hegel* (New York: Oxford University Press, 1983) 52.

[14] Hegel, *Phenomenology of Sprit*, section 545, 331-2. *PhG*, 386.

[15] Horkheimer, *Eclipse of Reason* (New York: Continuum, 1974) 119.

As J. M. Bernstein correctly notes, Hegel's dialectic of pure insight and faith is an implicit critique of Kant. According to Bernstein's interpretation of Kant, concepts without intuitions are empty (pure insight), while intuitions without concepts are blind (certain types of religious faith).[16] There is a necessary interconnection between concepts (*a priori*) and intuitions for the purpose of judgment for Kant.[17] Bernstein thus implies that Hegel's dialectic of pure insight and religious faith evolves into Adorno and Horkheimer's dialectic of enlightenment and myth.[18] This dialectical tension ultimately collapses onto itself—myth is revealed as such by enlightenment and banished, while that fleeting moment of enlightenment often returns into myth.[19] James Schmidt, citing Horkheimer, writes:

> While Horkheimer and Adorno were concerned with the struggle between enlightenment and mythology rather than between enlightenment and faith, their argument mirrors Hegel's. The goal of the enlightenment, as they understood it, was "to dissolve myths and to depose imagination through knowledge." (MH, GS 5: 25). Yet, "the myths which fell victim [*zum Opfer fallen*] to Enlightenment were its own product." (MH, GS 5: 30)[20]

---

[16] Hegel "understood the moments of faith and pure insight to point back to a more fundamental antagonism. One can conceive of faith and pure insight as highly refined epistemic crystallizations of more fundamental anthropological moods: faith expresses unconditional *trust* in the other or, at least, the yearning or need for unconditional trust. Hence the figure of God is just the figure of an object of unconditional trust." J. M. Bernstein, "Negative Dialectic as Fate: Adorno and Hegel," in *The Cambridge Companion to Adorno*, ed. Tom Huhn (Cambridge: Cambridge University Press, 2004) 24.

[17] Bernstein, "Negative Dialectic as Fate," 23-4.

[18] "[T]he dialectic of enlightenment is, finally, a transformed embodiment of Hegel's causality of fate doctrine." Bernstein, "Negative Dialectic as Fate: Adorno and Hegel," 21.

[19] Lambert Zuidervaart makes the important point that "A fundamental mistake in many interpretations of *Dialectic of Enlightenment* occurs when readers take such theses [concerning myth and enlightenment] to be *theoretical definitions of unchanging categories rather than critical judgments about historical tendencies.*" "Theodor W. Adorno," by Lambert Zuidervaart, in *The Stanford Encyclopedia of Philosophy (Summer 2011 Edition)* ed. by Edward N. Zalta; emphasis added. URL: <http://plato.stanford.edu/archives/sum2011/entries/adorno/>. Accessed 9/12/2011.

[20] James Schmidt, "Language, Mythology, and Enlightenment: Historical Notes on Horkheimer and Adorno's *Dialectic of Enlightenment*," in *Social Research* 65:4 (1998) 825.

This modified dialectic, Bernstein suggests, is the basis of the dialectic of enlightenment Adorno and Horkheimer eventually articulate in their collaborative work.[21]

Thirdly, the dialectic of intersubjective recognition found in Hegel's master-slave dialectic critically informs another crucial application of Hegel (via Marx) by Adorno, Horkheimer, and Tillich. In the quest for self-consciousness, the subject seeks recognition from another, as Hegel shows in the dialectic of master and slave.[22] Since there is inherent risk and a mimetic rivalry between parties which could lead to death,[23] subjects have historically accepted less-than-perfect relations in which slave consciousness exists *in itself* while the master consciousness exists *for itself*, without reciprocity. Hegel notes the irony of the master who lacks agency and thus freedom in an important sense because of their passivity; truth at this point is found only in slave consciousness.[24] This uneven relationship develops through labor, through which the worker "comes to see in the independent being its *own* independence."[25] This is one of the central insights Karl Marx takes from Hegel: freedom can arise as a product of labor through the process of the slave consciousness becoming self-conscious.[26] Again Hegel writes:

> ...being-for-self is present in the bondsman himself; in fashioning the thing, he becomes aware that being-for-self belongs to *him*, that he himself exists essentially and actually in his own right.... [T]he bonds-

[21] Adorno and Horkheimer's adaptation of Hegel's dialectic of pure insight and faith is "one fundamental expression of the dialectic of desired independence from nature and disavowed dependence." Bernstein continues, "Reason or enlightenment seeks through knowing and labor to master nature and become independent of it without acknowledging its pervasive dependence." Bernstein, "Negative Dialectic as Fate: Adorno and Hegel," 26.

[22] Hegel, *Phenomenology of Sprit*, sections 190-3, 115-7.

[23] Hegel, *Phenomenology of Sprit*, section 187, 113-4.

[24] Hegel, *Phenomenology of Sprit*, section 194, 117.

[25] Hegel, *Phenomenology of Sprit*, section 195, 118. "...das arbeitende Bewusstsein kommt also hierdurch zur Anschauung des selbständigen Seins, *als seiner selbst*." *PhG*, 148. Emphasis in original.

[26] Concerning this, Bernstein compellingly argues that "Adorno and Horkheimer's fundamental strategy is to appropriate Hegel's analysis of the dialectic of master and slave, independence and dependence, both directly *and* by turning it back into the logic of reason and object. Reason (the master concept) depends on object (the slave intuition)." Bernstein, "Negative Dialectic as Fate: Adorno and Hegel," 25; emphasis in original.

> man realizes that it is precisely in his work wherein he seemed to have only an alienated existence that he acquires a mind of his own.[27]

Fourthly, Adorno and Horkheimer accept Hegel's understanding of dialectics as the attempt to heal enlightenment division, while flatly denying any actual 'fulfillment' or 'reconciliation' of the dialectic. As was suggested in the opening of this chapter, Adorno and Horkheimer come to reject any fundamentally *positive* reading of enlightenment as a consistent possibility for individual and social change,[28] yet they cling to the idea of enlightenment as perhaps the only remaining possibility through critical emancipatory reason. Tillich, on the other hand, accepts dialectic as a means for—at least potentially—healing such division, and he seems to accept an ultimate reconciliation of the dialectic, although importantly, not as a utopia within history. Tillich retains hope for an ultimate eschatological consummation of history beyond the confines of the finite and the historical, rooted in his theology of God as the unconditioned ground of Being itself.

Reason engages in a dialectical conversation, rooted in the Greek *dialektikos*: the art of discourse or conversation in which the self is constituted as other. For Hegel, it is through such 'conversation' that truth can be disclosed, and dialectic is the means through which reason realizes itself. The three steps for Hegel are: unreflective unity of subject and object, reflective division of the subject from the object via negation, and finally a synthetic, reflective unity in which the subject overcomes the negation. It is this third step that is rejected so thoroughly by Adorno in particular that Joel Whitebook can declare: "Adorno was vehemently anti-Hegelian. He was also one of the most thoroughly Hegelian thinkers of the century."[29] Adorno strongly rejects any concluding moment of *Aufhebung* for reasons that will become clearer in chapters four and five. Horkheimer largely rejects the presumed (if only temporary) finality; Tillich offers a nuanced critique of Hegelian reconciliation.

In a significant review written for the *Institut's* journal in 1941, Tillich agreed with critical theory that Hegel's thought was

---

[27] Hegel, *Phenomenology of Sprit,* section 196, 118-9. *PhG*, 148-9. Emphasis in original.

[28] Individual agency and the possibilities and limitations of social change are addressed extensively in the third chapter.

[29] Joel Whitebook, "Weighty Objects: On Adorno's Kant-Freud Interpretation," in *The Cambridge Companion to Adorno*, 51.

> originally motivated by the conviction that the given facts that appear to common sense as the positive index of truth are in reality the negation of truth, so that truth can only be established by their destruction. The driving force of the dialectical method is this critical conviction.[30]

Tillich continues, arguing that Hegel's understanding of reason undergirds critical theory and functions as "the bridge from Kant and the bourgeois revolution to Marx and the proletarian revolution, with critical dialectics serving as the main cable of that bridge."[31] Both Adorno and Horkheimer would likely agree with Tillich's assessment here.

Dialectic, for Hegel, is the structure by which Spirit (*Geist*) unfolds as freedom and becomes self-aware within time and space. The abstract idea of freedom becomes concrete in particular individuals, finally leading to the concrete universality of freedom as a political narrative in history. For Hegel, subject and object ultimately achieve a type of self-reflective unity and the dialectic ends theoretically with the 'whole as the true.' For Horkheimer, as well as for Tillich, the tension between subject and object allows patterns of domination via instrumental reason to destabilize any effective relationship between subject and object, master or slave. Adorno rejects Hegel here, arguing pointedly in *Minima Moralia* that the "whole is the false"[32] because the unfolding of the dialectic has resulted in profound unfreedom—the calamitous barbarism of modernity.

I.2 The Influence of Karl Marx

Karl Marx's philosophy of history mirrors, among other things, Hegel's 'stages': an original unity marked by a "primitive kind of communism,"[33] followed by disruption via developments in production which lead to the alienation of workers from the means of production, and concluding with an ideal reconciliation; the separation exacerbated by rigid class distinctions is finally overcome by increasing equality through communism.[34] For Marx, the quest for emancipation

[30] Tillich, "Review of *Reason and Revolution: Hegel and the Rise of Revolution*," by Herbert Marcuse, in *Studies in Philosophy and Social Science* 9 (1941) 476.

[31] Tillich, "Review of *Reason and Revolution: Hegel and the Rise of Revolution*," 476.

[32] Theodor W. Adorno, *Minima Moralia: Reflections from Damaged Life*, trans. E.F.N. Jephcott (New York: Verso, 2002). "Das Ganze ist das Unwahre," in *GS* 4, 55.

[33] Sherratt, 36.

[34] For a nuanced account of Marx's understanding of the stages of history, see G. A. Cohen, *Karl Marx's Theory of History: A Defense* (Princeton: Princeton University Press, 2001).

is always an unfolding process because social realities and subjective perceptions constantly change. As Marx wrote in critique of idealism: "It is not the consciousness of men that determines their existence, but their social existence that determines their consciousness."[35] To be clear: while Adorno, Horkheimer, and Tillich can be said to agree broadly with Marx's diagnosis, each challenges Marx's prognosis.

The influence of Marx appears in Adorno, Horkheimer, and Tillich not only in the common critique of capitalism, but also in a dialectical philosophy of subjectivity (consciousness) and structure (society) with an emancipatory goal. Marx argues for a "categorical imperative to overthrow all circumstances in which man is humiliated, enslaved, abandoned, and despised...,"[36] and one can discern essential agreement in the writings of all three thinkers. Adorno and Horkheimer sought to integrate Hegelian and Marxian thought without the Hegelian moment of reconciliation in their fight against 'identity theory.' Relentlessly pushing philosophy to engage the social sphere—one of his greatest legacies to critical social thought—Marx writes in *Communist Manifesto*: "Does it require deep intuition to comprehend that man's ideas, views, and conceptions, in one word, man's consciousness, changes with every change in the conditions of his material existence, in his social relations and in his social life?"[37] In agreement with Hegel, Marx understands history to be an unfolding process of development, but contra Hegel, Marx argues that it is not driven so much by *Geist*, but rather by "*human labour* and by the *socio-economic relations* within which that labor occurred,"[38] according to Sherratt.

---

[35] Karl Marx, "Preface to *A Contribution to the Critique of Political Economy*," in *Early Writings*, trans. by Rodney Livingston and Gregor Benton (New York: Vintage Books, 1975) 425. "Es ist nicht das Bewusstsein der Menschen, das ihr Sein, sondern umgekehrt ihr gesellschaftliches Sein, das ihr Bewusstsein bestimmt." "Zur Kritik der politischen Ökonomie: Vorwort" (1959) in *Marx-Engels Werke* (Berlin: Dietz Verlag, 1961) bd. 13, 9. This 1859 Preface was not included with the *Critique of Political Economy* or *Capital* during Marx's lifetime.

[36] Karl Marx, "Towards a Critique of Hegel's *Philosophy of Right*: Introduction," in *Selected Writings*, ed. by David McLellan (New York: Oxford University Press, 1977) 69. "Der Kritik der Religion endet mit der Lehre, dass der Mensch das höchste Wesen für den Menschen sei, also mit dem kategorischen Imperativ, alle Verhältnisse umzuwerfen, in denen der Mensch ein erniedrigtes, ein geknechtetes, ein verlassenes, ein verächtliches Wesen ist...." *Marx-Engels Gesamtausgabe* I:2 (1) 177.

[37] Karl Marx, "Communist Manifesto," in *Selected Writings*, 236. *Das kommunistische Manifest* (Frankfurt/Main: Heinrich Reinhardt, 1946) kapitel 2, 24.

[38] Sherratt, 35; emphasis in original.

Marx's view of history, like that of Hegel, is largely teleological.[39] In one of the most important developments arising from Hegel's thought, Marx takes Hegel's dialectic and applies it to concrete and transformative practice achievable in the *present or near future*, rather than hypothesizing a lengthy dialectical process in which workers and eventually Spirit itself will come to self-consciousness. Marx understands the working proletariat as the vehicle of this coming transformation. It is the proletariat which will negate the negation of the master-slave dialectic and eventually come to self-awareness and freedom by overpowering the industrial masters. Informed by Ludwig Feuerbach's critique of religion, but critical of his abstract anthropology, Marx further develops a Hegelian materialism which profoundly influenced Adorno, Horkheimer, and in a different way, Tillich. Tillich finds Marx's infamous dictum concerning the need for philosophy to *transform*, not just analyze the world, inspiring: for Tillich this meant increasing political action from the 1920s to the 1940s. A final important development from Hegel to Marx is the focus on dimensions of power and reason's subservience to it.[40] Orthodox Marxism in this way arguably disguises its own normativity and ideology. This is in part what Tillich means by the "inner conflict of socialism," which is explored in the third chapter.

Distinct from the Marxian reception of Horkheimer and Adorno, Tillich reacts strongly against the presumption that materialism necessarily implies atheism. It was important to Tillich that the "young Marx had emphasized humanism as the core of socialism."[41] Tillich sought to demonstrate, among other things, that Marx naively equated the humanistic with the atheistic, and this may reflect an implicit critique by Tillich of Horkheimer and Adorno as well.

---

[39] According to Sherratt, "Marx's thought represents a crucial stage of development in the trajectory of German thought from Kant and Hegel to the Frankfurt School. Marx's motivation was a continuation of the enlightened one of Kant in the eighteenth century, to ground philosophy in reason, and Hegel, in the nineteenth century, to ground reason in a philosophy of history. However, Marx's philosophy was deeply *politically* engaged and although indebted in most ways to Hegel, took a *materialist* turn." Sherratt, 35; emphasis in original. She continues: "In [Marx's] model, history achieves its goal: it is a complete process, a 'totality.'" Sherratt, 37.

[40] Sherratt writes: "Unlike Hegel, for Marx, society is only rational and complete when the material conditions of society are fully developed, until then reason is part of the 'ideology' of the ruling class: 'the ruling ideas [are]...the ideas of its ruling class.'" Sherratt, 36.

[41] Heinrich Meng, *Leben als Begegnung* (Stuttgart, 1971) 78; as cited in Wiggershaus, 55. Tillich described religious socialism as a version of Christian humanism, and Tillich often spoke of the early Marx and his humanistic structure with approval.

Marx's trenchant social and economic analyses, along with his later secular materialism are not incompatible with religious faith, according to Tillich, and taking Marx seriously need not imply or lead to atheism. Although Tillich's anthropology differs in some key ways from Marx, as will be seen in detail in the following chapter, the important step philosophically in which "Marxism perceives the human situation, including human history, as bound completely to time,"[42] resonates deeply with Tillich as an organically 'religious' analysis of the human condition.

Tillich argues that although socialism "depends neither upon a specific economic theory nor upon the realization of *one* specific form of economy,"[43] his preferred 'religious socialism' "stands fundamentally on the grounds of Marx's analysis of capitalist culture."[44] It is primarily Marx's social analysis that interests Tillich and lies in the purview of religious socialism. Tillich writes:

> Religious socialism is not 'Marxism,' neither political Marxism in the sense of communism nor 'scientific' Marxism in the sense of economic doctrines. We have, however, learned more from Marx's dialectical analysis of bourgeois society than from any other analysis of our period.[45]

Marx's anthropological presuppositions and his philosophy of history were particularly appealing to Tillich and other religious socialists.[46] Equally important, Marx's philosophy helped Tillich bring questions of structural oppres-

---

[42] Paul Tillich, "Christianity and Marxism," in *Political Expectation*, trans. Victor Nuovo (New York: Harper & Row, 1971) 96.

[43] *PE*, 49; emphasis in original. "Der Sozialismus ist weder abhängig von einer bestimmten ökonomischen Theorie noch von der Verwirklichung *einer* bestimmten Wirtschaftsform." "Religiöser Sozialismus II," in Tillich, *Gesammelte Werke*, bd. II, 167.

[44] Tillich, "Religious Socialism," in *Political Expectation*, 48. "Der Religiöse Sozialismus steht grundsätzlich auf dem Boden der von Marx gegebenen *Analyse der kapitalistischen Gesellschaft*." "Religiöser Sozialismus II," in *GW* II, 166. Tillich further notes: "The agreement of religious socialism with Marx's sociological analysis of capitalism does not as a matter of course imply its assent to his economic theory." *PE*, 49. Cf. "Religiöser Sozialismus II," in *GW* II, 167.

[45] Tillich, "Author's Introduction" to *Protestant Era*, ed. and trans. James Luther Adams, intro. R.H. Daubney (London: Nisbet & Co., 1951) xviii.

[46] Tillich writes in the Author's Introduction to *Protestant Era*: "We have found in it an understanding of human nature and history which is much nearer to the classical Christian doctrine of man with its empirical pessimism and its eschatological hope than is the picture of man in idealistic theology." Tillich, *Protestant Era*, xviii.

sion and alienation into Christian theological reflection on sin.[47] Religious socialism was in part an attempt to revive the original religious impetus of Marxism and to overcome Marx's mistake of too easily equating all religion with idolatry.

I.3 The Influence of Max Weber and the 'Late Marxism' of Georg Lukács

Bureaucratization, Max Weber argued, is analogous to the precision of a machine, and as cold and calculating as a machine in its logic.[48] Although Weber acknowledged the inevitability of bureaucratization, he lamented its permeation of society and the concomitant loss of autonomy. With the "bureaucratic ideal of life," Weber argued, modern people become "specialists without spirit, sensualists without heart."[49] Weber's 'steel-hard casing'[50] of bureaucratized instrumental reason broadly characterizes the perception of and response to modernity and human agency for Adorno and Horkheimer; somewhat less so for Tillich. Each operates with implicit (and often explicit) norms starting from what they take to be a given: the present order of society is fundamentally flawed and unjust, and that society can, if not should, be different.[51] Rationalization is a non-linear process (because it vacillates from disenchantment to reenchantment) affecting all areas of modern existence which simultaneously enhances and limits freedom and agency through efficiency and utility.

---

[47] Tillich suggests that he and other religious socialists "realized more than most Christian theologians ever did that there are social structures that unavoidably frustrate any spiritual appeal to the people subjected to them." *Protestant Era*, xviii.

[48] Max Weber, *Economy and Society*, trans. Ephriam Fischoff (New York: Bedminster, 1968) vol. 3, 973.

[49] Max Weber, *The Protestant Ethic and the Spirit of Capitalism*, trans. Talcott Parsons (New York: Scribner, 1958) 182. "Fachmenschen ohne Geist, Genussmenschen ohne Herz." *Die protestantische Ethik: Eine Aufsatzsammlung*, 189.

[50] Translated by Talcott Parsons and widely known as 'iron cage,' the German *stahlhartes Gehäuse* is more accurately a 'steel-hard casing' or 'shell as hard as steel.' *Die protestantische Ethik: Eine Aufsatzsammlung*, 188. See Max Weber, *The Protestant Ethic and the 'Spirit' of Capitalism and Other Writings*, trans. by Peter Baehr and Gordon C. Wells (New York: Penguin Books, 2002) 121. See also "The 'Iron Cage' and the 'Shell as Hard as Steel:' Parsons, Weber and the *stahlhartes Gehäuse* Metaphor in *The Protestant Ethic and the Spirit of Capitalism*," by Peter Baehr, in *History and Theory* 40 (2001) 153-69.

[51] These implicit and explicit norms will be explored in chapter four.

Weber's understanding of modern capitalism included several central characteristics, all mediated by the acquisitive drive to commodify and exchange anything and everything. Derek Sayer summarizes these Weberian categories as follows: private enterprise, profit through exchange, organized provision of wants and desires, rational organization of labor, rational accounting, and formal calculative rationality.[52] Weber made the important distinction between purposive/instrumental rationality (*Zweckrationalität*) and subjective/value rationality (*Wertrationalität*), a distinction that influenced Adorno, Horkheimer, and Tillich's own understandings of reason. Instrumental rationality focuses on means, often regardless of the ends, while value rationality is more prescriptive but retains a critical awareness of the implications of evaluations and actions.

Another central Weberian thesis of critical significance for Adorno and Horkheimer is the disenchanted (*entzaubert*) nature of modernity. This thesis is a key to *Dialectic of Enlightenment* where Adorno and Horkheimer suggest, going beyond Weber, that whatever exposes a myth itself becomes the next orienting social mythology. While Weber locates this dialectic of disenchantment and reenchantment[53] in the dawn of modernity and the Protestant Reformation, Adorno and Horkheimer locate this process of disenchantment and desacralization at the dawn of human history, and within the human person *qua* social being.

Influenced by Weber's concept of bureaucratic administration and by Marx, Georg Lukács explored the challenges arising from industrialization in a more nuanced manner than one sees in Marx's idealism. Lukács is a representative of 'Late Marxism,' in the late 19th and early 20th centuries, in which thinkers influenced by Marx sought to explain why the revolution predicted by Marx had failed to materialize. This 'Late Marxism' profoundly influenced Tillich and several of the early Frankfurt School members including Adorno. Nevertheless, both Tillich and Horkheimer, as late as 1930, still expected some type of revolution. Adorno, on the other hand, was influenced by Lukács soon after the publi-

---

[52] Derek Sayer, *Capitalism and Modernity: An Excursus on Marx and Weber* (London: Routledge, 1991) 92-5.

[53] Weber's emphasis is solely on disenchantment, which seems to be a linear process. For Weber himself, re-enchantment is not a positive thing, but it is something which he considers likely for individuals in society as they come to terms with the results of disenchantment. Myth, magic and religion return in different guises to fill the void, for example. For secondary scholarship on re-enchantment, see chapter 3.

cation of *History and Class Consciousness* in 1923 and Adorno draws heavily from Lukács in his early work.[54]

Lukács argues that the commodity structure "takes on the character of a thing" and is thereby reified through a "phantom objectivity."[55] Commodity structure "becomes the universal structure of society as a whole," according to Lukács. He continues: "in this context...the reification produced by commodity relations assume[s] decisive importance both for the objective evolution of society and for the stance adopted by men towards it."[56] Adorno in particular was persuaded by Lukács' argument that Marx's understanding of the proletariat as the revolutionary subject was in error and this aspect of Marx's philosophy needed to be re-examined.[57] Buck-Morss notes that Adorno's *Habilitation* on Kierkegaard's aesthetics "was heavily indebted to Lukács' concepts of 'reification,' 'commodity structure,' and 'fetishism.'"[58] These three concepts, but particularly reification, were important well beyond Adorno's *Habilitation* and were also crucial to Horkheimer and Tillich's respective understandings of alienation and domination in modernity.[59]

---

[54] Adorno cites Lukács in his 1931 inaugural address, "The Actuality of Philosophy," in which Adorno engages a thought experiment concerning commodity structure, and in his 1932 lecture to the Kant Society, "The Idea of Natural History." The Lukácsian concept of reification is crucial to Adorno's 1938 essay "On the Fetish-Character in Music and the Regression of Listening." It is also important to Adorno's analysis of fascism as late as 1951 in "Freudian Theory and the pattern of Fascist Propaganda."

[55] Georg Lukács, *History and Class Consciousness* (Cambridge: MIT Press, 1972) 83.

[56] Lukács, 86.

[57] Susan Buck-Morss suggests that this "does not necessarily prove that Adorno never placed his hope in the proletariat...." Nevertheless, it does show that Adorno "refused to incorporate [the proletariat] within the foundation of his theory, to allow theory's validity to be in any way dependent upon the existence of a collective revolutionary subject or the possibility of its direct application to political praxis." Buck-Morss, 25.

[58] Buck-Morss, 27. Buck-Morss also points out that the sole concrete example Adorno gives in his inaugural lecture is "borrowed from Lukács," critiquing the Kantian *Ding an sich*. Buck-Morss, 27.

[59] Tillich, for example, in his Introduction to *The Socialist Decision*, describes the results of class struggle in terms of "Entmenschung" and "Verdinglichung," or 'dehumanization' and 'reification,' all while hoping for the fulfillment of a "realer Humanismus." See *GW* 2, 225, n. 3. Of course Marx uses the term *Verdinglichung* as well, and although Tillich knew Marx better than he did Lukács, Marx was interpreted through the lens of Lukács. In a May 1942 radio broadcast into Nazi Germany, Tillich succinctly claimed: "Entrechtung ist Entmenschung." Paul Tillich, *An Meine deutschen Freunde: Politische Reden* (Stuttgart: Evangelisches Verlagswerk, 1973) 40. In the 1944 preface to *Dialectic of Enlightenment*, Adorno and Horkheimer write: "Intellect's true concern is a negation of

Social transformation depends on the maturation of the proletariat's class-consciousness, according to Lukács. Yet because of commodification, the fate of the individual worker is "typical of society as a whole in that this self-objectification, this transformation of a human function into a commodity reveals in all its starkness the dehumanised and dehumanising function of the commodity relation."[60] While this transformation from self-consciousness to revolutionary action was a given for Marx, influenced by Hegel's dialectic of history, for Lukács, this revolutionary potential is not. Lukács examined the problem of agency and revolutionary subjectivity, and although he still agreed with Marx, at least in theory, that social transformation comes through the proletariat, he was increasingly dubious concerning the *capacity* of the proletariat to fulfill this role because of occluding factors of commodification and reification. In his *Habilitation* on Kierkegaard's aesthetics, Adorno employs Lukács' categories: "The efficient cause" of the Kierkegaardian 'situation' "is none other than the reification of social life, the alienation of the individual from a world that comes into focus as a mere commodity."[61] Horkheimer, too, was influenced by Lukács' social analysis, and commodification is particularly important in the *Dialectic of Enlightenment's* analysis and critique of the culture industry.

Distinguishing between the actual and the imputed [*zugerechnete*] consciousness of the proletariat, i.e., "what the proletariat *would* think if they had an accurate awareness of their objective position,"[62] Lukács argues that the party best exemplifies the "common will"[63] of the proletariat. The Communist Party, according to Lukács, is "distinguished from the rest of the proletariat by the fact that it has a clear understanding of the historical path to be taken by the proletariat as a whole."[64] Adorno, Horkheimer, and Tillich each reject this position, but they concur with Lukács that the quest for emancipation leads—almost inevitably—to new modes of domination. Tillich particularly agrees with Lukács

---

reification." Max Horkeimer and Theodor W. Adorno, *Dialectic of Enlightenment: Philosophical Fragments,* ed., Gunzelin Schmid Noerr, trans., Edmund Jephcott (Stanford: Stanford University Press, 2002) xvii. "Sein wahres Anliegen ist die Negation der Verdinglichung."

[60] Lukács, *History and Class Consciousness*, 92. *Geschichte und Klassenbewusstsein*, 183

[61] Theodor W. Adorno, *Kierkegaard: Construction of the Aesthetic*, trans. and ed. Robert Hullot-Kentor (Minneapolis: University of Minnesota Press, 1989) 39. *GS* 2, 59.

[62] Buck-Morss, 29; emphasis in original.

[63] Lukács, *History and Class Consciousness*, 321.

[64] Lukács, *History and Class Consciousness,* 325. *Geschichte und Klassenbewusstsein*, 494.

that modern bourgeois society ends up reifying the human person, choking life from, rather than emancipating the human spirit, as socialism purports to do.[65]

In the early 1930s, Tillich and Horkheimer still basically accept Marx's idea of the proletariat as the revolutionary class. According to Tillich, "Along with Marx, religious socialism sees in the proletariat the place given by fate for resistance to the capitalist structure of society."[66] By contrast, Adorno accepted the conclusion of Lukács that something had inhibited the progress Hegel and Marx anticipated and the proletariat had failed to bring about revolution, when and as it should have on Marx's analysis. Horkheimer came to hold this view by the late 1930s. Influenced by Lukács, and particularly by Lukács' reading of Weber and Marx, Horkheimer and Adorno took this revolutionary failure of the proletariat as a given by the 1940s and sought to diagnose what went wrong. Tillich, by contrast, still retains some cautious hope for social transformation, effected in part by religious socialism.[67]

Drawing upon Lukács and others, dehumanization became a central category for Tillich. Tillich argues in 1944 that existentialism is characterized as a "rebellion against the dehumanization of man in society."[68] The next chapter will return to dehumanization, along with reification and the anthropological impli-

---

[65] Marx and Weber had not anticipated the full extent of modern bureaucratic and ultimately instrumentalized reason, according to Lukács. Sherratt writes: "Lukacs developed the Weberian turn towards an analysis of modern forms of reason, as a possible explanation for history's stunted growth and communism's failure to emerge." Sherratt, 39. "Following Weber, modern socio-economic conditions entailed, for Lukacs, specific *undeveloped* forms of reason related to the narrow, procedural and repetitive modes of thought that had inevitably arisen to accompany industrial production and its administration. These narrow forms of reason meant that the proletariat could not develop from 'false consciousness' into fuller, truer forms of 'consciousness.' As a result, their political development [toward revolution] was also retarded." Sherratt, *Adorno's Positive Dialectic*, 40; emphasis in original.

[66] *PE*, 49. "Religiöser Sozialismus II," in *GW* II, 167.

[67] "Religious socialism is also aware of the fact, however, that the disposition of the proletariat by fate cannot be subject to calculation, and therefore can be lost." Tillich, *Political Expectation*, 49. "Religiöser Sozialismus II," in *GW* II, 167. Tillich understands class division to be entrenched within the capitalist system (*The Religious Situation*, 109, inter al.) This view of social transformation or revolution is, of course, still a process for Tillich. O'Keefe writes "To believe in the instant achievement of the classless society is, says Tillich, a belief in miracles, not in dialectics." Terrence O'Keefe, "Paul Tillich's Marxism," *Social Research* 48:3 (1981) 483.

[68] Tillich, "Existentialist Philosophy," in *The Journal of the History of Ideas* 5:1 (1944) 44-70.

cations of both. It is important to note in advance that, unlike Adorno and Horkheimer, Lukács does *not* think that reification fundamentally affects the core of humanity, and Tillich agrees with Lukács on this critical point, revealing a sharp theoretical divide concerning emancipatory agency between Tillich on the one hand and Adorno and Horkheimer on the other.

Lukács claims that the commodity-structure of society clearly affects "the relation between people"[69] and argues that reification shapes how people understand themselves and interact with others. Reification affects consciousness, but it has other important limits *vis-à-vis* humanity. Thus, Lukács suggests that the process of reification *does not necessarily* circumscribe humanity. He writes:

> ...[W]hile the process by which the worker is reified and becomes a commodity dehumanizes him and cripples and atrophies his 'soul'—as long as he does not consciously rebel against it—it remains true that precisely his humanity and his soul are not changed into commodities.[70]

Significantly, Lukács also suggests that reification can, at least theoretically, be overcome.[71] Tillich implicitly agrees with this important claim, while Adorno and Horkheimer, as will be seen in the next chapter, argue that reification fundamentally and perhaps inalterably affects human persons, not only interpersonal relations.

Despite the conclusions Adorno and Horkheimer drew from his work, there remains in Lukács an important residue of optimism and hope for rational and emancipatory resistance to modern structures of commodification. In an

---

[69] Lukács, *History and Class Consciousness*, 83.

[70] Lukács, *History and Class Consciousness*, 172. *Geschichte und Klassenbewusstsein*, 300.

[71] Lukács writes: "Reification is, then, the necessary, immediate reality of every person living in capitalist society. It can be overcome only by *constant and constantly renewed efforts to disrupt the reified structure of existence by concretely relating to the concretely manifested contradictions of the total development, by becoming conscious of the immanent meanings of these contradictions for the total development.*" Lukács, *History and Class Consciousness*, 197; emphasis in original. *Geschichte und Klassenbewusstsein,* 338-9. Note that Douglas Kellner disagrees with this interpretation in *Critical Theory, Marxism and Modernity.* Kellner thinks reification affects humanity more fundamentally than I do. Kellner describes reification as: "the process through which human beings are turned into things." Douglas Kellner, *Critical Theory, Marxism and Modernity* (Cambridge: Polity Press, 1989) 10; see also p. 53. In my view, Kellner is insufficiently nuanced in his interpretation of Lukács; reification clearly affects humans and alters class-consciousness, but it is not all pervasive (as Adorno and Horkheimer later suggest) or inextricably determinative of human subjectivity.

important distinction, Lukács does not see commodification inevitably or inextricably infecting humanity in the way that Horkheimer and Adorno will. The human subject can resist commodification for Lukács and for Tillich, and there is thus some room, however limited, for freely expressed subjectivity and even resistance. Horkheimer and Adorno, particularly in their joint writings, powerfully reject this premise.

II. The Idea of a 'Critical Theory': Max Horkheimer

Max Horkheimer's early writings reveal a relatively hopeful outlook on the possibilities of rational social transformation, in marked contrast to his individual and joint works in the 1940s. The tone of Horkheimer's 1931 inaugural lecture "was marked...by a measured hope that real discoveries as opposed to transfigurative ideology could serve humanity as a means of bringing meaning and reason into the world,"[72] according to Wiggershaus. This cautious optimism arguably remains a key feature of Horkheimer's thought until the mid-1940s. Nevertheless, the gradual transition in Horkheimer's thought is better understood not in terms of optimism and pessimism, but rather in terms of seeking to maintain dialectical tension between emancipatory possibilities and oppressive social realities.

Horkheimer's definitive early essay in which he defines critical theory, "Traditional and Critical Theory," was published in 1937, the seventieth anniversary of Marx's *Capital*, and it retained some important Marxian elements.[73] Nevertheless, the reception and aftermath of this essay marked an important transitional moment in Horkheimer's thought; from this point forward, he moves gradually away from Marx. The work of Horkheimer as well as the *Institut* more broadly prior to this essay was more directly influenced by Marx and was regularly referred to as 'historical' or 'dialectical materialism;' only in the wake of this essay does 'critical theory' become increasingly synonymous with the *Institut's* program and the idea of a 'Frankfurt School.'

---

[72] Wiggershaus, 39.

[73] Horkheimer himself saw this essay on theory as an 'anniversary essay' for *Capital*, as he expressed in a letter to Henryk Grossmann. "Horkheimer was justified in seeing his article as an anniversary essay on *Capital* because, although he did not mention the anniversary in it, it presented dialectical logic expressly as the logical structure on which the critique of political economy was based." Wiggershaus, 186.

Already in his 1934 essay, "The Rationalism Debate in Contemporary Philosophy," Horkheimer presaged many of the points later associated with critical theory. He writes:

> Rational action is oriented to a theory of society that…is no mere summation of abstract conceptual elements. Rather, it is the attempt, with the aid of all the various disciplines, to reconstruct an image of the social life process that can assist in understanding the critical condition of the world and the possibilities for a more rational order.[74]

Indeed, one of the most basic functions of critical theory as envisioned by Horkheimer is a trenchant critique of the status quo in all forms and on all levels, with a transformative social goal of envisioning society as it 'otherwise could be.'[75] In a 1939 essay in the *Institut's* journal, Horkheimer wrote what could serve as an epigraph to early critical theory: "The real social function of philosophy lies in its criticism of what is prevalent."[76]

In "Traditional and Critical Theory," Horkheimer seeks to distinguish between 'traditional theory' and 'critical theory,' and he levels a sustained attack on Otto Neurath and other logical positivists of the 'Vienna School,'[77] a debate important to the normative and metaphysical assumptions arguably undergirding critical theory, explored in chapter four. The difference Horkheimer suggests between traditional and critical theory, and between logical positivism and critical theory draws, in part, upon Weber's distinction between instrumental and value rationality. 'Traditional theory' is reflected in an axiomatic, deductive system wherein facts support theories; facts are purely descriptive, not evaluative. It is represented by Cartesianism, positivistic science (where there is an assumption

---

[74] Max Horkheimer, *Between Philosophy and Social Science: Selected Writings,* trans. G. Frederick Hunter et. al. (Cambridge: MIT Press) 259.

[75] According to Birgit Recki, "By the beginning of the 1940s Horkheimer had clearly already realised that there is no critical consciousness without some relation to the 'wholly other,' and especially that no genuine intention to transform current reality can be sustained without such a relation." Birgit Recki, "The Metaphysics of Critique: On the Relationship Between Metaphysics and Experience in Max Horkheimer and Theodor W. Adorno," trans. Nicholas Walker, in *Theodor W. Adorno: Critical Evaluations in Cultural Theory*, ed. Simon Jarvis (New York: Routledge, 2007) 116.

[76] Max Horkheimer, "The Social Function of Philosophy," in *ZfS* 8 (1939) 331.

[77] The logical positivism of the Vienna School and Horkheimer's debate with Otto Neurath will be treated in chapter 4. See especially John O'Neill and Thomas Uebler, "Horkheimer and Neurath: Restarting a Disrupted Debate," in *European Journal of Philosophy* 12:1 (2004) 75 ff.

of unmediated reality as a starting point), and often a near-fixation upon mathematics and formal logic.[78] While 'traditional theory' engages subjective reason and instrumental rationality, Horkheimer understands 'critical theory' to be unmasking the simple yet pernicious fact that in the modern era, as a result of philosophical dependence on one mode of theory (traditional), *domination has become the sole meaning of subjectivity* (instrumental reason).

'Traditional theory' is atemporal and totalizing while 'critical theory' is historically situated and necessarily fragmented. Horkheimer came to realize by the mid-1930s that mere sociological description cannot help liberate reason—sociological analysis alone is both epistemologically superficial and conceptually weak, lacking emancipatory potential[79] and the normative scope necessary to critically engage an instrumentalized and increasingly barbaric social tapestry. 'Critical theory,' on the other hand, understands its own historical context and regards itself as an object. While traditional theory allies itself with the natural sciences and mathematics, it is not the case that critical theory simply aligns itself with the social sciences or rejects the 'pure' sciences. Rather the difference between traditional and critical theory "springs in general from a difference not so much of objects as of subjects."[80] Critical theory reflects interdisciplinary social analysis that seeks to go beyond the Scylla of positivism and the Charybdis of idealism.

The critical theory of Horkheimer and his colleagues in the Institute of Social Research seeks to engage the intellectual trajectory of Hegel and Marx along with the critiques of Nietzsche and Freud. Here there is no Cartesian split; the knower is transformed by the act of knowing. 'Critical theory' is a dialectical process of constant self-critique through which both subject and object are transformed by the encounter. Nor does it assume or accept Hegelian reconciliation. 'Critical theory' assumed that in the modern (western) world, there is no more 'nature' independent of human labor—everything bears the marks of human transformation—humanity inhabits a world of its own creation (Lukács posits this as a 'second nature').[81]

'Critical theory,' along with its vanguard theorists, arguably comes to take the structural place of the proletariat in traditional Marxist theory, and in so

---

[78] Max Horkheimer, "Traditional and Critical Theory," in *Critical Theory*, 190 ff.; "Traditionelle und kritische Theorie," in *KT*, II, 137-91.

[79] Darrow Schechter, 84.

[80] *CT*, 209. "Traditionelle und kritische Theorie," in *KT* II, 158.

[81] This will be further explored in the following chapter on anthropology.

doing, it runs the risk of privileging theory over practice, as one arguably sees particularly in the case of Adorno. The stated goal of critical theory is to engage in multi-disciplinary research and reflection which analyzes the complex and ongoing relationship between humanity and history and between nature and society.[82] Further, critical theory is "dominated at every turn by a concern for reasonable conditions of life,"[83] according to Horkheimer. Any philosophy adequate to address the challenges of modernity must be critically aware of the social realm, both in terms of contexts and consequences, and have as a goal the amelioration of and ultimate emancipation from oppressive conditions. Interestingly, Tillich's own 'religious socialism' of the late 20s and early 30s, anchored by rational and prophetic criticism, coincides with the emancipatory criteria for critical social theory set by Horkheimer several years later; this will be further explored below.

Although inherently interdisciplinary, the vision of critical theory espoused in "Traditional and Critical Theory" led to an increasing independence from traditional social scientific disciplines, perhaps reflecting a reaction against the rigid disciplinarity of logical positivism. Wiggershaus insightfully suggests that this may be due to the influence of Freudian thought on Horkheimer since, "in the way in which it had been presented in its classical period [Freudian psychoanalysis] could not be classified as a specialized scientific discipline."[84] The interdisciplinary freedom of Horkheimer and his cohort could also be seen as a certain freedom *from* traditional disciplines, beginning with the 1937 essay. If this is so, this "was a central factor in giving Horkheimer…the sense that important insights could also be achieved—or even better achieved—by skipping over the specialized disciplines,"[85] according to Wiggershaus.

In the social realm, instrumental rationality is one of the primary diagnoses of critical theory, when not only objects but also subjects are reduced to utility, drawing upon one reading of Lukács. Horkheimer's critical theory seeks to un-

---

[82] As Stanley Aronowitz puts it in his 'Introduction' to Horkheimer's *Critical Theory*: "The task of critical theory, according to Horkheimer, is to penetrate the world of things to show the underlying relations between persons…to see 'the human bottom of nonhuman things' and to demystify the surface forms of equality." *CT*, xiii.

[83] TCT, 199. "…die vom Interesse an vernünftigen Zuständen durchherrschte kritische Theorie der bestehenden Gesellschaft." "Traditionelle und kritische Theorie," in *KT* II, 147.

[84] Wiggershaus, 186.

[85] Wiggershaus, 186.

mask the unacknowledged presuppositions at work in social structures which serve various power interests. Horkheimer writes:

> The aim of [critical] activity is not simply to eliminate one or another abuse, for it regards such abuses as necessarily connected with the way in which the social structure is organized. Although it itself emerges from the social structure, its purpose is not...the better functioning of any element in the structure. On the contrary, it is suspicious of the very categories of better, useful, appropriate, productive, and valuable...and refuses to take them as nonscientific presuppositions about which one can do nothing.[86]

This rejection of utility and productivity as valid social norms becomes crucial for articulating and exploring the intersection of religious studies and critical theory, as will be seen in the fifth and final chapter. Critically engaged religious discourse and critical theory both challenge the modern category of utility and suggest alternative standards of evaluation.

Some of the central concerns and tenets of critical theory identified above from Horkheimer's essay include: 1.) a multi- and inter-disciplinary approach to the challenges facing reason from social domination and oppression within modernity, 2.) a self-critical awareness of historicity and situatedness, 3.) a dialectically based process of engagement through which subject and object are both affected, 4.) a negative critique of the status quo which does not require a positive metaphysic, 5.) a rejection of utility and productivity as understood in the present order, 6.) a philosophy of history influenced not only by Hegel and Marx, but also by Nietzsche and Freud as well, and 7.) an epistemologically rich and conceptually strong critique with normative force and emancipatory goals, striving for freedom and justice. Each of these themes can be seen, albeit to different degrees, permeating the work of Horkheimer, Tillich, and Adorno, along with the work of the majority of the members of the *Institut*.

III. Theodor Adorno's Critical Theory: Aesthetics and Negation

Adorno works within and from the central tenets of critical theory identified above, but he goes beyond Horkheimer's articulation of critical theory in several

[86] *CT*, 206-7. "Traditionelle und kritische Theorie," in *KT* II, 155-6.

important ways.[87] Adorno brings a unique perspective from his musical background and this adds a level of aesthetic critique to his social analysis which is hlacking in Horkheimer and Tillich. Trained as a musician under Alban Berg in Vienna in the 1920s, Adorno conveys a distinctively aesthetic perspective in his philosophical critique of the alienation and domination of modern society that moves beyond purely rational critique.

Adorno's analysis of the 'culture industry' criticized the locus of production and false satisfaction of bourgeois desire. Across the culture industry, Adorno discerns reification at all levels of human action and expression.[88] The plasticity of 1940s Los Angeles and the movie culture in Pacific Palisades (as well as some forms of 'pop' music and astrology) further fueled Adorno's ire. He argued that culture cannot be reduced to economic causality; Adorno offers a humanistic argument for culture for culture's sake because culture's (partial) transcendence is a moment of at least potential truth. In "The Schema of Mass Culture," Adorno writes:

> The neon signs which hang over our cities and outshine the natural light of the night with their own are comets presaging the natural disaster of society, its frozen death. Yet they do not come from the sky. They are controlled from the earth. It depends upon human beings themselves whether they will extinguish these lights and awake from a nightmare which only threatens to become actual as long as men believe in it.[89]

While other Frankfurt theorists were interested in "the criticism of the ideological, social function of ideas,"[90] Buck-Morss claims that Adorno's early project was distinct.[91] This aesthetic version of critical theory, rooted in the cri-

---

[87] Stefan Breuer, in *On Max Horkheimer: New Perspectives*, ed. Seyla Benhabib, et. al. (Cambridge: MIT Press, 1993) 266-70.

[88] "Thus, the culture industry, and its products, mass culture and mass consumption, themselves became elements in the symbolic reproduction of commodified subjectivities that are empty of any normative and thus moral content." Eduardo Mendieta, in *The Frankfurt School and Religion: Key Writings by the Major Figures*, ed. Eduardo Mendieta (New York: Routledge, 2005) 5.

[89] Theodor Adorno, 'The Schema of Mass Culture,' in *The Culture Industry: Selected Essays in Mass Culture*, ed. by J. M. Bernstein (London: Routledge, 1991) 83. "Das Schema der Massenkultur," in Adorno, *GS* 3, 335.

[90] Buck-Morss, xiii.

[91] "Adorno not only wanted to demonstrate the untruth of bourgeois thinking; he wanted to show that precisely when the bourgeois project—the idealist project of establishing the identity of mind and material reality—failed, it expressed, unintentionally,

tique of culture, is perhaps unique to Adorno among the Frankfurt School affiliates. Importantly, however, Adorno categorically refused to idealize the aesthetic throughout his work; he denied that the cultural sphere could be isolated from the social or the economic. Yet Adorno's often trenchant critiques of the 'culture industry' do not pretend to carve out any separate or protected sphere of culture, value, or beauty.[92]

As has been noted, Adorno and Horkheimer focus heavily on the critical edge of social critique, with a central emphasis on negativity. The Hegelian emphasis on determinate negation was pursued to the exclusion of the possibility of reconciliation, wherein negation would itself be negated. This is particularly so for Adorno, and is quite deliberate. In his 1931 inaugural address in Frankfurt, "Die Aktualität der Philosophie," Adorno stated:

> I am not afraid of the reproach of unfruitful negativity.... If philosophical interpretation can in fact only prosper dialectically, then the first dialectical point of attack is given by a philosophy which cultivates precisely those problems whose removal appears more pressingly necessary than the addition of a new answer to so many old ones.[93]

The theme of negativity is consistent throughout Adorno's oeuvre: 35 years later in *Negative Dialectics*, Adorno would write: "philosophy is obliged to ruthlessly criticize itself."[94] Yet even in the midst of Adorno's focus on negation, Susan Buck-Morss discerns a positive intention: Adorno's emphasis on

---

social truth, thus proving the preeminence of reality over mind and the necessity of a critical, dialectical attitude of nonidentity toward it—proving, in short, the validity of dialectical, materialist cognition." Buck-Morss, xiii.

[92] Jeffrey Paris challenges this assessment somewhat: "By some accounts, [Adorno and Horkheimer] appear to have lost what Horkheimer had seen in 1937 as the transformative power of critical theory, exchanging it—especially in Adorno's case—for an aesthetic preservation of the hopes of the past in autonomous works of art." Paris, "Obstinate Critique and the Possibility of the Future," in *New Critical Theory: Essays on Liberation*, ed. William S. Wilkerson and Jeffrey Paris (Lanham: Rowman & Littlefield, 2001) 25.

[93] Hullot-Kentor's translation is used here: "The Actuality of Philosophy," in *Telos* 60 (1984) 130. Adorno, "Die Aktualität der Philosophie," (1931) in *GS*, 339.

[94] Theodor W. Adorno, *Negative Dialectics*, trans. E. B. Ashton (London, Routledge, 1973) 3. "Nachdem Philosophie das Versprechen, sie sei eins mit der Wirklichkeit oder stünde unmittelbar vor deren Herstellung, brach, ist sie genötigt, sich selber rücksichtslos zu kritisieren." *GS* 6, 15.

> negation at the same time *redeemed* philosophy by transforming ontology, epistemology, metaphysics, ethics, and aesthetics from self-enclosed, idealist systems into dialectical, materialist activities of thought which participated self-consciously in the process of social change.[95]

The prospect of a reconciling intention animating Adorno's consistent negation is explored in chapter four, where I explore the possibility of implicit normative or perhaps even metaphysical assumptions undergirding Adorno's unwillingness to give negation the final word.

Holding onto negativity, yet contemplating all things from a hypothetical standpoint of a future redemption was, for Adorno, coterminous with any potential hope for justice for the living and the dead. This vivified Adorno's persistent and indeed prophetic adherence to the negative moment. In *Minima Moralia*, Adorno advocates "the attempt to contemplate all things as they would present themselves from the standpoint of redemption. *Knowledge has no light but that shed on the world by redemption*."[96] Like Walter Benjamin's concern for the *Jetztzeit* in his final thesis on the philosophy of history, Adorno's negative dialectics[97] seek emancipation and liberation from the crushing vice of instrumentality and domination, longing that "every second of time was the straight gate through which the Messiah might enter,"[98] as Benjamin put it.

IV. Paul Tillich's Critical Social Theory: Religious Socialism

In Paul Tillich's discussion of religious socialism in the late 1920s and early 1930s, enhanced by his distinction between rational and prophetic criticism, which will be explored below, one can discern each of the themes around which Horkheimer's later critical theory would congeal. What does it mean that a philosopher of religion like Tillich anticipated Horkheimer's social critique and

---

[95] Buck-Morss, 111.

[96] Adorno, *Minima Moralia*, 247, emphasis added. *GS* 4, 283.

[97] "Negative dialectics, which became another name for critical theory, was a form of thinking that dwelled on the edge of reason, not because reason is not to be found in the world and the only alternative is irrationalism, but because reason is always being exiled from the world by the reifying power of identity thinking and commodity fetishism." Eduardo Mendieta, in *The Frankfurt School and Religion*, 6.

[98] Walter Benjamin, *Illuminations: Essays and Reflections*, ed. by Hannah Arendt, trans. by Harry Zohn (New York: Schocken, 1985) Thesis 18 B, 264. *Illuminationen*, 279.

thus some of the impetus of critical theory? This question will be more fully addressed in the final chapter and conclusion. Although the normative force in Tillich's critical social theory derives from a metaphysical base quite distinct from Horkheimer and Adorno—the subject of chapter four—Tillich presciently engages the type of critical social theory advocated by Horkheimer in his essays on 'religious socialism,' nearly a decade before Horkheimer produced his foundational essay on critical theory.

Before explicating Tillich's social critique, a brief explication of religious socialism is necessary. 'Religious socialism' was never affiliated with any particular political party, and it was not intended to be, although its outlook was clearly socialist in a specific sense. Denying that it was a mere theory, Tillich often referred to religious socialism as a "*movement*"[99] of something cultural which transcended, while including the political. Tillich insisted that religious socialism had supporters in numerous parties across the political spectrum. He also insisted that it was not uniquely or uniformly 'religious' in any sense: religious socialism was not exclusively Christian. Tillich's friends, Eduard Heimann and Adolf Löwe, both Jewish economists and later affiliates of the Frankfurt School, were similarly committed to religious socialism from the early 1920s. Others who identified with the movement of religious socialism, according to Tillich, were not personally religious, and some were "extremely suspicious of traditional theology or philosophy."[100] Uniting religious socialism, according to Tillich, is a "political faith" and a "political will"[101] to re-connect the original impetus of socialism to its 'depth dimension.'

When Hitler came to power in 1933, Tillich was the chair of the philosophy faculty at the University of Frankfurt.[102] *The Socialist Decision*, also released in 1933, challenged National Socialist ideology and denounced anti-Semitism; the book was banned and burned for this reason. Tillich understood the 'political romanticism' exemplified equally by National Socialism and communism to

---

[99] Paul Tillich, "Man and Society in Religious Socialism," in *Main Works/Haupt Werke*, ed. Carl Heinz Ratschow (Berlin: De Gruyter, 1998) vol. III, 489.

[100] MSRS, 488-9.

[101] MSRS, 488-9. The three convictions of the "political faith" of religious socialism were: 1.) the conviction of the end of an age and the beginning of a new age marked by wars, 2.) the coming age would involve "a new collectivism, based on social planning," and 3.) that the coming age required some religious foundation.

[102] Although, as Erdmann Sturm suggests, Tillich already planned as of November 1932 to return to the theology faculty in Berlin. "Historische Einleitung," in Paul Tillich, *Frankfurter Vorlesungen (1930-1933)* ed. Erdmann Sturm (Berlin: De Gruyter, 2013) xix.

be held in check largely by prophetism and principles of Enlightenment.[103] Tillich presciently wrote: if "political romanticism and, with it, militant nationalism proves victorious, a self-annihilating struggle of the European peoples is inevitable. *The salvation of European society from a return to barbarism lies in the hands of socialism.*"[104] Socialism was not merely a political ideology for Tillich; it was, much more, a religious (prophetic) and cultural *duty* in the pursuit of justice and equality. To this effect, Tillich writes: "Religious socialism is the attempt to bring into awareness the element of faith at work in socialism, to reveal socialism's inner conflict, and to lead it to a solution that has symbolic power."[105] The greatest flaw of socialism in its purely secular guise, according to Tillich, is its proclivity to ignore the 'unconditioned,' the religious dimension of human experience. Marsden suggests that Tillich believed "socialism had identified the kairos, but missed its depth"[106] and significance.

The socialist rejection of 19th century dogmatic materialism presented one avenue of common ground. Following the horrors of World War I, in which Tillich served as a chaplain in the western trenches, Marsden notes that "Tillich quickly set himself the task of attempting to overcome the split between Lutheran transcendentalism and secular immanent hopes of socialist utopianism."[107] In contrast to the Lutheran doctrine of two kingdoms—one of heavenly justice and one of earthly sin and travail—Tillich attempts "to unite the radical nature and the transcendence of the religious perspective with the concreteness of an immanent will to shape the world."[108] Acknowledging the role of Christoph Blumhardt[109] in his own formulation of religious socialism, Tillich articulates the

---

[103] Paul Tillich, *The Socialist Decision*, trans. Franklin Sherman (New York: Harper & Row, 1977) 25-26.

[104] *SD*, 161. *GW* 2, 364. Emphasis in original.

[105] *SD*, 71. *GW* 2, 285.

[106] "Paul Tillich and the Theology of German Religious Socialism," by John Marsden, in *Political Theology* 10:1 (2009) 36.

[107] Marsden, 34. Marsden identifies Tillich's unique contribution to the turbulent era following the collapse of the Empire as an attempt "to steer a middle way between the exaggerated utopian hopes of socialists and the otherworldliness of so much of mainstream Christianity." Marsden, 35.

[108] *PE*, 57. "Religiöser Sozialismus II," in *GW* II, 174.

[109] German theologian Christoph Blumhardt (1842-1919) was instrumental in the Christian Socialist movement in Germany and Switzerland. His political action resulted in his removal from his pastorate, and he was influential on Tillich, as well as Karl Barth, Hermann Kutter, and Leonhard Ragaz, among others.

common ground that is at least potentially accessible between religion and socialism in general terms. He writes:

> The decisive idea of religious socialism is that religion does not have to do with a specific religious sphere but with God's dealing with the world, and that it is therefore possible that God's activity may be more clearly seen in a profane, even anti-Christian, phenomenon like socialism than in the explicitly religious sphere of the church.[110]

This insight for Tillich suggests the possibility of a greater alliance between religion and socialism. From his collaborative work with the diverse *Kairos Circle* in Berlin and through an important insight from Blumhardt, Tillich came to realize "that God may speak for a time more powerfully through a nonreligious, and even anti-Christian, movement, such as early social democracy, than through the Christian churches."[111] This idea of socialism as a potentially revelatory moment was not widely shared by other Christian thinkers.

Within these parameters, religious socialism as a movement sought with Marx to interpret, engage, and transform society. The focus here is on the social analysis and critique of Tillich in particular, although his was by no means the only religious socialist voice in this arena or at the time. Negatively, Tillich's social critique discerns at least four challenges or limitations to reason and the human subject: sin, finitude, estrangement, and the 'demonic.'[112] Positively, he acknowledges the importance of the critique of social structures, with the vital addition of two distinct types of critique: rational critique and prophetic critique. Rational critique and prophetic critique, while analytically distinct, are insepara-

---

[110] *PE*, 44. "Religiöser Sozialismus II," in *GW* II, 162.

[111] Paul Tillich, "The Formative Power of Protestantism," in *Protestant Era*, ed. and trans. James Luther Adams (London: Nisbet & Co., 1951) 213. Similarly, in his 1930 essay "Religious Socialism," Tillich writes: In the struggle *against* a demonized society and *for* a meaningful society, religious socialism discerns a necessary expression for the expectation of the kingdom of God. But it repudiates the identification of socialism with the kingdom of God just as it rejects religious indifference towards constructive tasks within this world. It regards the unity of the socialist dialectic, a unity of expectation and demand of that which is to come, as a conceptual unity and at the same time as a concrete and contemporary transformation of the Christian eschatological tension." Tillich, "Religious Socialism," in *PE*, 50, italics in original. "Religiöser Sozialismus II," in *GW* II, 168.

[112] These themes are diffuse throughout Tillich's early writings found in *PE, Protestant Era, Socialist Decision*, etc.

ble for Tillich;[113] one without the other reinforces, rather than challenging the status quo. Rational criticism is exemplified by "any scientific result…measured by that standard of scientific evidence which is valued in the particular field in question."[114] In prophetic critique, on the other hand, "the structure of science as such is brought into question—and perhaps justified—by what is beyond all human knowledge, by what is 'higher than all reason,'"[115] that source of 'ultimacy' upon which criticism must rest for Tillich. In some sense, this echoes Horkheimer's later distinction between traditional and critical theory. Rational criticism for Tillich needs prophetic criticism to supplement its inherent weaknesses and limitations; similarly, critical theory supplements (if not eclipses) traditional theory for Horkheimer.[116]

Prophetic criticism is always connected to the foundational theological principle of grace for Tillich, and it brings the 'depth dimension' of the 'Unconditioned'[117] to rational critique. In this vein, Tillich writes: "Prophetic criticism can become concrete only if the existential embraces the entire sphere of being…. Therefore the prophetic criticism of the Old Testament, the criterion of all genuinely prophetic criticism, always includes a concrete rational criticism."[118] This prophetic emphasis distinguishes Tillich's conception of criticism somewhat from contemporaneous theologians like Karl Barth who sometimes isolated themselves within theological language rather than addressing pressing social problems, like the rise of the Nazis to power,[119] perhaps inadvertently marginal-

---

[113] Tillich, "Protestantism as a Critical and Cultural Principle," in *PE*, 14. *GW* 7, 32.

[114] *PE*, 10-11. *GW* 7, 29.

[115] *PE*, 11. *GW* 7, 29.

[116] Gary Simpson writes: "Rational criticism's disciplined concreteness contests the temptation of prophetic criticism to become abstract." Gary Simpson, *Critical Social Theory: Prophetic Reason, Civil Society, and Christian Imagination* (Minneapolis: Fortress Press, 2002) 130.

[117] This is one of Tillich's earliest descriptions of God and it will be explored more fully in the final chapter.

[118] *PE*, 13. *GW* 7, 31.

[119] The early Barth was more actively involved in political and social causes; see Barth's *Epistle to the Romans*. Tillich later comes to critique Barth and neo-Orthodoxy for limiting their dialectical method to the theological realm. This is particularly the case in the Protestant church's 1935 meetings, resulting in the Barmen Declaration. Barmen made an eloquent theological defense of divine sovereignty but the document did not reach an audience much wider than theologians; Tillich critiqued the position reached at Barmen for failing to offer a critique of Nazism with a more broad-based and inclusive appeal to resistance.

izing other religious and secular groups who may otherwise have joined forces in a common critique of Nazism. The theological cannot do without the rational upon which it is based for Tillich. Likewise, prophetic criticism does not belong to a separate sphere as the dialectical theology of Barth suggested,[120] but is inextricably linked to and grounded in rational criticism for Tillich.

In his incisive review of Marcuse's *Reason and Revolution* for the *Institut's* journal in 1941, Tillich wrote: "Even a critical social theory cannot avoid an 'ultimate' in which its criticism is rooted because reason itself is rooted therein."[121] Concerning Tillich's review, Gary Simpson writes, "without basis in an 'ultimate,' rational criticism runs into a wall.... Only an ultimate ground can empower critical revolutionaries beyond critical fatigue."[122] This crucial critique concerning a normative source for social critique will be discussed further in subsequent chapters.

At the heart of Tillich's critical social theory is what he terms the 'Protestant principle.' Central to this are both the important distinction between rational and prophetic criticism and a necessary foundation of 'ultimacy'[123] upon which any critical social theory should stand. Tillich claims that the 'Protestant principle' arises from Judaism and its critical source is rooted in the Hebrew prophets. Tillich is not so much referring to 'Protestant' as a branch of Christianity, but rather to the spirit of 'protest' that compels all humans to seek justice.[124] Glenn Earley claims that 'prophetism,' the 'spirit of Judaism,' and the

---

[120] "The effectiveness of dialectical theology was limited because it overlooked the indissoluble relationship between the theological ideal and all other ideals, and therefore of theological criticism and all other rational criticism; thus it unintentionally relegated everything having to do with theology to a separate domain of prophetic criticism. The effect of this was to weaken to some extent the religious criticism that had been directed against other cultural spheres, for example, the criticism that had been advanced by 'religious socialism,' and therefore to strengthen the existing forms and powers of secular life." *PE,* 13-14. *GW* 7, 32.

[121] Tillich, "Review of Marcuse's *Reason and Revolution*," in *ZfS* 9 (1941) 478.

[122] Simpson, 34.

[123] This important critique of ultimacy will be dealt with further in chapters 4 and 5.

[124] The 'Protestant Principle' is the essence of all prophetic religion, according to Tillich, and as such, it exemplifies the central prophetic message in Judaism, although it must also be understood in terms of Tillich's doctrine of justification. It reflects the eternal spirit of prophetic justice, and Tillich sometimes referred to it as the capacity to distinguish between the Absolute and the finite.

'Protestant principle' are functionally interchangeable for Tillich.[125] Tillich himself considers Jewish prophecy the first and best historical example of the 'Protestant principle.'

In "The Protestant Principle and the Proletarian Situation" of 1931, Tillich offers his most thorough explication of the critical category of the 'Protestant principle.' There he writes:

> The Protestant principle...contains the divine and human protest against any absolute claim made for a relative reality, even if this claim is made by a Protestant church. *The Protestant principle is the judge of every religious and cultural reality*, including the religion and culture which calls itself 'Protestant.' The Protestant principle, the source and judge of Protestantism, is not to be confused with the 'Absolute'[126] of German idealism or with the 'Being' of ancient and recent philosophy. It is not the highest ontological concept derived from an analysis of the whole of being; it is the theological expression of the true relation between the unconditional and the conditioned or, religiously speaking, between God and man. As such, it is concerned with what theology calls 'faith,' namely, the state of mind in which we are grasped by the power of something unconditional which manifests itself to us as the ground and judge of our existence....[127]

Tillich seeks to distinguish the 'Protestant principle' from Protestantism as the "true relation between the unconditional and the conditioned," or between the divine and the human. That which points beyond itself to the infinite ground of being serves as a critique of any attempt to reify or otherwise elevate that which is finite. Tillich continues, relating the 'Protestant principle' to the contemporary socio-political situation:

> The Protestant principle is...the guardian against the attempts of the finite and conditioned to usurp the place of the unconditional in thinking and acting. *It is the prophetic judgment against religious pride, ecclesiastical arrogance, and secular self-sufficiency and their destructive consequences.* The Protestant principle in this sense is not strange to the situation of the proletariat in modern society. It is, on the contrary, *the exact expres-*

---

[125] Earley, Glenn David, An 'Everlasting Conversation:' Judaism in the Life and Thought of Paul Tillich (Ph.D. diss.: Temple University, 1987) 250.

[126] Hegel's Absolute Spirit is likely meant here, although Schelling could be the intended referent.

[127] "The Protestant Principle and the Proletarian Principle," in *The Protestant Era*, 163; emphasis added. *Protestantisches Prinzip und proletarische Situation*, 8.

> *sion of its religious significance as an outstanding example of man's situation.* The inadequacy of Protestantism in the face of the proletarian situation is, accordingly, the result of the contradiction between the Protestant principle and Protestantism as it actually is.[128]

At the intersection of rational and prophetic critique, resisting the cold calculus of utility, the 'Protestant Principle' lies at the heart of Tillich's social analysis and critique. Unfortunately, Tillich does not explicate the concept as thoroughly as he could have, and the practical application of this principle is subject to a variety of interpretations.

V. Enlightenment and its Negation

Enlightenment, particularly for Adorno and Horkheimer, is a *process*, not merely an event or historical period at the origin of 'modernity.' Enlightenment is simultaneously that which can free one from myth, and that which returns to myth by binding freedom in modes of control, reification, oppression, and domination. Enlightenment is a dialectical process and the *telos* of dialectic is emancipation. Wiggershaus notes the terminological ambiguity of 'enlightenment' in Adorno and Horkheimer's central collaborative work: the term 'enlightenment' functions "sometimes in a negative, sometimes in a positive sense, sometimes in the sense of subjective reason, sometimes in that of objective reason."[129] At certain points, Adorno and Horkheimer suggest that enlightenment is a largely positive force accessible within one's consciousness, liberating the mind and potentially society as well. There appears to be at least vestigial potential for critical emancipatory rationality as a means to resist, if not overcome, instrumental rationality. At other points, however, enlightenment seems decidedly negative, possessing inherently regressive (*rückläufige*) tendencies. What is one to make of this tension?

The negative—dreadful even—specter of enlightenment as simultaneously the source of and solution to the problems of people from the days of Homeric accounts of Ulysses up to modern anti-Semitism, can be seen clearly in the thought of Adorno and Horkheimer in the year before *Dialectic of Enlightenment* was first published. In a letter to Friedrich Pollock dated May 7, 1943, Horkheimer responded to a project undertaken by Pollock, Adolf Lowe, and Tillich concerning the labor relationships between contemporaneous managers and the

[128] "The Protestant Principle and the Proletarian Situation," in *The Protestant Era*, 163-4; emphasis added. *Protestantisches Prinzip und proletarische Situation*, 8-9.

[129] Wiggershaus, 333.

masses compared with those in earlier times. Reacting to a written account of the conversation, Horkheimer suggested to Friedrich Pollock:

> The process to which they should refer instead is the one which I have been dealing with during the last two years... the process of enlightenment as it was marked out in the first thought a human being conceived, that same process of which Hegel says that if started it is irresistible.[130]

The remarkable language here was foregrounded above in remarks on Hegel and pure insight as a *disease*; this will be explored further below. In his letter to Pollock, Horkheimer notes—the immediate context is 'clerks' and whether they are 'better' or 'worse' than in previous eras—"we have to understand this development [enlightenment as irresistible process] and we can understand it only if there is something in us which does not submit to it."[131] Horkheimer then quotes from Hegel's *Phenomenology of Spirit* (cited above) to demonstrate his thesis:

> ...the struggle against [pure insight, which leads to enlightenment] betrays the fact that the infection has occurred. The struggle is too late, and every remedy adopted only aggravates the disease, for it has laid hold of the marrow of spiritual life... there is no power in consciousness which could overcome the disease.[132]

Horkheimer and Adorno use this same passage from Hegel again, to the same purpose, in *Dialectic of Enlightenment.* That text opens with the authors' claim that the earth is "radiant with triumphant calamity [*strahlt im Zeichen triumphalen Unheils*]"[133] because of the 'disease' of enlightenment which is a fundamental human process, not a uniquely modern development. As Adorno and Horkheimer describe the function of negation in *Dialectic of Enlightenment*, "knowledge does not consist in mere perception, classification, and calculation

---

[130] Horkheimer, letter to Pollock, 7 May 1943. Horkheimer, *GS* 17, 446.

[131] Horkheimer, *GS* 17, 446. Horkheimer thinks Tillich and Lowenthal missed something important in their discussion of 'clerks' in the May 7, 1943 letter from Horkheimer to Pollock. Horkheimer argues that one can only understand enlightenment if there is something in the person which resists enlightenment, lauding Pollock for his essential agreement, while likely taking a jab at Tillich and Lowenthal for not seeing, or worse, for not possessing this "something in us which does not submit to" enlightenment.

[132] *Phenomenology of Spirit* (545) 331-2. *PhG*, 386.

[133] *DE*, 1; *DA*, 9.

but precisely in the determining negation of whatever is directly at hand."[134] They critique Hegel's postulation of totality arising from determinate negation as itself myth:

> With the concept of determinate negation, Hegel gave prominence to an element which distinguishes enlightenment from the positivist decay to which he consigned it. However, by finally postulating the known result of the whole process of negation, totality in the system and in history, as the absolute, he violated the prohibition and himself succumbed to mythology.[135]

Similarly, Horkheimer's ominously titled 1941 essay, "The End of Reason," begins thusly: "The fundamental concepts of civilization are in a process of rapid decay."[136] Likewise, in *Eclipse of Reason* a few years later, reason as such is described as a disease, akin to Hegel, and is taken by Horkheimer to be based in the drive to dominate nature: "The disease of reason is that reason was born from man's urge to dominate nature, and the 'recovery' depends on insight into the nature of the original idea, not on a cure of the latest symptoms."[137] On June 3, 1945, Adorno wrote to Leo Lowenthal concerning revisions of Horkheimer's *Eclipse of Reason*, again hinting at some extent of collaborative work on this project:

> The text [*Eclipse of Reason*], particularly in the first chapter, describes the process of formalization and instrumentalization of reason as a necessary and irresistible one, in the sense in which Hegel dealt with enlightenment in *Phenomenology*. But after that the book only contains a critique of this form of reason. The relationship between the critical point of view and the point of view being criticized has not been made theoretically clear. It often seems as though we were professing objective reason 'dogmatically' to a certain extent, having previously determined that subjective reason is ineluctable.[138]

While Adorno clearly had a hand in this project, based as it was in part on their collaborative work in the mid-1940s, and was in this context working on Horkheimer's behalf in revising *Eclipse of Reason*, two points are worth noting.

---

[134] *DE*, 20. *DA*, 33.

[135] *DE*, 18. *DA*, 30.

[136] Horkheimer, *ZfS*, 9 (1941) 366.

[137] *ER*, 176.

[138] Adorno, 3 June 1945 letter to Lowenthal, cited in Wiggershaus, 332. This letter appears to exist only in the Löwenthal Archive at the University of Frankfurt.

First, in the midst of their most constructive period of collaboration, Adorno and Horkheimer chose to co-author *Dialectic of Enlightenment*, but *Eclipse of Reason* bears Horkheimer's name alone.[139] Second, Adorno simultaneously identifies with the argument by using the first-person plural—"often seems as though *we* were professing," while perhaps subtly distancing himself from its conclusions and noting oversights of 'the book,' not 'our' book. Whether and on what points the two may agree and disagree on these particular points will be discussed below. Schmidt understands the metaphor of 'enlightenment as disease' to be central for Horkheimer. Following Hegel's account in the *Phenomenology of Spirit*, enlightenment for Horkheimer and Adorno "defeats faith, but in doing so, undermines itself by revealing that it is nothing more than a faith of a different sort. Subjecting everything in the world to a cold calculus of utility, enlightenment culminates in...furious destruction"[140] according to Schmidt.

For Tillich, there is a fundamental shift in modernity—"in the pre-capitalist era there was something transcendent in man's relation to things"[141]—which stands in stark contrast to Adorno and Horkheimer's assertion that instrumental reason pre-dates the Enlightenment era, and is perhaps coterminous with human thought itself. Nevertheless, Tillich shares Adorno and Horkheimer's profound concern for the ways in which domination has inscribed itself within the individual and society. In 1926 Tillich argues that the manifestations of capitalism:

> correspond to the rationalistic methods of natural science and lead to the same results in the relations between things and in social relations. In the free market economy the attitude toward material things comes to be dominating, loveless, without the sense of community with them. Things become wares—objects whose meaning lies in the production of profits in transactions of buying and selling, not in the enrichment of the personal life. They are acquired and disposed of by their masters, not by beings who have some kind of community with them.[142]

---

[139] Horkheimer considered including Adorno's name since the materials largely came from their joint work, but he eventually decided to publish it in his name alone. See Wiggershaus.

[140] James Schmidt, "Genocide and the Limits of Enlightenment: Adorno and Horkheimer Reconsidered," in *Enlightenment and Genocide: Contradictions in Modernity*, ed. James Kaye and Bo Strath (New York: Peter Lang, 2000) 84.

[141] Paul Tillich, *The Religious Situation*, trans. H. Richard Niebuhr (Henry Holt and Co, 1932) 73. *Die Religiöse Lage der Gegenwart*, 64.

[142] Tillich, *The Religious Situation*, 72. *Die Religiöse Lage der Gegenwart*, 64.

Horkheimer and Adorno diagnose a shift in modernity, but not a qualitative shift; enlightenment pre-dates modernity but the two are not synonymous. However, in his 1939 essay "Die Juden und Europa," Horkheimer linked capitalism and fascism: "Whoever does not want to speak about capitalism must also remain silent on fascism."[143] For Horkheimer, late capitalism may be especially pernicious, but it is not qualitatively distinct from the human propensity to reify through instrumental reason.

VI. *Dialectic of Enlightenment* as Philosophy of History[144]

Much of the emancipatory hope in social progress seen in Horkheimer's earlier writings, including his programmatic essay "Traditional and Critical Theory," seems to have dissipated by the time of *Dialectic of Enlightenment*. Nevertheless, 'enlightenment' is a highly ambiguous category for Adorno and Horkheimer, as has been noted. At times, there appears to be hope that through commitment to ongoing, self-aware, and self-critical enlightenment, along with the critical emancipatory capacity of the rational mind in community, real change could take place. At other points, this is severely called into doubt. What is clear is that, like Hegel and Marx before them, Adorno and Horkheimer are engaging in a dialectical presentation of a philosophy of history, exploring enlightenment's moves from emancipatory openness to reifying oppression. Enlightenment is primarily a transhistorical process, dating back to the dawn of history; indeed, as Horkheimer claims in the 1943 letter cited above, it is seen in the infectious and irresistible "process of enlightenment as it was marked out in the first thought a human being conceived." There is no sphere of human thought or action that is not somehow infected by domination in the guise of instrumental rationality. Yet the barbarism of the 20th century is, according to Adorno and Horkheimer, different in quality and scope, and it requires a critical reexamination of Hegel's dialectic of subject/object or humanity/nature.

143 Horkheimer, "Die Juden und Europa," in *ZfS* 8:2 (1939) 115. Author's translation, "Wer aber vom Kapitalismus nicht reden will, sollte auch vom Faschismus schweigen." The essay begins similarly, with a direct connection between anti-Semitism and Nazism. "Wer den Antisemitismus erklären will, muss den Nationalsozialismus meinen." Tillich, *The Religious Situation*, 72. *Die Religiöse Lage der Gegenwart*, 64.

144 The philosophy of history in *Dialectic of Enlightenment* draws upon the work of Giambattista Vico, but this is outside the scope of this chapter.

Another crucial influence on the thought of Adorno and Horkheimer is Freud, whose influence was not addressed in the first section of this chapter but must be mentioned here. In seeking to integrate some of the insights of Freudian psychoanalytic theory in *Dialectic of Enlightenment*, Horkheimer and Adorno came to see that it is not merely individual desires which are repressed as a necessary component of the legal-social contract without which society could not function, but that history itself is a manifestation of repression and domination.[145] They write: "The achievements of civilization are a product of sublimation, of the acquired love-hate for body and earth, from which domination has violently severed all human beings."[146] While sublimation appears to be one manifestation of repression, the enduring power of myth and religion is another. Of less concern is the truth or falsehood of religion on a meta-level; Freud's focus is on the illusory character of religion which provides a (necessary) salve for civilization. Adorno and Horkheimer ultimately agree with Freud that civilization as a process is both inevitable and largely self-destructive. Some form of repression or sublimation appears inescapable to both as well. Although they were able to articulate the underlying causes of the intersection between civilization and repression, neither Freud nor Adorno and Horkheimer were able to adequately delineate the *mechanisms* of societal and cultural repression which mark western technical rationality and civilization.

According to Horkheimer and Adorno, the *telos* of the Enlightenment as a historical movement was to enhance human knowledge such that humans could attain greater mastery of self and nature. The Enlightenment 'self' was intended to be a beacon of lucid rationality and "legislating authority of action."[147] Under the conditions of modernity and late capitalism, however, this

---

[145] Freudian anthropology also informs *Dialectic of Enlightenment* according to Marianna Papastephanou, in "Ulysses' Reason, Nobody's Fault: Reason, Subjectivity and the Critique of Enlightenment," in *Philosophy and Social Criticism* 26:6 (2000) 47-59. Freud suggests that in society, individuals choose to renounce certain desires in order to join a society. As such, according to Papastephanou, "With a materialist twist, Freudian essentialism is accommodated in critical theory." Papastephanou, 52.

[146] *DE*, 194. *DA*, 248-9. Immigrants, upon arriving in a new land seek to make a fresh start and acclimate themselves to and assimilate in the new culture, leaving the old behind. Such individuals, as exemplars of humanity in general according to Adorno and Horkheimer, "repress history in themselves and others, out of fear that it might remind them of the disintegration of their own lives, a disintegration which itself consists largely in the repression of history." *DE*, 179.

[147] *DE*, 22.

idealized self has not come to fruition.[148] Knowledge oriented toward control is the beginning of the modern scientific revolution, and for Horkheimer and Adorno, "[t]echnology is the essence of this knowledge."[149] In the pursuit of such knowledge, like Francis Bacon's quest to liberate reason from idolatry, things like myth, religion, and metaphysics are excluded and the world becomes 'disenchanted.'[150] Indeed, on "the way toward modern science human beings have discarded meaning."[151] Efficiency trumps morality and utility vanquishes purpose. Yet this is the tragedy and poignant irony of enlightenment—as human knowledge and mastery over self and nature increased, the human individual must submit to the social norms derived from this knowledge. This repression of the self, emblematic of the Enlightenment pursuit, engenders new myths at the same time it seeks to vanquish the old.

In the midst of this ongoing process of enlightenment, disenchantment, and re-mythologizing, the human subject struggles to locate itself. Adorno and Horkheimer write:

> The human being's mastery of itself, on which the self is founded, practically always involves the annihilation of the subject in whose service that mastery is maintained, because the substance which is mastered, suppressed, and disintegrated by self-preservation is nothing other than of the living entity...in other words, self-preservation destroys the very thing which is to be preserved.[152]

Their argument is concerned with the *process* of enlightenment, which they trace back to the foundations of human society. That is to say, the alienation of individuals and the employment of rationality as a means rather than as an end (seeking truth) is by no means a modern phenomenon. Rather, the instrumental rationality they identify as co-extensive with the birth pangs of modernity is actually part and parcel of the emergence of human society, or, more accurately, the subject in and over against society.

---

[148] When individual self-preservation meets the collective drive for self-preservation in capitalist society, this process ironically "enforces the self-alienation of individuals, who must mold themselves to the technical apparatus body and soul.... [T]he transcendental subject of knowledge, as the last remainder of subjectivity, is itself seemingly abolished...." DE, 23.

[149] *DE*, 2.

[150] This is in line with, and in reference to Max Weber's *Wissenschaft als Beruf*.

[151] *DE*, 3.

[152] *DE*, 43. *DA*, 62.

By the mid-1940s, Horkheimer and Adorno have given up on revolution but they still seek to transform society from within to an extent—they still seek to re-enlighten enlightenment: "freedom in society is inseparable from enlightenment thinking."[153] The challenge and pressing question to be asked of Adorno and Horkheimer *vis-à-vis* subjectivity following *Dialectic of Enlightenment* is whether there is any agency left in their theorized subject.[154] The opening sentences of *Dialectic of Enlightenment* serve to establish the authors' understanding of the *telos* of critique: liberation of the human subject through the use of critical reason. Adorno and Horkheimer write: "Enlightenment, understood in the widest sense as the advance of thought, has always aimed at liberating human beings from fear and installing them as masters. Yet the wholly enlightened earth is radiant with triumphant calamity."[155] Already in the second sentence of the work, originally published as *Philosophical Fragments* in 1944,[156] the authors apparently despair of the capacity of emancipatory reason. Enlightenment seeks to liberate the subject from myth by liberating it from nature, but it is a doomed process. Domination becomes the primary meaning and vehicle of subjectivity. The Odysseus myth as treated in *Dialectic of Enlightenment* is a narrative of bourgeois domination. In Odysseus' escape from the Cyclops, Odysseus becomes *Udeis*: 'no-man;' his emancipation is simultaneously his self-negation. Similarly, in order to bypass the Sirens' alluring song, Odysseus is tied to the mast and the rowers' ears are plugged. The human subject is simultaneously Odysseus, impotent to act because of social structures of domination, and the

---

[153] *DE*, xvi.

[154] Leszek Kolakowski argues: "The authors do not offer any way out of the state of decadence. They do not say how man can become friends with nature again, or how to get rid of exchange value and live without money and calculation. Failing a positive Utopia, [their] final response to the human condition can only be an inarticulate cry." Leszek Kolakowski, "The Frankfurt School and Critical Theory," in *Foundations of the Frankfurt School of Social Research*, 111, 114. In a 1943 letter to Pollock, Horkheimer wrote that the opening chapter of what became *Dialectic of Enlightenment* was necessary and significant because the *Odyssey* "is the first document on the anthropology of man in the modern sense, that means, in the sense of a rational enlightened being." Horkheimer to Pollock, 20 March 1943. Cited in Wiggershaus, 323. This does not appear in Horkheimer's *Gesammelte Schriften*.

[155] *DE*, 1. *DA*, 9.

[156] The text was originally published as *Philosophical Fragments* in 1944. In 1947, it was republished as *Dialectic of Enlightenment*, with relatively minor structural changes (including the excision of much of the Marxian terminology) and the addition of the chapter on anti-Semitism.

rowers, unable to hear the Sirens' call. This reflection on the nature of human subjectivity in modernity is the subject of the following chapter.

Dialectic of Enlightenment was written in and is a powerful expression of despair of socially transformative and emancipatory possibilities.[157] Joan Alway notes that "amid the wreckage of the Marxian emancipatory vision, one finds little but despair, and what traces of optimism can be found bear little relationship to the traditional Marxian view on agents and actions."[158] Any remaining hope in reason as inherently emancipatory is muted at best in *Dialectic of Enlightenment*. Adorno and Horkheimer write:

> The hope for better conditions, insofar as it is not merely an illusion, is founded less on the assurance that those conditions are guaranteed, sustainable, and final than on a lack of respect for what is so firmly ensconced amid the general suffering.... The light of reason, which dawned in that impulse and is reflected in the recollecting thought of human beings, falls, even on the happiest day, on its irresolvable contradiction: the calamity which reason alone cannot avert.[159]

Although they claim in the Preface that "freedom in society is inseparable from enlightenment thinking,"[160] it is difficult to imagine what form of emancipatory reason or social freedom is possible based on their trenchant diagnosis and critique of capitalism, instrumental reason, and identity thinking.[161]

---

[157] According to Alway, the "image of a better world, and claims concerning agents and action which might realize such a world, are almost entirely absent" from *Dialectic of Enlightenment*. Joan Alway, *Critical Theory and Political Possibilities: Conceptions of Emancipatory Politics in the Works of Adorno, Horkheimer, Marcuse and Habermas* (Westport: Greenwood Press, 1995) 31.

[158] Alway, 31-2. While Alway is essentially correct, she does not address the process of composition of *Dialectic of Enlightenment*. The original 1944 manuscript, published as *Philosophical Fragments* without the final section on anti-Semitism, contained substantially more Marxian language than the final 1947 version of *Dialectic of Enlightenment*. See "The Disappearance of Class History in 'Dialectic of Enlightenment:' A Commentary on the Textual Variants (1944 and 1947)" by Willem van Reijen and Jan Bransen, in *Dialectic of Enlightenment* (Stanford: Stanford University Press, 2002). See also James Schmidt's "Language, Mythology and Enlightenment," and Martin Jay, *Dialectical Imagination*, 256, *inter al.*

[159] *DE*, 186-7. *DA*, 236-7.

[160] *DE*, xiii. *DA*, 3.

[161] Even in some of his early writings, Horkheimer expresses a deep skepticism of the existence of social power sufficient for emancipation. Horkheimer writes in "Authority and the Family:" "Bourgeois thought begins as a struggle against the authority of tradition and replaces it with reason as the legitimate source of right and truth. It ends with

It is important to recall that *Dialectic of Enlightenment* was originally meant to be the first half of a larger work. In their original 1944 preface to *Dialectic of Enlightenment*, Adorno and Horkheimer still retain some muted hope for positive social transformation of some sort: "The critique of enlightenment…is intended to prepare a positive concept of enlightenment which liberates it from its entanglement in blind domination."[162] The text was intended to be followed by a sequel which would take up the issues involved with seeking to reclaim certain parts of enlightenment, and to use the liberative potential of enlightenment against the forces of oppression which occluded this emancipatory possibility.[163] The planned sequel, *Rettung der Aufklärung*, was intended to provide a "positive theory of dialectics" which would seek to outline a "rescue of the enlightenment," as Horkheimer put it.[164]

James Schmidt traces the ways in which the original 1944 manuscript sloughed off much of the remaining Marxian language for the 1947 publication, completing what Martin Jay called the "last leg" of Horkheimer and Adorno's "long march away from orthodox Marxism."[165] Notably, the 1944 description of the "object of exploitation" became "subject" in the 1947 version.[166] 'Capitalism' and 'capital' become 'the economic system' and 'economy', respectively.[167] Noting the importance of the change from 1944's 'class society' to 1947's 'society,' Schmidt argues that "[t]he 1947 text is making a claim that applies to all societies at all times. The 1944 text is making a rather specific claim about class dom-

the deification of naked authority as such…since justice, happiness, and freedom for mankind have been eliminated as historically possible solutions." Horkheimer, *CT*, 72. *KT* I, 303.

162 "Preface," *DE*, xviii. *DA*, 6.

163 Schmidt writes: "While Horkheimer and Adorno's attempt to write a sequel to the *Dialectic of Enlightenment* that would elaborate a 'positive' program by which the Enlightenment might be 'rescued' remained unfinished and while none of the material that was said to have been completed has yet been found, there is one crucial point on which all of Horkheimer's descriptions of the work agree: it was to begin with a discussion of the nature of truth." Schmidt, "Language, Mythology and Enlightenment," 820.

164 Tillich, Lowe, and Horkheimer letters, Aug. 1947; Horkheimer *GS* bd. 17: 873, fn. 3, 884, also 892-3; referenced in "Language, Mythology and Enlightenment: Historical Notes on Horkheimer and Adorno's *Dialectic of Enlightenment*," by James Schmidt, 835, fn. 3.

165 Jay, 256. See Schmidt, "Language, Mythology and Enlightenment," 811. See also "The Disappearance of Class History in 'Dialectic of Enlightenment:' A Commentary on the Textual Variants (1944 and 1947)" by Willem van Reijen and Jan Bransen, in *DE*.

166 *GS* 5, 36.

167 *GS* 5, 26, 62.

ination."[168] Schmidt cautions against drawing many conclusions from these changes, noting that the 1944 version reflected incomplete *Philosophische Fragmente*, while the 1947 version was a polished and relatively coherently unified argument. Schmidt writes:

> *Dialectic of Enlightenment* traced the process by which the dreams of the enlightenment had turned into a nightmare. The unwritten *Rettung der Aufklärung* would awaken the enlightenment from its nightmare, restore it to consciousness, and set it back on its path. Any reading of *Dialectic of Enlightenment* that is unaware of the incompleteness of its argument runs the risk of misunderstanding the intentions of its authors. And any attempt to remain faithful to the project begun by Horkheimer and Adorno can find no better starting point than the question that stymied them half a century ago: How can the enlightenment be rescued?[169]

In letters to Tillich and Adolph Löwe as late as August 1947, Horkheimer indicated that the intended sequel would provide a "positive theory of dialectics" which would seek to outline a "rescue of the enlightenment."[170] Other than *Diskussionsprotokollen* from 1946, nothing concrete has survived of what may have been part of that sequel—if the project ever began—but in Horkheimer's descriptions one can see a clear emphasis on truth as the orienting lens for this second work.[171] What is known about this proposed sequel to *Dialectic of Enlightenment* is that Adorno argued that as "theoreticians of reason" they should interrogate "transcendental-logical categories" according to "their own meaning." To this, Horkheimer retorted:

> Is this not mythical metaphysics? The claim that one follows the true interest of the subject is an illusion. Hegel had fulfillment as a guide to the absolute Truth. What do we have as a guide?[172]

---

[168] Schmidt, "Language, Mythology and Enlightenment," 812.

[169] Schmidt, "Language, Mythology and Enlightenment," 835 [*DE*, 29].

[170] Max Horkheimer's letters to Adolph Lowe and Paul Tillich, Aug. 1947; *GS* bd. 17: 873, n. 3, 884; also see reference to this dialogue in "Language, Mythology and Enlightenment: Historical Notes on Horkheimer and Adorno's *Dialectic of Enlightenment*," by James Schmidt, 835, fn. 3.

[171] The '*Diskussionsprotokolle*' of October 1946 represent all that seems to have survived of this project. See Horkheimer, *GS*, 12, 594-605.

[172] Horkheimer, *GS* 12, 604. Author's translation, "Ist das nicht mythische Metaphysik? Die Behauptung, dass man dem wahren Interesse des Gegenstandes folge, ist

Adorno then suggested that the 'illness' of reason itself (*die Vernunft erkrankt ist*) could function as such a norm, foundation, or guide:

> We must bring together the thought of the disease of reason and the possibility of its recovery by means of the sickness with the demand to bring the forms of consciousness themselves and their social or anthropological reality that are simultaneously their own meaning and the reason for the inadequacy of each form of consciousness.[173]

Yet Horkheimer definitively responded that *Dialectic of Enlightenment* had already pursued this argument, and it alone was not sufficient to warrant or ground a sequel.[174] For Horkheimer, if not yet for Adorno as well, work on the proposed sequel to *Dialectic of Enlightenment* evidently was leading to a dead end.[175]

The more fundamental question is what philosophical warrant Horkheimer and Adorno might have had to express any emancipatory hope following *Dialectic of Enlightenment*; this question will be pursued more fully in chapters four and five. Habermas, among others, suggests that they were left with none.[176] Similarly, Papastephanou argues that critical theory's treatment of reason is self-defeating and undermines its emancipatory potential. She writes: "to turn reason against itself by rationally demonstrating that the history of thought functions as an organ of domination neutralizes critique from within and allocates it to a

---

eine Täuschung. Hegel hatte als Leitfaden die absolute Wahrheit, die Erfüllung. Was haben wir als Leitfaden?"

[173] Adorno, cited in the final *Diskussionsprotokol* concerning a possible sequel to *Dialectic of Enlightenment*, in Horkheimer, *GS* 12, 604. Author's translation, "Den Gedanken von der Erkrankung der Vernunft und der Möglichkeit ihrer Gesundung durch die Krankheit hindurch müssen wir zusammenbringen mit der Forderung, die Bewusstseinsformen selber auf ihre gesellschaftliche oder anthropologische Realität zu bringen, die zugleich ihr eigener Sinn sind und der Grund der Unzulänglichkeit jeder einzelnen Bewusstseinsform." This complex comment from Adorno will receive greater interpretive attention near the conclusion of the next chapter, which deals with anthropology.

[174] Horkheimer, *GS* 12, 604.

[175] Horkheimer's letters to Lowe and Tillich, and particularly the *Diskussionsprotokolle* of 1946 demonstrate this. Schmidt's "Language, Mythology and Enlightenment" hints at this as well.

[176] "On their analysis, it is no longer possible to place hope in the liberating force of enlightenment." "The Entwinement of Myth and Enlightenment: Max Horkheimer and Theodor Adorno." Jürgen Habermas, in *The Philosophical Discourse of Modernity*, trans. Frederick B. Lawrence (Cambridge: MIT Press, 1991) 106.

sphere of ineffable otherness."[177] Both Habermas and Papastephanou offer strong critiques, but to address these critiques and to explore the implicit and explicit responses of Horkheimer and Adorno requires analysis of metaphysical assumptions and norms, which will come in the following chapters.

Although it is an overwhelmingly pessimistic work, *Dialectic of Enlightenment* is not an entirely hopeless work.[178] In support of his reading of *Dialectic of Enlightenment* as a text containing at least a few rays of hope, Schmidt writes: "...each of the three chapters of what was to form the *Dialectic of Enlightenment* ends with an image of awakening from a dream, of returning to consciousness, of a coming to possession of one's powers."[179] The question of the legitimacy of a 'positive' reading coming out of *Dialectic of Enlightenment* requires further analysis of the metaphysical and religious presuppositions Horkheimer and Adorno were working with; this will be treated in chapters four and five.

VII. Diagnoses and Prognoses

In the period on which this study primarily focuses, namely 1929-1944, the diagnoses offered by Tillich, Adorno, and Horkheimer are often—understandably given world events—quite bleak. The ninth of Walter Benjamin's "Theses on the Philosophy of History" is perhaps exemplary of the position of Horkheimer and Adorno toward the end of this period. Reflecting on Paul Klee's painting *Angelus Novus*, Benjamin describes "a storm blowing from Paradise" in which the angel is caught. "This storm irresistibly propels [the angel] into the future toward which his back is turned, while the pile of debris before him grows skyward. This storm is what we call progress."[180] While Tillich retained some hope for change, and worked obliquely for political change in his critique of National

---

[177] Marianna Papastephanou, "Ulysses' Reason, Nobody's Fault: Reason, Subjectivity and the Critique of Enlightenment," in *Philosophy and Social Criticism* 26:6 (2000) 57. She also notes: "in order to attack reason and Enlightenment, [critical theory] employs means that go beyond its conceptual horizons failing to spell out the conditions of its own commitment to a rational critical standpoint.". Habermas, in *The Philosophical Discourse of Modernity*, 48.

[178] Schmidt notes: "The opening chapter closed by suggesting that, by bringing about a massive extension of human powers over nature, enlightenment had created the preconditions for a situation in which the subject that exercised this rule would no longer be a single class, but instead 'everyone.'" Schmidt, 833.

[179] Schmidt, 835.

[180] Benjamin, *Illuminations*, 257-8. *Illuminationen*, 273.

Socialism, both in Germany and in exile in the U.S., Adorno and Horkheimer largely focused on theory itself as critique.

Critical theory as exemplified by Adorno and Horkheimer in the 1940s regards resignation to the status quo and identity thinking as constitutive of late capitalism. Identity thinking, according to Jonathan Joseph, "is the belief that things are as they are or…it is the inability to see things differently to how they appear in their immediacy."[181] The immanent ideology critique characteristic of Adorno and Horkheimer seeks to reject identity thinking; according to Joseph,

> the aim is to show that what exists does not have to be as it is, that things are not given, that things are contradictory and that possible alternatives exist. Dialectical theory questions the immediacy of empirical facts by seeking out the underlying structural conditions and social processes.[182]

In the work of Horkheimer and Adorno, one sees several sustained critiques of modernity's one-dimensional society and fully administered world, going well beyond simple bourgeois capitalism denounced in Marxism.

VII.1 Horkheimer

The viewpoint from which critical theory arises "derives from historical analysis as the goals of human activity, especially the idea of a reasonable organization of society that will meet the needs of the whole community, are immanent in human work but are not correctly grasped by individuals or by the common mind,"[183] according to Horkheimer. Given his diagnosis of modernity and subjectivity within modernity, it is to be expected that Horkheimer's prognosis for society is somewhat bleak, although throughout his corpus, Horkheimer expresses glimmers of hope, more so in his early and very late writings. The movement between emancipatory expectation and the memory of oppression guides his work, although Horkheimer comes to emphasize domination and instrumentality more than emancipatory rationality by the 1940s. He writes in 1937 that through analysis of the Marxist categories, "the meaning of this whole is to be sought not in the preservation of contemporary society but in its trans-

---

[181] Jonathan Joseph, *Social Theory: An Introduction* (New York: NYU Press, 2004) 140.

[182] Joseph, *Social Theory*, 141.

[183] *CT*, 213. *KT*, II, 162.

formation into the right kind of society."[184] In the same essay, he emphasizes emancipatory praxis: "The issue...is not simply the theory of emancipation; it is the practice of it as well."[185] In an early entry in *Dawn and Decline*, Horkheimer expresses hope for a "rationally organized socialist society which regulates its own existence."[186] Nevertheless, any actual change for Horkheimer belongs to a hypothetical better future, toward which society should work but which can never be anticipated.[187] Horkheimer implies but does not emphasize as strongly as he could have that incremental change for the better is possible, even if only on the micro-level.

VII.2 Adorno

Instead of seeking to articulate a positive notion of reason and autonomy under the conditions of modernity, Adorno focuses on a sustained critique of a 'totally administered society' in which reason and autonomy are threatened by the oppressive logic of identity thinking. Stefan Müller-Doohm summarizes Adorno's diagnosis and prognosis for society: "Through critical thinking, social theory has the task of helping to overcome internally contradictory social conditions, just those conditions that could be other than they are."[188] This awareness of 'things as they otherwise could be' is crucial to Adorno's diagnosis of modernity (as well as that of Horkheimer) and his prognosis for human subjectivity within it, along with any hypothetical future change. Müller-Doohm continues: "With the help of...theory, it is possible to construct a model depicting how the world could be different—different than it is. These possibilities of otherness are not otherworldly utopian projects."[189] Adorno's prognostic goal is interpreting society *as it otherwise could be*,[190] but his diagnosis of modern society and of human subjectivity relies heavily on aesthetics and negativity. This is not so much a weakness as

---

[184] *CT*, 218. *KT*, II, 167.

[185] *CT*, 233. *KT*, II, 181.

[186] Horkheimer, *Dawn and Decline*, 51.

[187] Horkheimer writes: "In regard to the essential kind of change at which the critical theory aims, there can be no corresponding concrete perception of it until it actually comes about. If the proof of the pudding is in the eating, the eating here is still in the future." *CT*, 220-1. *KT*, II, 169.

[188] Müller-Doohm, 281.

[189] Müller-Doohm, 281.

[190] "The difference between the real and the possible makes necessary both a critique of historically superfluous unfreedom and a critique of social relations in which domination of humans over other humans perpetuates itself." Müller-Doohm, 286.

it is a strength, however. Adorno's emphasis on negation seeks to preserve room for potential breaks in identity thinking, as will be seen in chapters four and five. He does not accept Marx's view of the proletariat as the revolutionary class but rather locates the operative agency of a society 'different than it is' in the critical use of reason against unfreedom. Adorno's unyielding focus on negativity is intended to preserve the possibility of emancipatory rationality and indeed at least the possibility of transcendence; this is explicated more fully in the final chapter.

VII.3 Tillich

In their joint writings, Adorno and Horkheimer diagnose a dialectic between reason or enlightenment and myth, a dialectic which collapses upon itself. Similarly, Tillich diagnoses an original dialectic between critical and prophetic rationality and passive assimilation of Christianity into culture. Just as Adorno and Horkheimer understand the quest for enlightenment through reason to inevitably devolve into a new mythology, so too by analogy Tillich understands prophetic reason to have devolved into a bland assimilation of religion into modernity.[191]

For Tillich, because Christianity has assimilated into the "economic and political…[,] Christianity's standpoint for possible opposition to capitalist society has disappeared. Christianity and modern society have been brought to the point of identity."[192] Protestantism thereby loses its ability to critique modernity's epistemology and, in agreement with Weber, Tillich notes that Protestantism's dogmatic stasis provided fertile ground for the social development of capitalism, ultimately identifying itself with capitalism. "Western Protestantism leaves autonomous culture untouched in the realm of knowledge, but also preserves untouched its own dogmatic fundamentals, in the social realm it creates capitalism with which it identifies."[193] As a result, "a critical opposition to modern society has become impossible"[194] for Protestantism. While Tillich does not believe that critical reason and prophetic critique are strictly speaking impossible, he is increasingly cautious about claiming too much transformative social potential on the macro level. Protestantism, as Tillich understands it, should be

[191] Tillich writes: "Religion was transformed into the economic and technical mastery of the world, into humanitarianism and the worldly development of personality." *PE,* 5-6. *GW* bd. 10, 104.

[192] *PE*, 6. *GW* bd. 10, 104.

[193] *PE*, 6. *GW* bd. 10, 104.

[194] *PE*, 6. *GW* bd. 10, 104.

the source of a clarion call to modernity in its prophetic critique of the increasing instrumentality and social domination and alienation, rather than a willing, if largely passive participant in those unjust structures.

In *The Socialist Decision*, Tillich pleaded for the "awakening of a realistic expectation of a just society that would fulfill, not simply contradict, the origin,"[195] according to Champion. Tillich argued that humanitarian solidarity was necessary to withstand the brutal cunning of unreason. His early philosophy of religious socialism rejects any notion of linear progress within history or uniformly positive societal evolution.[196] In "Storms of our Times" (1942) Tillich writes: "The cultural life after the period of the Enlightenment was based on the presupposition that the intellectual and moral development of the individual would lead to a cultural 'common sense,' able to create a harmonious and progressive civilization."[197] Tillich regards such naïve belief in progress to have been destroyed by World War I, resulting in "a complete cultural disintegration"[198] of Western Europe by 1937. Tillich understands this breakdown in culture to be manifest in four distinctively modern sentiments: fear (economic, political, cultural and religious), uncertainty, loneliness, and meaninglessness.[199] Tillich's religious socialism functions as a prophetic interruption of these modern challenges.

Tillich ultimately thinks a critical social theory engaging religious socialism and grounded in an awareness of 'ultimacy' can overcome the three loci identified earlier as manifestations of oppression within modernity: alienation, domination, and reification. This nexus becomes increasingly clear in the following chapters and together raise an increasingly central question arising from this study: is religious socialism contextually bound to the 1920s and 1930s—its centrality diminishes profoundly in Tillich's writings in the United States in the 1940s—and thus irrelevant, or is there any remaining life in it, possibly germane today?

---

[195] "Tillich and the Frankfurt School: Parallels and Differences in Prophetic Criticism," by James W. Champion, in *Soundings* 69:4 (Winter 1986) 521.

[196] This rejection reflects a consistent position throughout Tillich's thought, and the eschatology in the 3rd volume of the *Systematic Theology* articulates essentially the same position, rejecting any inner-historical utopia.

[197] Tillich, Paul, "Storms of our Times," in *The Protestant Era*, 244. First published in *Anglican Theological Review* 25:1 (1943).

[198] "Storms of our Times," in *The Protestant Era*, 245.

[199] "Storms of our Times," in *The Protestant Era*, 245-246.

VIII. Conclusions

Considering Weber's work and his diagnosis of the disenchanted 'steel-hard casing' of modernity, is there any possibility left for social freedom? Is there any escape from Lukács' diagnosis of commodification? The context of National Socialism profoundly shapes the social, philosophical, and cultural interpretations and diagnoses of all three thinkers. Nevertheless, given Horkheimer and Adorno's reticence to articulate norms for a critical social theory beyond critical reason itself, one must wonder whether criticism can lead to emancipatory reason given the grip of alienation, domination, and reification. Both Adorno and Horkheimer think critical reason can make important steps in an emancipatory direction, but cannot overcome these ultimately; as time wore on, they grew increasingly concerned that the disease of enlightenment had inoculated modern subjects to the cure of reason. Tillich argued by contrast that only a critical social theory fully aware of its 'depth dimension' and an 'ultimate' as its source and norm could overcome the oppression characteristic of modernity. Further uniting the three is an emphasis upon the important link between knowledge and freedom, which appears to be the common thread of hope for how society could otherwise be, as will be explored in chapters four and five.

The early essays of Adorno, and particularly those of Horkheimer, are hopeful to the extent that society could be (re)ordered by a renewed focus on emancipatory reason. In Horkheimer's work one sees the most change, from a positive conception of reason and its emancipatory capabilities in the 1930s to a bleak prognosis for reason by the 1940s. In several of Horkheimer's essays in the 1930s one sees some hope that socialism could offer the vehicle for transformation. His seminal essay "Traditional and Critical Theory" envisions some space for a strengthened and renewed rationality in society. Influenced by the bleak news coming out of Europe, Horkheimer and Adorno increasingly despaired of reason's capacities for transcendence and emancipatory valence. By the time of *Dialectic of Enlightenment* (1944, 1947), there is an increasing focus on oppression rather than emancipatory reason. Tillich, by contrast, still envisions a future in which reason, oriented toward its 'depth dimension,' can at least potentially orient and radically transform society.

In conclusion, one might ask why Adorno and Horkheimer urge us to take note of the 'disease' of enlightenment if there is little faith in the presumed cure of reason? How is one to account for normative inflections of emancipatory reason and critique itself? At stake is nothing less than freedom within one's historical moment. Does one escape, transcend, or endure modernity and seek emancipation by going 'up' to get 'out'? Or is liberation possible horizontally? Does critical social theory imagine itself as a contemporary *ascesis*, as if scraping the rust from pure metal? These and other questions will be dealt with in the last two chapters, where the importance of emancipatory norms and language will be suggested. The apparent resignation of Adorno and Horkheimer during the 1940s suggests that the 'disease' and 'infection' of enlightenment cannot be adequately dealt with in purely adjectival terms like 'emancipatory.' There are many ways to refuse normative accounts of emancipation, but what can be seen in Adorno and Horkheimer's work is a quest to find new ways of imagining emancipatory potential while minimizing normative language.

The following chapter examines the effects of modernity and instrumentality upon the human subject *qua* individual and in society. It shows how the effects of alienation, domination, and reification play out in the quest for an emancipated human subject, both individually and collectively. This explication also brings to the fore one of the central differences between Adorno, Horkheimer, and Tillich—anthropology. The common conception of the critical capacities of reason shared among the three begins to fray when it comes to the capacities of the human subject, individually and collectively, to enact critical reason with an emancipatory goal.

3.

Anthropological Differences Among Tillich, Adorno, and Horkheimer

> To be radical is to grasp things by the root.
> But for man the root is man himself.
>
> —Karl Marx, "A Contribution to the Critique of Hegel's Philosophy of Right," in *Early Writings*[1]

Introduction

One of the central concerns of Tillich in the late 1920s through the end of the war is virtually identical to perhaps *the* crucial contemporaneous question for Horkheimer, Adorno, and other members of the *Institut für Sozialforschung*—what is happening to humanity in modernity and why? Their respective conceptions of what 'humanity' is, the limitations humanity faces, and the possibilities for seeking emancipation simultaneously reveal sharp lines of contrast and fertile ground for constructive engagement. Tillich, Horkheimer, and Adorno each attempt to articulate the conditions for the possibility of human emancipation; their common challenge is doing so in a way that takes full account of the limitations of human nature and the uses and abuses of rationality. Crucial to all three thinkers is the goal of human emancipation in the face of dehumanization. In the previous chapter alienation, domination, and reification and their effects on rationality were identified as central problems, with similar diagnoses shared by Adorno, Horkheimer, and Tillich. The effect of such dehumanization on reason has been explored; here I explore that multitude of ways in which alienation, domination, and reification affect the human subject *qua* individual and in society. The anthropological distinctions explored in this chapter—some of which are substantial—are nevertheless rooted in a common diagnosis of the problems facing the subject in modernity, particularly the effects of alienation, domination, and reification. Exiled from their native Germany in the build-up to World War II, these concerns were more than abstractions.

---

[1] Karl Marx, "A Contribution of the Critique of Hegel's Philosophy of Right. Introduction," in *Early Writings*, 251.

This chapter examines and explores the fertile intellectual and theological terrain out of which three distinct philosophical anthropologies arose in the shadow of the ascent of National Socialism in Germany in the early 1930s. In this, the central chapter of the work, it becomes clear that the goal of both critical theory and religious socialism—emancipatory reason—both affects and is profoundly affected and limited by conceptions of human subjectivity under modern conditions of dehumanization. Who is the subject of emancipation for each thinker? If one thinks people are self-interested and bound by sin (Tillich), what kind of agency do they have? Similarly, if one thinks people are neutral but society itself is inhuman, as Horkheimer and Adorno imply, how did society—itself composed of neutral individuals—get to be inhuman in the first place? Holding such a position, how does one theorize the capacity of individual subjects to change an inhuman society and to work toward emancipation of self and society? Can such a capacity be adequately theorized in the absence of a concept of human nature?

Tillich thinks that socialism has failed thus far, in large part, because of an unwillingness to engage in the re-imagination of the modern subject it aims to liberate. By slighting anthropology, socialism has insufficiently theorized the potential for individual, much less social, transformation. Early on, Horkheimer apparently agrees with Tillich, albeit implicitly. This chapter argues that a rough conception of human nature is necessary for funding adequate emancipatory praxis. The absence of nuanced theoretical engagement with anthropology leads to an insufficiently theorized subject and a weakened conception of emancipatory agency.

With the presumption of human worth and an explicit valuing of human happiness, the existence of injustice and awareness of human needs serves as the foundation for an ethically normative judgment concerning humanity. Horkheimer and Adorno—along with Tillich—assume that exploitation and injustice are morally wrong, and they think emancipation is a desirable outcome. Being committed to the project of emancipation and enlightenment, both Horkheimer and Adorno articulate a desire for transformation toward a better society. The possibility of socialism—and emancipatory transformation more generally—requires at least an implicit conception of human nature, as Marx had noted.[2]

[2] Marx claimed that "it is possible to achieve real liberation only in the real world and by real means...in general, people cannot be liberated as long as they are unable to obtain food and drink...." Marx, *Collected Works,* vol. 5, 38. Marx further wrote: "Men have history because they must produce their life, and because they must produce it

The epigraph to this chapter indicates the importance of anthropology to Marx. Norman Geras' interpretation seems correct: "*Historical materialism itself, this whole distinctive approach to society that originates with Marx, rests squarely upon the idea of a human nature.*"[3] At the same time, this idea problematically suggests something like human nature anterior to its social development.

There is an implicit and important assumption in Marxian anthropology that people are capable of developing or sustaining the qualities needed for the envisioned future, and a more just order.[4] Thus, there is an important and often unacknowledged presumption in Marxian theory, which can be seen in the early Horkheimer, that humans have the capacity to engage and transform the social order. Horkheimer writes: "In materialist theory, the main point is...to improve the lot of humanity."[5] While present in the early Horkheimer, this assumption virtually disappears from Adorno and Horkheimer's collective works in the 1940s, when they move further away from Marxian theory. Particularly important in this earlier period is the Marxian notion of *Entfremdung*, or 'alienation.' Lukács' 1923 *History and Class Consciousness* and the understanding of 'reification' (*Verdinglichung*) therein provide crucial background and context.

Although largely in agreement with the diagnoses of Marx and Lukács concerning the reification and commodification of objects, there are important differences among Adorno, Horkheimer, and Tillich concerning the effects this has on human subjectivity. Significantly, however, Lukács does *not* think that commodification fundamentally and inextricably affects human subjectivity, as

---

moreover in a certain way: this is determined by their physical organization; their consciousness is determined in just the same way." Marx, *Collected Works*, vol. 5, 43. Based upon his interpretation of Marx's "Sixth Thesis on Feuerbach," which is commonly misinterpreted as denying the concept of human nature in Marx, Norman Geras argues Marx's thought relies upon a conception of "human nature, or the nature of man," which is conditioned by or "manifested in the ensemble of social relations." Norman Geras, *Marx and Human Nature: Refutation of a Legend* (New York: Verso, 1983) 46-7.

[3] Geras, 108; italics in original. For Marx, human nature includes the social, linguistic, reasoning, productive and transformative forces that are common to all humans. See e.g. Geras, 99.

[4] "A concept of human nature, encompassing at once the common needs and the general and distinctive capacities of humankind, plays...a quite fundamental, explanatory role there in accounting for those specifically human social relationships that are production relations and for that specifically human type of process of change that is history." Geras, 106.

[5] "Materialism and Morality," BPSS, 37. *KT* I, 97.

noted in the previous chapter,[6] unlike Horkheimer and Adorno, and contrary to Douglas Kellner's interpretation of Lukács, also cited in the previous chapter. I argue that Lukács retains a degree of hope for resistance that Adorno and Horkheimer increasingly cannot grant by the 1940s. Tillich's view on this matter mediates, in a way, between Lukács' latent hope and the apparent resignation of Adorno and Horkheimer. While Tillich knew Lukács' work, he does not directly engage Lukács on the issues of subjectivity and commodification. Tillich does acknowledge that the hegemony of 'instrumental reason' dominates not only the means employed by humanity for given ends, but by eclipsing consideration of ends, instrumental reason also—at least implicitly—influences human relationships. Although reification and commodification influence human subjectivity, Tillich does not suggest that social forces turn subjects (*qua* human, not *qua* worker) into commodities, agreeing with Lukács. Adorno and Horkheimer, in their increasingly bleak understanding of the 'fully administered society,' suggest by contrast that human subjectivity and social relations are affected to the core—perhaps even ontologically—by commodification.

Early on, in the 1930s, Horkheimer acknowledges numerous human commonalities and he uses the language of 'human nature' and 'human essence,' as long as such concepts are not universalized or thought to be unchanging.[7] Horkheimer is not essentializing human nature, but his language is peculiar for a

---

[6] Lukács, *History and Class Consciousness*, 172, 197; see ch. 2.

[7] The English term 'human nature' is overly laden with connotations of universality across time. The three authors—notably Horkheimer and Tillich—routinely use both *Natur* and *Wesen*, along with the more generic *Menschen* (humanity). Both German words are most commonly translated as 'human nature' (rather than 'essence' for *Wesen*) in English. While 'human essence' is an acceptable translation of both terms, I have chosen not to use 'essence' in the constructive discussion here, since it may connote something of metaphysical or ontological permanence, arguably intended in part by Tillich, but almost certainly unintended by Horkheimer. Furthermore, Horkheimer uses *Wesen* more frequently than Tillich, who more often uses *Natur*. It is not necessary for the purposes of the argument here to provide precise definitions to this and similar terms. While ambiguous, 'human nature' for both Tillich and Horkheimer roughly denotes the psychological and social qualities that characterize humans in contrast to other living things. Horkheimer uses 'human essence' nearly synonymously with 'human nature.' For Tillich, the term 'essence' (*Wesen*) although used seemingly interchangeably with 'nature' (*Natur*) is more ontological, suggesting fundamental features without which humans would lose their identity as human. In this literal sense, Tillich's anthropology could perhaps be said to be essentialist, but unlike many anthropological essentialists, Tillich understands the nature of humanity to be socially mediated and, in large part, under ongoing renegotiation.

modern philosopher and somewhat unusual for a Marxist. More importantly for the argument of this chapter, Adorno loathes such language and excoriates Tillich for using similar language, while ignoring Horkheimer's language. This is especially striking since Horkheimer and Adorno claim to be thinking with common purpose, even this early. This disconnect is addressed at the end of the chapter. In one sense, why would it matter that Horkheimer used the language of 'human nature' or that he did so ambiguously? It does matter because the ways Horkheimer uses these terms in the 1930s reveal that he was thinking about humanity, subjectivity, etc. in parallel ways to Tillich, and it sets the stage for an important distinction from Adorno.

Tillich's anthropology is nuanced, and he cannot easily be categorized as a pure essentialist. Following Marx, he argues that humans can be understood, at least in part, by their use of reason and language and similar structures of consciousness, needs, production, etc. He also sees transformative potential located in the proletariat, which he hopes to supplement with 'Christian humanism' via 'religious socialism.'[8] Of particular import is Tillich's claim that materialistic socialism faces an 'inner conflict' because it cannot adequately account for human transformation vis-à-vis social transformation. In 1943, Tillich defines humans as 'finite freedom'—not *having* finite freedom, but *being* finite freedom. Humans for Tillich are not infinite like God, but neither are they bound by necessity in important ways; humans are free with infinite longing yet bound within a finite form. The question is whether Tillich's formulation of 'finite freedom,' rooted deeply in his ontological assumptions, reflects in a limited way, an essentialized anthropology.

Adorno address anthropology less frequently than either Horkheimer or Tillich. Following his rejected initial *Habilitation* that engaged psychoanalysis and anthropological themes to an extent, Adorno veered away from sustained treatments of and engagement with anthropology during much of the period covered by this study. Some of Adorno's early musicological essays make provocative insights and claims about humans—and arguably about a 'nature of humanity'—but these are almost uniformly *ad hoc* and are not easily comparable with the relatively more sustained treatments of Horkheimer and Tillich in the

[8] Cited above, Tillich notes in 1930: "Along with Marx, religious socialism sees in the proletariat the place given by fate for resistance to the capitalist structure of society." *PE*, 49. *GW* 2, 167. Emphasis in original.

1930s and 40s.[9] Likewise, Adorno's study of Husserl completed at Oxford engages anthropological themes, but again, not in a systematic fashion. Although his reticence should not be understood as an opposition to the abstract concept of anthropology, it presents a challenge as he tries to sufficiently theorize the subject his philosophy seeks to emancipate. Adorno vehemently disagrees with Tillich's use of the terms 'man,' 'human nature,' etc.—the same terms Horkheimer used, although there is no evidence Adorno ever challenged Horkheimer on it. Employing concepts like the 'human' or 'human nature' etc., is, per Adorno, to risk becoming bound up in ideology, romanticism, power games, and to reinforce the status quo. Particularly intriguing is that Adorno's caustic *Entwurf contra Paulum* was never sent. It is hypothesized that the letter was never sent because Adorno showed it to Horkheimer first. Horkheimer almost certainly told Adorno to not send it to Tillich, arguably because it was strangely close to Horkheimer's own, earlier position. What is clear is that Horkheimer greatly curtails his use of such terminology after that point and the joint works of Horkheimer and Adorno, notably *Dialectic of Enlightenment*, do not engage anthropology in any constructive or extensive way.[10]

The first section of this chapter explores Horkheimer's anthropological assumptions in the 1930s, in conversation with several contemporaneous essays of Tillich. It initially attempts to decipher the former's abstract understanding of humanity under the conditions of modernity and his use of terms like 'essence' and 'human nature' to describe humanity. The goal is to demonstrate that in his early essays, Horkheimer consistently rejects any *unchanging* understanding of 'nature' or 'essence,' but he ambiguously retains the concepts as helpful frameworks for explicating his understanding of the relationship between the individual and society. Subsequently, the particulars of Horkheimer's understanding of the 'nature of humanity'[11] and his understanding of the concrete capacities and limitations of individuals in society, particularly regarding moral and social agency, are explored.

The second part of this chapter turns to some of the fundamental differences between Tillich and Adorno on anthropology in the early 1940s. Previous-

---

[9] The absence of analysis of these early materials in Adorno should not suggest that this is not a productive line of inquiry; its episodic nature renders much of this slightly outside the scope of this chapter however.

[10] In another sense, however, one could also argue that the treatments of theories of nature, body, and mimesis reference or reflect an anthropology.

[11] See below.

ly unexamined correspondence between Tillich and Adorno shows profound and perhaps irreparable division in their respective thoughts concerning anthropology; this material is translated as an appendix. I argue that while Adorno may have been right to reject the universalizing trans-historical abstraction of a "human nature," he was an astute enough student of human history and culture to carefully consider general historical trends. Despite Adorno's trenchant critique of Tillich's essentializing of human nature in the 1940s, which will be thoroughly explored in the second section of this chapter, the position of Horkheimer in the overall debate about anthropology is less clear. It will be demonstrated that Tillich's position, harshly criticized by Adorno, is similar to the contemporaneous anthropological position of Horkheimer, and the question as to why Adorno chose to overlook this similarity in Horkheimer's thought will be raised. The chapter concludes with a brief reflection on the engagement with anthropology implicit and explicit in *Dialectic of Enlightenment*.

I. Max Horkheimer's Early Anthropology

The Frankfurt School theorists, as noted in chapter two, lament modernity's deeply paradoxical 'glorification of means.' Already at the beginning of the twentieth century, Weber's analysis of instrumental rationality had noted the increasing parity between rationality and efficiency. To a certain extent, a self-regulating system arose within modernity in which the originary philosophical and human question 'is it good?' was eclipsed by the instrumental question 'is it efficient?' This shift had profound effects on questions of truth, both sociological and metaphysical. As explored in the previous chapters, Horkheimer, Adorno, and Tillich argue in distinctive, yet complimentary ways that the hegemony of instrumental reason in modernity comes to dominate not just the means employed by humanity for given ends, but in eclipsing the ends, it comes to affect human relationships to others and even one's self-understanding. As noted above, with regard to Lukács, Horkheimer (and Adorno) took the stronger position that human subjectivity itself was directly affected by commodification.

Horkheimer's evolving conception of emancipatory reason explored in the previous chapter can be further nuanced by analyzing his assumptions about human subjectivity and the uses and limits of rationality in modern society. In light of the transition away from materialism articulated in "Traditional and

Critical Theory" in 1937 and his increasing critical conflict with positivism,[12] Horkheimer realized that the burgeoning critical theory he and his colleagues sought to articulate must develop a new epistemology and a new anthropology. This shift marks an important step in what Horkheimer called a necessary and "radical reconsideration…of the knowing individual as such."[13] Who, or what, is the subject of modernity for Horkheimer? This important question is addressed by beginning with an examination of Horkheimer's use of the language of 'nature' and 'essence' in his early writings.[14]

I.1 'Nature,' 'Essence,' and 'Nature of Humanity'[15] in the Early Horkheimer

The radical reconsideration of the knowing subject had already begun in Horkheimer's writings dating back to at least 1930. Indeed, Horkheimer's inaugural address in Frankfurt noted that the "final goal of social philosophy is the philosophical interpretation of human fate—insofar as humans are not merely indi-

---

[12] This move is explained more fully in the following chapter on metaphysics where I focus on Horkheimer's debate with Otto Neurath and the 'Vienna School.'

[13] *CT*, 199. *KT* II, 148.

[14] Most translations of the works of the three authors elide these two terms and Horkheimer, while using both *Natur* and *Wesen*, among other terms, does not seem to have any major distinction in mind. He is broadly critical of both terms even though he implicitly relies upon them as a framework for subjectivity. The use of these terms by Horkheimer and Tillich is not uniform, as I will demonstrate. Horkheimer generally challenges 'nature' or 'essence' as static concepts because of their link to metaphysics, the presumption of static (and therefore totalizing) knowledge, and the abuses of Fascist rhetoric concerning 'nature' and 'essence.' Horkheimer likely thinks that any reified language such as 'nature' disguises ideology and in fact any veiled appeal to the 'natural' disguises a harmful ideology.

[15] I have chosen to use the phrase 'nature of humanity' instead of 'human nature' or 'essence' as widely as possible and appropriate in the following discussion. *The 'nature of humanity' here suggests a composite, socially mediated substance and some commonality among humanity which is neither permanent nor unchanging, and is directly shaped by social and historical factors.* This formulation has the advantage of articulating the subject in such a way that she or he has a basic level of emancipatory agency. This is not necessarily true for Adorno, and by the time of *Dialectic of Enlightenment*, Horkheimer and Adorno's understanding of humanity differs from the conception of the 'nature of humanity' I have articulated here. By the mid-1940s, for Horkheimer and Adorno, the emancipatory potentiality of the subject is called severely into question. Both Tillich and Horkheimer use the phrase 'nature of humanity' (*Wesen des Menschen*) but I am also loosely following Norman Geras' distinction between 'human nature' and the 'nature of man' in his introductory 'Definitions' in *Marx and Human Nature: Refutation of a Legend*, esp. 23-5.

viduals but members of a community."[16] As Horkheimer and his colleagues wrestled with human fate, they had to address contemporary metaphysical and ontological questions[17] concerning the existence and extent of a human 'nature' or 'essence.' In his earlier essays, Horkheimer had little hesitation utilizing the terms 'human nature' or 'human essence,'[18] unlike the anthropological position sketched more than a decade later in collaboration with Adorno in *Dialectic of Enlightenment*, where such language is notably absent. The challenge in interpreting this language is that Horkheimer is inconsistent with his approach to and use of the terminology of human 'nature' or 'essence.' For this reason and others this chapter will largely use 'nature of humanity'[19] in the constructive discussion. The full significance of Horkheimer's willingness to engage such terminology at all will only become clear in the second section of this chapter, where Adorno excoriates Tillich for using nearly identical categories, even in a nuanced manner.

Although Horkheimer rejects any *static* anthropological pronouncements in his early essays, always insisting upon social context, he does not fundamentally oppose the idea of 'nature of humanity' *per se*. In Horkheimer's 1930 *Habilitation*, "Beginnings of the Bourgeois Philosophy of History," he writes: "We can, of course, only speak of the essence of humanity [*Wesen des Menschen*] insofar as it manifests itself."[20] There are even unapologetically positive manifestations of a 'nature of humanity' for Horkheimer as long as such "attempts strictly adhere to the state of current empirical research and...recognize their provisional nature." Horkheimer further notes that such conceptions of humanity, while limited, "have the value of broadening the range of questions and inquiries

---

[16] Horkheimer, "The State of Contemporary Social Philosophy and the Tasks of an Institute for Social Research," in *Critical Theory and Society: A Reader*, 25.

[17] These will be addressed in the following chapter.

[18] Horkheimer's willingness to engage some ideas of human nature corresponds with Norman Geras' influential thesis concerning Marx's view of human nature. Geras writes that "Marx—like everyone else—did reject certain ideas of human nature; but he also regarded some as being true." Geras, 14-15.

[19] It is impossible to completely separate these terms in our discussion below, but I maintain that the argument is not weakened if 'nature,' 'essence,' and 'nature of humanity' are seen as functionally interchangeable. In direct citations from the three central authors, the English translation (most often 'human nature') is left unchanged, but my interpretation of this phrase in almost all cases is closer to the description above of the 'nature of humanity,' connoting a basic level of human connection which is contextually informed.

[20] BPSS, 333. *Anfänge der Bürgerlichen Geschichtsphilosophie* (Stuttgart: W. Kohlhammer Verlag, 1930) 34.

emerging out of the specialized spheres of science and fruitfully applying them to a framework for examining the interconnections of reality."[21] Despite limitations, a concept of the 'nature of humanity,' as long as it is not regarded as absolute or unchanging, can provide a helpful framework for understanding individuals and society, and it is arguably crucial for articulating emancipatory agency.

At certain points, Horkheimer appears to presume the concept of a 'nature of humanity' which is in flux: in "Authority and Family" (1936), he juxtaposes idealism with his own evolving materialism and writes that materialism "tries to comprehend the historical transformations of human nature [*menschlichen Natur*] in terms of the ever-varying shape of the material life-process in each society."[22] While Horkheimer's emphasis on 'historical transformations' undermines any stable concept of a 'nature of humanity,' he does not reject the underlying terms themselves. Here Horkheimer also counsels "realism in the face of theories which turn human nature, conscience, or reason…into stable, independent essences and try to explain the functioning of society by the influence of one or more of them."[23] The central problem for Horkheimer is attempting to turn reason, conscience, or 'human nature' [*Menschennatur*] into a stable essence, *not* with the concepts themselves as long as they are understood to be social and in flux. Emphasizing the transitional nature of humanity several years later, Horkheimer echoes Rousseau when he writes in "Art and Mass Culture" (1941): "evil does not stem from nature, but from the violence committed by society against human nature striving to develop."[24] While he is clear that humanity is constantly undergoing crucial transformations, individually and socially, drawing on the concept of instrumentality, Horkheimer nevertheless claims that *society itself is a source of violence against human nature as it develops*. In each of these cases, something like a 'nature of humanity' appears to serve as a useful framework for the early Horkheimer.

Despite his use of the terminology of 'nature' and 'essence,' Horkheimer consistently argues against any stable 'nature of humanity,' suggesting that any "doctrine of a particular human nature [*menschlichen Wesenart*] that consists of definitive pronouncements about some immutable concept of human essence [*Idee des Menschen*] that is untouched by history, is thus impossible."[25] Again,

[21] BPSS, 333. *Anfänge der Bürgerlichen Geschichtsphilosophie*, 33.
[22] BPSS, 51. *KT* I, 281.
[23] BPSS, 55. *KT* I, 286.
[24] BPSS, 276.
[25] BPSS, 333. *Anfänge*, 33.

Horkheimer's objection is to a concept of the 'nature of humanity' *which presumes finality or immutability.*[26] While one can profitably describe aspects of a socially constructed 'nature of humanity,' dangers arise if and when those are reified, as can be seen in Horkheimer's language above, in terms like 'definitive' and 'immutable.' Anticipating Tillich's language below, there seems to be little fundamental difference between the two concerning the situatedness and provisionality of human existence. Nevertheless, a rift was perceived and perhaps exacerbated by Adorno, as will be explored in the next section.

Horkheimer is willing to acknowledge some common human characteristics, even as he criticizes any presumption of humanity as 'eternally fixed.' He writes:

> The doctrine of an eternally fixed human nature [*die Lehre von der ewig gleichen Menschennatur*]—an idea that turns up again and again in the historical-philosophical thinking of the modern age—this doctrine of the same instincts and passions is a mistake. Of course, neither can we maintain the opposite, that people of different times and cultures differ radically from one another....[27]

Here he juxtaposes two equally false premises: all people at all times are somehow the same—suggesting an 'eternally fixed human nature'—and all people at all times are 'radically' distinct. He is implying that an 'eternally fixed' human nature cannot account for the clearly fungible characteristics of humanity, such as instincts and passions, and that one can neither claim fundamental, transtemporal unity nor disunity among individuals and across cultures. Echoing Marx, Horkheimer further suggests that social constructs (like capitalism) affect and can even modify 'human nature.'[28] In 1935, Horkheimer writes: "The social relationships involved in economic processes affect the entire spiritual nature and intellectual world and thus the constitution of human nature [*menschlichen Natur*]."[29] This is a position he will come to reject by the mid to late 1940s, and which Adorno vehemently rejects.

---

[26] In his 1930 *Habilitation* Horkheimer wants to jettison any assumption of an "unalterable human psyche" but he admits this does not require "renounc[ing] psychological explanations in history." BPSS, 333.

[27] BPSS, 331. *Anfänge*, 31.

[28] Marx writes: the human person "acts upon external nature and changes it, and in this way he simultaneously changes his own nature." *Capital*, vol. 1, 283.

[29] BPSS, in *Collected Works*, 164. *KT* I, 216. When it is used in contemporary society, the concept of 'human nature' is often so enmeshed in transient social and political

Early on, Horkheimer similarly is willing to describe a process of 'human development,'[30] although he clearly locates this in a dialectical relationship to nature. Nature is not external to humanity but is conditioned by, and can only be understood in relationship to, a historically situated understanding. Human existence has at least epistemic primacy, according to Horkheimer's 1930 *Habilitation,* "Beginnings of the Bourgeois Philosophy of History."[31] In this and in other essays written in the 1930s, Horkheimer demonstrates that in the Renaissance, the advent of modern technology led indirectly to political domination, most notably in Machiavelli, for whom domination of the natural world logically entailed domination of political subjects.[32] Horkheimer criticizes Machiavelli's understanding of the 'nature of humanity' as dogmatic; "it disregards the fact that both psychical and physical elements, which determine the structure of human nature [*menschlichen Natur*], are incorporated into historical reality."[33] Civilization itself changes nature, Horkheimer suggests, contra Machiavelli. Furthermore, Horkheimer argues that human self-conception changes across time. "The doctrine is false that even though the times change, the psychological makeup of human beings [*die Beschaffenheit der Menschen*] remains the same."[34] Martin Jay points out that a consequence of Horkheimer's argument here is that history and nature are not irreconcilable.[35] Adorno echoes a similar point of view two years later in his Kant Society lecture, "The Idea of Natural History," and

structures as to render it senseless, according to Horkheimer. He writes: "in many social groups, as today among the lower classes and the peasants in many parts of Europe, everything that seems to be human nature or character is so compounded of intimidation, powerless desires, distorted ideas, and oppressive conditions, that radical changes in the economic and social spheres could extinguish and transform within a few years what had previously been regarded as an eternal essence." *CT*, 66. *KT* I, 297.

[30] BPSS, 332, 334, *inter al.*

[31] "What we call nature is dependent upon human beings [*Menschen*] in a twofold sense: first, humanity's process of development [*Entwicklungsprozess der Menschheit*] continuously transforms nature through the course of civilization; second, the very conceptual elements through which we give content to the word 'nature' depend upon the epoch in which humanity [*Menschheit*] finds itself. In other words, the object of the knowledge of nature, like this knowledge itself, is conditioned." BPSS, 334. *Anfänge*, 36.

[32] Here Horkheimer begins to implicitly claim that human subjects are affected by commodification, distinct from Lukács, for whom commodification does not directly affect humanity.

[33] BPSS, 330. *Anfänge*, 29.

[34] BPSS, 331. *Anfänge*, 31

[35] Jay, 257.

the connection between humanity and nature is an important point in the analysis in *Dialectic of Enlightenment*.

In his 1935 essay, "Remarks on Philosophical Anthropology," one can see Horkheimer exploring the implications of abstract anthropology for his developing critical theory through the assumption of common human characteristics. This and other contemporary essays offer invaluable insight into the assumptions Horkheimer was making about the 'nature of humanity' at the time. He writes: "Human beings satisfy their changing needs and desires and defend themselves from death not because they believe that by doing so they are fulfilling an absolute imperative, but rather because they cannot escape from the longing for happiness and the fear of death."[36] Horkheimer also may have Freud's distinction between *eros* and *thanatos*, the death drive, in mind.[37] Regardless, the implication in 1935 is that there are clearly common human characteristics, such as the desire for happiness and the fear of death, even if no exhaustive, universal human nature or essence can be precisely characterized, as a sum of attributes or otherwise. Similarly, in "Materialism and Metaphysics," Horkheimer claims that "man's striving for happiness is to be recognized as a natural fact requiring no justification."[38] In addition to common human characteristics, Horkheimer sees some aspects of humanity as 'natural facts,' such as 'striving for happiness,' avoidance of pain, etc.

Horkheimer suggests that an abstract conception of the 'nature of humanity' can profitably be understood as a provisional framework of a dynamic social process of dialectical development, much like Tillich's anthropological understanding in *The Socialist Decision*, as will be seen below. In 1935, Horkheimer writes in "Remarks on Philosophical Anthropology:"

> Of course, human beings [*Menschen*] have been similar to one another in every epoch as well as in the entire history of mankind. They not only have certain practical needs in common, but they coincide in their

---

[36] BPSS, 155. *KT* I, 204.

[37] Horkheimer's 1936 essay "Egoism and Freedom Movements" explicitly cites this Freudian distinction several times. See Freud's 1920 essay "Beyond the Pleasure Principle" and his 1930 book, *Civilization and its Discontents*. David Held, in *Introduction to Critical Theory: Horkheimer to Habermas*, sees a direct link between Horkheimer and Freud's respective anthropologies. Held, 197.

[38] *CT*, 44. *ZfS* 2 (1933) 31. The same year (1933) in "Materialism and Morality," Horkheimer echoed a similar sentiment: "it appears as if all living beings have a claim to happiness, for which [humanity] would not in the least ask any justification or grounds." BPSS, 34-5.

> beliefs and perceptions.... Nevertheless, these similarities among various groups are not the result of a consistence in human nature [*ein einheitliches Menschenwesen*]. The social life process in which they emerge involves both human and suprahuman factors [*menschliche und aussermenschliche Faktoren*].[39]

Despite the numerous commonalities shared by all humans across time, Horkheimer is seeking to provide some necessary nuance in describing subjectivity vis-à-vis engagement with nature and social forces—'suprahuman factors.' The lack of 'consistence' does not suggest something fundamentally distinct—on an ontological level. Despite all similarities and commonalities among humans, there is no absolute common essence (*ein einheitliches Menschenwesen)* since all people and all groups are shaped by distinct contexts. Is Horkheimer perhaps implying that "human nature" (*Menschen*) reflects the context-less and seemingly universal human 'longing for happiness and fear of death,' along with the accretions of 'needs, beliefs and perceptions'? This would not indicate an 'essence' necessarily, but at the very least, Horkheimer suggests that such base characteristics reflect something definitively 'human.' Continuing his discussion of the social life process, Horkheimer writes that the life process:

> consists not simply in the representation or expression of human nature in general [*des Menschen überhaupt*], but rather a continuous struggle of individual human beings [*bestimmter Menschen*] with nature. Furthermore, the character of every individual within a group originates not only in the dynamic that pertains to him in his capacity as a representative product of human nature [*in ihm selbst als diesem menschlichen Wesen*], but in his individual fate within society as well.[40]

Horkheimer's point here is unclear. Is he suggesting a dual-element, in which humans are simultaneously representatives of 'human nature' (presumably via the common characteristics of longing for happiness, fear of death, needs, beliefs, and perceptions) but also socially constructed individuals as well? He juxtaposes 'human nature in general' (*des Menschen überhaupt*) to 'individual human beings' (*bestimmter Menschen*), who, somewhat confusingly, can still be understood, at least in part, as a 'representative product of human nature' (*in ihm selbst als diesem menschlichen Wesen*).

---

[39] BPSS, 152. *KT* I, 201.
[40] BPSS, 152. *KT* I, 201.

Horkheimer continues his complex 1935 characterization and critique of 'human nature,' writing:

> The relationships among social groups arise from the changing constellations between society and nature.[41] These relationships are determining factors in the creation of the spiritual and psychological makeup of individuals, while this resulting character in turn affects the social structure. Human nature [*menschlichen Qualitäten*] is thus continuously influenced and changed by a manifold of circumstances. One could even understand the existence of a human nature [*menschliche Züge*] that is invariable in time as a result of processes that continuously renew themselves, processes in which human beings form an inextricable part. However, one cannot understand [human nature/*menschliche Züge*] as the expression of a person in and for itself [*nicht als Äußerung des Menschen an und für sich*].[42]

The important distinctions and factors manifest in differing social groups reflect the situatedness and contextual aspects of all human groups, and Horkheimer again suggests that there is a dual-element or process operating here. The human longings and fears, 'practical needs' and 'beliefs and perceptions' which inhere in all human groups across time are always needs, beliefs, and perceptions in definite social, cultural, political, and linguistic contexts. Horkheimer is here still essentially in line with Marx.[43] The 'nature of humanity,' despite all its weaknesses, is a helpful framework for an abstract understanding of the dynamic encounters with social contexts that shape individuals and groups.[44] When Horkheimer claims in the above passage that "human nature is...continually influenced and changed by a manifold of circumstances," he uses *menschlichen Qualitäten,* suggesting something more like 'human qualities or attributes.'

Horkheimer also uses *menschliche Züge*, or distinct 'human features,' though 'human courses,' implying direction and/or progress, could be meant by *Züge* as well. Of course Horkheimer does not think this is likely, and even if humans could take an active role in shaping a non-instrumental future independent from

---

[41] This formulation concerning "changing *constellations* between society and nature" may reflect the influence of Walter Benjamin, or perhaps even of Adorno, who used the concept of 'constellations' in his 1931 inaugural address, "The Actuality of Philosophy."

[42] BPSS, 152. *KT* I, 201.

[43] See, inter al., Marx's *Collected Works*, vol. 5, 38. Cited above.

[44] "Only a transparent and adequate relationship between individual action and the life of the society can provide a foundation for individual existence." BPSS, 155. *KT* I, 204.

the logic of domination, such human 'features' or 'courses' would likely remain inadequate to encapsulate the human person, in and for itself.[45] In his final remark in the passage above, Horkheimer again notes that one cannot reach a general or collective 'humanity' starting from the isolated individual, but must always start from the specificity of the human person within a social context. Abstract descriptions of a 'human nature' or 'essence' are not sufficient to characterize the individual.

Interestingly, Horkheimer's use of such terminology continues into the 1940s. In his 1941 essay, "Vernunft und Selbsterhaltung,"[46] or "Reason and Self-Preservation," which will be explored below, Horkheimer continues to freely use terms like "humanity" (*Menschheit*[47]); he describes "human qualities" (*menschliche Qualitäten*)[48] and he suggests that "the destruction of humanity has become complete."[49] He suggests that humans can be defined—to a certain extent—by the use of reason which he believes distinguishes humans from animals.[50] Interestingly, approximately one year later, Adorno harshly criticizes Tillich for making similar statements and claims.

In response to Horkheimer's essay "Vernunft und Selbsterhaltung," Tillich wrote a letter, "Comments Concerning 'Reason and Self-Preservation" in 1942.[51] This letter curiously mirrors Adorno's subsequent arguments against

---

[45] "There is no formula that defines the relationship among individuals, society, and nature for all time. Even if we are not justified in interpreting history as the unfolding of a consistent, unchanging human nature [*eines einheitlichen Menschenwesens*], the contrary and fatalistic formulation—that of a necessity that is independent of human beings and that governs the course of things—would be just as naïve." BPSS, 153. *KT* I, 202.

[46] Max Horkheimer, "*Vernunft und Selbsterhaltung*," in *Walter Benjamin zum Gedächtnis* (New York: Institute of Social Research, 1942). This essay obtained from the Hannah Arendt Archives at Bard College, NY, was later updated and published in an emended form in Horkheimer's *Gesammelte Schriften*, bd. 5. The German essay is based on Horkheimer's original English essay, "The End of Reason," published in *ZfS* in 1941. See The *Essential Frankfurt School Reader*, 26-48.

[47] Horkheimer, "Vernunft und Selbsterhaltung," 35; from the Bard College manuscript of *Walter Benjamin zum Gedächtnis*, 35.

[48] Horkheimer, "Vernunft und Selbsterhaltung,"36.

[49] "*Der Destruktion des Menschlichen ganz eine geworden ist.*" Horkheimer, "Vernunft und Selbsterhaltung," 37.

[50] Horkheimer, "Vernunft und Selbsterhaltung," 57.

[51] 1942 Letter from Tillich to Horkheimer. Paul Tillich Archives, Andover-Harvard Theological Library, Cambridge, MA. In *Das Feld der Frankfurter Kultur und Sozialwissenschaften vor 1945*, Manfred Bauschulte and Volkhard Krech write: "Hork-

Tillich, which will be demonstrated in the second section of this chapter. After challenging portions of Horkheimer's interpretation of medieval and Reformation theologians, particularly concerning the function of reason, Tillich draws attention to what he understands to be Horkheimer's assumption of a "pure humanity" or a "pure dehumanization."[52] In this 1942 letter, Tillich writes to Horkheimer:

> I do not believe that there is pure dehumanization just as I do not believe that there can be pure humanity. I believe that there is fragmentary humanity that is based in widespread and constantly new embodiments of inhumanity. And I believe that this fragmentary humanity is strong enough to disclose and withstand every new development and dehumanizing structure, but only in the power of the already existing fragmentary humanity.[53]

The phrase "pure dehumanization" (*reine Entmenschlichung*) does not appear in any existing version of "Vernunft und Selbsterhaltung," and Horkheimer rejects the term in a letter to Tillich written August 12, 1942.[54] Even though the

heimer hatte Tillich den Aufsatz 'Vernunft und Selbsterhaltung' zugesandte…und der als seine Art theoretische Mikrozelle für die spätere 'Dialektik der Aufklärung' dienen sollte. Tillich antwortet auf die Zusendung zunächst mit einer detaillierten Korrektur der im Text enthaltenen kirchengeschichtlichen und theologischen Irrtürmer." "Saulus-Situationen: zum Verhältnis von Kritischer Theorie und Religiösem Sozialismus," Manfred Bauschulte und Volkhard Krech, in *Das Feld der Frankfurter Kultur und Sozialwissenschaften vor 1945*, hrsg. Richard Faber und Eva-Maria Ziege (Königshausen & Neumann, 2007) 56.

[52] As is noted below, this precise language does not appear to exist in any extant version of Horkheimer's essay. Horkheimer does, however, use the phrase *Entmenschlichung* on numerous other occasions, and in his response to Tillich, he accepts the phrase *Menschlichkeit* in a highly nuanced fashion. It may simply be that this characterization is Tillich's alone and does not accurately reflect Horkheimer's terminology; Horkheimer suggests as much in his response.

[53] 1942 Letter from Tillich to Horkheimer, p. 8-9, author's translation. Paul Tillich Archives, Andover-Harvard Theological Library, Cambridge, MA. "Ich glaube nicht, dass es reine Entmenschlichung gibt, wie ich nicht glaube, dass es reine Menschlichkeit auf dem Boden breiter und sich immer neu verkörpernder Unmenschlichkeit gibt. Und ich glaube, dass diese fragmentarische Menschlichkeit stark genug ist, jede entstandene unmenschliche Struktur zu enthüllen und zu überwinden, aber nur in der Kraft der immer auch vorhandenen fragmentarischen Menschlichkeit."

[54] See "Paul Tillich und Max Horkheimer im Dialog. Drei bisher unveröffentlichte Texte (1942/45)" hrsg. Erdmann Sturm, in *Zeitschrift für neuere Theologiegeschichte* 1:2 (1994) Text 2. The term *Entmenschlichung does* appear in Adorno's critique of Tillich, however, as will be seen below.

phrase "pure humanity" (*reine Menschlichkeit*) does not appear in "Vernunft und Selbsterhaltung," Horkheimer appears surprisingly willing to claim it, 'in its theoretical function,' in the same 1942 letter to Tillich. Horkheimer writes:

> While you deny the view of *pure dehumanization*, which the article does not maintain, by the way, you assume at the same time the concept of *pure humanity* which you nevertheless want to reject in the interest of the doctrine of radical evil.[55] However, if one allows this concept of the truth to count, even as a theoretical function, never mind as a basic motive of thought, one will indeed find that the negating power constitutes the life of the spirit.[56]

Through a consideration of 'pure humanity' *in its theoretical function*, Horkheimer argues, one will find that negating strength constitutes the life of the spirit or mind. Exactly what he means by this is unclear, but Horkheimer's willingness to contemplate 'pure humanity,' even in its purely theoretical function, is somewhat surprising. Nevertheless, it is consistent with an interpretation of Horkheimer's early understanding of an evolving, contextual conception of the 'nature of humanity' as a useful framework for social critique, even if only as negation.

In *Eclipse of Reason*, which is based partly on Horkheimer's collaborative work with Adorno in the early 1940s, Horkheimer again engages the 'nature of humanity.' In the Preface, he writes "progress threatens to nullify the very goal it is supposed to realize—the idea of man." Whether this will lead further to barbarism or toward glimpses of freedom "depends at least in part on our ability to interpret accurately the profound changes now taking place in the public mind and in human nature."[57] Horkheimer also notes: "Under totalitarianism, when an individual or group is singled out by the elite for discrimination, it is not only

---

[55] Horkheimer is referring to the Kantian notion of 'radical evil,' which in a slightly different form, is accepted by Tillich as a description of human sinfulness and separation from God.

[56] Horkheimer, "Paul Tillich und Max Horkheimer im Dialog. Drei bisher unveröffentlichte Texte (1942/45)" 293. Author's translation, "Indem sie nämlich die Ansicht von der *reinen Entmenschlichung* verneinen, die der Aufsatz übrigens nicht behauptet, setzen sie zugleich den Begriff der *reinen Menschlichkeit*, den sie doch im Interesse der Lehre vom radikal Bösen ablehnen wollen, voraus. Wenn man aber diesen Begriff oder den der Wahrheit auch nur als theoretische Funktion gelten lässt, geschweige denn als Grundmotiv des Denkens, so wird man finden, dass seine negierende Kraft in der Tat das Leben des Geistes ausmacht." Empahsis added.

[57] ER, iii-iv.

deprived of the means of livelihood, but it's very human essence is attacked."[58] Here the terms 'human nature' and 'human essence' are again used ambiguously,[59] which is all the more remarkable given Adorno's collaborative role in the essays which became *Eclipse of Reason.* Adorno would counter that there is no human 'essence' to attack—only concrete individuals, in concrete historical groupings and contexts.

Despite Horkheimer's consistent critique, something like a 'nature of humanity' seems to be his early shorthand for the ongoing mediation between natural, common human features (longings, fears, needs, beliefs, and practices), and their social contexts. While apparently willing to acknowledge an evolving human 'nature' or 'essence'[60] as a useful framework, what Horkheimer challenges—and what Adorno vehemently rejects—is any presumption of a static 'nature of humanity' which does not consider these unique contexts and irreducible individuality.

One could plausibly argue that the early Horkheimer's ambiguity deliberately reflects a philosophically performative redefinition of the term 'human nature' in order to negate it, as can arguably be seen in Horkheimer's response to Tillich concerning the negating theoretical function of 'pure humanity.' Yet in his early essays, Horkheimer is not willing to go far enough in either direction, neither completely rejecting the language of 'human nature' and 'essence' as a framework, nor accepting it. He does, however, accept and operate on the assumption of a 'nature of humanity,' connoting a composite, socially mediated historical being. This ambiguity qualifies Horkheimer's argument somewhat, and it arguably affects his depiction of human subjectivity, particularly the moral and social agency of the individual who seeks to resist the encroachment of instrumental rationality. By 1943 Horkheimer comes to see instrumental rationality itself as constitutive of the 'nature of humanity,' and from that point forward, he ceases to be able to adequately theorize emancipatory subjectivity or to empower liberative agency.

---

[58] ER, 105.

[59] See e.g. ER, 90, 105, 114.

[60] In "Remarks on Philosophical Anthropology," Horkheimer also appears to deny an evolving concept of human nature: "The attempt to conceive of human beings either as a fixed or as an evolving unity is futile," although the explicit denial is of a *unity.* BPSS, 174. *KT* I, 226.

I.2 From the 'Nature of Humanity' to Human Agency

Although in line with Marx, it is rather surprising that Horkheimer is willing to engage conceptions of a human 'nature' or 'essence' at all, even though it is interrelated with the social and political. Yet whatever benefits are gained from a nuanced, abstract conceptualization of humanity, subjectivity for Horkheimer can only be adequately grasped and grounded by addressing concrete individuals and groups within social and political contexts. In "Remarks on Philosophical Anthropology" (1935), Horkheimer writes:

> The denial of an unchanging, constant human nature [*Menschenwesens*] should, on the other hand, not be taken as an absolute to the extent that the belief in a universal human nature [*menschliche Natur*] appears only as a slight error. One must also recognize that happiness and misery run constantly through history; that human beings as they are have their limits and deserve consideration; and that there is a price to be paid for overlooking those limits.[61]

Even if, or even though, there is no fixed, unchanging "human nature," Horkheimer is equally adamant that there can be no excuse for treating people as means to any end, a central emphasis of his anti-instrumentalist position throughout his life and work.

Domination, reification, injustice, and instrumental rationality occupy much of Horkheimer's writings, and it is inevitable that this influences his thoughts on human subjectivity and agency. In his "Remarks on Philosophical Anthropology" (1935), Horkheimer notes that:

> anthropology...asks for and seeks a definition of human nature [*Wesenbestimmung des Menschen*] that extends from prehistory to the end of humanity, and it avoids *the anthropological question par excellence, namely: how can we overcome an inhuman reality* (since all human capacities [*menschlichen Fähigkeiten*] that we love suffocate and decay within it)?[62]

The supreme anthropological question, Horkheimer claims, is how can humans overcome an inhuman reality? The central assumption is that society is the problem, hindering an inherently neutral, if not good, humanity from self-actualization. Inhuman (social) realities suffocate human capacities that decay

[61] BPSS, 175. *KT* I, 227.

[62] BPSS, 160; emphasis added. *KT* I, 210.

within it. Horkheimer's view of a neutral, if not inherently good, humanity would not last long.

"Egoism and Freedom Movements: On the Anthropology of the Bourgeois Era" (1936) continues the work Horkheimer began in his *Habilitation,* further exploring the bourgeois context and history of the term 'human nature,'[63] including religious interpretations. He slightly amends his own claim concerning humanity of one year prior:

> The same absolute rejection of every egoistic instinct is an obvious presupposition, both in the cynical pronouncement that human nature [*menschlichen Natur*] is evil and dangerous and has to be kept in check by a powerful system of domination (with the corresponding Puritan doctrine of the sinfulness of the individual...) and also in the opposite declaration, that human nature [*Menschen*] is originally pure and harmonious, and has merely been disturbed by the restrictive and corrupt conditions of the present age.[64]

Here Horkheimer criticizes both the idea that humanity is inherently evil, needing correction, and the notion that humanity is inherently good, turned astray by society. A version of the latter view, hypothesizing humanity as inherently neutral, is something Horkheimer comes close to espousing at other points, including his observations cited above.[65] Attempting to mediate between the two extremes, he argues in "Egoism and Freedom Movements" for "free pleasure which is sought without justification"[66] and the "demand for general happiness along with hostility to carefree pleasure."[67]

Horkheimer makes a striking claim in his 1937 essay "Traditional and Critical Theory," where he again hints at innate human neutrality, tarnished by social corruption. He writes:

---

[63] "Egoism and Freedom Movements: On the Anthropology of the Bourgeois Era," in BPSS, 49-110. "Egoismus und Freiheitsbewegung: Zur Anthropologie des bürgerlichen Zeitalters," in *ZfS* 5 (1936) 161-234.

[64] Translation taken from Wiggershaus, 180. For an alternate English translation, see BPSS, 52. *KT* II, 4-5.

[65] See, for example, Horkheimer's insight in "Art and Mass Culture," cited above, that "evil does not stem from nature, but from the violence committed by society against human nature striving to develop." *CT*, 276.

[66] BPSS, 57. *KT* II, 12.

[67] BPSS, 62. *KT* II, 18. This essay has strong Freudian elements and Horkheimer makes explicit reference to Freud's distinction between *eros* and *thantos*, the death drive.

> Critical thinking...is motivated today by the effort...to transcend the tension and abolish the opposition between the individual's purposefulness, spontaneity, and rationality, and those work-process relationships on which society is built. *Critical thought has a concept of man as in conflict with himself* until this opposition is removed. If activity governed by reason is proper to man, then existent social practice, which forms the individual's life down to its least details, is inhuman [*unmenschlich*], and this inhumanity affects everything that goes on in the society.[68]

Here, Horkheimer juxtaposes individual "purposefulness, spontaneity and rationality" with social and labor processes which create conflict within the human subject. Like Tillich, Horkheimer describes the human person in conflict with itself (analogous to sin) and social practice as tending toward the inhuman (analogous to structural sin). Horkheimer claims that the human person—seemingly all humans—is in conflict not unless, but *until*, the opposition between individual self-determination and social-labor coercion ends. This suggests that as late as 1937, Horkheimer retained some cautious optimism concerning the human capacity to engage and transform society. This position changed by the 1940s where Horkheimer increasingly discussed human complicity with unjust and inhuman social processes.[69]

While he rejected any totalizing narrative concerning the 'nature of humanity,' Horkheimer's own conception of instrumental rationality perhaps challenges these early concerns by universalizing the effects of instrumental rationality. Here, the general concern is examining how Horkheimer conceptualizes the human subject so that one retains some degree of agency without violating his own concerns about the 'nature of humanity.' First, one must understand how Horkheimer's increasing awareness of instrumental rationality affects his understanding of humanity. In the previous chapter on critical emancipatory reason, I noted the curious remark made by Horkheimer in a 1943 letter to Pollock, concerning a dialogue with Tillich and Lowenthal dealing with 'clerks.' There, Horkheimer suggested:

---

[68] *CT*, 210; emphasis added. *KT* II, 158-9.

[69] Indeed, the position can arguably be seen changing already in a 1938 essay in *ZfS*, "Montaigne and the Function of Skepticism," where Horkheimer writes: "The negative moment—knowledge of the darker traits of human beings—is not absent from dialectical thought; critique is its element." BPSS, 303. *ZfS* 7 (1938) 42. On the other hand, later in that same essay, Horkheimer writes: "Despite all the horror, the superficial appearance of a depraved humanity...is deceptive." BPSS, 308. *ZfS* 7 (1938) 48.

> The process to which they should refer instead is the one which I have been dealing with during the last two years... the *process of enlightenment as it was marked out in the first thought a human being conceived*, that same process of which Hegel says that if started it is irresistible.[70]

Horkheimer's implicit claim concerning the irresistible progress—echoing the language of disease—of enlightenment as an unavoidable process of disintegration once it has begun, is bleakly pessimistic. One should be cautious not to read too much into this statement, but Horkheimer's language is fascinating: "in the first thought a human being conceived," enlightenment—i.e. instrumental reason—was present. This is even more radical than the claim later in *Dialectic of Enlightenment*, where Adorno and Horkheimer make the subtler point that enlightenment is part of the social process wherein they show the acquisitive and mimetic functions of human beings in society competing for scarce resources (whether physical or more abstract).

Horkheimer's position suggests a conception of enlightenment as, in part, a mimetic process of competition and treating an 'other' as less than what they deserve. The assumption of human worth is taken for granted, but instrumental rationality appears to be not merely a component of competitive social processes but a fundamental and inevitable part—Horkheimer's core presupposition perhaps—of humanity.[71] The further assumption is that instrumental rationality is coterminous with human thought or perhaps with human nature. Is this an *ersatz* 'essence'—something inevitable and invariable across humanity, defined by instrumental rationality? In his 1943 letter to Pollock, Horkheimer's implication is that instrumental rationality is a chief manifestation of the disease of enlightenment and it is hard-wired into the individual human. This goes back to the archetypal and mythical first human and is co-extensive with human thought.[72]

---

[70] Horkheimer, *GS* 17, 446; emphasis added.

[71] This is also how Habermas interprets Horkheimer and Adorno on this point. He writes that Horkheimer and Adorno "expand instrumental reason into a category of the world-historical process of civilization as a whole, that is, to project the process of reification back behind the capitalist beginnings of the modern age into the very beginnings of hominization." Jürgen Habermas, *Theory of Communicative Action*, trans. Thomas McCarthy (Cambridge: Polity Press, 1991) vol. 1, 366.

[72] Horkheimer notes: "The disease of reason is that reason was born from man's urge to dominate nature, and the 'recovery' depends on insight into the nature of the original disease, not on a cure of the latest symptoms." *ER*, 119. This is the project and goal of *Dialectic of Enlightenment* and of critical theory generally.

Horkheimer offers an implicit re-reading of the mythical origins of humanity, suggesting that the instrumental nature of enlightenment thought is somehow hard-wired into each human person. The fundamental problem of enlightenment as a process which originated in the "first thought a human being conceived" is the human propensity to seek utility, to reify the 'other' and the concomitant focus on instrumental means. This is true not only of the modern Enlightenment, but the process of enlightenment (and myth with it) all the way back to the archetypal 'beginning' is presented as coterminous with the 'nature of humanity.' Horkheimer implies that the propensity toward domination is part and parcel of the 'nature of humanity;' the modern European Enlightenment and its legacy is merely the most recent manifestation of this primal urge to dominate. It is interesting to note in passing how analogous this is to the Judeo-Christian conception of sin as a plague which, once it has begun, spreads like a disease and infects humanity individually and collectively, down to the thought of an individual. Instrumental reason and accompanying reification take the structural place of individual and structural sin as the transgressions that mark or stain all subsequent humanity.

I.3 Self-Preservation and Subjectivity

The disease of reason is also apparently morally culpable in some sense for Horkheimer, furthering the comparison with the Judeo-Christian conception of sin. Suggestions of humanity's inherent neutrality or goodness, corrupted only by an unjust social structure, are almost entirely gone by the 1940s. In exchanging reason for self-preservation, the human subject surrenders what is original and 'good.'[73] This can be seen in Odysseus' encounter with Polyphemus, where Odysseus must betray and deny himself in order to preserve his life.[74] While understandable, this seems to be morally culpable for Horkheimer, and in their joint work, for Adorno as well. From the moment in which the individual decides to, and realizes the necessity of, repressing the self in order to preserve the self in society, instrumental reason takes over and distorts human subjectivity

[73] Papastephanou writes, "oppressive reason is the subject's fault from time immemorial, since the latter exchanges freedom for security." Marianna Papastephanou, "Ulysses' Reason, Nobody's Fault: Reason, Subjectivity and the Critique of Enlightenment," in *Philosophy and Social Criticism* 26:6 (2000) 54.

[74] While outside of the scope of this chapter, an analysis of the Odysseus section of *Dialectic of Enlightenment*, examining Odysseus as the 'prototype' of modern subjectivity for Adorno and Horkheimer would be fruitful.

and relations.[75] All individuals are born into and formed by linguistic contexts and social groups that already operate based on reification and collective repression.

Horkheimer's 1941 essay "Vernunft und Selbsterhaltung" was included in a limited-release publication of the *Institut* in New York, *Walter Benjamin zum Gedächtnis,* which was published in 1942 in honor of Benjamin.[76] This essay surveys much of the conceptual ground explicated in and through the Odysseus narrative in *Dialectic of Enlightenment* several years later, in a section commonly believed to have been the brainchild of Adorno.[77] In this 1941 text, which foreshadows *Dialectic of Enlightenment* in several ways, Horkheimer articulates a further anthropological presupposition which again draws on Freudian anthropology.[78] Rooted etymologically in the German *Enthaltung*, or 'abstinence,' *Selbsterhaltung* implies a conscious 'self-limitation,' or perhaps even a degree of abstinence from some aspect of the self required for rationality. Horkheimer is suggesting that there is a conscious limitation of the self that is necessary for the operation of rationality, which is the price of maintaining the ego.[79]

Horkheimer then argues that self-preservation comes at the expense of reason and that the collapse of individual autonomy and the collapse of reason are coterminous. He writes:

> The category of the individual to which, despite all tension, the idea of autonomy was attached has not stood firm to big industry. Reason has gone to ruin, in so far as it was the ideological projection of decayed community, to the apparently autonomous subjects now experiencing

[75] "Calculation and reification are built into language and appear time-transcendent and ineluctable" for Horkheimer. Papastephanou, 55.

[76] Wiggershaus notes that many of the earliest readers of these three essays by Horkheimer and Adorno found them so Benjaminian that they were mistakenly thought to have been written by Benjamin himself. Wiggershaus, 311.

[77] This text complicates a common and simplistic understanding of Adorno as the primary source of the Odysseus section of *Dialectic of Enlightenment.*

[78] Also important for this discussion of critical anthropology is the influence of Freud and his understanding of the requisite repression of the self for the sake of the self-in-society. Freud held that the individual 'pleasure principle' must be subsumed under the 'reality principle' in order for society to function. See Freud, *Civilization and its Discontents* (1930).

[79] In a more Freudian and existential vein, Horkheimer writes of death as the absolute limit in 1941 in "Vernunft und Selbsterhaltung:" "*Der Tod war die Grenze schlechthin des durch Selbsterhaltung konstituierten Individuums.*" Horkheimer, "*Vernunft und Selbsterhaltung*" (Bard manuscript) 52.

> negation. *The decay of reason and of the individual are one and the same. 'The self is irrecoverable' and self-preservation disappears from its subject.*[80]

Not only are the decay of reason and of the subject coterminous, Horkheimer makes the further claim that the self or subject (*das Ich*) cannot be saved, retrieved or preserved. The very attempt of self-preservation under the conditions of modernity causes the subject itself to disappear.

Despite this bleak portrait of the modern subject, Horkheimer retains some hope in communal social action, and above all, in collective solidarity. He writes:

> With the decay the self and its reflective reason, human relationships approach a limit where the control of all personal relations are overturned by the economic, the universal mediation of coexistence through the commodity in a new way of immediacy.[81]

Horkheimer implies that despite the decline or decay of the subject, the universal mediation of co-existence through commodities can be transformed into a new manner of immediacy, namely solidarity. In a 1941 letter to Marcuse, Horkheimer writes that his essay on reason ("Vernunft und Selbsterhaltung") offers "an examination of the prospects for a change from individual self-preservation to universal solidarity."[82] Whether this intention comes through in the essay is debatable, but Horkheimer aimed to show human solidarity as a defense mechanism against the pervasiveness of self-preservation and the accompanying repression.

---

[80] Horkheimer, "Vernunft und Selbsterhaltung" (Bard manuscript) 37-8; emphasis added. Author's translation, "Die Kategorie des Individuums, an die trotz aller Spannung die Idee der Autonomie geknüpft war, hat der großen Industrie nicht standgehalten. Die Vernunft ist soweit verfallen, wie sie die ideologische Projektion eben der schlechten Allgemeinheit war, an der die scheinbar autonomen Subjekte jetzt ihre Nichtigkeit erfahren. *Der Zerfall der Vernunft und der des Individuums sind eines. 'Das Ich ist unrettbar' und der Selbsterhaltung entschwindet ihr Subjekt.*"

[81] Horkheimer, "Vernunft und Selbsterhaltung," 44. Author's translation, "Mit dem Verfall das Ichs und seiner reflektierenden Vernunft nähern die menschliche Beziehungen einer Grenze sich an, wo die Beherrschung aller persönlichen Verhältnisse durch die ökonomischen, die universale Vermittlung des Zusammenlebens durch die Ware, in eine neue Weise von Unmittelbarkeit umschlägt."

[82] Letter, Horkheimer to Marcuse, 6 December 1941; cited in Wiggershaus, 297.

Horkheimer's 1941 English-language essay, "The End of Reason,"[83] makes a similar positive argument, maintaining some critical power for resistance within reason itself. He writes: "through reason man frees himself of the fetters of nature. This liberation, however, does not entitle man to dominate nature (as the philosophers held) but to comprehend it.... Reason could recognize and denounce the forms of injustice and thus emancipate itself from them."[84] Even in the midst of Horkheimer's increasingly desperate accounts of subjectivity and domination, he makes room for possibilities of emancipatory reason, increasingly through social solidarity.

The theme of self-preservation at the expense of reason is also important in *Eclipse of Reason*, and there, again, the concept of solidarity surfaces. The emergence of subjectivity comes at the expense of the repression of the individual necessary for self-preservation within society. This difficulty is compounded under the conditions of modern capitalist society and Horkheimer's view that under such conditions, even the human subject can easily become a commodity. Horkheimer writes: "self-preservation can be achieved only in a supra-individual order, that is to say, through social solidarity."[85] The individual must repress their own nature and form an uncertain alliance with other individuals in order to survive.

A similar formulation describing the modern subject can be seen in *Dialectic of Enlightenment*: "The awakening of the subject is bought with the recognition of power as the principle of all relationships."[86] For Horkheimer, reason becomes instrumental within humanity; a (or perhaps *the*) means of preserving the self is the rational calculation of repressing one's own nature. Yet the fundamental problem is not self-preservation itself, but rather the means and forms necessary for such preservation. In a similar vein, Horkheimer writes in *Eclipse of Reason*: "It is not technology or the motive of self-preservation that in itself accounts for the decline of the individual; it is not production *per se*, but the forms in which it takes place—the interrelationships of human beings within the specific framework of industrialism."[87]

---

[83] This English essay is widely understood as a model for the slightly later German essay "Vernunft und Selbsterhaltung."

[84] Horkheimer, "End of Reason," in *The Essential Frankfurt School Reader*, 47.

[85] *ER*, 119.

[86] DE, 5. *DA*, 15.

[87] ER, 103-4.

Again, in *Eclipse of Reason*, Horkheimer writes: "The fully developed individual is the consummation of a fully developed society. The emancipation of the individual is not an emancipation from society, but the deliverance of society from atomization...."[88] By contrast, a society which denies the flourishing and full development of subjects is at best undeveloped. The emancipation of the subject frees the individual to more fully participate in society, allowing greater agency. These and other hints toward Horkheimer's conception of solidarity show that subjectivity can lead to agency, as will be seen in the following chapter dealing with metaphysics and norms.

Arguing in the 1930s that social realities can be changed, even by the titular 'little man' of the entry in *Dawn and Decline*, Horkheimer underlines the significance of human agency and responsibility over what are fatalistically regarded as laws of the market or laws of nature. These "phenomena... depend on men and the way they arrange their social existence. They can therefore be changed."[89] Under the conditions of modernity and capitalistic class stratification, what is required to change the situation is to realize that "the subject does not exist. Everything therefore depends on creating the free subject that consciously shapes social life. And this subject is nothing other than the rationally organized socialist society which regulates its own existence."[90] At that point, Horkheimer still believed that 'creating a free subject' was possible, despite his claim that the 'subject does not (currently) exist.' As can be seen even in some of his works from the early 1940s, such as *Eclipse of Reason*, Horkheimer still retains some hope for human subjectivity in solidarity.

In "Remarks on Philosophical Anthropology" (1935), Horkheimer suggests that social transformation is in principle possible, and can even be buttressed by examining certain common human characteristics:

> [In looking at] historically determined human beings...instead of with man as such...*we want to stress the existence and transformation of characteristics that may determine the actual course of history.* The concept of man [*Bild des Menschen*] here appears not as uniform, but as consisting in characteristics that designate certain groups. These characteristics arise together with the social life process, are transmitted from one class

---

[88] ER, 92.

[89] DD 50-1. *Dämmerung: Notizen in Deutschland*, Heinrich Regius (Zürich: Verlag Oprecht & Helbling, 1934) 98.

[90] DD, 51. *Dämmerung*, 99-100.

> to another, and under certain circumstances are either absorbed by the entire society and given new meanings or else disappear.[91]

It is worth wondering whether Horkheimer is here suggesting that focusing on certain human characteristics, within their proper context, can reveal strategies for resistance?

Despite all of his explicit anti-utopian commitment, already in his 1933 "Materialism and Metaphysics," Horkheimer articulates the hope for "the idea of a better reality which will emerge from the presently prevailing state of affairs."[92] Similarly in "Remarks on Philosophical Anthropology" (1935) one encounters other trends, whereby Horkheimer suggests that critical theory commits itself in solidarity to the mission of "a freer humanity [*einer Menschheit*]."[93] This tension between Horkheimer's quasi-utopian hopes for solidarity in the future[94] and his denial of such hopes will be explored in the following chapter.

Finally, Horkheimer acknowledges in 1935's "Remarks on Philosophical Anthropology" that the only necessary motivation for continuing anthropological reflection and study is "the realization that real sufferings must be eliminated," although he goes on to warn against "new acts of theological fantasy."[95] This acknowledgement in the two above quotations, linking the elimination of suffering to ongoing anthropological reflection, is significant. A decade later, Horkheimer no longer would acknowledge such a connection, but it speaks clearly to the central thesis: some conception of the 'nature of humanity' is necessary to fund emancipatory theory and praxis.

---

[91] BPSS, 161; emphasis added. *KT* I, 211-2.

[92] *CT*, 45. *ZfS* 2 (1933) 33.

[93] BPSS, 166. *KT* I, 217.

[94] "Solidarity refers not just to human beings as they are, but as they might be as well." MH, BPSS, 303. *ZfS* 8 (1938) 42.

[95] BPSS, 161. "Das Motiv zu solchen Studien liegt weniger in der fragwürdigen Ansicht[en] der Anthropologie selbst..., sondern in wirklichen Qualen, die es zu beendigen gilt. Dass die Bilder des ewigen Lebens verblassen und die Formen des zeitlichen völlig der Harmonie entbehren, bedeutet keineswegs, dass die Zeit für neue Taten der theologischen Phantasie gekommen sei." *KT* I, 212.

II. Paul Tillich's Early[96] Anthropology

Like Horkheimer, and similar to Marx, Tillich initially locates the 'nature of humanity' in reason and consciousness, along with instincts and passions. He writes in *The Socialist Decision*: "The capacity for rationality is the primary characteristic of human being [*menschlichen Seins*]; the other aspects of human nature [*Wesens*] must be made subject to reason."[97] Also like Horkheimer, Tillich analyzes the bourgeois and Enlightenment view of human nature. The bourgeois view of human nature was stuck between empirical and rational poles, believing either that reason alone or education and progress would suffice to provide stability for humanity.[98]

Similar in many ways to the position of Horkheimer articulated above, Tillich rejects the prospect of an 'eternal human nature.' In *The Socialist Decision*, he writes:

> [I]t is certainly not necessary to posit an eternal human nature [*'ewigen Wesen' des Menschen*]; but it is necessary to understand humanity [*Menschen*] living in encounter and in history, as a unity, since otherwise nothing at all could be asserted, even about the most concrete historical phenomenon. Most significantly, every norm would thereby be invalidated.[99]

Note here the similarities with Horkheimer (and the contrast with Adorno's characterization of Tillich seen below)—for Tillich, humanity is characterized in terms of dynamic *encounter*, not eternal nature, although he does refer to human being (*menschliche Sein*), suggesting an ontological element which Horkheimer denies.

---

[96] The first half of the chapter looks, almost exclusively, at Tillich's writings in the 1930s in conversation with Horkheimer. While Tillich's writings from the 1920s, including his dissertation, *Habilitation*, and other writings on Schelling deal with anthropological themes, there is not significant correlating work by Horkheimer at the same time, in part because Tillich was several years older than Horkheimer. The second half of the chapter looks primarily at a 1943 essay by Tillich and a response from Adorno.

[97] Paul Tillich, *The Socialist Decision*, trans. Franklin Sherman (New York: Harper & Row, 1977) 71. *GS*, bd. 2, 285. Tillich continues: "Being, even human being, must be formed by consciousness. Thus arises the image of humanity as steadily and progressively raising being to the level of consciousness; as gaining an ever clearer self-understanding, as analyzing things and acting on the basis of this illumination (earlier called 'enlightenment') in a reasonable, orderly manner...." *GW* 2, 286.

[98] *SD*, 71-2.

[99] *SD*, 165, n. 7. *GW* 2, 231, n. 7.

In *The Socialist Decision*, Tillich suggests that in the human person, there is a dynamic interconnection between being and consciousness of being, between self-awareness and consciousness of one's self-awareness. He writes: "Political thinking proceeds from human nature [*Menschen*] as a whole. It is rooted simultaneously in being and in consciousness, more precisely in the indissoluble unity of the two."[100] Tillich goes on to say: "*Every element of human and social being* [*menschliches Sein*], *down to the most primitive emotional drive, is shaped by consciousness.* Any effort to dissolve this connection ignores the first and most important characteristic of human nature [*Wesenszug des Menschen*]...."[101] This foundational principle of the 'nature of humanity,' articulated in the opening pages of *The Socialist Decision*, is distinct from Horkheimer in that it reflects a dynamic unity of being and consciousness. The awareness of one's situatedness, coupled with a simultaneous drive to transcend that situatedness is foundational to Tillich's claims about the necessity of presupposing a basic operative anthropology. This is an important clue as to the basis of Tillich's argument a decade later that the human person is 'finite freedom,' which bears the brunt of Adorno's critique.

For Tillich, the human subject is distinguished not only by reason, but also by a level of self-conscious reason which renders the subject a question to him or herself: Who am I? How did I get here? What should I do? How can I make the world a little more just? Distinct from animals because of an "internal duality [*gedoppeltes Wesen*]" Tillich writes, echoing Hegel, "[h]umanity [*der Mensch*] is a life-process that questions itself and its environment, placing demands on itself and its environment.... [I]t has these two aspects: to exist in itself and simultaneously to stand over against itself, thinking about itself and knowing itself."[102] Tillich is not affirming a Cartesian dualism, but rather positing that in humanity, "there is *one* being but twofold in its unity."[103] For the sake of simplicity, this is described as the 'existential' aspect of the 'nature of humanity.'

---

[100] *SD*, 2. *GW* 2, 226.

[101] *SD*, 3; emphasis in original. *GW* 2, 226.

[102] *SD*, 2. *GW*, bd. 2, 226.

[103] *SD*, 2. *GW* 2, 226. While the influence of Heidegger on Horkheimer and Adorno is limited and negative, Heidegger's influence on Tillich was profound. Here it suffices to note the apparent influence of Heideggerian phenomenology on Tillich's anthropological portrait in *The Socialist Decision*, particularly relating to questions of existence, awareness of death, and existential probing of the 'whence' of existence.' While the influence of Tillich's former colleague in Marburg (1925-7) should not be overstated, it behooves us to recall that Heidegger's own understanding of his presuppositions led him to

Tillich seems to understand this awareness as a universal human feature, so although it appears to be a descriptive, heuristic framework, one might also plausibly argue that he 'essentializes' humanity in this way. Rather than proposing a universal, trans-temporal anthropological claim, Tillich makes an assertion about observed common experience and characteristics within his specific context, or a claim about subjectivity under the conditions of modernity. Regardless, the existential experience Tillich thinks is common within modernity reflects one of the ways he engages the human subject's freedom and the possibility of ethical agency, and it is this nexus that now comes into focus.

The important analysis and critique of the 'myth of origin' in *The Socialist Decision* reflects Tillich's 'existential' concern and zeroes in on key questions of ethics and agency. Myth in general for Tillich, through the cycle of birth and death, seeks to clarify the 'whence' of human existence, the existential and metaphysical conundrum of humanity's self-conscious curiosity as to origin and purpose. In *The Socialist Decision*, he writes:

> Every myth is a myth of origin, that is, an answer to the question about the 'Whence' of existence and an expression of dependence on the origin and on its power. *The consciousness oriented to the myth of origin is the root of all conservative and romantic thought in politics.*[104]

Tillich here emphasizes the connection between the myth of origin and the conservative and romantic political nationalism manifest in National Socialism. Romantic and nationalistic politics exploit the myth of origin by narrowly circumscribing the existential question raised which each individual must answer, and instead provide a composite social alternative. In the case of National Socialism, the mythology of blood, soil, and Fatherland demonstrates this subterfuge.

---

a profoundly different conclusion about humanity and the political realm. Less than a year after Tillich wrote *The Socialist Decision*, Heidegger became *Rektor* of Freiburg University as a member of the Nazi party and Tillich's book was banned and burned before it was widely distributed. Tillich was expelled from his teaching position in Frankfurt, and soon thereafter effectively exiled from Germany for his critique of National Socialism and his support for Jewish students and colleagues. Adorno rejects most of Heidegger's thought, and much of Adorno's later work, notably *Negative Dialectics*, explicitly has Heidegger as its source of critique. The early essays of Adorno, however, explored in the next chapter on metaphysics, betray a more positive, if still ambiguous relation to Heidegger and ontology.

[104] *SD*, 4; emphasis in original. *GW* 2, 227-8.

How does he understand the human subject as a dynamic 'life-process,' a unity of being and consciousness in the context of (nationalistic) myths of origin? For Tillich, not unproblematically, the pervasiveness of the existential question of 'whence,' when not misdirected by romantic 'myths of origin,' directs the human subject to its goal by raising questions of a source—the 'whither' of existence—which thereby grounds any ethical *ought*. Tillich writes:

> [H]uman beings [*der Mensch*] not only find themselves in existence; they not only know themselves to be posited and withdrawn in the cycle of birth and death, like all living things. They experience a demand that frees them from being simply bound to what is given, and which compels them to add to the question 'Whence?' [*Woher*] the question 'Whither?' [*Wozu*]. With this question the cycle is broken in principle and human kind is elevated beyond the sphere of merely living things. For the demand calls for something that does not yet exist but should exist, should come to fulfillment. A being [*Wesen*] that experiences a demand is no longer simply bound to the origin.... Through the demand, humanity is directed to what ought to be.[105]

Tillich makes the strong claim that this ethical demand constitutes the responsible individual and breaks the myth of origin, in large part through the subject's consciousness that it is not bound by perceived ties to the 'origin,' whatever it may be. Freedom and agency become possibilities which can be actualized when the subject consciously breaks the ties to one's 'origin.'[106] He writes:

> For the human person [*der Mensch*] is not only an individual, a self, but also has knowledge about himself or herself, and thereby the possibility of transcending what is found within the self and around the self. This is human freedom, not that one has a so-called 'free will,' but that as a human being [*als Mensch*] one is not bound to what one finds in existence, that one is subject to a demand that something unconditionally new should be realized through oneself. Thus the cycle of birth and death is broken; the existence and the actions of human beings [*sein Dasein und sein Tun*] are not confined within a mere development of their origin. Wherever this consciousness prevails, the tie to the origin has been dissolved in principle and the myth of origin has been broken

---

[105] *SD*, 4. *GW*, bd. 2, 228.

[106] In a limited sense, Horkheimer and Adorno might agree with Tillich here. Their emphasis on critical thought—critical consciousness—as the primary vehicle of resistance seems to find an echo in Tillich's claims.

> in principle. *The breaking of the myth of origin by the unconditional demand is the root of liberal, democratic, and socialist thought in politics.*[107]

Tillich here uses the Heidegger-influenced term *Dasein* to describe the human person in a particular context; this is distinct from Horkheimer and Adorno who generally reject Heideggerian language.[108] Human subjects here in the context of myth are defined in large part by free possibility and characterized by consciousness of ethical demands. With that critical consciousness comes the possibility of transcending a given context or status quo, quite to the contrary of myths of origin such as Nazi mythology. Important for my purposes, Tillich concludes the above quote by tying together critical consciousness, ethical agency, and socialist political theory and practice. After a brief examination of the explicitly theological presuppositions about anthropology in his early work, a shift is made to Tillich's understanding of religious socialism, particularly as it relates to and draws upon a critical conception of anthropology.

The human individual[109] who is subject to the ethical 'demand' of the 'whither?' is "a unity of body and soul, and the meaning of [one's] existence cannot be separated from the meaning of [one's] bodily existence."[110] According to Tillich, this unity, always under the threat of disunity, "represents the original intentions of the Old and the New Testaments."[111] Despite the perpetual threat to human existence posed by the disruption of the vital and the spiritual, he claims that this "view rejects every utopia, that is, every expectation of perfection within history."[112] This statement is crucial and appears to have been overlooked by both Horkheimer and Adorno, who mistakenly criticize Tillich for what they presume to be his privileging of an inner-historical utopia. Tillich, like Hork-

---

[107] *SD*, 5; emphasis in original. *GW* 2, 228.

[108] Adorno freely uses *Dasein* in the early 1930s, including his *Habilitation* on Kierkegaard, and Horkheimer uses the term *Dasein* at least until 1938. Tillich continues to use this term for as long as he writes in German.

[109] Despite Adorno's critique that Tillich is overly individualistic, Tillich isn't solely concerned with the individual and he is well aware of the individual's situatedness within social structures. While Tillich does seek to provide a framework for the 'human as such,' most of Tillich's anthropological sketch is concerned with historically determined individuals and groups within society, hence the collective goal of religious socialism, for example.

[110] *PE*, 47. *GW* 2, 165.

[111] *PE*, 47. *GW* 2, 165.

[112] *PE*, 47. *GW* 2, 165. Emphasis in original.

heimer and Adorno, rejects any inner-historical utopia, while nevertheless striving to bring about change in the midst of the mundane and the barbaric.

In his 1930 essay "Religious Socialism," Tillich rejects both utopianism and essentialism, claiming that, "In the light of the brokenness of man's being, religious socialism rejects every utopian ethic. That man is good and that only social circumstances make him bad is as a generalization as false as it may be relatively true for a concrete situation…."[113] Unlike Horkheimer, Tillich does not maintain human neutrality or argue for inherent social corruption of an otherwise neutral, if not good, human subject. Here one can profitably compare his position on human sin and brokenness to Horkheimer's relative optimism about people, combined with his pessimism about society. While Horkheimer presupposes that the human person is neutral, driven astray by a society which causes violence to 'human nature,' Tillich rejects such a conception because of his understanding of sin and his relative optimism (compared with Horkheimer and Adorno) concerning transformative social possibilities.

It is instructive to note at this point that Tillich's early anthropology is somewhat more of a philosophical anthropology than a traditional theological anthropology. When addressing humanity, some contemporary Protestant theologians began from, or built to, Jesus as the paragon of humanity—the ideal, faultless human and the model for a human life rightly lived before God—because Jesus is understood to be perfectly divine and perfectly human, the paragon and ideal manifestation of the 'nature of humanity.'[114] Writing as a professor of philosophy in the early 1930s, Tillich does not directly address the incarnation and the effect it has on anthropology in his more philosophical discussion in *The Socialist Decision* or in his later, more explicitly religious address, "Man and Society in Religious Socialism."[115] In his early essays, the primary theological motifs relevant to anthropology are sin and prophetic expectation. He posits

---

[113] *PE*, 52. *GW* 2, 169.

[114] Theologians have wrestled for centuries with the question of what it means that God—in the incarnate form of Jesus—became human and 'dwelt among us.' Following the Chalcedonian formula, Jesus is understood to be fully God, yet also human 'without confusion, change, division or separation.'

[115] In the early 1930s when Tillich wrote "Religious Socialism" and *The Socialist Decision*, the two primary texts analyzed here, he was a professor of philosophy in Frankfurt, so it is perhaps not as surprising that he does not explicitly engage theological anthropology in either text. By 1943, when he wrote "Man and Society in Religious Socialism," however, Tillich was a professor of philosophical theology at Union Theological Seminary.

humanity's condition—based on his theological conviction concerning human sinfulness—as 'broken'[116] and argues that no social structure or system can change this fundamentally, although social structures can exacerbate human brokenness. In a 1931 essay, he wrote: "The Protestant principle implies a judgment about the human situation, namely, that it is basically distorted."[117]

Tillich accepts and affirms what he describes as "the prophetic element of Marxist anthropology, namely the relatedness of man's being to a transcendent [*die Beziehung des menschlichen Seins auf ein transzendentes*] principle that is unconditionally valid and fulfilling."[118] It is this prophetic element of expectation—a Jewish category[119]—that he wants to re-instill in socialism. In *The Socialist Decision*, he writes: "*Both prophetic and socialist expectation are a witness of life to its fundamental openness. They are a protest of life against false concepts of transcendence that inevitably call forth, in opposition, false concepts of immanence.*"[120] One of his most controversial claims is that the human person is somehow related to that which is beyond both being and freedom, and he claims this as a manifestation of "the prophetic-eschatological element in socialism."[121] Tillich also expresses sympathetic agreement with the Freudian critique of religion: "prophetic religion is inherently suspicious of religion that is based on man's wishes, of the 'self-made God' [Luther], and of the unconscious use of the divine in the service of the will to power."[122] Further, he insists prophetic religion "must adopt this constant suspicion of ideology and apply it to itself."[123] Constant self-critique for Tillich, as for Adorno and Horkheimer, is a hallmark of a healthy theory as well as theology.

---

[116] Another important way the early Tillich understands human beings is as the locus of the interconnection of "essential goodness, existential estrangement, and the possibility of a 'third' beyond essence and existence." Paul Tillich, *Theology of Culture*, ed. Robert C. Kimball (New York: Oxford University Press, 1964) 119.

[117] Tillich, *The Protestant Era*, 165. "Protestantische Prinzip und der proletarischen Situation," 11.

[118] *PE*, 46. *GW* 2, 164.

[119] The central Jewish element of prophetic critique and expectation is explored in chapter 5.

[120] *SD*, 111; emphasis in original. *GW* 2, 319.

[121] *PE*, 48. Religious socialism sees "die Wurzel des prophetisch-eschatologischen Elementes im Sozialismus…." *GW* 2, 165-6.

[122] *PE*, 46. *GW* 2, 164.

[123] *PE*, 46. *GW* 2, 164. Emphasis in original.

II.1 Religious Socialism and the 'Nature of Humanity'

Tillich's early understanding of the 'nature of humanity' is profoundly connected to the constructive socio-political program that he was actively seeking to implement from the mid-1920s through the mid-1940s, namely 'religious socialism.' Tillich's religious socialism arises in tandem with his understanding of the 'nature of humanity' and the functions and limitations of human rationality in modernity. Described most generally as a "manifestation of *Christian humanism*,"[124] religious socialism in Tillich's understanding provides, or perhaps seeks to reclaim, a Christian substance (*Gehalt*) to "the universal and rational forms of that which is human...."[125] Because he maintains in this 1930 essay that there is "no such thing as humanism in general," Tillich reasons that neither can there be any "simple opposition between Christianity and humanism."[126] Tillich explored and developed this argument in conversation with Erich Fromm in the Frankfurt Institute of Psychoanalysis in the early 1930s.[127]

Tillich argues that humanism, along with much of socialism, in the modern era has "cut itself off from its religious background and from its intrinsically religious origins...reject[ing]the transcendent orientation, and since an empty humanistic form does not exist, it opened itself in this way to anti-Christian elements."[128] Tillich also places some blame for the presumed and actual opposition on Christian churches' 'fixation' with and 'adaptation' to "profane humanism."[129] Tillich's immediate goal, then, is to challenge the presumed opposition between 'Christian' and 'humanism,' and between 'religion' and 'socialism.' He is essentially suggesting that the nouns 'humanism' and 'socialism' lack some fundamental depth and traction in their ability to sustain critique in the attempt to improve society, and that each can be strengthened, respectively, by the adjectives 'Christian' and 'religious.' This is comparable to Tillich's critique of Marcuse examined in the previous chapter, and by extension, the Frankfurt School's critical theory in general, concerning the need for an 'ultimate' source and foun-

---

[124] *PE*, 42; emphasis in original. Religious socialism "ist eine Erscheinung des '*christlichen Humanismus*.'" *GW* 2, 160.

[125] *PE*, 42. *GW* 2, 160.

[126] *PE*, 42. *GW* 2, 160-1.

[127] In these discussions with Fromm and other members of the Frankfurt Institute of Psychoanalysis, "Tillich emphasized the necessity of radical social change for human existence to be fulfilled," according to Wiggershaus, 55.

[128] *PE*, 42. *GW* 2, 161.

[129] *PE*, 42. *GW* 2, 161.

dation of critique.[130] Tillich is well aware of the ambiguity and pitfalls of the terms 'Christianity' and 'religion,' and his understanding of these terms is neither simplistic nor univocal.

Religious socialism seeks to revive the Christian *Gehalt* at the origins of humanism and socialism, and thereby offer a supplement to materialist socialism's critique, analysis and prescription for a better society. Tillich argues that the apparent opposition between religious socialism and materialist socialism "appears…in their respective *conceptions of man [Auffassung des Menschen].*"[131] It is in the respective anthropological presuppositions where an "ambiguous state of affairs" most clearly comes to light and could drive a wedge between religion and socialism. Tillich challenges this apparent disjunction, not to argue that distinctly 'religious' and 'socialist' anthropologies are operating from the same presuppositions or toward identical goals, but rather to note the points of commonality and prospects for dialogue.

Having briefly explicated what he means by Christian humanism, Tillich readily acknowledges that 'religion' and 'socialism' are not self-evidently related or happy bedfellows. Yet he claims that much of the presumed opposition between 'religion' and 'socialism' rests on a common misunderstanding and oversimplification rooted in (mis)interpretation of Marx's anthropology. In his dialogues with Fromm and other members of the Institute of Psychoanalysis in the early 1930s, Tillich emphasized "how strongly the young Marx emphasized humanism as the core of socialism."[132] The 'core of socialism' Tillich identifies is Marx's social analysis and critique of capitalism along with the underlying power dynamics of class society.[133] With regard to the economic theory behind Marx's social analysis of capitalistic structures, Tillich claims that religious socialism

---

[130] See chapter two for a discussion of Tillich's comments concerning the necessity of an "ultimacy" to ground and sustain critique in his 1941 *ZfS* review of Marcuse's *Reason and Revolution.*

[131] *PE*, 45. *GW* 2, 163, emphasis in original.

[132] This reflection comes from the autobiography of the co-director of the Frankfurt Institute of Psychoanalysis, Heinrich Meng, recalling his interaction with Tillich in the 1930s. Heinrich Meng, *Leben als Begegnung* (Stuttgart, 1971) 78; cited in Wiggershaus, 55.

[133] In 1930 (and into the 1940s) Tillich still viewed religious socialism as providing a conception of emancipatory agency similar to that of Marx. He writes: "Along with Marx, religious socialism sees in the proletariat the place given by fate for resistance to the capitalist structure of society." *PE*, 49. Original cited above.

"takes no position whatsoever;"[134] religious socialism is primarily concerned with engaging Marxian anthropology to support its emancipatory theories.[135]

Tillich understands religious socialism as a challenge to forms of socialism which revert to utopian idealism or positivistic rationalism. Most forms of materialist socialism operate on a misinterpretation of Marx's anthropology, according to Tillich. He argues that materialist socialism[136] mistakenly neglected Marx's conception of the 'nature of humanity,' on which Marx's own emancipatory theory rests, and thus created a false opposition. It accepts Marx's appropriation of Feuerbach's anthropological analysis of the "limitlessness of human drives" and the "formation of religious ideas by means of the projection and objectivization of the contents of these drives,"[137] but it draws the false conclusions that there is no 'nature of humanity' and that religion is inimical to socialism. Tillich further suggested to Adorno in 1936 that a new "'Communist or Socialist' Manifesto could be written with religion."[138]

Although anthropology is not the primary concern of his 1933 manifesto against National Socialism, Tillich, in *The Socialist Decision*, recognizes that he must ground his philosophy of action and agency via a brief discussion of the 'nature of humanity,' informed by his assumptions about and interactions with phenomenology and psychology. The problem with many secular theories, Tillich argues, is that without some understanding of the 'nature of humanity'—even as a heuristic device—the transformative aspect of agency and ethics comes unmoored. To be clear: Tillich's proposal is *not* the imposition of a fideistic

---

[134] *PE*, 49. Tillich goes on to say that "It is not the task of religious socialism to solve concrete economic and political problems. It can, however, influence their solution indirectly by means of its total position." *GW* 2, 167.

[135] Tillich arguably has in mind Marx's assertion cited above: "To be radical is to grasp things by the root. But for man the root is man himself." Marx, *Early Writings*, 251. Transformative social action is rooted in anthropology, Tillich emphasizes and claims support from Marx for his position.

[136] By 'materialist socialism,' I am grouping together all forms of socialism which are rooted in secular materialism; Tillich also refers to this general grouping as 'vulgar' socialism. The term is very loosely defined and is intended to connote juxtaposition with religious socialism.

[137] *PE*, 45. *GW* 2, 164.

[138] This is Adorno's account of a conversation with Tillich in May 1936 in a letter to Horkheimer. *Theodor W. Adorno und Max Horkheimer Briefwechsel 1927-1969, Band I: 1927-1937,* hrsg. Christoph Gödde und Henri Lonitz (Frankfurt am Main: Suhrkamp, 2003) 145. Author's translation, "'kommunistisches oder sozialistisches' Manifest geschrieben werden mit Religion."

framework in opposition to such secular theories, but rather a cooperative reevaluation of the emancipatory resources available in and for modern society.

Materialist (or secular) socialism portrays humanity in an "idealistic" and "materialistic" form, which "is opposed to Christian anthropology,"[139] according to Tillich. Religious socialism, by contrast, shares and "adopts the decisive intention of Marxist anthropology and radicalizes it by shedding"[140] materialistic and idealistic elements of Marxism. Tillich's religious socialism rejects the idealism in many Marxist anthropologies, including those with utopian elements which hold "that human nature [*Menschenwesens*] will be transformed and completely subjected to the idea of justice."[141] Seeking to go beyond the materialistic and idealistic aspects of Marxist anthropology, Tillich claims a 'dual starting point' for a religious-socialist anthropology, "namely, the *unity of that which is vital and spiritual* in man, and the simultaneous *disruption of that unity* which is the source of the threat to man's being [*menschlichen Seins*]."[142] The 'threat' Tillich describes is existential or spiritual; that which provides meaning and transcendent context to or for an individual or community is threatened.

In the early 20th century, this threat came from the "loss of a meaningful and vital mode of existence in the typically proletarian situation" which both "points to the threat to, and the reality of the loss of, meaningful existence."[143] When the proletarian situation reflects "the shattering of the meaning of life in general"[144] then not only is the vital aspect of humanity shattered, but so too is the spiritual dimension imperiled. In the face of this threat, the source of transformation or transcendence, as Tillich puts it, "cannot arise from the human situation, but originates from that which is beyond man's being and its brokenness, from beyond being and freedom, and beyond the vital and the spiritual."[145] The threat of the loss of meaning means a threat to the human subject and to religious socialism. This points to what Tillich calls the 'inner conflict of social-

---

[139] "Religious Socialism," 45. *GW* 2, 163.

[140] *PE*, 46. *GW* 2, 164.

[141] *PE*, 46. *GW* 2, 164.

[142] *PE*, 46-7. *GW* 2, 165, emphasis in original.

[143] *PE*, 47. *GW* 2, 165. Tillich continues: "In the face of meaninglessness in the vital dimension of existence there is no validity in the demand on the part of the church or of a philosophical idealism for compensation in a spiritual world separated from that dimension." *PE*, 47.

[144] *PE*, 47. *GW* 2, 165.

[145] *PE*, 47. *GW* 2, 165.

ism;' secular socialist theory alone cannot account for transformation in the world and within history; it must be interrupted prophetically.

Reiterating his position in *The Socialist Decision*, Tillich writes: "Appealing to both Marx and to the prophetic, early Christian end-expectation, [religious socialism] devoted itself to uncovering the element of faith in socialism and making it explicit."[146] Religious socialism for Tillich reflects "the attempt to bring into awareness the element of faith at work in socialism, to reveal socialism's inner conflict, and to lead it to a solution that has symbolic power."[147] The "inner conflict"[148] in socialism to which he refers is reflected in socialism's disjunctive utopianism, its eschatological belief (devoid of a religious substance) that the present world must be fundamentally transformed into something which does not yet exist in order to attain its goals, and its refusal to acknowledge its own implicit, usually unacknowledged anthropological presuppositions.[149] Tillich writes: "*If socialism expects the coming of a harmonious world, it must reckon with a leap that can in no way be explained in terms of present reality.*"[150] The core problem is that in abandoning the idea of harmony, secular socialism must "posit a leap from a present irrational situation to a future rational situation."[151] Tillich does not give us enough information to make a definitive assessment as to whether he would have included Adorno and Horkheimer among those whose theories fall into this 'inner conflict.' Nevertheless, in Tillich's critique of the Frankfurt School's avoidance of 'ultimacy,'[152] Tillich may have included many of them among those who finally could not satisfactorily account for the transformation of the human subject should a radical transformation of society take place. By the 1940s, Adorno and Horkheimer had argued compellingly that the "present irrational situation" described by Tillich was profoundly barbaric, effectively reifying the subject and limiting agency. They had done this

---

[146] *SD*, 70. *GW* 2, 284-5.

[147] *SD*, 71. *GW* 2, 285.

[148] *SD*, 70 ff. *GW* 2, 281 ff.

[149] Tillich writes: "When one examines the content of socialism's final expectation more closely, one finds that it presupposes a radical transformation of human nature [*Menschennatur*], and in the last instance—since human nature [*menschliche Natur*] constantly grows out of nature as such—a transformation of nature and its laws." *SD*, 111; *GW* 2, 318-9.

[150] *SD*, 69; emphasis in original. *GW* 2, 283.

[151] *SD*, 132. *GW* 2, 338.

[152] See Tillich's review of Marcuse's *Reason and Revolution* in *ZfS* (1941) which was addressed in the previous chapter.

so well that they were unable to do anything more than, as Tillich points out above, "posit a leap...to a future rational situation." The implicit utopian hopes for a future that could be 'otherwise' are central to the inquiry in the following chapter.

Tillich claims that 1920s socialist thought, looking back to Marx and in comparison to the Bolshevik experiment in Russia, could not adequately account for any hypothetical rational social transformation within the present order, and they were thus forced to rely on a hypothesized total utopian break with the present order. Tillich argues: "When socialist theory asserts that it is the transformation of the social situation that will transform human beings, it avoids the question of how a transformed social situation is possible without the transformation of human beings."[153] In this vein, both Horkheimer and Adorno avoid the question of transformed subjectivity and cling to negativity and hope as critical concepts. Admittedly, Horkheimer and Adorno do so justifiably since they saw the developments in Germany from the 1930s onward to be so oppressive and inhuman that a total transformation is required, even if it cannot be rationally grounded. Tillich saw and condemned the same corruption and barbarism, but he maintained that there were latent possibilities for goodness and transformative agency in individual humans and society—despite the pervasive reality of sin. This meant that incremental change for the better was at least theoretically possible within the present order, though not a complete utopian transformation, either within history or without. In *The Socialist Decision*, Tillich writes: "Viewed from the perspective of the psyche, there are three powers that resist the rationality of the Enlightenment: *eros, fate,* and *death*."[154] It is within the context of these resistant features of the 'nature of humanity' that Tillich's later constructive systematic theological project was formed.

Because German socialism, according to Tillich, tried to combine elements of the bourgeois and Enlightenment conceptions of humanity and to retain the rationalist belief in harmony, its anthropology reaches a point of contradiction. As Tillich puts it:

> Human reality encounters us in the form of what [Marx] calls prehistory or the history of class struggles. The person who lives in the class struggle is a person whose being is characterized better by Nietzsche's doctrine of the will to power than by Lessing's doctrine of the educa-

[153] *SD*, 74. *GW* 2, 288.
[154] *SD*, 25. *GW* 2, 246.

> tion of the human race [*Menschengeschlechtes*].... For this reason, Marxism, in spite of its hostility to utopianism, has never been able to defend itself against the suspicion that it has a hidden faith in utopia.[155]

This applies not only to Marxism, but to the historical materialism characteristic of Horkheimer and Adorno during this period as well. It will be demonstrated in the following chapters that these utopic elements never disappear, but are not entirely rationally convincing either, as Tillich suggests. If there is irrationality in the world—as any Marxist, along with Horkheimer and Adorno would unequivocally agree—the problem, according to Tillich, is that there "*is nothing to mediate the leap from unreason to reason. Between reality and expectation lies an abyss.*"[156]

The other central manifestation of socialism's "inner conflict" is that in its overt denial of anthropology, it unreflectively continues to operate on a series of unexamined anthropological assumptions. In seeking to articulate an emancipatory theory and praxis, all forms of socialism necessarily make assumptions about human needs, desires, and capabilities.[157] Each implicitly operates with assumptions about the 'nature of humanity,' according to Tillich. In his Introduction to *The Socialist Decision* Tillich argues:

> *The roots of political thought must be sought in human being [menschlichen Sein] itself.* Without some notion of human nature [*Bild des Menschen*], of its powers and tensions, one cannot make any statements about the foundations of political existence and thought. Without a doctrine of human nature [*Lehre vom Menschen*], there can be no theory of political tendencies that is more than a depiction of their external form.[158]

Later in the same text, in his assessment of historical materialism[159]—which is here juxtaposed to idealism—Tillich writes:

---

[155] *SD*, 73. *GW* 2, 287-8.

[156] *SD*, 73; emphasis in original. *GW* 2, 287.

[157] Tillich, like Adorno and Horkheimer, rejects any mechanistic or purely biological account of human needs and desires. Tillich rejects any deterministic view: "The human person is not a mechanism determined by simple pleasure and pain reactions." *SD*, 133.

[158] *SD*, 2, emphasis in original. *GW*, bd. II, 225.

[159] Tillich uses this phrase somewhat loosely to connote a "*materialistic interpretation*" through which humanity "*seeks to satisfy its needs through a common productive enterprise.*" *SD*, 114; emphasis in original. It is not entirely clear whether Tillich equates this with a form of socialism or not, but it, like all forms of socialism, operates with anthropological assumptions, many unacknowledged. Historical materialism, in Tillich's mind, is

> with respect to the character of [human] needs and, consequently, the direction of the common productive enterprise, general statements can be made only insofar as a particular concept of human nature [*Menschen*] is assumed. For a theory will shape its assertions concerning the tendency and nature of the productive enterprise according to the image of human nature [*Bild des Menschen*] which that theory involves, whether consciously or unconsciously.[160]

Tillich's point in both cases is that any socially engaged philosophy must make assumptions about the 'nature of humanity' and it is preferable to acknowledge and critically engage those assumptions.

Socialism has thus far failed, in part, because of an imaginative failure in anthropology, according to Tillich. By slighting anthropology, socialism has not understood the subject and consequently has been unable to effectively reach its intended audience. It has failed to sufficiently theorize the hoped-for social transformation in terms of individual transformation. It has completely underestimated "the charismatic personality"—Tillich specifically mentions the *Führer* here—by overestimating the capacities of reason. Socialism has not sufficiently theorized or equipped subjects to analyze and resist charismatic political romanticism and empty rhetoric lauding 'myths of origin.' Finally, socialism has failed to engage human subjects as creative, aesthetic beings, manifest through a "*dearth of impressive symbols* within the socialist movement."[161] As such, secular socialism finds itself fighting on behalf of the bourgeois by ironically fighting *against* the bourgeois.

II.2 Introduction to Anthropological Differences Between Tillich and Adorno

Tillich's primary anthropological concern in the 1930s and early 1940s is rooted in his understanding of religious socialism. The overarching concern of Tillich is with articulating a "'nature of man' that transcends all possible variations of human nature," rather than with engaging particular nuances of interpretations of "human nature" *per se*.[162] Tillich was seeking to articulate what has been called a 'nature of humanity,' accounting for human similarities and contexts and to ar-

---

clearly secular. The more challenging question is whether Tillich would include Horkheimer and Adorno under the rubric of historical materialism.

160 *SD*, 114. *GW* 2, 321.

161 *SD*, 74; emphasis in original. *GW* 2, 288.

162 *MSRS*, 490.

ticulate the conditions for transformative and emancipatory praxis, while simultaneously eschewing any claim to a trans-temporal or utopic 'human nature.' The contemporaneous social analysis of Adorno is also arguably grounded in implicit anthropological concerns, though far more subtly.[163] This is in part because he claims to reject any metaphysical grounding instructive of what 'humanity' is or might ideally be. Adorno clearly rejects any essentialized 'human nature,' but he nonetheless operates on certain assumptions about the 'nature of humanity.'[164] Following on the work of other Frankfurt School thinkers in the 1930s, Adorno examines the individual *qua* member of a social group in his study of the 'authoritarian personality' in the 1940s.

Some of the prevailing scientific and particularly empiricist accounts of anthropology in the 1920s and 30s saw humanity as something fundamentally knowable and reducible to data; this somewhat mechanized scientific view diminished subjectivity and led to an atomistic individualism. Like Horkheimer, Adorno realized that critical theory must develop a new epistemology and anthropology, as the first step in what Horkheimer had called a necessary and "radical reconsideration...of the knowing individual as such."[165] Yet Adorno fundamentally and consistently rejects the development of any 'positive' anthropology.[166] Whether he operates with a 'negative' or an implicit anthropology is an open question that is addressed below.

Adorno is clearly far less concerned with the 'nature of humanity' than was Horkheimer. As early as a 1930 letter to Kracauer, Adorno openly doubts the possibility of Marxian revolution and its hoped-for transformation of humans in society: "I only see, if possible, the reality still darker than you do, because I do not believe that any change of the human person can come and that there is no

[163] As was briefly noted above, Adorno's engagement with anthropological themes is more common in his very early writings, and exists episodically in his musicological essays and Husserl study in the 1930s, but his treatment of the subject is not nearly as extensive as that of Horkheimer or Tillich.

[164] These assumptions will become clearer only gradually throughout the remainder of this chapter and into the next. First and foremost, Adorno assumes inestimable human worth and the right to self-determination. He believes that oppression and suffering are fundamentally and universally wrong. The centrality of critical rationality and the negating function of reason are also clearly important anthropological assumptions.

[165] *CT*, 199. *KT* II, 148.

[166] Martin Jay agrees with this assessment, as do the majority of Adorno interpreters. See e.g., *Dialectical Imagination*, 266.

serious chance."[167] In his 1931 inaugural lecture, Adorno claims that anthropology is not centrally important to his philosophy. He writes: "I will not decide whether a particular conception of man and being [*eine bestimmte Auffassung vom Menschen und vom Dasein*] lies at the base of my theory, but I do deny the necessity of resorting to this conception."[168] A "conception of humanity" is not identical with anthropology, and a dismissal of speculative anthropology is not the same as a rejection of anthropology *per se*. Nevertheless, anthropology is implicit at best in much of Adorno's early work. His conception of anthropology is drawn in explicit connection to—or rejection of—Tillich's presentation in a 1943 essay. Adorno's critical essay has not received significant scholarly attention and it is for this reason that the remainder of the chapter focuses centrally on this exchange. Tillich's essay is treated first, since it was nominally the source of Adorno's critique.

II.3 Paul Tillich's "Finite Freedom"

The most substantive and fascinating differences between the anthropologies of Tillich and Adorno can be illuminated and analyzed through a comparison of Tillich's 1943 essay "Man and Society in Religious Socialism" with an important essay written in response by Adorno. The latter is a long-forgotten twenty-six page letter from Adorno to Tillich, published with introductory remarks by Erdmann Sturm in the *Zeitschrift für Neuere Theologiegeschichte* in 1994, evincing Adorno's strong critique of Tillich's anthropological assumptions.[169] This document, translated in English as an appendix, casts valuable light on a period of

---

[167] Letter, Adorno to Kracauer, 12 May, 1930. In *Adorno-Kracauer Briefwechsel, 1923-1966,* hrsg. Wolfgang Schopf (Frankfurt am Main: Suhrkamp Verlag, 2008) bd. 7, 207. Author's translation, "Nur sehe ich, womöglich, die Realität noch schwärzer als Du, da ich nicht glaube, dass die Änderung der Menschen kommt und gar keine ernstliche Chance gibt."

[168] AP, 132. *GS* 1, 343.

[169] The *Entwurf* can also be found at the end of the second volume of the *Adorno-Horkheimer Briefwechsel* (also published in 1994) as it was sent to Horkheimer along with a letter. Central among the very few scholarly commentaries on this textual exchange is Erdmann Sturm's textual history note from 1998: "Die tiefe Differenz zwischen Tillich's anthropologisch fundiertem Religiösem Sozialismus und der Kritischen Theorie Horkheimers und Adornos zeigt sich eindrücklich gerade in diesen beiden Texten. Aus Adornos Sicht war die Kluft, die an diesem Punkt zwischen ihnen bestand, unüberbrückbar." "Zur Textgeschichte," von Erdmann Sturm, in MW/HW III, 488.

transition, as the tide of the war began to change, in western culture generally, and in Tillich's thought *vis-à-vis* Adorno and Horkheimer in particular.

Tillich's essay "Man and Society in Religious Socialism" was part of a larger working-group project wrestling with anthropology, of which Horkheimer and Adorno almost certainly were part.[170] Adorno's *Entwurf*[171] suggests that this anthropological disagreement was part of a larger, ongoing debate about subjectivity and ontology.[172] Tillich's essay was written in English for a theological audience, and it is divided into four themes: the 'being of humanity,' the 'historicity of humanity,' 'creative freedom,' and the 'spiritual and material powers in the historical existence of humanity.' Tillich begins by claiming that humanity is signified by both contingency and transcendence: "Man is a being which is able to have historical change.... Man not only *has* history but he also knows that he has history."[173] Positing that "freedom is the possibility of transcending a given situation,"[174] Tillich suggests that freedom implies an inherent insecurity, because it is experientially finite. In articulating a vision for a more just society, Tillich's religious socialism discloses that its "ultimate criterion is the nature of man; and therefore the basic structure of man's being: 'finite freedom.'"[175] This terse summation must be unpacked, as it bears the brunt of Adorno's critique.

Encompassed by the possibilities of both freedom and transcendence, Tillich makes the claim that human beings—or 'the nature of humanity'—can be

---

[170] The immediate context of the essay was a presentation Tillich gave to the "National Council of Religion in Higher Education," in Haverford, PA, in September, 1943. It was initially published in *Christianity and Society*, a journal edited by Reinhold Niebuhr.

[171] Adorno's letter is commonly referred to as his '*Entwurf contra Paulum*.' The German word *Entwurf* can mean a range of things in English: outline, design, project, draft, concept, blueprint, etc.

[172] Guy B. Hammond thinks the anthropological debate which came to a head in Tillich's "Man and Society in Religious Socialism" and Adorno's *Entwurf* is rooted in a series of conversations concerning differing accounts of subjectivity dating back to the early 1930s in Frankfurt discussion groups. Hammond suggests that there is a conception of subjectivity in Adorno's *Kierkegaard*, which is in tension with Tillich's anthropology in *The Socialist Decision*. The tension, which we see in Adorno's letter (since Tillich never received it and could not have responded) is likely a reflection of and continuation of that older debate, according to Hammond. Guy B. Hammond, "Tillich, Adorno, and the Debate About Existentialism," in *Laval théologique et philosophique* 47:3 (1991) 343-55.

[173] *MSRS*, 491.

[174] *MSRS*, 493.

[175] *MSRS*, 492. Note that Tillich had used the phrase "schöpferische Freiheit" in his early (1922) essay "Kairos." See *GW* 6, 23.

defined as 'finite freedom:' the "*structure of man is the structure of 'finite freedom.'* It is wrong to say that man has finite freedom.... Man is finite freedom."[176] The question of whether such a formula is essentializing or not is not immediately relevant. Tillich continues to readily acknowledge the inherent problems with any doctrine of the 'nature of humanity,' as he had in his writings in the 1930s, examined in the first section of this chapter. He admits that all such doctrines "cannot escape finitude, error, and tragedy,"[177] but he understands the attempt to situate the human person as the subject of emancipatory theory and praxis as necessary nonetheless, for some of the reasons discussed above. Although Tillich attempts to proffer a relatively 'positive' description of the 'nature of humanity,' he understands the tension between human freedom and finitude—indeed, they are polarities[178]—to be tragic; freedom often leads to estrangement.[179] Humans are finite, "and if that which is finite acts in an infinite way it becomes tragic. The tragic is the finite, exercising an infinite freedom."[180] Tillich's understanding of humanity as 'finite freedom,' although tragic, "shows also the way to action."[181]

Tillich continues, noting that the 'nature of humanity,' insofar as it can be known, has a structure not only of 'finite freedom,' but also of "creative freedom,"[182] where creativity is characterized as the upshot of finitude. Although it is tragic, finite freedom suggests, if not its own solution, at least one means toward authentic action under the conditions of such freedom and limitation. Tillich writes: "Every act of freedom is finite but as a creative act it also has infinite significance."[183] Despite the finite and tragic nature of such freedom, it is also creative and active, and creative free action has "the full weight of the participation in divine creativity. This feeling alone can overcome the trend towards res-

---

[176] *MSRS*, 492; emphasis in original.

[177] *MSRS*, 491.

[178] *MSRS*, 493.

[179] "Theology," according to Tillich in a 1946 essay, "in dealing with man's nature as that of 'finite freedom,' shows that man's freedom drives him into a tragic estrangement from himself, from the other beings, and from the ultimate ground and meaning of his existence." Paul Tillich, "The Nature of Man," in *Journal of Philosophy* 43 (1946) 676.

[180] *MSRS*, 493.

[181] *MSRS*, 494.

[182] *MSRS*, 496.

[183] *MSRS*, 494.

ignation and cynicism which is the shadow of Utopianism."[184] Tillich's rejection of this-worldly utopianism was noted above, and will be hinted at below, but it will also be dealt with more systematically in the two concluding chapters.

Estrangement and dehumanization for Tillich reflect the denial of the natural human right to actualize one's natural creative freedom. Thus, the rampant power inequalities of modernity, whether political, (in Fascism) economic, (capitalism), or social possibilities (class, education) disclose modern sources of alienation and dehumanization,[185] concretely reflecting finite freedom and its limitations in modernity. As was noted above, Tillich wrote to Horkheimer in 1942: "I do not believe that there is pure dehumanization just as I do not believe that there can be pure humanity. I believe that there is fragmentary humanity that is based in widespread and constantly new embodiments of inhumanity."[186] Despite his denial of "pure dehumanization" Tillich clearly recognizes the insidious effects of dehumanization very early on. Already in *The Socialist Decision*, Tillich emphasized that in the fight against dehumanization society must engage, and seek to reclaim the 'nature of humanity.'

Religious socialism, as an evolving Christian political theology, reflects Tillich's understanding of the way forward in authentic and creative free action, even in the midst of dehumanizing contexts and circumstances. Describing socialism generally (including religious socialism), Tillich writes:

> Socialism is precisely the counter-movement against this process of dehumanization [*Verdinglichung des Menschen*], against the tendency of capitalism to turn people into psychological mechanisms possessing calculable pleasure-pain reactions. The socialist concept of human nature [*Menschenauffassung*] has set forth at the level of theory an image of the human against the practical consequences of which the whole social movement is directed: the person who has become a thing [*den Menschen, der Dinge geworden ist*].[187]

This 'socialist conception of human nature' struggles against the image of a reified, dehumanized subject, seeking to theorize a subject with agency capable of *resisting* reification. Religious socialism argues passionately that socialism can

---

[184] *MSRS*, 494. What exactly Tillich meant by the provocative claim of "participation in divine creativity" is not clear.

[185] *MSRS*, 497.

[186] 1942 Letter from Tillich to Horkheimer, p. 8-9. Paul Tillich Archives, Andover-Harvard Theological Library, Cambridge, MA. Cited above.

[187] *SD*, 133. *GW* 2, 338. Emphasis in German only.

and should serve as a counter-balance against dehumanization, but Tillich rejects the idea that dehumanization *necessarily* results in the reification of human subjects; Adorno and Horkheimer, particularly from the mid-1940s onward, would likely accept this position more readily. Here it is important to recall that Georg Lukács, despite diagnosing rampant reification in society and noting its effects on subject, did not think this fundamentally or inextricably affected human subjects or circumscribed their ethical agency. Adorno and Horkheimer make the strong claim that modern dehumanization has made human subjects into reified objects, dominated by an 'administered society.' As was mentioned at the beginning of this chapter, Tillich does not go as far as Adorno and Horkheimer; he does not think the human subject has yet been, or could ever be fully reified. In agreement with Lukács, Tillich retains some hope for individual and social agency and transformation.

As was demonstrated in the first section of this chapter in terms of social agency, Tillich analyzes ways in which "the doctrine of man is decisive for social reconstruction."[188] It is important to emphasize that the concept of a 'nature of humanity' is for Tillich not merely for descriptive or analytical purposes, but rather to ground the possibility of socially transformative action against reifying agents. Contrary to Adorno's, and perhaps some of Horkheimer's, concerns about Tillich's use of such concepts, the goal is *not* an essentialized or strictly ontologized humanity. For Tillich, the primary reason for articulating a 'nature of humanity' is to articulate the potentialities for and challenges to transformative, emancipatory praxis.

III. Theodor W. Adorno's '*Entwurf contra Paulum*'[189]

Adorno's critique of Tillich's essay "Man and Society in Religious Socialism" was written as a letter to Tillich, although there is no indication that Adorno ever sent it. It is worth noting that the word *Entwurf* can mean draft or outline,

---

[188] *MSRS*, 492.

[189] Adorno's *Entwurf* is translated into English for the first time here in the appendix. All citations from this document are my own translations, utilizing the German pagination. Note that I am not claiming to represent a systematic treatment of Adorno's views on anthropology here. This is largely because Adorno does not—quite intentionally—have any clearly demarcated position which could be articulated in a parallel fashion to the above presentations of Horkheimer and Tillich. The focus here is solely on the text of Adorno's letter to Tillich and its engagement with Tillich's essay "Man and Society in Religious Socialism," which is representative of Adorno's sparing references to and engagements with philosophical anthropology in the period on which the study focuses. This results in a slight but unavoidable imbalance in this chapter, as I can only engage Adorno's critique of Tillich.

indicating a preliminary position which Adorno did not complete and of which Tillich had no knowledge. Written February 16, 1944 in Los Angeles, it does not seem that Adorno's initial intention was to send the letter to Tillich. Tillich likely did not receive the letter because Adorno first showed the *Entwurf* to Horkheimer to get the latter's critiques and suggestions; the two were living and working in close proximity at the time in Pacific Palisades, California.[190] Erdmann Sturm supports this hypothesis in his *Textgeschichte* of "Man and Society in Religious Socialism,"[191] writing that Adorno

> [S]ent his '*Entwurf*,' together with a letter dated 17 February 1944, to Max Horkheimer for his revisions. Horkheimer's opinion of Adorno's '*Entwurf*' is unknown. Horkheimer obviously did not join Adorno's discussion with Tillich, although he could only agree to Adorno's critique of Tillich. Thus it seems Tillich had no knowledge of Adorno's '*Entwurf*.'[192]

Although Sturm claims Horkheimer's response is unknown, there is an unsigned, very brief letter in English, apparently from Horkheimer to Adorno, in which he claims to have "glanced over" the *Entwurf*. Horkheimer praises it, based on a superficial reading, as a "most brilliant essay,"[193] but he asks that it not be sent. He promises to read and comment on it thoroughly in the immediate future, but no further records exist. That Horkheimer praises the essay as brilliant does not, of course, mean that he agreed with all or any of its specific contents, particularly based on a 'glance.' Indeed, based on this 'glance,' Horkheimer asks Adorno to *not* send the letter to Tillich yet. Sturm casually suggests that Horkheimer 'obviously' could not *fully* concur with Adorno's position, "although he could only agree," and leaves it at that. Indeed, the historical record ends there.

---

[190] Horkheimer was briefly back in New York at the time, and acknowledges receipt of the *Entwurf* from Adorno in a brief letter dated 26 February 1944.

[191] See Tillich's MW/HW, vol. 3.

[192] *MSRS*, 487-8. Author's translation, "sandte seinen 'Entwurf' zusammen mit einem Schreiben vom 17.2.1944 an Max Horkheimer, der ihn überarbeiten sollte. Von einer Stellungnahme Horkheimers zu Adornos 'Entwurf' ist nicht bekannt. Horkheimer hat sich aber offensichtlich Adornos Auseinandersetzung mit Tillich nicht angeschlossen, obwohl er Adornos Tillich-Kritik nur zustimmen konnte. So hat Tillich von Adornos 'Entwurf, ' so scheint es, keine Kenntnis erhalten."

[193] Letter, Horkheimer to Adorno, 29 February 1944. *Adorno-Horkheimer Briefwechsel*, bd. 2, 317.

It is quite possible that Horkheimer deliberately avoided responding further, since on a more detailed reading, he would have realized—the 'brilliance' of the essay notwithstanding—that the critique of Tillich therein in some ways applied to his own position. That there is no record of further conversation alone proves nothing, but the fact that the *Entwurf* was never sent to Tillich does very likely show that Horkheimer did not agree with its content and particularly its first person plural form. Further supporting the hypothesis that Adorno's letter was read and subsequently rejected by Horkheimer, resulting in the *Entwurf* not being sent to Tillich, is the letter's inclusive language. Although it was written by Adorno alone, it is written throughout in the first-person plural—'it is our position' and 'we contend,' etc. It is conceivable that Adorno may have originally thought that he was writing for both of them; it is not known whether Horkheimer read Tillich's original essay, and only Sturm hypothesizes—briefly—on Horkheimer's likely reaction to Adorno's response to Tillich's essay.

That same year (1944), when they were completing their *Philosophical Fragments*, Adorno and Horkheimer somewhat hyperbolically asserted the profound interpenetration of their thought and mutual interdependence.[194] That this 'we' is more than a straightforward rhetorical device is evident early in the *Entwurf*,[195] where Adorno quotes from Horkheimer's earlier writings from the 1930s, later compiled and published as *Dawn and Decline*. Adorno criticizes Tillich by pointing out—using Horkheimer's words in *Dämmerung*—something "*we* anticipated...before the breakout of the Third Reich."[196] It is highly unlikely that Adorno had anything to do with the composition of Horkheimer's *Dawn*

---

[194] See, for example, the Introductions to both *Eclipse of Reason* and *Dialectic of Enlightenment*.

[195] Adorno refers to "our teacher Cornelius" on p. 282. Hans Cornelius was the teacher of Horkheimer and Adorno, and was Tillich's predecessor in the philosophy chair in Frankfurt. Tillich and Cornelius were very different people and thinkers, and Adorno likely uses the reference to Cornelius to emphasize this disjoint he perceives—even though he disagrees with Cornelius on the point in question. Interestingly, Tillich was also Adorno's teacher and *Habilitation* supervisor, so Adorno would seem to be making a quite pointed jab at Tillich.

[196] Author's translation of Theodor W. Adorno, "Theodor W. Adorno contra Paul Tillich: Eine bisher unveröffentlichte Tillich-Kritik Adornos aus dem Jahre 1944," hrsg. von Erdmann Sturm, in *Zeitschrift für Neuere Theologiegeschichte*, bd. 3, 1996, 280. This essay is also known as the "*Entwurf contra Paulum*" (henceforth, Entwurf). Emphasis added.

and Decline,[197] yet Adorno does not hesitate—more than a decade later—to claim this in some sense as his own, or to identify himself as part of Horkheimer's thought retrospectively.[198] This is a most curious hermeneutical move and claim.[199] In another joint claim in the *Entwurf*, referencing *Dialectic of Enlightenment*, on which he and Horkheimer did fully collaborate, Adorno writes: "In the terminology of one of our last works we would say: your notion of history has fallen back into mythology."[200] Adorno at least implies that the collaboration in *Dialectic of Enlightenment* is analogous to what he claims about the collaborative composition of *Dawn and Decline*, which is extremely difficult to accept on face value.

Based on the letters exchanged between Adorno and Horkheimer, it is almost certain that Horkheimer had nothing to do with the composition of Adorno's letter, and when he read it, he likely found the letter too acerbic, even if he agreed with certain points of Adorno's critique, for a number of reasons. It was probably due to Horkheimer's misgivings—the specifics of which remain a mystery—that Adorno's *Entwurf* was never sent to Tillich. Horkheimer initially cautions Adorno against sending it and there are no records of it in the Paul Tillich Archives at Harvard. It is therefore most likely that Tillich never knew of the critique therein.[201] The remainder of this section and the accompanying analysis therefore entails a certain level of creative interpretation, attempting to

---

[197] Adorno and Horkheimer were obviously in common circles and were briefly both on the philosophy faculty in Frankfurt during the time Horkheimer composed the aphorisms published pseudonymously as *Dämmerung*. Nevertheless, there is little evidence of substantial collaboration between the two men in this early period. They were separated from 1933 until being reunited in 1938 in New York, when Adorno joined the *Institut* for the first time, and thereafter, collaborative work slowly began to take shape.

[198] Interestingly, however, this affinity with Horkheimer is declared by Adorno as early as 1934 in a letter (July 6, 1934) to Leo Lowenthal, also concerning Horkheimer's publication of the *Dämmerung*.

[199] See Agnes Heller's excellent essay on the nature of 20th century philosophical 'schools,' especially the Frankfurt School. Heller identifies several features of a modern school which lead to the first person plural identifier seen in Adorno's letter and throughout much of Horkheimer and Adorno's works in the 40s. "The Frankfurt School," by Agnes Heller, in *Rethinking the Frankfurt School: Alternative Legacies of Cultural Critique*, ed. Jeffrey T. Nealon and Caren Irr (Albany: State University of New York, 2002) 207-222.

[200] "In der Sprache einer unserer letzten Arbeiten würden wir sagen: Ihr Geschichtsbegriff ist in die Mythologie zurückgefallen." *Entwurf*, 291.

[201] *Zur Testgeschichte*, editorial preface to "Man and Society in Religious Socialism," in MW/HW III, 487-8.

pull together threads of a conversation that likely never occurred. This will be used as a backdrop to highlight some tensions and inconsistencies between Horkheimer and Adorno, when seen in the light of Adorno's critique of Tillich's anthropology and Horkheimer's refusal to support it.

Adorno's critique in his *Entwurf contra Paulum* cuts to the heart of the debate between the two thinkers, and it perhaps drives a small wedge between Adorno and Horkheimer in retrospect. Tillich's central claim, cited above, that "the structure of man is the structure of 'finite freedom'" is met almost immediately in Adorno's *Entwurf* where he pointedly argues: "Every sentence which takes the form of 'the human is…' implies that a content is already written through just this form: the human person is filth [*der Mensch ist Dreck*]."[202] Despite Horkheimer and Tillich's early willingness to engage some formulations beginning with 'the human is…', disclosed in various forms in the first part of this chapter, positive and essentializing claims about 'human nature' and 'essence' had been used and abused by the Nazis, *inter al.*, and Adorno was rightly concerned about such language and the power dynamics disclosed and disguised therein.

Although Adorno prefaces his critique of Tillich's anthropology with the stated desire to not resume an ongoing debate about ontology,[203] it appears to be largely on the basis of ontology that Adorno criticizes Tillich's anthropology. Adorno implies that Tillich tries to ground the idea of the human person in the idea of being itself. Adorno writes: "Bringing the idea of the person back to the existence of being is a gesture of authority which is to be greeted with contempt in the convenient pre-decision which dissects the human."[204] He goes on to challenge what he understands to be Tillich's ontological assumptions about humanity, suggesting that linking the subject to 'being' (whether as its 'ground,' etc.) is merely an authoritarian gesture which serves to try to control, rather than free the subject. To define the human by means of any proposed 'nature of humanity' serves ironically to emphasize the gap between the actuality of human existence and any concept of it.[205] For Adorno, any and all positive anthropolo-

---

[202] "Jeder Satz, der nach der Form 'Der Mensch ist…' verläuft, schreibt bereits durch eben diese Form den Inhalt vor: der Mensch ist Dreck." *Entwurf*, 281.

[203] *Entwurf*, 281.

[204] "Die Zurückführung des Menschen auf sein Sosein ist die Geste der Autorität, von Verachtung nicht zu trennen: die in ihr gelegene Vorentscheidung schneidet das Menschliche ab." *Entwurf*, 281.

[205] *Entwurf*, 281.

gies contain disguised power dynamics.[206] In a superficial sense, as was noted, Adorno does not deny that something like a 'nature' or 'essence,' encapsulated in a doctrine of humanity, *could* exist, but rather he emphasizes that the *assumption of its existence* is the problem. Since claims of and access to knowledge concerning a hypothetical 'nature of humanity' routinely serve forces of oppression rather than those of liberation, Adorno reasons that all such claims should be rejected. Any claims concerning a hypothetical 'nature of humanity' are inherently and poorly disguised power claims, and Adorno (somewhat inaccurately) takes Tillich to task for not acknowledging this outright.[207]

Tillich's third thesis or 'article of political faith' within religious socialism in the essay, "that without the acceptance of a religious foundation and the symbols expressing it no system of a planned society can escape a speedy self-destruction,"[208] proves, in Adorno's mind, that Tillich's religious socialism only "pretends to deepen socialism" but is "in truth decayed pragmatism."[209] This 'decayed pragmatism' operates with a series of anthropological assumptions and assertions which, according to Adorno, work directly *against* their stated goal—the emancipation of human subjects under the conditions of modernity, but he provides scant specificity or explanation.

Adorno initially acknowledges a clear "connection between religion and the doctrine of humanity which exists beyond question," but he quickly goes on to say that it is "precisely on the basis of this connection that organized religion has

---

[206] Adorno made a similar critique of Tillich in a 1936 letter to Horkheimer, concerning Tillich's review of Kurt Goldstein's *Der Aufbau des Organismus*. That this review, in which Tillich discusses the issue of humanity at the center of Goldstein's thought, appeared in the *ZfS* 5 (1936) particularly incensed Adorno, who referred to it as "einen Skandal und eine Unverschämtheit." Adorno's concern with a review *of Goldstein* in the *ZfS* makes far more sense than Adorno's apparent concern *with Tillich's review* of Goldstein, however. Adorno's critique of Tillich actually refers to Tillich's characterization of Goldstein and others for whom anthropology was a central concern, not necessarily to Tillich's own views. *Adorno-Horkheimer Briefwechsel*, 150. C.f. Tillich, in *Zeitschrift für Sozialforschung* 5 (1936) 111.

[207] Tillich acknowledges this at the beginning of his essay (and in other writings) in a quote cited above: all doctrines concerning a hypothetical 'nature of humanity' "cannot escape finitude, error, and tragedy." *MSRS*, 491.

[208] *MSRS*, 489.

[209] Das "zeigt, dass eben die Richtung, die den Sozialismus zu vertiefen prätendiert, in Wahrheit dem Pragmatismus verfallen ist." *Entwurf*, 281.

positioned itself in the service of repression."[210] Exactly how this follows is not entirely clear, particularly in light of Tillich's nuanced discussion of the relationship between religious socialism and the 'nature of humanity' above. Religion, or perhaps the church in Adorno's understanding, ascribes a "nullity before God"[211]—an emphasis on the infinite qualitative gap between divine goodness and human fallenness—perpetuating the repression of humanity "into an object of discipline and manipulation."[212] Such an emphasis disempowers human subjects and indirectly reaffirms structures of social control.

Anthropological conceptions that perpetuate disempowerment originate at least in part with organized religion, according to Adorno. He writes:

> The institution that controls [the human] to such an extent—the church—adjusts [the human] by virtue of the power of the doctrine [of humanity] as an administrative object and grasps it. The pathos with which [the church] always knows better what the human is than itself knows and recommends and entitles it at the same time to the administration [of the human].[213]

The church has been allowed—by its own parishioners—to define the 'nature of humanity' for them, thereby strengthening the institution's power over the subject. In light of the German experience of the *Deutsche Christen* and Pope Pius XI's 1933 pact with Hitler, Adorno's critique is both reasonable and compelling. Yet given Tillich's consistent support for the Jews (including Adorno), even against the church at times,[214] along with his "Ten Theses Against National Socialism" and his reaction against sympathizers like Emmanuel Hirsch, there would seem to be more agreement than disagreement between the two on this point.

---

[210] "…die Lehre vom Menschen anlagt…uns an den Zusammenhang der Religion mit der Lehre von der Menschennatur halten, der ja ohne alle Frage besteht. Es ist aber eben dieser Zusammenhang, kraft dessen organisierte Religion von je in den Dienst der Unterdrückung sich gestellt hat." *Entwurf*, 281.

[211] "Nichtigkeit vor Gott." *Entwurf*, 281.

[212] Es "macht sie virtuell zu Objekten von Disziplin und Manipulation." *Entwurf*, 281.

[213] "Die Institution, die dergestalt über ihn verfügt—die Kirche—visiert ihn kraft der Lehre von 'ihm' als Verwaltungsobjekt und erfasst ihn. Das Pathos, mit dem sie immer besser weiss, was er ist, als er selber, empfiehlt sie zugleich als zu seiner Verwaltung berechtigt." *Entwurf*, 281.

[214] Tillich fundamentally rejected the idea of Christian churches seeking to convert Jews to Christianity.

Adorno's critique of Tillich continues, now implicitly challenging the latter's Marxian assumptions.[215] Adorno writes: "If we really only call 'human' the one existing in class society, it is easy to design an anthropology that excludes everything else that would be different."[216] The human subject and agent must be understood as more than a subject of class distinctions and definitions, although Tillich clearly agrees in the essay in question and in other writings. Nevertheless, Adorno reprimands him for using "a static, naive logic that ridicules the factual history of humankind. You argue as if the terms were fixed forever per definition...."[217] It is unclear what aspect(s) of factual human history Adorno thinks Tillich is slighting, but again, the narrow focus misrepresents Tillich's thought. In other works, from the 1930s up to and including some contemporaneous with "Man and Society in Religious Socialism," Tillich consistently argues *against* the static, unchanging 'human nature' Adorno accuses him of espousing.

Veering close to an *ad hominem* attack, Adorno compares Tillich's thought and presentation to a sermon, rather than real philosophy or critical thought.[218] Adorno writes, "You possess a belief in definitions (less from modern ontology and more from the homiletic tradition) that goes along much better with the common sense demand for clear and identically conserved terms than with philosophy."[219] Is he accusing Tillich of philosophical laziness in working from staid

---

[215] Adorno focuses solely on the essay "Man and Society in Religious Socialism" and he misses Tillich's nuance elsewhere. As will be seen below, some of Adorno's critiques, when placed in the larger context of Tillich's analysis of Marxian anthropology and religious socialism (with which Adorno was likely, familiar) are less trenchant when read within the wider context and other relevant texts.

[216] "Wenn man den Menschen wirklich nur das Wesen nennt, das in der Klassengeschichte vorkommt, dann hat man es in der Tat leicht, eine Anthropologie zu entwerfen, die alles ausschließt, was anders wäre." *Entwurf*, 282.

[217] "Aber man bedient sich dabei einer statischen, naiven Logik, die der inhaltlich vertretenen Historizität des Menschenwesens geradezu Hohn spricht. Sie argumentieren, als wären die Begriffe jeweils durch ihre Definitionen ein—für allemal festgelegt...." *Entwurf*, 282.

[218] The essay "Man and Society in Religious Socialism" *was* written for a theological audience and thus was arguably more 'homiletic' than critically philosophical, and it seems highly unlikely Adorno was unaware of this. Even if he was not explicitly told about the original context of the essay, Adorno likely ascertained that this was not intended as pure philosophy. This continues to raise the question of why Adorno was so harsh in his response, which will be addressed below.

[219] "Sie haben, und zwar weniger aus den modernen Ontologen als aus der homiletischen Tradition, einen Glauben an Definitionen, der mit der common sense-Forderung

definitions, or is there something more at stake? Adorno cites Hegel's *Logik* against what he sees as Tillich's essentializing of the 'nature of humanity.' Any deduction of a human 'essence' must arise from concrete human experience, not from any *a priori* definition;[220] defining the human person as 'finite freedom,' according to Adorno, is superficial and arbitrary. Adorno implicitly compares Tillich's error (pre-defining the 'nature of humanity' in abstract categories) to *eisegesis*, reading into a text, rather than proper *exegesis*, deducing conclusions from the text itself. In his mind, this leads Tillich right into the trap that Hegel had demonstrated clearly nearly a century before—external determination is insufficient to address the concrete whole, precisely because it arises externally to the thing which it seeks to define. In theory, Adorno offers a fair critique, yet Tillich *does* start from concrete human experience, even when he summarizes claims with apparently essentializing statements like 'the human is finite freedom.'[221]

Quoting again from Hegel's *Logik*, Adorno writes: "you make the mediated into a pure matter of immediacy. This is a form of action that is not too different from what politically happens if fascists claim the highly mediated society of late capitalism as the immediacy of the 'people.'"[222] In short, by working from and then essentializing the immediacy of human existence, i.e. as 'finite freedom,' Adorno suggests Tillich neglects the dialectical element of human encounter, though again, the critique does not quite hit the mark. Is Adorno suggesting that Tillich's essentializing of the 'nature of humanity' by working from *a priori* concepts and definitions—assuming he does this—is alike in kind to National Socialist essentializing of *das Volk* for propagandistic purposes? Or is this a rhetorical construct to emphasize the extent and import of the fallacy which Adorno believes Tillich is making? The latter is far more likely, given not

---

nach klaren, identisch bewahrten Termini weit besser übereinkommt als mit der Philosophie." *Entwurf*, 282.

[220] *Entwurf*, 283.

[221] Other than 'finite freedom,' the definitions of humanity offered in *The Socialist Decision* by contrast, claim primarily that humanity is a 'fragmented' unity, constituted by dynamic encounters in and with history.

[222] "Sie aber machen das Vermittelte logisch zu einer Sache der bloßen Unmittelbarkeit. Das ist als Verfahrungsart gar nicht so verschieden von dem, was politisch geschieht, wenn die Faschisten die höchst vermittelte spätkapitalistische Gesellschaft als die Unmittelbarkeit des 'Volks' reklamieren." *Entwurf*, 284.

only the personal relationship and mutual respect between the two, but more immediately, in comments Adorno makes on the same page.[223]

Adorno attempts to step back and emphasize that his critique of philosophical anthropology is not solely tied to his distrust of or distaste for metaphysics or ontology. As Adorno writes, "in the sense of Hegel, it would be as abstract to positively anticipate the image of the freed human within the definition. It is this double-impossibility, not the obstinate hatred towards metaphysics that excludes the possibility of a philosophical, positive anthropology."[224] There is, first and foremost, according to Adorno, the impossibility of defining an unchanging 'nature of humanity,' for some of the reasons already indicated, although Tillich denies such a 'static' essence or nature as well. There is also a second impossibility, rooted in the first, which would seek to articulate the conditions of the possibility for the liberation of the human subject based on a definition which, inherently and counter to its intentions, binds the subject rather than aiding in liberation.

Concerning Tillich's attempt to distinguish humans within a hierarchy of beings, from angels to animals, in part based on his understanding of the uniquely human existential challenge of death as one's known end, Adorno finds Tillich's intention undermined by his own logic. Adorno writes: "It seems that this classification in the world of creatures comes to one conclusion: the principle that binds the human as original sinner to that determination for one and all time is the same (principle) that lifts the human out of nature."[225] Adorno wryly comments, "If humans would learn not to insist on the difference between themselves and animals, they would probably not need to humiliate themselves so much in front of angels."[226] While Adorno's pithy insight is provocative and

---

[223] Adorno writes: "You are much too shrewd to overlook the dubiousness of the definitional method. Yet you take a back seat by suspending the demand of truth at a central passage and make knowledge into a matter of expediency." *Entwurf*, 284.

[224] "Nur freilich wäre es im Hegelschen Sinne ebenso abstrakt, etwa das Bild des befreiten Menschen im Begriff positiv vorwegzunehmen. Diese doppelte Unmöglichkeit, nicht der Sture Hass auf die Metaphysik ist es, der die Möglichkeit philosophischer, positiver Anthropologie ausschließt." *Entwurf*, 284.

[225] "Es will uns nämlich scheinen, als ob diese Klassifikation im Reich der Wesen in beiden Fällen auf das gleiche hinausliefe: das Prinzip, das den Menschen als Erbsündigen ein für alle Mal bei dieser Bestimmung festhält, ist das gleiche, das ihn aus der Natur heraushebt...." *Entwurf*, 285.

[226] "Wenn die Menschen es lernen würden, nicht mehr auf ihre Unterschiedenheit von den Tieren zu pochen, brauchten sie sich vielleicht nicht mehr derart vor den Engeln zu demütigen." *Entwurf*, 285.

almost certainly correct, he evidently chose to overlook the similar comments of Horkheimer, who, a year or so prior, in "Vernunft und Selbsterhaltung," had also distinguished between animals and humans, based on the inherence and use of reason. Adorno's omission of critique directed at Horkheimer is discussed below.

Finitude and estrangement are Tillich's ways of describing the primary external limitations on humanity. Following the existentialist paradigm and Heidegger's *Sein zum Tode* (being-towards-death), Tillich understands death as the known orientation and limit concept, much as Horkheimer had in his 1935 "Remarks on Philosophical Anthropology."[227] For Tillich, death is the limit concept which contains life and provides the conditions for its meaning. Adorno's central challenge to the understanding of the human subject as limited by sin or estrangement is that "established power benefits from the doctrine of the radically corrupted nature of the human."[228] That is, defining the human person in terms of limitations serves to reinforce latent social power structures rather than to challenge them by emphasizing the human potential to overcome such limitations. This is valuable as a philosophical and a theological critique of Tillich, and of the social function of the Christian doctrine of sin in general. As Tillich would almost certainly agree, the doctrine of sin has all too often been used to justify and exculpate entrenched laziness and undisciplined action, where it should perhaps better be understood as a wake-up call and challenge to continually strive toward that perfection which Paul called the Christian goal, fully aware of the limitations of the Christian. For Adorno, "this world is not the one of humankind, but an alienated, mediated, objective one, and...every attempt to directly hear the human voice within the fossilized relations certifies society through what it lacks."[229]

---

[227] This is not to suggest that Horkheimer was overtly influenced by Heidegger at this point (1935). Rather, it is simply to note that Horkheimer, like Tillich, understands death as a necessary feature of anthropology.

[228] "...in der Tat die Lehre von der radikal verderbten Menschennatur des bestehenden Mächten von je zugutegekommen ist." *Entwurf*, 285.

[229] "...diese Welt gar nicht die der Menschen ist, sondern eine von ihnen entfremdete, vermittelte, dinghafte, und weil jeder Versuch, in den versteinerten Verhältnissen die Stimme des Menschen unmittelbar zu vernehmen, dieser Gesellschaft gerade das attestiert, was sie nicht hat." *Entwurf*, 285-6.

III.1 Anthropology, Dehumanization, and Suffering

The heart of the disagreement with Tillich expressed in the *Entwurf*, according to Adorno, arises from Tillich's undialectical assertions and assumptions concerning the possibility and source of a positive anthropology arising from the negative limitations of existing society. Yet even this profound disagreement arises from a common awareness of the limitations of existing society. Adorno writes:

> Our distinct philosophical difference lies in the sentences: 'And Marx could not talk permanently about the dehumanization in early capitalism without a vague picture of a really human society. They all have a doctrine of man.' According to that, you need something 'positive' to be able to articulate the negation. But the only positive thing you 'have' is the givenness in its depravity beyond which our knowledge cannot go other than by identifying the depravity through its immanent contradiction to the given. The positive is the negative and only the negative, the definite negation, is actually positive. *What the human is can only be said by what it is not.* To presume a necessary positive means to deify the world.[230]

Here Adorno echoes sentiments found throughout *Dialectic of Enlightenment* and in his later work, *Negative Dialectics*. This is indeed a crucial point of difference: must there be some positive which functions to critique the negative, understood as the given, or is it only through the experience of the negative, negated, that it is possible to imagine a positive? For Adorno, a positive anthropology was neither possible nor desirable, particularly given the extent of dehumanization and barbarism he saw. Pure negation was the safest—and importantly in Adorno's view—the most legitimate path in the light of damaged life.

---

[230] English emphasis added. "Unsere entscheidende philosophische Differenz dürfte beschlossen liegen in den Sätzen: 'And Marx could not talk permanently about the dehumanization in early capitalism without a vague picture of a really human society. They all have a doctrine of man.' Danach müsste man etwas 'Positives' haben, um die Negation aussprechen zu können. Aber das einzig Positive, das man 'hat,' ist das Gegebene in seiner Schlechtigkeit, über das die Erkenntnis mit nichts anderem hinausgeht als damit, dass sie die Schlechtigkeit durch den immanenten Widerspruch des Gegebenen bestimmt. Das Positive ist das Negative, und nur das Negative, die bestimmte Negation, eigentlich positiv. Was der Mensch ist, kann nur gesagt werden vermittelt durch das, was er nicht ist. Demgegenüber ein Positives als notwendig vorgegeben annehmen heißt die Welt vergotten." *Entwurf*, 286.

With Horkheimer and Adorno, Tillich agrees that claims concerning the 'nature of humanity'—or such denials—are always already claims of power and authority, but the two differ in their conclusions. Tillich understands this as a responsibility; such claims will inevitably be made and an elitist pretention to the contrary will accomplish little. Those who are aware of the implicit power dynamics have perhaps a special responsibility and opportunity.

Tillich points out that while both Barthians and Marxians claim to reject any positive anthropology, they both in fact have an implicit operative anthropology; they "always speak and act as if they had a doctrine of man."[231] This is identical to Tillich's position in *The Socialist Decision*, cited above.[232] Barthians claim to be able to diagnose a clear problem in human nature, though they claim that human nature cannot authentically be known apart from the 'cure' of the divine Word. Marxians similarly describe both the de-humanizing aspects of modernity and an ideal revolutionary human society, using both as a critique of other operative anthropologies. While both Barthians and Marxians claim to not have operative anthropologies, Tillich argues that every ideology reflects anthropological presuppositions, whether implicit or explicit, static or dynamic.[233] Nevertheless, Tillich writes, "they do not want to confess [their anthropology] for reasons of political or religious strategy."[234] His point, and implicit charge, is that Adorno operates from a series of anthropological assumptions, whether he acknowledges them or not. The centrality of reason and importance of negating critique are among the more overt assumptions, though Adorno is quite subtle with them. Yvonne Sherratt suggests that Adorno is operating with the anthropological presumption of a "psychological essence to humanity... [which] consists in human beings having a drive for 'aesthetic experience.'"[235] Returning to

---

[231] *MSRS*, 491.

[232] E.g.: "the direction of the common productive enterprise, general statements can be made only insofar as a particular concept of human nature is assumed." *SD*, 114.

[233] See again, *The Socialist Decision*: "For a theory will shape its assertions concerning the tendency and nature of the productive enterprise according to the image of human nature which that theory involves, whether consciously or unconsciously." *SD*, 114.

[234] *MSRS*, 491.

[235] Sherratt continues her provocative argument, suggesting that "As a consequence," of this assumed 'drive for aesthetic experience,' Adorno makes a stand "against a society that marginalises the aesthetic by relegating it to the realm of 'leisure,' 'pleasure' or the *autonomous* aesthetic realm rather than seeing it as an essential part of all aspects of human life." Sherratt, 17; emphasis in original. She continues, noting that Adorno's notion of the 'nature of humanity' comes from "his own revised reading of Freud... [It]

the quotation from Adorno above, the only way Marx could diagnose the maladies of bourgeois capitalism and seek a liberative solution, according to Tillich, was to juxtapose present maladies with an idealized other situation in which workers and the means of production were more harmoniously aligned. For Tillich, the estrangement and dehumanization experienced by the human subject defined as 'finite freedom' is best understood and overcome by opposing it with a concept of justice which he derived from the Christian tradition.

Adorno's critique is that all such idealized concepts, even if not utopian, are *a priori* rather than originating in the concreteness of human experience. Like the medieval Nominalists, God could not be spoken of in terms of attributes, but solely by a *via negativa*. One should not say that God is goodness itself, but it would be incorrect to assume or assert that God is not good. Ideas like 'God is love,' while not strictly false, are imperfect insofar as they ensnare God within human concepts and predications. As Kant would later put it, 'existence is not a predicate,' and Nominalists like Scotus and Ockham sought to limit human predication of the divine. Adorno is essentially correct in his critique, and Tillich should have been more consistent on this point. Adorno and Horkheimer, as the next chapter demonstrates, engage *a priori* concepts like justice in order to ground their critiques of the status quo. Adorno critiques Tillich from the point of view of the silenced, suffering masses, and as such, Adorno uses the silence of the suffering as the foundation of his critique and his implicit vision of a different future.

The final sentence in the extended quote from Adorno above, "to presume a necessary positive means to deify the world,"[236] is particularly telling. The positive for Adorno, if it exists, can be known only by negation. This is why, by the time of *Minima Moralia*, the 'whole is the untrue,' because critique can focus only on negation. One can clearly see this theme of negation throughout Adorno's corpus.

Although Adorno will not speak about the 'human,' he is comfortable discussing dehumanization. This is an interesting tension, if not an outright contradiction with Horkheimer, since Horkheimer rejects 'pure dehumanization' (*Entmenschlichung)* in his 1942 response to Tillich, at the same time that he ac-

generates a Utopianism which consists of incorporating aesthetic experience into all the foundational dimensions of human life, including reason itself." *MSRS*, 491.

[236] "Demgegenüber ein Positives als notwendig vorgegeben annehmen heißt die Welt vergotten." *Entwurf*, 286.

cepts 'pure humanity' (at least in its theoretical form).[237] There, Tillich rejected both 'pure dehumanization' and 'pure humanity,' although he clearly identifies episodic and extensive manifestations of dehumanization vis-à-vis 'fragmentary humanity.' Responding to Tillich in the 1944 *Entwurf*, Adorno writes:

> In the sense of dialectical logic, dehumanization [*Entmenschlichung*] precedes the term of the human. This term ['human'] can only be won by the ongoing, deeper insight into dehumanization, not by subtracting everything 'dehumanized' from the static sum of qualities and carrying home the beggarly rest, 'the human being,' as eternal possession.[238]

Dehumanization is and can only be known *a posteriori* and the human person, according to Adorno, can only be known following the experience of dehumanization. Would this suggest that the human person could be understood as the social locus of dehumanization for Adorno?

Adorno then returns his critical attention to Tillich's understanding of the human person as 'finite,' bound up in history. This seems unobjectionable at first glance—why would Adorno deny that the human is finite, or that it is in and has a history? But this is not the basis of Adorno's critique. The quarrel is not with the historicity of the human person, with which Adorno agrees, but rather with Tillich's means of arriving at this understanding of the human person. There is no 'static' self as the subject of historical change, as Horkheimer (and Tillich) repeatedly maintained, even as both engaged the language of human 'nature' and 'essence.' Adorno argues that to further claim that the human subject is itself historical is to say nothing whatsoever about the 'nature of humanity.' He writes:

> The source of error is not the particular way of defining the human and how you want to tie that up by dynamic sampling, but the philosophical method that always looks for the 'first,' no matter what is chosen as this first. 'Having a history' is also no ontological quality of the human, nothing that belongs to the person 'as such,' and that is prescribed to the world. Having a history means to be involved in dialectics, in the

[237] Adorno admittedly does not differentiate 'pure dehumanization' (from dehumanization) as Tillich and Horkheimer had done in their 1942 letter exchange.

[238] "Im Sinn der dialektischen Logik geht in der Tat die Entmenschlichung dem Begriff des Menschen voraus, und ein solcher ist nur in der fortschreitenden Einsicht in die Entmenschlichung zu gewinnen, nicht aber, indem man alles 'Entmenschlichte' von der statischen Summe der Qualitäten abzieht und den Rest, der kümmerlich genug wäre, als 'den Menschen,' als ewigen Besitz nach Hause trägt." *Entwurf*, 286.

> subject-object relation. In other words, history is constituted not by life as pure life of the human, but by extra-humanization and alienation. To put it more simply, one could say that history is not a characteristic quality of the human, but is rather the embodiment of suffering.[239]

History is thus the social locus in which the human person is subject to suffering, with which Horkheimer would undoubtedly agree. Adorno continues, "To know history and to have a history is not the same and on the bottom line of history, suffering, knowledge has changed very little. On the other hand, having a history reaches far beyond consciousness and every part of nature, as a suffering part, has an eternal part in it."[240] Tillich's claim that knowledge of history is already an indication of freedom from history is pure illusion, according to Adorno. Suffering is what constitutes human experience and knowledge of suffering is unfortunately not identical with its negation, as Adorno quotes Pascal, contra Tillich's apparently essentializing portrait of the human.

III.2 Limitations of Adorno's *Entwurf*

Adorno's critique is exacting and had he sent it in some form to Tillich, there may have been an opportunity for a fascinating conversation between the two thinkers and the potential for development in either of their positions. Yet as insightful as the *Entwurf* is, it is acerbic and somewhat myopic, perhaps because it was merely a 'draft' or 'outline' of what Adorno intended in conjunction with Horkheimer. The critique focuses solely on Tillich's short essay "Man and Society in Religious Socialism," and it overlooks the context and nuance of Tillich's broader writings about anthropology with which Adorno was very likely famil-

---

[239] "In der Tat ist die Fehlerquelle nicht die besondere Weise, in der der Mensch umgrenzt wird und die Sie durch Dynamisierung feuerfest machen wollen, sondern vielmehr das philosophische Verfahren, das auf der immerwährenden Suche nach dem 'Ersten' sich befindet, ganz gleich was als dies Erste gewählt wird. Auch 'Geschichte haben' ist keine ontologische Qualität des Menschens, nichts was ihm 'an sich,' und aller Welt vorgeordnet, zukäme. Sondern Geschichte haben heißt in die Dialektik verflochten sein, in die Subjekt-Objekt-Beziehung. Mit anderen Worten, Geschichte besteht darin, dass das Leben des Menschen nicht rein 'dessen' Leben ist, sondern durch Außermenschliches und Entfremdetes sich konstituiert. Einfacher könnte man sagen, Geschichte sei nicht eine auszeichnende Qualität des Menschen, sondern vielmehr der Inbegriff allen Leidens." *Entwurf*, 287.

[240] "Geschichte wissen und Geschichte haben ist nicht dasselbe, und am Entscheidenden der Geschichte, dem Leiden, hat das Wissen bis heute wenig genug geändert. Andererseits aber reicht das Geschichte-haben unvergleichlich weit über das Bewusstsein hinaus, und alle Natur hat, als leidende, daran unendlichen Anteil." *Entwurf*, 287.

iar.[241] Adorno ignores the context and intended audience of Tillich's essay, accusing him of 'sermonizing.'

Tillich does not go so far as to claim any knowledge of an extra-temporal humanity, and in fact, he states the opposite on several occasions. Adorno had very likely read and was familiar with Tillich's *The Socialist Decision,* having been Tillich's student and teaching assistant at the time, but he overlooked or forgot Tillich's consistent refrain about the dynamic nature of humanity as a dynamic 'encounter' in and with history in that text. A brief reminder of Tillich's position in *The Socialist Decision* (1933) is germane:

> [I]t is certainly not necessary to posit an eternal human nature [*einem 'ewigen Wesen' des Menschen*]; but it is necessary to understand humanity [*Menschen*] living in encounter and in history, as a unity, since otherwise nothing at all could be asserted, even about the most concrete historical phenomenon.[242]

Similarly, Tillich's 1942 letter to Horkheimer, cited above, clearly states: "I believe that there is fragmentary humanity that is based in widespread and constantly new embodiments of inhumanity."[243] Adorno thus missed—or ignored—the broader context of Tillich's account of the intersection of religious socialism, Marxian anthropology, and the 'nature of humanity,' along with the lecture's intended audience. Tillich's conception of humanity as 'finite freedom' must be understood in light of his rejection of an eternal, unchanging 'human nature' in *The Socialist Decision*, and in light of his insistence upon the fragmentary nature of humanity constantly facing the threat of existential disruption and dehumanization.

Having explored Adorno's letter in detail, it is both necessary and fruitful to pause and wonder why[244] Adorno would draft such a caustic letter to his

---

[241] In fairness to Adorno, he may not have been familiar with any of Tillich's other works on anthropology, although this seems unlikely given the numerous seminars they co-taught in Frankfurt. Adorno deliberately only responds to Tillich's 1943 essay, so critiquing him for missing the wider context should not be taken too far.

[242] *SD*, 165, n. 7. ***GW*** 2, 231, n. 7.

[243] 1942 letter from Tillich to Horkheimer, Harvard Paul Tillich Archives, p. 8-9. Cited above.

[244] The question at hand is not why someone would critique Tillich's essay—there is much which could be called into question in it. Eugen Rosenstock-Huessy wrote a critical letter to Tillich concerning "Man and Society in Religious Socialism" in March of 1944. Rosenstock-Huessy's letter does not survive and, based on Tillich's response, both the penmanship and substance of the critique within the letter were hard to decipher. See

Doktorvater and the man Adorno credited with saving his life.[245] As indicated in the first chapter, Adorno had (largely) fond reminisces and high accolades for Tillich as a person and as a teacher. It is important to note that Adorno's rather acerbic critique of Tillich in his *Entwurf* is not entirely unique and certainly reflects Adorno's personality and writing style. As noted in the first chapter, Adorno's assessments of his friends and colleagues in personal correspondence could be incredibly harsh. Adorno's comments about Marcuse in a 1935 letter to Horkheimer are much more extreme than anything Adorno wrote to or about Tillich, for example. In a letter dated May 13, 1935, Adorno not only tied Marcuse to Heidegger, but shockingly suggested that there was little more than Marcuse's Judaism which kept him from being a fascist.[246]

Similarly, Adorno had known Walter Benjamin since 1923 and the two were friends who respected one another, but in light of Benjamin's "contacts with a Brechtian Marxism which Adorno felt to be a crude species of vulgar materialism," Adorno wrote "a series of letters to [Benjamin] which strongly objected to...Benjamin's positive views of the new mass media and...undialectic approaches."[247] Adorno published numerous attacks on Benjamin, his close friend and mentor, including "On the Fetish-Character in Music and the Regression of Listening" (1938) in which Adorno strongly criticizes Benjamin's "Work of Art in the Age of Mechanical Reproducibility." Adorno's letters to Benjamin are admittedly more constructive critiques than Adorno's *Entwurf*

Ergänzungs- und Nachlassbände zu den Gesammelten Werken von Paul Tillich, bd. 6, 297-8. Rather the question is why Adorno would write such a caustic letter to his *Doktorvater*, a man he respected greatly and later claimed he owed his life to Tillich, and why he then chose not to send this letter after its composition. These latter two issues are the focal point of this section.

[245] *Lectures on Negative Dialectics*, cited in chapter 1. As far as we know and from what can be discerned from other letter exchanges and first-hand accounts, Adorno and Tillich were relatively close. Tillich was among a very small group of people who were allowed to refer to him as 'Teddy.' Tillich's daughter Erdmuthe fondly recalls visits from 'Onkel Teddy' in the Tillich's New York City apartment. Personal conversation with Erdmuthe Tillich in San Diego, CA, November 2007.

[246] Concerning Marcuse, Adorno commented to Horkheimer in 1935, "...den ich schließlich für einen durch Judentum verhinderten Faszisten halte...." *Adorno-Horkheimer Briefwechsel*, bd. 1, 65.

[247] Eugene Lunn, *Marxism and Modernism: An Historical Study of Lukács, Brecht, Benjamin, and Adorno* (Berkeley: University of California Press, 1982) 150-1. Lunn suggests that "a number of Adorno's most important essays written from 1936-1945...were attempts, among other things, to refute Benjamin's analyses of the 'popular arts.'"

contra Paulum, and the difference in tone is notable. Nevertheless, Adorno's *Entwurf* is best seen, in large part, in light of his published critiques of Benjamin and other friends and colleagues. This merely begs the question, however, as to why Adorno would react so caustically against Tillich, while ignoring potentially significant differences with Horkheimer with respect to anthropology, subjectivity, and agency.

III.3 Why did Horkheimer's Anthropology Escape Adorno's Critique?

One curious element of this debate, particularly given Adorno's vehemence against Tillich, is Horkheimer's use of the phrases 'human nature' and 'human essence,' in almost exactly the same period as Tillich. In fact, this the same period during which Horkheimer hyperbolically claimed that his and Adorno's ideas were so interwoven (especially in *Eclipse of Reason* and *Dialectic of Enlightenment*) that it would be difficult to tell which idea started with which person. Despite the obvious interweaving and interpenetration of the thought of the two in the 1940s, Adorno's acerbic critique of Tillich seems incongruent with his silence concerning Horkheimer's writings engaging language of human 'nature' or 'essence' a few years earlier. Horkheimer did not repudiate his earlier remarks, and in fact presumed and used similar language, albeit sparingly, in his individual writings in the mid-1940s. Not surprisingly, but also lacking consistency, Adorno's vitriol escaped Horkheimer, at least in print.[248]

Throughout Horkheimer's early essays, he engages and employs language of the 'nature of humanity' in a manner similar to Tillich. Adorno's *Entwurf* is a scathing rebuke of Tillich for such language, but Adorno remains silent with regard to Horkheimer's analogous and contemporaneous usage.[249] In his 1941-42 essay "Vernunft und Selbsterhaltung," Horkheimer claims that the primary

---

[248] Agnes Heller offers one possible insight into the reasons for Adorno's apparent unwillingness to critique Horkheimer in her essay on the Frankfurt School qua philosophical school. With Horkheimer at the center of the 'school,' Heller describes Adorno as Horkheimer's "faithful knight" who willingly remained in the latter's shadow. Heller, 216.

[249] We may easily hypothesize conversations between Horkheimer and Adorno on the topic, and may even surmise that, based on Horkheimer's retreat from such language after the mid-1940s, that Horkheimer agreed with Adorno's critique in such hypothetical discussions. The central point is simply that Horkheimer never retracted his earlier language, making Adorno's silence with regard to this language peculiar, particularly as the two thinkers claim to be thinking in tandem.

difference between humans and animals is reason. He demurs somewhat with respect to his conception of humanity in his 1942 remarks in response to Tillich's critique of *Reason and Self-Preservation,* though in some senses, his argument is stronger, noting the potential benefits of examining "pure humanity" in its theoretical form. Less than two years later, Adorno's wrath is unleashed on Tillich for making similar statements and claims. Even later, in the lectures published in *Eclipse of Reason* (1944) during the time when Adorno and Horkheimer were at the height of their collaborative efforts, Horkheimer would again use the phrases 'human essence' and 'human nature,' with some qualifications, but without apparent problem. Significantly, Adorno had nothing to say about this, at least in print.

Horkheimer might not criticize Tillich in the same way as Adorno did, and Horkheimer's apparent refusal to co-sign or forward the *Entwurf* supports such a reading, which is also in line with Erdmann Sturm's findings and assessment. It is simply not known whether, and to what extent, Horkheimer agreed with Tillich, and he quite conceivably found in Adorno's *Entwurf* a tacit rebuke of his own writings in the 1930s and early 1940s. It is also possible that Horkheimer was simply busy with travel and other obligations and did not see the *Entwurf* as significant.

One important caveat is that while Tillich was still influenced by Marxian social critiques in the early 1940s, Adorno and Horkheimer were less so. While portions of *Dialectic of Enlightenment*, notably the sections on Odysseus and anti-Semitism, reveal vestiges of Marxian concepts,[250] *Dialectic of Enlightenment* is part of the 'second' or 'third wave' of critical theory, and is distanced from Marxian analysis and categories—particularly concerning anthropology—more than Tillich's work in the mid-1940s. Tillich's commitment to and reliance upon Marxian categories through an anthropological lens is an important feature of Adorno's critique in the *Entwurf.*

Furthermore, Tillich's anthropological presuppositions changed little from his 1943 essay to his magnum opus, the three-volume *Systematic Theology*, released over the following two decades. In his *Systematic Theology*, Tillich's understanding of the human person and the 'nature of humanity' remained oriented toward 'finite freedom.' Had Adorno's letter been slightly less acerbic,

---

[250] The first edition, *Philosophische Fragmente* (1944) had a much stronger Marxian tone and vocabulary than the revised 1947 version. See "The Disappearance of Class History in '*Dialectic of Enlightenment*': A Commentary on the Textual Variants (1944 and 1947)" by Willem van Reijen and Jan Bransen, in *Dialectic of Enlightenment*, 248-252.

Horkheimer may have been more willing to co-sign and forward the letter to Tillich. There is little reason to suspect Tillich would have fundamentally altered his anthropological presuppositions even if a constructive debate had arisen on these issues, but it is impossible to know. Such a discussion, either on paper or in person, would likely have greatly benefited Tillich, and perhaps Adorno and Horkheimer as well.

In one sense, Tillich functionally essentializes the 'nature of humanity' with his language of 'finite freedom,' not because he seeks to limit humanity, but rather because this is the logical conclusion of his ontological method and presuppositions. Since Tillich believes all people are created by and rooted in 'God,' as the ground of their being, understanding humans as 'finite' and 'creative freedom' vis-à-vis God does, in a limited sense, presume a type of 'essence' common to humanity. Yet it is *only in this narrow sense*, however, that Tillich 'essentializes' humanity. As has been shown, his nuanced conception of a 'fragmentary' humanity, rejecting 'pure humanity' and conceptions of 'eternally unchanging nature,' etc. make a strong version of the argument for essentialism unsustainable.

If Tillich believes that the human person can be accurately described as 'finite freedom' but that there is no such thing as 'pure humanity,' is this simply Tillich's Christian understanding of sin, rendering humanity always fragmentary? Would Tillich suggest that humanity is both fragmentary and finite, or are the two roughly synonymous? His anthropology is clearly more essentialized than that of Adorno, and Tillich does maintain that humanity can be understood—to an extent—because humans are created in *imago Dei*. Yet Tillich's primary anthropological orientation is more focused on the experiential nature of finite freedom than a social concept of humanity. His theological anthropology, limited as it is, likewise focuses primarily on the individual.[251] Adorno appropriately critiques Tillich's analysis of the individual at the expense of the group, but here he may have strayed from Horkheimer.

If 'essence' reflects an essentialized definition of the 'nature of humanity' for Tillich, 'existence' describes the human experience of self and other humans that is, of course, subjective in nature. That being said, Adorno and others who reject any knowable, even if incomplete, 'essence' of humanity nevertheless expe-

---

[251] In a 1955 lecture, "The Theological Significance of Existentialism and Psychoanalysis," Tillich, would suggest three modes of human existence: "essential goodness, existential estrangement, and the possibility of a 'third' beyond essence and existence." In *Theology of Culture*, 119.

rience and claim to know something about the existence of the 'nature of humanity.' Thus Tillich notes that every society and culture, including modern socialism and liberalism, presuppose knowledge of the structure of humanity, even if only as the basis of critique.[252]

For both Horkheimer and Adorno, repression and *Entfremdung* reflect the knowable existence of the 'nature of humanity,' in much the same way that for Tillich, dehumanization and estrangement through sin reflect the knowable existence of such a 'nature of humanity.' The heart of the debate is whether knowing or making claims concerning the existence of humanity (as alienated, etc.) *necessarily* implies an 'essence' over and against which to judge contemporary existence wanting and in need of transformation. In other words, what is humanity estranged from? God? Self? The means of production? Self-determination? Tillich notes, in indirect response to Adorno that even "Marx could not talk permanently about the dehumanization in early capitalism without a vague picture of a really human society."[253] As Tillich notes at several points in his brief essay, he is merely pointing out the ways in which critics of any positive anthropology nevertheless *presuppose* an anthropological norm against which current existence is judged. For both Adorno and Horkheimer, suffering and injustice serve as such negative norms and limits; this will be further explored in the following chapter. Although in this essay, presented to a Christian audience, Tillich begins with essence and moves to existence, there seems to be little disconnect if, in dialogue with Horkheimer and Adorno, for example, Tillich were to begin with the agreed-upon structures of current human existence (suffering and injustice) and move from there to his Christian faith in a created humanity. Tillich's 'positive' anthropology is not simply an essentialized ontological norm (as Adorno suggests), but also reflects the (created) standard against which current existence (dehumanization, etc.) is measured and judged. His conception of the 'nature of humanity' is clearly more ontological than that of Horkheimer and especially that of Adorno. Regardless of the starting point, the 'third' part of humanity later suggested by Tillich, that which lies beyond essence and existence, presupposes both.

There is an inherent (though neutral) insecurity associated with finite freedom, and Tillich laments the existential "angst of our present social order, which is rooted in the threat of being prevented from any actualization of finite free-

[252] *MSRS*, 495, 497.
[253] *MSRS*, 491.

dom and of being thrown in to the horror of meaninglessness."[254] As a political theology, Tillich argues that religious socialism sees such *angst* or dread manifest on both individual and social levels. As their starting point, particularly in the period of and following *Dialectic of Enlightenment*, Horkheimer and particularly Adorno understand this *angst* to function primarily on the social level since they attempt to avoid any reifying concepts of the 'nature of humanity.'

On the individual level, according to Tillich, *angst* cannot be overcome because human freedom will always remain finite and *angst* is by no means unique to modernity. On the social level, it can and should be questioned and critiqued, given the essential nature of humanity as 'finite freedom,' and as a hopeful benchmark for concrete change. By comparison, Horkheimer and Adorno seem to err on the utopian side of hope for a future in which even social *angst* can be overcome. Recognizing the effects of social structures such as active and definitive sources of sin and estrangement on individual agency, Tillich's anthropology is able to locate a greater degree of agency than can either Horkheimer or Adorno, and with greater agency, there is greater potential for resistance in the individual.[255]

While Horkheimer and Adorno's critiques of Tillich's individualist anthropology clearly have merit, Tillich rejects atomistic individualism and as a Christian theologian, his anthropology is decidedly 'positive' and hopeful compared to the often bleak pessimism of Horkheimer and Adorno. In Tillich's Christian anthropological terms, sin is a denial or repression of the tragic freedom which is always already a central structural feature of human persons who are able to posit themselves and their own histories against an infinite horizon. Horkheimer and Adorno's critique is significant; they read Tillich as overly focused on the individual, which risks occluding the ways humans act within and adapt to social structures. Tillich's concern with the social sphere[256] almost always begins with the individual *qua* individual, while his analysis of the individual *qua* social being is secondary. Rationality is a determinative aspect of anthropology, and here we are looking at human rationality in terms of an ideal versus the actuality, given individual and structural limitations on reason.

---

[254] *MSRS*, 497.

[255] Tillich delineates at least four challenges or limitations to human rationality: sin, finitude, estrangement, and the 'demonic.'

[256] Tillich particularly addresses the social dimension in his work on religious socialism, and preeminently in his 1933 *Socialist Decision*.

Perhaps the central point of disagreement, particularly between Tillich on the one hand and Horkheimer and Adorno on the other is whether such limitations on human rationality are perceived to be external or internal. Horkheimer and Adorno did not sufficiently acknowledge their quasi-metaphysical assumptions, and this will be demonstrated in the following chapter. They did not reflect sufficiently upon the panoply of *internal* limitations on humanity and rationality, imposed in part by social structures over which individuals have little control. The lack of focus on internal agential limitations in the works of both Adorno and Horkheimer ironically suggests a more essentialized or reified notion of critical reason as the core of 'humanity.'

Since the structure of 'finite freedom' reveals that humanity is "inescapably...related to the infinite,"[257] Tillich's anthropological sketch raises the question of reuniting essence and existence. In the creative human act (necessity) of facing this question, one is met by God's answer through the method of correlation. Understood in the Tillichian sense of God as the 'ground of Being,' this appears to be the correlative answer implied by the question of human finitude, just as the awareness that humans are finite suggests an awareness of infinity as its antipode. And since all knowledge is mediated and limited by finitude, what one can say and know about God or the infinite or the ground of being is always symbolic. This creative yet finite freedom which characterizes human experience requires 'the courage to be,' a concept on which Tillich would focus in the following decade.

If Adorno had been more willing to engage Tillich's anthropology and had focused more directly on the internal limitations of human rationality and possibilities for resistance, particularly concerning estrangement and the 'demonic,' his critique may have been substantially more trenchant. On the other hand, if Tillich had employed a less idealistic notion of the 'nature of humanity' and had addressed questions of social agency more directly following his Frankfurt colleagues, his theology would have been strengthened. The expected future in Tillich's religious critical theory functions as a source of transcendence and orientation for justice—what Tillich called a 'dialectical eschatology'—which is at least potentially capable of funding a more potent critique of the status quo than can a secular critical theory. Significantly, his constructive approach to an anthropology oriented towards emancipation recognizes both internal and external limitations on the human person and on human rationality.

---

[257] *MSRS*, 501.

Before concluding this section, it is necessary to return to a comment made by Adorno to Horkheimer in October 1946, in the final *Diskussionsprotokol* concerning a potential sequel to *Dialectic of Enlightenment*, a more positive text which would hypothetically, based on the multiple diagnoses of modernity and enlightenment's illnesses, attempt a 'rescue of enlightenment.' Horkheimer feared that they had lost any practical 'foundation' or 'manual' (*Leitfaden*) on which to ground a positive critique, much less an attempt to 'rescue' enlightenment as they had hoped. Adorno responds by suggesting the illness of reason itself as a preliminary guide for articulating ways to go about seeking to 'cure' reason. Also cited in the previous chapter, Adorno suggested that the 'illness' of reason itself (*die Vernunft erkrankt ist*) could function as a foundational guide or orientation (*Leitfaden*) toward such a cure:

> We must bring together the thought of the disease of reason and the possibility of its recovery by means of the sickness with the demand to bring the forms of consciousness themselves and their social or *anthropological reality* that are simultaneously their own meaning and the ground for the inadequacy of each form of consciousness.[258]

I emphasize Adorno's curious phrase 'anthropological reality' for obvious reasons—this is not a phrase one would expect to come from Adorno, particularly in light of Adorno's excoriating attack on Tillich's assumption of the necessity of some type of anthropological reality as a foundation for critical social theory and political praxis. It is not suggested, by any means, that Adorno is here making a concession to Tillich, or to philosophical anthropology in general. The discussion ends within a page, and the *Rettung der Aufklärung* was never attempted. One cannot make too much of Adorno's off-hand comment in a private session with Horkheimer in 1946, but his suggestion of such a *demand* or *challenge* (*Forderung*) offers a typically elusive, yet fascinating glimpse into what kind of demand on social and anthropological reality Adorno might have had in mind.

---

[258] Adorno, in the final *Diskussionsprotokol* concerning a possible sequel to *Dialectic of Enlightenment*, in Horkheimer, *GS* 12, 604. Emphasis added.

IV. *Dialectic of Enlightenment* as Anthropology[259]

Although Adorno and Horkheimer are operating with an implicit philosophical anthropology of sorts, they are not essentializing any presumed 'nature of humanity' in *Dialectic of Enlightenment.* Rather, they offer a description of perceived actualities based on historical and social contingencies. The engagement of the relationship between humanity and nature, vis-à-vis mimesis, for example, is at the forefront, while a philosophical anthropology outlined in skeletal form above, is largely absent from *Dialectic of Enlightenment.*[260] What can be seen in Horkheimer and Adorno's joint writing is a reasonable blend of the two perspectives seen in the previous sections of this chapter. Horkheimer's free usage of seemingly essentializing phrases concerning humanity is not as evident as in some of his individual writings in the preceding years. Adorno is not as vociferously opposed to any implicit or explicit claims and assumptions about the 'nature of humanity' as he was in his *Entwurf* to Tillich a year earlier. Tillich's claims about humanity are, by contrast, much stronger.

Although Horkheimer and Adorno's project in *Dialectic of Enlightenment* might superficially appear to reject anthropology, the structure and overall project include several crucial assumptions about humanity. Myth and rationality are inseparable in *Dialectic of Enlightenment,* and more radically, they form a dialectically unfolding process. Although they reject any notion of historical pro-

---

[259] Given the length of this chapter, this section on the implicit and explicit functions of anthropology in *Dialectic of Enlightenment* is deliberately exceedingly brief. An entire study could focus on this question. The goal here is simply to provide context and reference to Adorno's critique of Tillich, which was written during the composition of *Dialectic of Enlightenment* and to serve as a reminder that the focus of this chapter has been unevenly distributed toward Horkheimer and Tillich. Adorno did reject much of what could be called 'positive philosophical anthropology,' and his *Entwurf* is a prime example of this. It is hoped that this very brief section will remind the reader that Adorno nevertheless engaged philosophical anthropology in his works, including his collaborative work with Horkheimer.

[260] Although much more could be said about the assumptions and assertions about humanity in *Dialectic of Enlightenment,* I have chosen, partially for the sake of space, to limit my remarks here. It seems clear that something distinct is going on in terms of the portrayal of human subjectivity and agency in this work than in earlier works. This difference may be characterized by the increasing rhetoric of domination and the decreasing attention to subjectivity and agency, although this is admittedly an oversimplification and would require substantial further explication. The primary goal is to demonstrate the shift in anthropology, particularly through a brief analysis of the Odysseus excursus, rather than attempting to adequately account for the complex reasons for this transformation.

cess or progress, Horkheimer and Adorno diagnose certain repetitive patterns in human history and society. According to Patrick Deneen, although they "do not intend to imply that the human condition, at least materially, has remained the same, they attribute a moral conformity throughout human history toward barbarity and fascism."[261]

What anthropological assumptions are Adorno and Horkheimer making? First, the transition from the animal to the human comes with a qualitatively distinct form of instinctual repression of the natural, the mythical, and the magical. Animals operate by instinct, while humans operate by reason controlling instinct for the sake of self-preservation. A second, implicit assumption is that the human self is constituted as a self by this transition to instinct under the regulative precept of reason. Third, the human has always been constituted by the 'choice' between the repression of nature and the repression of self. Finally, selfhood requires repression of nature, which comes at great cost to the self.[262]

Central to unpacking the thesis of cultural repression as it is employed by Adorno and Horkheimer is their version of the paradox of enlightenment: enlightenment presupposes the very myth which it seeks to eradicate. The drive to dominate external nature resulted in the unleashing of forces which dominated humans internally as well, forcing humanity to repress individual desires but also creating the conditions for the perceived means of liberation (enlightenment rationality) becoming the very mechanism of re-inscribed cultural repression and oppression. The domination of external nature has arisen from and been fueled by western norms and "technical rationality"[263] which emphasize absolute efficiency and domination. The result is that the domination of nature has become increasingly efficient through scientific and technological developments. Humanity's domination of external reality has unleashed a seemingly uncontrollable force that comes in turn to dominate internal reality and human self-regulation. Technology as the totality of means set to attain an arbitrary end in the most

---

[261] Patrick J. Deneen, *The Odyssey of Political Theory: The Politics of Departure and Return* (Lanham: Rowman & Littlefield, 2003) 185.

[262] Deneen discerns three anthropological themes in Horkheimer and Adorno's treatment of the *Odyssey*. First, because of the constant conflict between humanity and nature, "humanity continuously seeks nature's conquest and domination." Deneen, 189. Building off of the first, domination of nature is accomplished through a domination of the self, via repression, and domination of other humans. Thirdly, according to Deneen, the "drive to dominate self, humanity, and nature is born of humanity's ineluctable will toward self-preservation." Deneen, 189.

[263] DE, 95.

efficient manner possible gradually begins to perform its given function on its creators.

According to the Preface, the materials in *Dialectic of Enlightenment*, particularly the concluding 'Notes and Drafts,' were intended to sketch a "dialectical anthropology," together with its anticipated companion volume, *Rettung der Aufklärung*. As their conclusion to the 1944 Preface, Horkheimer and Adorno write: "In the last section we publish notes and sketches which, in part, form part of the ideas in the preceding sections, without having found a place in them, and in part deal provisionally with problems of future work. *Most of them relate to a dialectical anthropology*."[264] Of course the second volume never materialized,[265] and it is debatable what, if any, 'dialectical anthropology' guides the first volume.

V. Conclusions

This chapter has focused on early interactions among these three thinkers, particularly concerning the possibilities and limitations of a philosophical anthropology. The central anthropological assumption made by all three thinkers is the essential and incontrovertible value of humanity. Tillich, Horkheimer, and Adorno each sought to articulate norms of liberation, both for society and social philosophy. In terms of anthropology, for Tillich this means understanding the concept of the human being as a fractured manifestation of the *imago Dei*, bound by sin yet free through faith to embody and disseminate grace in the world. Horkheimer and Adorno's skepticism concerning the existence and knowability of a 'nature of humanity' is influenced in part by the Jewish prohibition against idolatry, as will be demonstrated more fully in the final two chapters. It is also reflective of critical theory's general prioritization of critical analysis of culture over speculative reflection on metaphysics, religion, or anthropology.

As the project of the *Institut* evolved from materialism to critical theory, Horkheimer understood the importance of the human subject in culture as the

---

[264] DE, Preface, xix. Emphasis added. "Im letzten Teil werden Aufzeichnungen und Entwürfe publiziert, die teils in den Gedankenkreis der voraufgehenden Abhandlungen gehören, ohne dort ihre Stelle zu finden, teils Probleme kommender Arbeit vorläufig unreissen. Die meisten beziehen sich auf eine dialektische Anthropologie." *DA*, 7.

[265] At the end of the Preface to *Dialektik*, in Horkheimer's *Gesammelte Schriften*, Horkheimer expresses hope that "in the not too distant future" they could complete the fragments. *GS* 5, 23.

locus of transformative possibilities in society. Implicitly in line with Marx in his early work, Horkheimer sees the importance of philosophical anthropology, and he accepts certain inevitable commonalities in terms of rationality and basic human needs, desires, and fears, *inter al.* Early in his writings, Horkheimer is willing to engage conceptions of a hypothetical 'nature of humanity,' although he consistently rejects any absolute, unchanging, static, or ahistorical interpretation of humanity. He understands the human subject to be neutral and society to be the stumbling block for the individual. Human subjects make certain rational calculations for self-preservation, which also limits agency. Horkheimer is even willing to acknowledge, in a letter to Tillich, the theoretical existence of a 'pure humanity,' even if only to demonstrate its negating function. By the time of his collaboration with Adorno in the mid-1940s, the language of a 'nature of humanity' diminished, but did not disappear from Horkheimer's work. Only after *Dialectic of Enlightenment* does Horkheimer appear to lose hope in the capacity of the subject's agency *vis-à-vis* society.

Similar to Horkheimer, Tillich in the 1930s presumes the importance of a 'nature of humanity' although he too rejects any eternal, ahistorical conceptions. Tillich makes a valiant attempt to re-instill a Marxian anthropology in socialism against an ominous backdrop. Religious socialism, drawing upon the anthropology of Marx, seeks to re-introduce Christian humanism into socialist discourse. Religious socialism does not intend to supplant socialism or to provide a simplistic fideistic framework, but rather to supplement the critiques of materialist socialism and work together in the quest for a more just society. Tillich argues for the centrality of reason, a critical self-consciousness, and some common psychological features shared among human beings in a certain period. Although a theologian by training, Tillich's anthropology in the period in question is largely philosophical and is limited to a discussion of sin and prophetic expectation. Tillich perhaps neglects some of the resources of theological anthropology, particularly dealing with the incarnation in his discussion. Tillich also diagnoses what he calls the 'inner conflict of socialism,' arguing that secular socialism cannot adequately articulate the grounds on which human transformation could occur, should social transformation take place.

The second section of the chapter focuses on a latent debate between Tillich and Adorno. Tillich argues in a 1943 essay that the human person can be understood as a manifestation of "finite" and "creative freedom," and Adorno takes serious issue with this essay and Tillich's assessment. Adorno engages in an extended and at times harsh critique of Tillich, focused narrowly on Tillich's

1943 essay and missing some important context. Although the 'draft' letter was written in the first-person plural, and at the height of the collaborative work between Adorno and Horkheimer, it appears that Horkheimer did not agree with Adorno's assessment and critique of Tillich, and the letter was never sent to Tillich. This raises interesting questions since, in many ways, Horkheimer's anthropology prior to the composition of *Dialectic of Enlightenment* was similar to that of Tillich. Why did Adorno seek to eviscerate the position of his own teacher and *Habilitation* advisor, while ignoring similar arguments made by Horkheimer? I suggest that, in addition to respect for his 'boss' and co-collaborator, Adorno kept a blind eye to Horkheimer's anthropology, which the latter never rescinded.

Although Tillich makes highly generalizing assumptions, notably concerning 'existential' consciousness common to human experience under the conditions of modernity, I argue that his anthropology, along with religious socialism's conception of the 'nature of humanity' *does not rely* on a static anthropology although it does have a much stronger sense of ontology. Tillich rejects any concept of an 'eternal' or 'unchanging' humanity and he argues for a 'fragmentary humanity,' historically and contextually situated. Tillich's anthropology can be accurately seen as essentialized *only in the limited sense of ontology*; because he assumes a common origin in God; 'finite' and 'creative freedom' describes the 'essence' of humanity vis-à-vis God. He does, however, refer to human beings (*menschliche Sein*) and at several points, refers to the subject using the Heideggerian term *Dasein*.[266] This use of Heideggerian terminology should not be overwrought, however—in contemporaneous writings, Horkheimer used the term *Dasein*, as did Adorno extensively in *Kierkegaard: Construction of the Aesthetic,* and in a more limited manner in "The Actuality of Philosophy."[267] Heideggerian philosophy and terminology were widespread in philosophical circles in the early 1930s; even those who ardently criticized Heidegger felt

[266] Of course, the term itself is not a Heideggerian neologism: *Dasein* is used by Hegel and Marx, for example. After the publication of Heidegger's *Being and Time* in 1927, however, *Dasein* took on new valences and references to the term thereafter could not have avoided the evocation of Heidegger.

[267] Horkheimer, for example: "Materialismus und Metaphysik" (1933) von Max Horkheimer, in *ZfS,* 2 (1933) 9; "Der neueste Angriff auf die Metaphysik" (1937) in *KT* II, 82, 113, usw.; "Traditionelle und kritische Theorie" (1937) in *KT* II, 159. For Adorno, see *Kierkegaard: Construction of the Aesthetic*, and "The Actuality of Philosophy" (1932) 131. Adorno again uses the term *Dasein*, albeit highly critically, in *Negative Dialectics*.

compelled to engage his work and terminology. Tillich was clearly more sympathetic to Heidegger, while it may be more accurate to say that Heidegger was an interlocutor in the youth of both Adorno and Horkheimer.

In this chapter, I have argued that a rough conception of the 'nature of humanity' seems to be necessary for a robust emancipatory theory and praxis. Horkheimer's early works are much more open to the possibility of social transformation, and it is not coincidental that in these early writings, Horkheimer more frequently engages human subjectivity and agency, even while rejecting any conception of an eternal human essence. Tillich maintained the most hope of the three for the possibility of social transformation, and his anthropology is the broadest and most robust. While he argues that there is something like a "human nature" in finite and creative freedom, he rejects the notion of an eternal human essence. While Adorno may have been right to reject the universalizing, power-corruptive aspects of "human nature" discourse, he would certainly caution us to pay attention to the lessons of concrete human history. Of the three, Adorno is the least open to transformative social potential, and although this chapter analyzed his work very narrowly, it is clear that he was also the most vehemently opposed to any form of philosophical anthropology, understanding it largely as a form of domination rather than a possible means for articulating emancipatory theory or practice.

4.

Metaphysics and Norms in Critical Social Theory

> The great question is...what can we oppose to this machinery in order to keep a portion of mankind free from this parceling-out of the soul, from this supreme mastery of the bureaucratic way of life. —Max Weber, "On Bureaucratization"[1]

Introduction

Along with Max Weber, Adorno, Horkheimer, and Tillich each wondered whether metaphysics was necessarily part of the machinery of social domination, a function of the 'steel-hard casing,'[2] or whether metaphysics could be a constructive partner of emancipatory reason, standing against the machinery of domination.[3] Metaphysics, for the purposes of this chapter, refers to rational inquiry into the structure of 'being' as encountered in reality and to the *a priori* presuppositions that animate such rational inquiry.[4] A more nuanced characterization of metaphysics, particularly for Adorno and Horkheimer, will be offered below. Can anything resist the encroachment of commodification and alienation in modernity diagnosed by Lukács? The question orienting this chapter is what kind of work, if any, metaphysics does for each thinker in light of Weber's ques-

---

[1] Max Weber, "On Bureaucratization," (1909) in J. P. Mayer, *Max Weber and German Politics* (London: Faber & Faber, 1962) 128.

[2] This was long known as the 'iron cage,' as was discussed in chapter two.

[3] Loosely defined, metaphysics was a problem even for Tillich, as I will show in this chapter. All three thinkers implicitly use or explicitly accept certain metaphysical assumptions, but in a general sense, metaphysics was seen as a challenge.

[4] As such, metaphysics and ontology are closely related and one could easily make the argument that for Tillich, metaphysics and ontology are functionally synonymous. Ontology is traditionally a branch of metaphysics dealing with the question of 'being.' For Adorno and Horkheimer, normative presuppositions seem to take the structural place of metaphysics, but norms should not be strictly equated with metaphysics. Metaphysics, as will be demonstrated, is an ambiguous enterprise in the history of philosophy with which both Adorno and Horkheimer wrestled, but could not completely abandon, even in their critiques.

tion in the epigraph above, and seen in Lukács' diagnosis from the previous two chapters. Does metaphysics still have immanent emancipatory valences? Did it ever have such power? Can metaphysics help the human subject and society at large overcome alienation and estrangement? For Adorno and Horkheimer, two central questions to be explored here are whether trenchant criticism is possible, and whether alienation can be overcome, without metaphysical presuppositions. This chapter will demonstrate that while Adorno and Horkheimer, to varying degrees, deny metaphysics as a discipline, they nevertheless continue to operate with a clearly implicit metaphysical hierarchy of necessary assumptions and norms in order to ground their social critique.

With the common intellectual legacy explored in the first two chapters, Adorno, Horkheimer, and Tillich share a similar concern for autonomy, justice, and the emancipatory expectation of critical reason as the primary hope for increased justice and rationality in the world. Although these thinkers have many common concerns and a shared intellectual milieu, furthered by personal friendships and decade-long debates, the way each arrives at and the presuppositions used to reach those shared concerns are often profoundly different. This is particularly the case with regard to metaphysical and religious ideas, the concern of this and the following chapter. While this and the following chapter deal with abstract questions of epistemology, metaphysics, and religion, they are grounded in the shared goal of addressing and overcoming these foundational challenges with the goal of emancipatory rationality and renewed subjectivity. In the previous chapter on anthropology, it was demonstrated that Horkheimer especially is willing to engage with language of a 'nature of humanity,' however critically. This debate concerning the 'nature of humanity' also has metaphysical implications and the anthropological assumptions made by Adorno as well as Horkheimer further disclose operative normative and metaphysical presuppositions.

The central concern of this chapter is to explore and elucidate the common ground, mutual critiques, and foundational distinctions among the three thinkers surrounding metaphysics, building upon the questions of rationality and agency raised in the previous chapters. This chapter will therefore identify the underlying epistemological assumptions and guiding metaphysical norms used—explicitly as well as implicitly—by Adorno, Horkheimer, and Tillich in the 1930s and 1940s. Identifying the different articulations of and rationale for these shared assumptions and methodologies will illumine the central areas of tension and disagreement among the three thinkers. The early Horkheimer critically engages metaphysics, albeit ambiguously, while for Adorno, an early interest in metaphysics significantly decreases in importance throughout the 30s and 40s.[5] As was demonstrated in chapter two, Tillich's concern is that a posited 'transcendence' that is devoid of 'ultimacy,' or some metaphysical or religious foundation, lacks the necessary critical weight for social critique and transformation. In chapter three, it became clear that anthropological concerns relate to foundational normative assumptions about the human subject and individual and collective agency in modernity. This chapter will focus on a reexamination of the questions of ultimacy, norms, and foundations of critique.

Horkheimer overtly rejects metaphysics in many of his early writings, but those same writings are fraught with metaphysical assumptions and they necessarily gesture toward explicitly metaphysical questions. Horkheimer argues that all philosophy and criticism is situated and finite and "opposes every attempt to play down the importance of insight into the earthly order of things by turning man's attention to a supposedly more essential order."[6] Yet despite this and other critiques of metaphysics, he continues to engage metaphysical questions, increasingly so in the 1930s and 40s. This chapter suggests that Horkheimer ultimately rejects one variety of metaphysics in order to preserve room for another kind of metaphysic, albeit unacknowledged. As will be demonstrated, his rejection of metaphysics is in part a matter of imprecision in terminology, but it originates in large part from his fundamental rejection of injustice and suffering. Through a re-cast, albeit implicit metaphysic, Horkheimer hopes to preserve room for alterity and justice. This theme will recur in the following chapter concerning religious discourse.

For Tillich, any valid metaphysic must be grounded upon the claim that the authentic human cannot exist independently of God as the 'Unconditioned' ground of her being and the foundation of truth, freedom, and justice. Adorno and Horkheimer's respective metaphysics—presupposing here that they each have one—are perhaps necessarily more social yet individualistic than Tillich's, beginning with a critical aesthetic orientation—rooted perhaps in something as

[5] Adorno's first dissertation, *Die Transzendenz des Dinglichen und Noematischen in Husserls Phänomenologie,* and his first *Habilitation*, *Der Begriff des Unbewussten in der transzendentalen Seelenlehre,* which was rejected by Hans Cornelius, along with his approved Habilitation on Kierkegaard's aesthetics, all deal with metaphysical and ontological themes. By the time of his 1932 lecture to the Kant Society, "Die Idee der Naturgeschichte," Adorno began separating his work from explicitly metaphysical themes, and this trend continues at least until *Dialectic of Enlightenment* in 1944. See volumes 1 and 2 of Adorno's *Gesammelte Schriften.*

[6] *CT*, 26. *ZfS* 2 (1933) 15.

simple as individual pleasure, the longing for justice, or the hope that things could be otherwise, although there is more than subjectivity in their critique of utility as a modern norm. Both also challenge the ontological structure of Tillich's metaphysic; for example, Adorno questions Tillich's notion of the tragic conflict between the finite and the infinite. Horkheimer finds Tillich's metaphysical presuppositions too enmeshed in the legacy of idealism,[7] and both are at least partially correct in their critiques of Tillich here. The argument of this chapter and the following is that some foundation for critique is almost unavoidable, whether metaphysical, religious, aesthetic, or otherwise.

Metaphysics for Tillich, rooted in an ontological framework, is "concerned with the demonstration that direction toward the Unconditioned is a necessary function constituting the fulfillment of meaningful reality."[8] Thus, the recovery of metaphysics is for Tillich part and parcel of the recovery of reason, and it is thus at least potentially emancipatory. A superficial reading of Adorno and Horkheimer might suggest, by contrast, that the eradication of metaphysics is the precondition of the emancipation of reason and subjects. This chapter aims to demonstrate, however, that both Adorno and Horkheimer not only engage, but also rely upon similar, if occasionally unacknowledged, metaphysical and normative presuppositions. Indeed, both thinkers realized, following the debate with logical positivism, that empirical questions and concerns could only take critical social thought so far and that normative valuations were, to some extent, necessary aspects of critical theory.

I. The Frankfurt School and the Vienna School

Otto Neurath was an economist and sociologist at the University of Vienna and the unofficial center of the equally unofficial 'Vienna School' of logical empiricism or logical positivism.[9] Other notable members included Rudolf Carnap,

---

[7] Stefan Breuer, *inter al.*, argues that Horkheimer was also profoundly indebted to German idealism, and that he was less than transparent about this influence. "The Long Friendship," by Stefan Breuer, in *On Max Horkheimer: New Perspectives*, ed. Seyla Benhabib, et. al. (Cambridge: MIT Press, 1993) 260. Horkheimer does acknowledge the legacy of German Idealism in critical theory in the 'Postscript' to *CT*, 245.

[8] James Luther Adams, *Paul Tillich's Philosophy of Culture, Science, and Religion* (New York: Schocken Books, 1970) 188.

[9] Like the 'Frankfurt School,' there is a wide variety of perspectives included under the general heading of the 'Vienna School.' While Neurath can be accurately described as a logical empiricist, this is best seen on a spectrum; Neurath's position cannot be conflated with the positivism of the early Wittgenstein or Ayer, e.g. Neurath represents a transi-

Herbert Heigl, Philipp Frank, and peripherally, Kurt Gödel and Ludwig Wittgenstein, the latter of whom was inspirational to the brand of social science pursued by the Vienna School.[10] Neurath himself was particularly concerned with philosophy of language and the unity of the sciences, including their social function, coupled with a rejection of metaphysical speculation. Despite early similarities, Neurath and his colleagues became the object of Horkheimer's mischaracterization and attack in both "The Latest Attack on Metaphysics" and "Traditional and Critical Theory." The historical relationship between Horkheimer and Neurath is minimal but has been well documented by John O'Neill and Thomas Uebel.[11] While there is significant overlap between the early materialist position of Horkheimer and that of Neurath, the positivism debate reflects an important shift within Horkheimer's thought and developing conception of critical theory and the role of metaphysics in critical theory.[12]

What Neurath and his Vienna School colleagues were offering was an alternative and complementary social critique to that of the early Horkheimer and the Frankfurt School. Both groups were materialists influenced by Marx who initially sought to unify philosophy and the sciences while dislodging false mythologies and myopically reflexive metaphysics.[13] Neurath and Horkheimer both rejected the mystical turn of the later Wittgenstein as well. With the Frankfurt

---

tional figure in the Vienna School's thinking. O'Neill and Uebel write: "With Neurath…logical empiricism assumed a form clearly distinctive from that which it was given by Schlick early on and from the strictly formalist one which Carnap gave it and which became ever more dominant in the movement." John O'Neill and Thomas Uebel, "Horkheimer and Neurath: Restarting a Disrupted Debate," in *European Journal of Philosophy* 12:1 (2004) 79.

[10] This group was also referred to as the Vienna Circle.

[11] O'Neill and Uebel. See also Hans-Joachim Dahms' *Positivismusstreit.*

[12] O'Neill and Uebel suggest that Horkheimer's early, more empirically-grounded position, and his refusal to articulate a strong distinction between philosophy and science reflects a 'positivist attitude.' O'Neill and Uebel, 87. See especially Horkheimer's "Traditional and Critical Theory."

[13] The Vienna School's critique of metaphysics was often much stronger than that of Horkheimer or Adorno, however, and in an important sense represents a difference. Both critiqued traditional metaphysics but Horkheimer thought some of the Vienna School thinkers went too far in their critique. Rudolf Carnap, for example, claimed: "In the domain of metaphysics, including all philosophy of value and normative theory, logical analysis yields the negative results that *the alleged statements in this domain are entirely meaningless.*" "The Elimination of Metaphysics through Logical Analysis," by Rudolf Carnap, in *Logical Positivism*, ed. A. J. Ayer (Glencoe: Free Press, 1959) 60-1; emphasis in original.

School's publication of its empirical study on *Authority and the Family* in the mid-1930s, some commonalities in terms of research subject and methodology can be seen.[14]

Already in "Materialism and Metaphysics," (1933)[15] Horkheimer criticizes Comte and likely Neurath and other positivists for being concerned with appearances rather than the nature of things. Horkheimer writes, "Positivism…is proud of the fact that it is not concerned with the 'nature' of things but only with appearances and thus with what things actually offer to us of themselves."[16] Appearances mislead; without focusing on the nature of things, one doesn't have enough critical force to supersede superstition, for example.[17] The formalized logic exemplary of the logical positivism of the Vienna School, in Horkheimer's estimation, fetishized facts. As Martin Jay puts it, for Horkheimer, "positivism of all kinds was ultimately the abdication of reflection. The result was the absolutizing of 'facts' and the reification of the existing order."[18] Worst of all "in Horkheimer's eyes was the positivists' pretension to have disentangled facts from values."[19] Horkheimer vehemently rejected any presumption of disinterested objectivity or social scientific value-neutrality.[20]

Horkheimer published Neurath's "Inventory of the Standard of Living" (which was also financially supported by the *Institut*) in the *Institut's* journal in 1937. He subsequently refused to publish Neurath's response to his two central essays critiquing logical positivism, "The Latest Attack on Metaphysics" and "Traditional and Critical Theory." In a 1936 letter to Adorno, Horkheimer began to worry that logical positivism led to irrationalism and possibly even to even barbarism.[21] "Traditional and Critical Theory" in particular marks a transition

---

[14] *CT*, 47-128. For an analysis of the Institute's *Studies on Authority and the Family*, see Wiggershaus, 137-41, 149-56.

[15] Horkheimer referred to the work of the Frankfurt School as historical or dialectical materialism prior to 1937. The early materialism of Horkheimer and the physicalist materialism of Neurath are not dissimilar.

[16] *CT*, 37. "Materialismus und Metaphysik," in *ZfS* 2 (1933) 25.

[17] O'Neill and Uebel note that here Horkheimer distorted Neurath's position. The distinction between appearance and reality is not the same as the distinction between the empirical and non-empirical, contrary to Horkheimer's portrayal. O'Neill and Uebel, 82.

[18] Jay, 62.

[19] Jay, 62.

[20] See, *inter al.*, Wiggershaus, 185.

[21] In a letter of 22 October 1936 to Adorno after meeting with Neurath in New York, Horkheimer wrote quite bluntly: "Im Grunde ist das Ganze nur ein elendes Rückzugsgefecht der formalistischen Erkenntnistheorie des Liberalismus, der auch auf diesem

point after which Horkheimer's work increasingly separated philosophy—as he understood it—from the social sciences and assumed a meta-philosophical view, reconsidering the nature of the task of philosophy.[22] Neurath rightly criticizes Horkheimer's latent idealism and asks the latter on what basis he can ground a philosophy increasingly independent from the sciences, or adjudicate between good and bad meta-philosophies.[23] Horkheimer's response is a further caricature of positivism and is unsatisfactory; this marks the end of the brief period of collaboration between the Vienna School and the Frankfurt School.[24] Horkheimer's assumptions and questions guiding the meta-philosophical project of critical theory, particularly the dogged insistence that immanence not have the last word, are explored more fully below.

Horkheimer accused logical positivists of being a-historical and a-social in their work, forfeiting the ability to effectively critique manifestations of instrumental rationality in society.[25] Yet despite Horkheimer's characterization, Neurath did take the historical and social aspects and context of the sciences seriously.[26] Neurath responded by accusing Horkheimer of retreating to idealist

Gebiet in offene Liebedienerei gegen den Faschismus übergeht. Bestand schon eine wichtige Funktion des Neukantianismus darin, durch die Apologetisierung des herrschenden Wissenschaftsbetriebs die Gesellschaft, deren Erhaltung ebendieser dient, zu verklären, so werden jetzt schamlos alle Sphäre der Kultur überhaupt dem Irrationalismus preisgegeben.... Was sich hier zeigt, ist eben das, was ich im Wahrheitsaufsatz angedeutet habe: die prästabilierte Harmonie von Fachwissenschaft und Barbarei." Horkheimer, *GS* 15, 688-9.

[22] This transition is, in part, a result of the interactions with Neurath.

[23] The term 'meta-philosophy' is not to be equated with metaphysics but instead reflects upon the nature and scope of the project of philosophy itself. Neurath was correct in this critique of Horkheimer's increasing idealism, which one can see Horkheimer acknowledging in the 'Postscript' to "Traditional and Critical Theory." Horkheimer suggests that critical theory is "the heir not only of German idealism but of philosophy as such." *CT*, 245.

[24] Horkheimer did publish a review of the *International Encyclopedia of Unified Science*, jointly written by many of the Vienna School members, in the *Zeitschrift für Sozialforschung* in 1939. Written by Marcuse, this critical review cited Horkheimer's own critique of Neurath, et. al., in the 1937 *ZfS* article "*Die neuste Angriff auf die Metaphysik.*"

[25] See *CT*, 145, 159, *inter al.* Thus Wheatland writes: "Positivism could merely describe the existing world, but it could not evaluate it or appreciate the constructive role that human beings played within it." Thomas Wheatland, *The Frankfurt School in Exile* (Minneapolis: University of Minnesota Press, 2009) 118.

[26] O'Neill and Uebel, 84.

metaphysics,[27] although Horkheimer denies this and in fact levels as much of his own critique at idealism as at positivism. O'Neill and Uebel note: "both Neurath's and the early Horkheimer's work were concerned to develop a programme that might be characterised as materialism without metaphysics."[28] Neurath's position, commonly referred to as 'physicalism,' seeks to disentangle and reclaim materialism from metaphysics through scientific 'protocol statements' rooted in the empirical world.

Essentially, Horkheimer mischaracterizes the crucial difference between the two 'schools,' claiming that logical positivism limited itself to the observation and categorization of facts while stopping short of social critique. Without its crucial critical function, according to Horkheimer, reason—here logical positivistic empiricism—merely reflects instrumentality.[29] In one of the most succinct critiques of this position, Adorno and Horkheimer write in *Dialectic of Enlightenment*, "This kind of neutrality is more metaphysical than metaphysics."[30] Yet this pithy assertion disguises an important assumption Horkheimer and Adorno seem to be making: if meta-philosophical neutrality is *necessarily* associated with the status quo, it would seem that both critique and change can only be effected on a meta-philosophical level. Positivist philosophy becomes a pawn of the status quo.[31] The logical positivism characteristic of many of the Vienna School thinkers attempted, in part, to limit the arena of reason to the realm of empirical facticity. For example, Neurath writes: "*we know of no court of appeal beyond the science that judges science and investigates its foundations....*"[32] Yet in Horkheimer's view, this served to functionally limit the critical social scope and capacity of reason.

---

[27] O'Neill and Uebel, 84-5. While Horkheimer came to understand the shift in his thought as showing increasing affinity with idealism, he still rejected the claim that it contained any metaphysic. This claim will be disputed below.

[28] O'Neill and Uebel, 85.

[29] Wiggershaus writes: "Although protest against authoritarian states, for example, was not excluded by positivists, it was treated as an 'evaluation,' which was beyond the boundaries of rationality or irrationality." Wiggershaus, 184.

[30] DE, 17. "Solche Neutralität ist metaphysischer als die Metaphysik." *DA, 29.*

[31] See Horkheimer's language in his letter to Adorno cited in footnote 21 above. O'Neill and Uebel suggest that the political impotence suggested as characteristic of positivism is inaccurate, at least in the case of Neurath who offered an explicit critique of 'technocratic politics.' O'Neill and Uebel, 96.

[32] Neurath, "Einheitswissenschaft und logischer Empirismus. Eine Erwiderung," ms., *Otto Neurath Nachlass, Wiener Kreis Archiv*, Rijksarchif Noord-Holland, Haarlem, 10; cited in O'Neill and Uebel, 83; italics in original.

Theodor Adorno also critically engages the Vienna School—although he focuses on Schlick and Carnap more than Neurath—as early as his 1931 inaugural lecture, "The Actuality of Philosophy." Just as Horkheimer initially found common ground with Neurath and other members of the Vienna School, so too Adorno's critiques are rooted in an appreciation for the work of positivist philosophy.[33] Nevertheless, the logical positivism of the Vienna School, according to Adorno, searches "for all propositions which in any way reach out beyond the circle of experience and its relativity, solely in tautologies, in analytical propositions."[34] In agreement with the position contra positivism that Horkheimer would reach six years later, Adorno suggests "every move beyond that which is verifiable by the power of experience is prevented"[35] by positivist philosophy. Adorno also implicitly challenges Horkheimer's early materialist phase, in which the latter also attempted to unify the sciences and philosophy. In 1931, Adorno holds on to the priority of autonomous philosophy, arguing via positivism that "philosophy becomes solely an occasion for ordering and controlling the separate sciences, without being allowed to append anything essential from itself to their

---

[33] Adorno carefully acknowledges the "extraordinary importance" of the Vienna School. He writes: "I view its significance less in that it might have successfully converted philosophy into science than in that its rigorous formulation of the scientific in philosophy sharpens the contours of the contents of philosophy not subject to logic and the separate sciences. Philosophy will not be transformed into science, but under the pressure of the empiricist attack it will banish from itself all questioning which, as specifically scientific, belongs of right to the separate sciences and clouds philosophic questioning." Adorno, "The Actuality of Philosophy," 125-6. "Ich erblicke ihre Bedeutung weniger darin, dass ihr nun tatsächlich die projektierte Überführung von Philosophie in Wissenschaft gelungen wäre, als darin, dass sie durch die Schärfe, mit der sie formuliert, was an Philosophie Wissenschaft ist, die Konturen alles dessen hervortreibt, was an Philosophie anderen Instanzen als den logischen und den einzelwissenschaftlichen untersteht. Die Philosophie wird nicht in Wissenschaft sich verwandeln, aber sie wird unter dem Druck des empiristischen Angriffs alle die Fragestellungen aus sich verbannen, die als spezifisch wissenschaftliche den Einzelwissenschaften gebühren und die philosophischen Problemstellungen trüben." *GS* 1, 333.

[34] AP, 125. "Mit Hilfe geschärfter erkenntniskritischer Methoden unternimmt es die fortgeschrittenste Logik—ich denke an die neue Wiener Schule, wie sie von Schlick ausging, heute von Carnap und Dubislav weitergeführt wird und in engem Zusammenhang mit den Logistikern und mit Russell operiert—alle eigentliche, weiterführende Erkenntnis der Erfahrung ausschließlich vorzubehalten und alle Sätze, die irgend über den Umkreis der Erfahrung und deren Relativität hinausgreifen, allein in Tautologien, in analytischen Sätzen zu suchen." *GS* 1, 332.

[35] AP, 125. *GS* 1, 332.

findings."[36] Horkheimer would not explicitly acknowledge the necessary autonomy of philosophy until his 1937 debate with Neurath.

Paul Tillich's more limited critique of logical positivism is very similar to those of Horkheimer and Adorno, though less trenchant and extensive. For Tillich, logical positivism prevents "philosophy from dealing with any problem which concerns us seriously;" it represents a "very comfortable flight of philosophical thought from the tremendous realities of our period."[37] Written after Horkheimer's 1937 break with positivism and arguably reflecting Horkheimer's mischaracterization of positivism, Tillich's comments may reflect the influence of Horkheimer.

II. Metaphysics and Transcendence

While Tillich's Lutheran understanding of human nature as limited by sin and estrangement is inherently somewhat pessimistic, his anthropology, as was demonstrated in the previous chapter, is tempered by an ultimate hope that God would make 'all things new.' Tillich also exhibited a cautious optimism concerning collective human agency, as one sees in his hopes for the collaboration of socialism and religion toward the betterment of individuals and society. By contrast, Adorno and Horkheimer's even more pessimistic anthropologies are united by a shared lament over modernity's deeply paradoxical 'glorification of means' wherein even human subjects are reduced to means; this is even more pessimistic, despite utopian undertones.

When Horkheimer and Adorno do engage the metaphysical or the religious, they rarely speak of 'transcendence' as such: there is no escape from history, and even when they write of longing for the 'Other' or the 'ineffable,' they never speak of any accessible sphere of 'transcendence,' as traditional religious theories often do. Sometimes Horkheimer will simply refer to a 'better future' for which he hopes, yet cannot rationally reach. In the conclusion to his 1938 essay, "Montaigne and the Function of Skepticism," Horkheimer writes:

> [T]he critical theory which we espouse, in contrast to skepticism, does not make an antitheoretical absolutism of the insight into the inadequacy of things as they are and the transitoriness of cognition. Instead,

---

[36] AP, 125. *GS* 2, 332.

[37] *Protestant Era*, 89. Written in English and delivered at Union Theological Seminary upon assuming the chair in Philosophical Theology. For Tillich, logical positivism is a result of the (unwarranted) separation of philosophy from theology.

> even in the face of pessimistic assessments, critical theory is guided by the unswerving interest in a better future.[38]

Horkheimer does not refer to this as a hope or a longing here, but rather claims to be "guided by the unswerving interest in a better future/*unbeirrten Interesse an einer besseren Zukunft*." What might this hypothetical 'better future' look like, or against what might it be juxtaposed?

Simultaneously, an implicit, and often unacknowledged prioritization of the hope for transcendence remains just below the surface of the relentless critique of the logic of immanence, particularly in the work of Adorno. As Rolf Wiggershaus insightfully notes, "Since all Adorno's criticisms were aimed at producing evidence of 'immanence,' the goal of his critique could only be termed transcendence, or simply: release—into the transcendent, into a realm free of intention, into what was new, unrestricted, open, non-identical."[39] 'Transcendence' here refers simply to the critical 'beyond,' toward which immanent critique gestures; such transcendence is obviously different from traditional theism. Adorno's immanent critique seeks to critically juxtapose ideals and potentialities against present actualities, comparing the way things 'could otherwise be' against the status quo. Opposed to transcendental critique, which presupposes some other standpoint from which to evaluate the world, immanent critique seeks to compare this-worldly ideals with this-worldly realities. Adorno and Horkheimer remained united in an abiding skepticism about any accessible metaphysical or religious 'truth.'

Here I roughly follow Birgit Recki's definition of metaphysics, coined in her incisive analysis of Adorno and Horkheimer's understandings of metaphysics and experience. Recki suggests that for both thinkers, metaphysics refers both to an attempt at "understanding *the whole*—or [that which] feels at least compelled to acknowledge a certain whole—and *thereby* already transcends what can be experienced as the measure of the empirical," and, secondly, the 'metaphysical' refers to "that which goes beyond the 'physis' of the existing society in a *utopian* sense."[40] The attempt to grasp the whole through a dogged insistence upon non-identical particularity in order to level a sustained critique, and the consideration of things, in a utopian vein, as they 'otherwise could be,' pointing toward a lim-

---

[38] BPSS, 311. "Montaigne und die Funktion der Skepsis," in *ZfS* 7 (1938) 52.

[39] Wiggershaus, 312.

[40] Recki, 120. Recki's analysis is not limited to the earlier period on which this study focuses, but her insights are germane to this early period.

ited transcendence, are the two major markers of the metaphysical assumptions operative in the early work of Horkheimer and Adorno. Brian Shaw rightly summarizes: "The goal at which Critical Theory aims and the means it seeks to assure it remain shrouded in mystery; they are matters solely of longing and belief."[41] That such longing and belief were largely unacknowledged does not change their metaphysical basis, and the tension between utopian drives and an expressed rejection of utopia presents an open challenge. As Tillich pointed out in *The Socialist Decision*, "Marxism, in spite of its hostility to utopianism, has never been able to defend itself against the suspicion that it has a hidden faith in utopia."[42] The questions of utopian hopes and transcendence will be engaged further below.

II.1 Horkheimer's Early Engagement with Metaphysics

Horkheimer's relationship to metaphysics is both complex and occasionally reductive; Recki accuses Horkheimer, and to a lesser extent Adorno, of a "vulgar reductionism"[43] in his engagement with metaphysics.[44] While Recki's claim is perhaps too strong, Horkheimer's ambiguity in addressing metaphysics reflects, among other things, his implicit reduction of most types of metaphysics into a single category, limiting both the scope and force of his critique somewhat. He is, however, more nuanced than some scholars are willing to acknowledge. Horkheimer is consistent and clear that materialism cannot remain indifferent to metaphysics,[45] yet while he often criticizes metaphysics, it is rarely clear exactly what he means by the term.[46] Even more challenging for the interpreter, Horkheimer often seems to criticize one type of metaphysics[47] while tacitly embracing another form of more qualified metaphysical presuppositions and foundation.

---

[41] Brian J. Shaw, "Reason, Nostalgia and Eschatology in the Critical Theory of Max Horkheimer," in *The Journal of Politics* 47:1 (1985) 167.

[42] *SD*, 73. *GW* 2, 287-8.

[43] Recki, 118.

[44] Horkheimer's early "programmatic essays express a decisive, indeed often highly polemical, rejection of metaphysics *as such*." Recki, 107.

[45] *CT*, 21. See "Materialismus und Metaphysik," in *ZfS* 2 (1933).

[46] Recki argues that the central reason for the "idiosyncratic repudiation of metaphysical reflection on the part of critical theory" comes back to Horkheimer's "overly reduced understanding of what metaphysics really is." Recki, 112.

[47] "Horkheimer recognises only *one* kind of metaphysics. For him *all* metaphysics represents a 'closed and conclusive dogmatism, 'completed theory of reality,' whose static

The quintessential modern challenge of articulating a basis of critique without metaphysics while relying on other, analogous and normative assumptions to ground such critique is markedly present in both Horkheimer and Adorno. For Horkheimer, this challenge is heightened by his realization that certain philosophical traditions (like the logical positivism of the Vienna Circle, as Horkheimer understood it) abnegated their capacity to critique and advocate for social transformation by eschewing questions of social value. To this point, Wolin writes: "What alarmed Horkheimer during the 1930s were 'anti-intellectual' theoretical currents that rejected metaphysics outright for along with metaphysics, they seemingly renounced all prospects for human betterment."[48] If there is an important connection between metaphysics and emancipation, this might highlight the ambiguity in Horkheimer's ambivalence toward metaphysics and his concerns with what might replace it.

Horkheimer's early remarks on metaphysics are indeed highly critical—the "abstract pretense of security"[49] and a handmaid of religion,[50] for example—but what he actually means by metaphysics is profoundly unclear. Yet at one point he claims that "there is some sense in which metaphysics means insight into the true nature of things."[51] In his debate with the Vienna School, Horkheimer rejected the positivism of Neurath and company, believing it could not adequately ground a historical critique of social realities.[52] At the same time, drawing upon Recki's characterization of metaphysics above, Horkheimer presumes that a critique focused on particularity *can* address, if not redress, the social whole. Such a critique could at least hypothetically thereby point toward critical transcendence

character, with the concomitant danger of 'absolutising' and 'hypostasing' historical conditions, cannot do justice in principle to the demands of dialectical theory." Recki, 114.

[48] Richard Wolin, *The Frankfurt School Revisited: and Other Essays on Politics and Society* (New York: Routledge, 2006) 2

[49] BPSS, 155. "...Metaphysik, diese gedankliche Vorspiegelung einer Sicherheit...." "Bemerkungen zur philosophischen Anthropologie," in *KT* I, 205.

[50] "Das metaphysische Bewusstsein verträgt sich in der Regel mit dem Glauben an die ewige Notwendigkeit eines harten Daseins für die Mehrzahl der Menschen...." *KT* II, 82.

[51] DD, 45. "Doch scheint mir, dass Metaphysik in irgendeiner Weise die Erkenntnis des wahren Wesens der Dinge bezeichnet." *Dämmerung*, 85.

[52] "While Horkheimer claims that the difference between critical social research and metaphysical reflection lies specifically in the appeal to experience, he is immediately forced to insist, in contrast to positivism, upon a form of thought that for its part always already transcends mere experience." Recki, 113. As was pointed out above, this belief of Horkheimer has been called into question by O'Neill and Uebel and others.

beyond the status quo, and could retain an 'unscientific hope' that things one day 'could be otherwise, in what Horkheimer calls a "future society."[53]

In "The Latest Attack on Metaphysics," Horkheimer wrote that "[w]hile it is true that metaphysics is wrong to feed mankind on hopes…it is also true that science becomes naively metaphysical when it takes itself to be *the* knowledge…."[54] He rejects any metaphysic which presents itself as an alternative to scientific knowledge, although his harshest critique is directed not against metaphysics per se—however understood—but rather against the false certainty of "allegedly indubitable ideas"[55] characteristic of some metaphysical theories. Yet the concept of truth remains crucial for Horkheimer. The concluding exhortation to Horkheimer's inaugural Frankfurt *Institut* lecture reads: "May the guiding impulse of this Institute be the unchangeable will to unflinchingly serve the truth."[56] Much of his critique presumes the 'truth' of critical theory, over against the manipulation of fascism, *et. al.*[57]

In an early entry from the 1930s on 'Metaphysics' in *Dawn and Decline*, Horkheimer again criticizes the abstraction of some metaphysics, noting acerbically that some metaphysicians overlook the mundane realities of class struggle and suffering in their postulations. Yet he does not attack metaphysics directly:[58]

> The number of things people mean by the term metaphysics is truly enormous. It is difficult to come up with a formulation which will appeal to all learned gentlemen and their views about ultimate things….

---

[53] *CT* see e.g. 198, 233, 240, 241.

[54] *CT*, 182-3; italics in original. "Aber wenn die Metaphysik auch im Unrecht ist, die Menschen durch ein Sein zu vertrösten, das mit den Mitteln der Wissenschaft grundsätzlich nicht festzustellen ist, so wird doch die Wissenschaft selbst naiv metaphysisch, wo sie sich mit Erkenntnis und Theorie überhaupt verwechselt und sogar den Namen der Philosophie, das heißt jeder ihr gegenüber kritischen Instanz, diskreditieren möchte." *KT* II, 132.

[55] *CT*, 132. "Der neueste Angriff auf die Metaphysik," in *KT* II, 82.

[56] "The State of Contemporary Social Philosophy and the Tasks of an Institute for Social Research," by Max Horkheimer, trans. Peter Wagner, in *Critical Theory and Society: A Reader*, 36.

[57] "Horkheimer's analysis of the dangers of fascism and his characterization of the struggle against it are permeated with eschatological language. The conflict between the 'truth' which Critical Theory reveals and authoritarianism in all its contemporary manifestations is a total and un-compromising one." Shaw, 166.

[58] Gunzelin Schmid Noerr, one of the editors of Horkheimer's *Gesammelte Schriften*, suggests that the early work of Horkheimer on metaphysics "does not so much deny the truth content of metaphysics but rather reveals its social function." Gunzelin Schmid Noerr, "Nachwort des Herausgebers," in *GS* 2, 462.

> And yet it seems to me that there is some sense in which metaphysics means insight into the true nature of things.... I don't know to what extent metaphysicians are right.... But I do know that ordinarily metaphysicians are not terribly impressed by what torments men.[59]

Recki claims that Horkheimer's initial "condemnation of metaphysics is motivated by an explicitly *historical consciousness* of the problems of *social* experience."[60] While Horkheimer may be seen to condemn metaphysics, he cannot reject it, as noted above: "it seems to me that there is some sense in which metaphysics means insight into the true nature of things." While Tillich would likely phrase it differently, there is no clear basis to suspect Tillich would fundamentally disagree with Horkheimer's assertion, as he too seeks to challenge some types as well. Metaphysics is important for discussing 'ultimate things,' as Horkheimer emphasizes, and without an acute awareness of injustice manifest in quotidian struggles and class relationships, Tillich's critique of such metaphysics would have been equally, if not more, harsh[61] than that of Horkheimer.

In an essay from 1935, Horkheimer writes more pointedly: "While solidarity with struggling, suffering human beings obviously tends to make one apathetic toward metaphysical assurances, a particular notion appears to reside in the passionate effort not merely to seek meaning in the world, but to contend that such a thing exists."[62] With this statement, Tillich could not possibly have agreed. Many traditional Lutheran theologians tended to withdraw from the world, and some of Tillich's colleagues could easily be accused of focusing on metaphysical assurances rather than solidarity with the suffering. The same cannot be said of Tillich, not even in his relative withdrawal from social and political action upon reaching the United States. Horkheimer's quip, by contrast, presumes a disjoint between action and reflection which is almost ironic given his distance from praxis and reliance upon theory.

---

[59] DD, 45-6. *Dämmerung*, 85-6.

[60] Recki, 110; emphasis in original. Something similar could be claimed for Adorno as well, particularly in light of his 1932 essay "The Idea of Natural History," seen in the tension between the historical and the metaphysical.

[61] A contemporaneous reflection from Benjamin is relevant here: only the divine enables humans to speak of justice. Walter Benjamin, *Zur Kritik der Gewalt und andere Aufsätze* (Frankfurt a.M.: Suhrkamp Verlag, 1971) 57.

[62] BPSS, 160. "Während die Solidarität mit den kämpfenden und leidenden Menschen offenbar dazu tendiert, die Person gleichgültig gegen metaphysische Sicherung zu machen, scheint dem leidenschaftlichen Bemühen, einen Sinn der Welt nicht bloß zu suchen, sondern zu behaupten...." *KT* I, 211.

In "Materialismus und Metaphysik" (1933), Horkheimer writes:

> Insofar as the metaphysical schools conceive of the unconditional not as being but as law-giving, as activity, or even as the quintessence of free acts, they also exact respect for the meaning of those acts, an adaptation of empirical human life [*Menschenlebens*] to the intelligible ground of personality [*intelligiblen Grund der Persönlichkeit*] to which philosophy penetrates. However, the underlying reality is regarded as normative not merely where the religious origins of the dependence relationship are still preserved in the form of the precept, but also in all cases where the accord between individual existence [*eines Daseins*] and its ground as discovered by metaphysics is regarded as valuable. For them, too, the being to which metaphysics gives 'the emphatic name of an actual existence' contains the rule for beings who dispose over themselves. The materialistic thesis excludes such inferences by its very nature. The principle it designates as actuality is not suited to provide norms. The material world is, in itself, senseless; no maxims for the shaping of life follow from its qualities [neither in the sense of a requirement [*eines Gebotes*] nor of a pattern.][63]

In contrast to (one type of) metaphysics, Horkheimer here claims his own 'materialistic thesis' is without norms, and that no maxims can be derived therefrom. While metaphysics seeks to draw rules for ethical action and provide meaning to life, materialism rejects any ultimate, accessible meaning or significance. It is interesting to note in passing that Horkheimer's phrase *den intelligiblen Grund der Persönlichkeit* carries potential echoes of Tillich's conception of God as *Grund*. Similarly, his use of *Dasein*, even in this early essay, should not be overlooked in light of the findings of the previous chapter.

It is justice—or the absence thereof—which is the guiding normative orienting principle of critical theory in the earliest formulations. In "Traditional and Critical Theory" (1937), Horkheimer writes:

> There are no general criteria for judging the critical theory as a whole, for it is always based on the recurrence of events and thus on a self-reproducing totality.... For all its insight into the individual steps in so-

---

[63] "Materialismus und Metaphysik," in *ZfS* 2 (1933) 8-9. This is John McCole's translation in "Dialectical Positivism of Happiness," in *On Max Horkheimer,* 76, which includes the three concluding sentences omitted from the slightly less-nuanced O'Connell translation in *Critical Theory.* The final clause, in brackets, is the author's translation, as it does not appear in either English translation.

> cial change…the critical theory has no specific influence on its side, except for concern for the abolition of social injustice.[64]

The pursuit of justice is the only norm Horkheimer will acknowledge for materialism and critical theory. In his "Postscript" to the essay collection of the same name, Horkheimer makes the further normative claim that "theory never aims simply at an increase of knowledge as such. Its goal is man's emancipation from slavery."[65] It is important to note that Horkheimer's consistent goal for social philosophy was neither mere description nor even critique in itself; he rather sought *transformation through critique*,[66] although he was reticent to acknowledge the sources and norms necessary for such transformation. Challenging this, Recki claims that Horkheimer's "failure to perceive that the principled conceptual grounding which is equally indispensable for a critical theory is itself metaphysical in character probably derives in the last analysis from his fixation with one specific form of metaphysical thought."[67] While he is slightly more nuanced than Recki claims, she is correct that Horkheimer's perception of the purview of metaphysics was overly narrow, often responding more to the reified forms of historical bourgeois metaphysics at the expense of claiming his own *a priori* presuppositions and normative assumptions.

The struggle against injustice, along with the insistence on the possibility of transcending, is rooted in Horkheimer's normative concern for the preservation of alterity, and in his refusal to allow the voices of the suffering and dead to pass from memory. In this normative focus on the critique and ultimate hope to overcome injustice, Horkheimer's longing for transcending stands at the center. The transcendence which remains his constant hope, over and against instru-

---

[64] *CT*, 242. The German original reads: "Allgemeine Kriterien für die kritische Theorie als Ganzes gibt es nicht; denn sie beruhen immer auf der Wiederholung von Ereignissen und somit auf einer sich selbst reproduzierenden Totalität.... Die kritische Theorie hat bei aller Einsichtigkeit der einzelnen Schritte und der Übereinstimmung ihrer Elemente mit den fortgeschrittenensten traditionellen Theorie keine spezifische Instanz für sich als dass mit ihr selbst verknüpfte Interesse an der Aufhebung des gesellschaftlichen Unrechts." *KT* II, 190.

[65] *CT*, 246. "…zielt sie nirgends bloß auf Vermehrung des Wissens als solchen ab, sondern auf die Emanzipation des Menschen aus versklavenden Verhältnissen." *KT* II, 194.

[66] Douglas Kellner writes: "Critical Theory is thus motivated by a dual interest in a rational society and the liberation of the individual from bondage to a system of exploitation and domination." Kellner, 49.

[67] Recki, 114.

mental rationality and a 'fully administered world,' makes Horkheimer's thought "fundamentally eschatological,"[68] according to Shaw. While it is not eschatological in a traditional Judeo-Christian theological framework, it echoes deeply the basic Judeo-Christian longing for transcendence, justice, and the hope for a messianic moment.

II.2 Adorno's Early Engagement with Metaphysics

Both Adorno's dissertation on Husserl and his rejected *Habilitation* deal with metaphysical issues, and to an extent, two of his important early essays, "The Actuality of Philosophy" and "The Idea of Natural History," both address metaphysical and ontological issues. After these writings from the early 1930s, Adorno largely avoids explicit engagement with metaphysics until the late 1950s. Noted above in his implicit response to the Vienna School, Adorno's inaugural lecture in 1931 insists upon the priority of autonomous philosophy. Unlike Horkheimer, whose materialist and interdisciplinary social scientific work in the early 1930s sought to articulate a unified system of science that included philosophy, Adorno early on "discerned a dialectical process *within philosophy itself*."[69] Only after his interaction and debate with Neurath in several essays in 1937 did Horkheimer clearly articulate the need for a distinctive field of philosophy, independent of the sciences. Adorno had recognized this need at least five years earlier, and he insisted that certain ethical questions occluded the central philosophical question of truth.[70] Adorno's consistent reliance upon critical philosophy sheds light on his own meta-theoretical commitments.

Although Adorno expressed an early appreciation for the Vienna School, he was concerned that positivist philosophy would retain only a regulatory function, unable or unwilling to bring the conclusions of the natural and social sciences under the unique critical eye of philosophy. In short, Adorno became concerned that positivist philosophy was abnegating its responsibility and retreating

[68] Shaw, 162. Shaw continues: "The constant intent in his writing is not to reform the world but to abolish it altogether. Worse yet, Horkheimer is a 'tragic' eschatologist. He can neither master his chiliastic impulses to remake the world, nor can he hide from himself the ultimate futility of such an enterprise."

[69] Benjamin Snow, "Introduction to Adorno's Actuality of Philosophy," in *Telos* (1977) 114.

[70] Snow argues that for Adorno, "not issues of right or wrong, but judgments of true or false were the necessary ground for the validation of theory. In an era when metaphysics had lost all validity, Adorno kept asking the metaphysical question…." Snow, "Introduction to Adorno's Actuality of Philosophy," 117

to social scientific observation. His understanding of philosophy, by contrast, can draw from and add to the observations of science, but it is not limited by science; most importantly, he argues for the necessity of interpreting the findings of science. While scientific inquiry can contribute to philosophy, Adorno suggests that science aims at "indestructible and static" facts while philosophy "perceives the first finding which it lights upon as a sign that needs unriddling."[71] Philosophy is faced with the paradox of the claim of truth balanced by an awareness that "nothing more is given to it than fleeting, disappearing traces [*als flüchtige, verschwindende Hinweise*];" philosophy, unlike science, "must always begin anew."[72] Adorno summarizes: "the idea of science [*Wissenschaft*] is research; that of philosophy is interpretation."[73]

Philosophy seeks to weave an interpretive, though always provisional, narrative of truth, as it interacts with scientific research. Adorno writes: "Philosophy has to bring its elements, which it received from the sciences, into changing constellations...into changing trial combinations, until they fall into a figure which can be read as an answer, while at the same time the question disappears."[74] Constellations are not to be confused with philosophical solutions; Adorno emphasizes that the goal is *dissolution*, rather than merely solving apparent problems or contradictions. Constructive interpretation of philosophy requires a certain degree of "manipulation of conceptual material," according to Adorno. Through the 'manipulation' of 'changing constellations,' the philosopher seeks to produce 'historical images' (*geschichtlichen Bilder*) which "do not

---

[71] AP, 126. "Die Differenz liegt vielmehr zentral darin: dass die Einzelwissenschaft ihre Befunde, jedenfalls ihre letzten und tiefsten Befunde als unauflöslich und in sich ruhend hinnimmt, während Philosophie den ersten Befund bereits, der ihr begegnet, als Zeichen auffasst, das zu enträtseln ihr obliegt." *GS* 1, 334.

[72] AP, 126. "Dabei bleibt das große, vielleicht das immerwährende Paradoxen: dass Philosophie stets und stets und mit dem Anspruch auf Wahrheit deutend verfahren muss, ohne jemals einen gewissen Schlüssel der Deutung zu besitzen; dass ihr mehr nicht gegeben sind als flüchtige, verschwindende Hinweise in den Rätselfiguren des Seienden und ihren wunderlichen Verschlingungen." *GS* 1, 334. Adorno overstates here; science, including that of the Vienna School, was and is provisional and always open to reconfirmation.

[73] AP, 126. "Die Idee der Wissenschaft ist Forschung, die der Philosophie Deutung." *GS* 1, 334.

[74] AP, 127. "...so hat Philosophie ihre Elemente, die sie von den Wissenschaften empfängt, so lange in wechselnde Konstellationen...in wechselnde Versuchsanordnungen zu bringen, bis sie zur Figur geraten, die als Antwort lesbar wird, während zugleich die Frage verschwindet." *GS* 1, 335.

constitute the meaning of being [*Dasein*] but dissolve and resolve its questions [and] are not simply given."[75] Such 'historical images' must "be produced by human beings and are legitimated in the last analysis alone by the fact that reality crystallizes about them in striking conclusiveness [*Evidenz der Wirklichkeit um sie zusammenschießt*],"[76] according to Adorno.

The most constructive relationship between philosophy and science involves an "exact form of imagination [*Eine exakte Phantasie*]."[77] Such imaginativeness remains strictly within the material science that offers it, but it transcends the sciences, even in the minutest aspects of its arrangement—aspects, admittedly, which necessarily originate in it. This conception of philosophical interpretation can be expressed as a demand to continually take account of questions arising from the reality which presents itself. One does so by applying a form of imagination which rearranges the elements of the question, but does not go beyond the range of those elements. The efficacy of this form of imagination can be measured by the disappearance of the question.[78] The constructive capacity of imagination described here reflects the task of philosophy for the early Adorno.

Having written his second *Habilitation* on Kierkegaard under a philosopher of religion, Paul Tillich, it is not surprising to find metaphysical themes in that work as well. Taking Recki's definition of metaphysics as a starting point, one can identify an early emphasis on metaphysical transcendence concerning what Adorno would later call identity thinking, along with a glimmer of utopian hope in his *Habilitation* on Kierkegaard. At the conclusion of the book on Kierkegaard, Adorno writes: "Longing is not extinguished in [images of beauty], but survives in them just as it emanates from them. By the strength of the imma-

---

[75] AP, 131. "Bei der Handhabung des Begriffsmaterials durch Philosophie rede ich nicht ohne Absicht von Gruppierung und Versuchsanordnung, von Konstellation und Konstruktion. Denn die geschichtlichen Bilder, die nicht den Sinn des Daseins ausmachen, aber dessen Fragen lösen und auflösen—diese Bilder sind keine bloßen Selbstgegebenheiten." *GS* 1, 341.

[76] AP, 131. "Vielmehr: [die geschichtlichen Bilder] müssen vom Menschen hergestellt werden und legitimieren sich schließlich allein dadurch, dass in schlagender Evidenz die Wirklichkeit um sie zusammenschießt." *GS* 1, 341.

[77] AP, 131; *GS* 1, 341. Here and in what immediately follows, I use Michael Robertson's translation of Wiggershaus—'imagination'—rather than Hullot-Kentor's 'fantasy.' Imagination arguably better reflects Adorno's *ars inveniendi (art of invention)* than does fantasy. See Wiggershaus, 94.

[78] *GS* 1, 342.

nence of their content, the transcendence of longing is achieved."[79] If utopia is the object of longing, it is an eschatological longing, a longing for a more just world which is not yet but which stands in contradiction to the present world for the early Adorno.[80]

In his 1932 lecture to the Kant Society in Frankfurt, "The Idea of Natural History," Adorno raises further interesting and implicitly normative questions.[81] Here Adorno critically engages Heidegger, freely using terms like "ontological situation"[82] and "ontological dignity."[83] He claims at the outset "the question of ontology, as it is formulated at present, is none other than what I mean by 'nature.'"[84] 'Natural history,' for Adorno, drawing upon Benjamin, seeks to collapse the apparent distinction between nature and history.[85] Here, his point is that nature is never purely 'natural'—it always contains historical traces. Therefore, ontology is never purely about being—it too always contains historical and social traces. Adorno's problem with neo-ontology, as later on, is that it often uncritically affirms being as a given, while ignoring social structures and historical con-

---

[79] Adorno, *Kierkegaard*, 140. "Sehnsucht endet nicht in den Bildern, sondern lebt fort in ihnen, wie sie aus ihnen kommt. Kraft der Immanenz ihres Gehalts vollzieht sich die Transzendenz der Sehnsucht." *GS* II, 199.

[80] In this vein, Guiseppe Tassone writes: "Metaphysical transcendence is, for Adorno, an epistemological necessity.... [The early] Adorno invokes theology to maintain the dialectical possibility of redemption in a world in which living processes have been reduced to dead things." Guiseppe Tassone, "The Politics of Metaphysics: Adorno and Bloch on Utopia and Immortality," in *European Legacy* (2004) 358.

[81] This lecture repeatedly references "the problems of the so-called Frankfurt discussion." AP, 111. According to Wiggershaus, the 'Frankfurt Discussion' was part of the Circle (*Kränzchen*) which included Adorno, Horkheimer, Tillich, and others. In particular, Kurt Riezler had defended Heidegger in one of the Circle's meetings, sparking the 'Frankfurt Discussion,' to which Adorno contributed through his lecture "The Idea of Natural History." Wiggershaus, 95.

[82] "The Idea of Natural History," by Theodor W. Adorno, trans. by Bob Hullot-Kentor, in *Telos* 60 (1984) 112. "Zunächst die Frage nach der gegenwärtigen ontologischen Situation." *GS* 1, 346.

[83] INH, 117.

[84] INH, 111-2. "Denn die Frage nach der Ontologie, wie sie heute gestellt wird, ist nichts anderes als das, was ich unter Natur gemeint habe." *GS* I, 346.

[85] Translator Robert Hullot-Kentor, in his introduction to Adorno's essay, writes: "Adorno wants to transform neo-ontology's mythically reconciling formulation of the interwovenness of nature and history into a dialectic in which their mutual and antagonistic conflict will collide and collapse." Robert Hullot-Kentor, *Things Beyond Resemblance: Collected Essays on Theodor W. Adorno* (New York: Columbia University Press, 2006) 237.

text. Neo-ontology's reliance upon autonomous reason reveals its idealism in two ways for Adorno: the attempt to grasp the whole and the "emphasis on possibility in contrast to reality."[86] One cannot examine being in its totality, as ontology seeks to do, but rather starting from particularity, philosophy aims at fleeting glimpses of the whole. In much the same way that Adorno argued for the necessity of imaginative interpretation in his inaugural lecture, in his 1932 lecture, he argues that interpretation requires the experience of 'shock,' and involves not merely synthesis, but a "change of perspective."[87] Following "The Idea of Natural History," however, as Adorno distanced himself even further from an early fascination with Heideggerian ontology, such themes receded as Adorno turned his energies to musicology for much of the next decade.[88]

Metaphysics is not a positive science for Adorno, but a (necessary) negative moment in the imagination of how things could otherwise be in a non-instrumental and non-reified society. This negative moment in the utopian quest for 'things as they otherwise could be' retains significant metaphysical valences,[89] and even though he does not explicitly acknowledge the necessity of metaphysics, even as a negative moment, Adorno's critique presumes it. The argument for 'imaginative interpretation,' 'shock,' and a 'change of perspective' in the early lectures reflects this implicit metaphysical need to go beyond the 'normal' limits of both the sciences and philosophy. Indeed, Adorno's second critique of neo-ontology—an "emphasis on possibility in contrast to reality"—could perhaps be applied to his own thought, betraying a similar idealist impulse. Adorno criticizes ontology and metaphysics for being insufficiently radical in their attempts to address and critique the structures of domination inherent in

---

[86] INH, 115-6. "Dies scheint mir für die Möglichkeit von Idealismus bei irrationalistischen Inhalten zu zeugen. Das andere Moment ist das Moment der Betonung der *Möglichkeit* gegenüber der Wirklichkeit. Es ist so, dass im Rahmen der neu-ontologischen Fragestellung ja selbst dies Problem des Verhältnisses von Möglichkeit und Wirklichkeit als die größte Schwierigkeit empfunden wird." *GS* 1, 353.

[87] INH, 118. "Naturgeschichte ist nicht eine Synthese natürlicher und geschichtlicher Methoden, sondern eine Perspektivenänderung." *GS* 1, 356.

[88] Adorno's second study of Husserl, completed as an 'Advanced Student' at Oxford in the mid-1930s is an exception. Although *Dialectic of Enlightenment* is not focused on metaphysics *per se*, it is inundated with normative assumptions.

[89] Recki insightfully points out that for Adorno, the "ultimately metaphysical character of critical theory itself finally emerges completely from the two-fold struggle to grasp society as a *whole* by reference to its own mediation of everything particular and individual, and to describe this whole from the visionary perspective of something *wholly other*." Recki, 120.

the status quo, always with a vision toward an emancipatory dissolution of such contradictions.

Horkheimer and Adorno often seem to reject both metaphysical foundations and religion as forms of 'magic,' and an attempt to 're-enchant' the world, as they argue in *Dialectic of Enlightenment.* Yet both operate with an implicit metaphysic grounding their critique. Some scholars like Papastephanou identify key ontological assumptions underlying Adorno and Horkheimer's critique of enlightenment, particularly in their joint work.[90] Papastephanou says of *Dialectic of Enlightenment*, "A blanket critique of reason based on ontological grounds can only promote the undemanded gestural vacuity of a mystical 'beyond.'"[91] The implicit metaphysic, or series of normative assumptions grounding the critique in *Dialectic of Enlightenment,* continues and even increases as the critique becomes more sustained and the outlook increasingly pessimistic. For example, Adorno and Horkheimer use terms like 'transcendence' and '*Unheilige*' as critical concepts, ostensibly voided of their religious pedigree.

In what is perhaps the central thesis of *Dialectic of Enlightenment*, following Weber's dialectic of disenchantment and reenchantment,[92] there lies a vital foundational and normative claim: *whatever seeks to uncover and expose myth, becomes itself a myth.* Adorno and Horkheimer in fact explicitly define this dynamic, with the example of metaphysics, at the heart of the 'philosophical fragments' compiled as *Dialectic of Enlightenment.* They write in the 1944 Preface:

> That the hygienic factory and everything pertaining to it, Volkswagen and the sports palace, are obtusely liquidating metaphysics does not matter in itself, but that these things are themselves becoming metaphysics, an ideological curtain, within the social whole, behind which

[90] See Papastephanou, 48ff.

[91] Papastephanou, 50. "Apart from being privatistic or elitist, appeals to an abstract 'ineffable' are also politically inoperative. Such is the major implication of the paradox of reason" in Horkheimer and Adorno. This critique is even more interesting when applied to Tillich, though that is beyond the scope here.

[92] Although Weber does not argue on behalf of such re-enchantment, his diagnosis of disenchantment suggests ways in which people have coped with disenchantment, by returning to myth and magic at the most superficial level. Weber's analysis would seem to imply that a consequence of disenchantment is a potential turn to new forms of social meaning. Secondary scholarship on Weber has taken re-enchantment seriously. See, e.g. "Weber, Re-Enchantment and Social Futures," by Raymond L. M. Lee, in *Time and Society* 19 (July 2010) 180-192, and Nicholas Gane, *Max Weber and Postmodern Theory: Rationalization Versus Re-Enchantment* (New York: Palgrave, 2002).

> real doom is gathering, does matter. This is the basic premise of our fragments.[93]

It is not metaphysics *per se*—or the absence of certain types of metaphysics—that is the problem for Adorno and Horkheimer; rather, it is the propensity of certain things which displace metaphysics to assume that structural space in society, effectively creating a new metaphysic, that disturbs Adorno and Horkheimer.

Although it stands slightly beyond of the period on which this study focuses, brief mention of Adorno's *Minima Moralia* (published in 1951) is fruitful. In line with Horkheimer's early position, Adorno praises Nietzsche, who, he claims, "voiced the strongest argument not merely against theology but against metaphysics, that hope is mistaken for truth; that the impossibility of living happily, or even living at all, without the thought of an absolute, does not vouch for the legitimacy of that thought."[94] Perhaps Adorno believed that in many instances metaphysical hope was mistaken for truth, but he himself could not operate philosophically without a similar, tacit hope. Recki notes that "Adorno's theory is based from the first, despite his own explicit self-understanding, on metaphysical speculations of considerable complexity."[95] The implicit metaphysic operative in Adorno's work not only preserves space for transcendence of the given and serves as a place holder for a type of utopian hope that things could be otherwise; it also importantly serves an ethical function. J. M. Bernstein summarizes the ethical valences of Adorno here well:

> If there is a recuperative moment in Adorno's otherwise negative philosophy it is to be located in the insistence upon the question of the possibility of metaphysical experience: only as a temporal experience is metaphysics possible, and only as metaphysics, as what transcends existence now, is experience possible. Because in thinking metaphysical experience Adorno is thinking what would answer the problem of nihilism, then metaphysical experience inscribes the space of the ethical.[96]

Bernstein is correct in his assessment that Adorno, much like Horkheimer, operates with an implicit and largely negative metaphysic and deep apprehension

---

[93] DE, xviii. *DA,* 5.

[94] *Minima Moralia,* 97. *GS* 4, 109.

[95] Recki, 125.

[96] J. M. Bernstein, *Adorno: Disenchantment and Ethics* (New York: Cambridge University Press, 2001) 426.

about normative bases and presuppositions, even in his early critical theory. This should not be seen as a weakness in Adorno's thought, however. While overtly decrying metaphysics, Adorno valiantly sought to limit the effects of relativism and nihilism by reinserting imagination and shock into the heart of critical theory and the philosophical enterprise in general. Although he rejects the speculative basis of traditional metaphysics as naïve, Adorno's critique of metaphysics actually creates space for ethical action oriented toward a hypothetical moment of transcendence. Bernstein's insight that metaphysical experience preserves space for the ethical—and resists the nihilistic impulse beyond universal metaphysical assumptions—merits further consideration.

Beyond this brief early engagement with metaphysics, the theme is almost completely absent from Adorno's work within the period on which this study focuses. He only directly lectured on metaphysics in 1965, with the exception of his analysis of Kant's *Critique of Pure Reason* in 1959. Later, Adorno would offer a trenchant critique of Heidegger's ontology and metaphysics in *Negative Dialectics* (1966), yet he did so in part to preserve metaphysical experience. He would famously claim in *Negative Dialectics* that his own mode of thought was in "solidarity with metaphysics in the moment of its downfall."[97] Although it was written well after the period on which this study focuses, Adorno's 1966 *Negative Dialectics* offers an interesting insight into critical theory's broader interaction with metaphysics. In this late text, Adorno speaks of 'emphatic concepts' such as freedom—and by extension concepts like humanity, justice, transcendence, truth, and reconciliation—which are both descriptive and prescriptive insofar as they go beyond what can be definitively said and known from the concept itself.[98] Critical theory of necessity makes such (metaphysical) postulations of things as they 'otherwise could be' in full knowledge that such things do not (yet) exist. The presumption of such critically nebulous 'emphatic concepts' is intended to preserve conceptual space for non-identity and transcendence in the midst of 'damaged life.'

---

[97] *Negative Dialectics*, 408. "Solches Denken ist solidarisch mit Metaphysik im Augenblick ihres Sturzes." *GS* 6, 400.

[98] "Emphatically conceived, the judgment that a man is free refers to the concept of freedom; but this concept in turn is more than is predicated of the man, and by other definitions the man is more than the concept of his freedom. The concept says not only that it is applicable to all individuals defined as free; it feeds on the idea of a condition in which individuals would have qualities not to be ascribed to anyone here and now." *Negative Dialectics*, 150. *GS* 6, 153-4.

II.3 Tillich and Theonomy

As has been demonstrated, when focused on the human person and persons in society, and thus the formal determination of the good, Adorno, Horkheimer, and Tillich share a common diagnosis of social problems, as well as a common set of goals, and similar overarching prescriptions for change. Yet in terms of the material determination of the good, and the specifics of their respective social prescriptions, Adorno and Horkheimer advocate autonomy in a decidedly secular social critique, while Tillich advocates theonomy in the guise of religious socialism. Theonomy is a central feature of rational inquiry into the structure of 'being' for the individual and society in Tillich's thought, and it is thus one of his primary metaphysical orientations and ideals.[99] His early theonomous metaphysic[100] reflects an attempt to see the unconditioned ground of all being through the lens of the finite. Yet this can only be grasped by the faith of 'belief-ful realism,' and only expressed as symbol.

Well aware of most modern critiques of metaphysics, Tillich expressed his dissatisfaction with the term and with many of its modern associations and implications.[101] He understood 'God' through the *intuitive* experience of that which is 'unconditional.' Tillich writes that religion is "more than a system of special symbols, rites, and emotions, directed toward a highest being; religion is ultimate concern; it is the state of being grasped by something unconditional, holy, absolute."[102] God is the 'ground of being' and the ultimate referent of humanity's ultimate concern.[103] Tillich rejects any theology or metaphysics which

---

[99] Theonomy for Tillich also relates to culture. In a theonomous situation, "the arts play much greater role than in a scientific or technical age." *Protestant Era*, 44. Tillich's conception of theonomous culture would appear to be profoundly at odds with Adorno's characterization of the commodification inherent in the culture industry.

[100] Tillich's early *Das System der Wissenschaften nach Gegenständen und Methoden* defined theology as 'theonomous metaphysics.' Tillich came to regard this as a "first and rather insufficient step toward what I now call the 'method of correlation.'" Author's Introduction to *Protestant Era*, xxvi.

[101] In modern philosophy, Tillich agreed that metaphysics "in spite of the testimony of all textbooks and lectures on philosophy that it means the book after the physics in the collection of Aristotelian writings, has [come to mean] something beyond human experience, open to arbitrary imagination.... It is time to dismiss this abused and distorted word 'metaphysics,' the negation of which has become an excuse for a terrific shallowness of thought...." *Protestant Era*, 86.

[102] *Protestant Era*, 59.

[103] God is the "Ground of Being...who is the a priori of all thinking...and emerges theonomously from the depths, both to sustain and shatter (break-through) individual

"speaks of God as a being beside others, subject to the structure of being…the highest being but not being itself."[104] As such, he is not quite a metaphysical foundationalist, since God is understood not as *a* being, but rather as *the ground of* being. Instead, he operates with what Reimer has described as an "ontological foundationalism premised on a very distinct understanding of the Unconditioned as the a priori of all that is conditioned."[105] Thus, metaphysics and ontology are functionally synonymous and inextricably interwoven for Tillich. It is worth noting that in his own critique of traditional metaphysics, Tillich seeks to articulate a transcendence that goes beyond traditional theism. Similarly, I argue that Horkheimer and Adorno seek to retain a type of transcendence that is also distinct from traditional theism. Nevertheless, any such transcendence for Horkheimer or Adorno must be grounded within human history and accessible through human agency.

Although Tillich expresses concerns similar to many of Adorno and Horkheimer's critiques of the instrumental rationality characteristic of modernity, he asserts that reason and critique can—and indeed must—be grounded in a metaphysical or religious presupposition;[106] his ideal is 'theonomous' reason. Theonomy is a mediating position between autonomy, on the one hand, and heteronomy, or, between the potential extremes of an isolating individualism and a collective mentality that can play into Fascist manipulation. Theonomy recognizes that personal identity is rooted in God, and identity is thus united with the 'Unconditioned' as the 'ground of its being.'

Theonomy is not the simple acceptance of a divine law, as its name might suggest; it rather reunites reason with its ultimate ground.[107] Autonomy "means obedience to reason, i.e., to the 'logos; immanent in reality and mind,"[108] and it can be seen particularly clearly in ancient Greece and the Enlightenment, where

and corporate existence." A. James Reimer, *Paul Tillich: Theologian of Nature, Culture and Politics* (Münster: LIT Verlag, 2004) 175.

[104] "Philosophy and Theology," in *Protestant Era*, 89.

[105] Reimer, 181.

[106] As such, religious self-interpretation "is a turning toward reality, a penetrating into existence, a driving to the level where the world points beyond itself to its ground and ultimate meaning." *Protestant Era*, 217.

[107] Describing a theonomous age in rather ideal terms, Tillich writes: "We shall call such a situation 'theonomous,' not in the sense that in it God lays down the laws but in the sense that such an age, in all its forms, is open to and directed toward the divine." "Kairos," in *Protestant Era*, 44. *GW* 6, 21.

[108] "Kairos," in *Protestant Era*, 44. *GW* 6, 21.

it prevailed, at least temporarily, in its struggle with theonomy. This is not to suggest any rigid antagonism, and Tillich insists that autonomy "is not necessarily a turning-away from the unconditional."[109] Theonomy functions as the mediation between and unity of autonomy and heteronomy, the imposition of "an alien law, religious or secular, on man's mind."[110] While heteronomy resists autonomy, seeking to "suppress it and its freedom of creativity,"[111] theonomy does not. Tillich argues that theonomy "is the answer to the question implied in autonomy, the question concerning a religious substance and an ultimate meaning of life and culture."[112] At stake in the distinction between theonomy and autonomy is the question of orientation: the theonomous is directed toward the unconditional while the autonomous is directed toward the finite.[113]

Tillich understands theonomy to be grounded in 'the Unconditioned' (God), yet intimately personal insofar as in theonomy, reason is united with its depth in the unconditioned. It is thus not fully 'other'—external to or imposed on the individual, given Tillich's unyielding insistence on the necessity of moral decision.[114] In essence, theonomy is the ideal against which Tillich evaluates modernity, instrumental reason, capitalism, and the bourgeois spirit.[115] Theonomy is the goal of religious socialism,[116] and it is manifest in the Protestant Principle, although it is neither limited to nor by Protestantism or Christianity more generally. Central to his work following World War I, theonomy is linked to his

[109] "Kairos," in *Protestant Era*, 45. *GW* 6, 22.

[110] "Kairos," in *Protestant Era*, 46. "Die Heteronomie unterwirft den menschlichen Geist einem fremden Gesetz, sei es religiös oder profan." *GW* 6, 23.

[111] "Kairos," in *Protestant Era*, 46. Es ist nicht "den Versuch, sie und ihre schöpferische Freiheit zu unterdrücken." *GW* 6, 23. Note that in this early essay, first published in 1922, Tillich uses the phrase "schöpferische Freiheit" which he rendered in English "finite freedom" in "Man and Society in Religious Socialism," much to the consternation of Adorno.

[112] "Kairos," in *Protestant Era*, 46. *GW* 6, 23.

[113] "Kairos," in *Protestant Era*, 45.

[114] This position is in contrast to other contemporaneous Protestant theologians like Karl Barth, who Tillich critiqued on a similar point in a 1935 essay on dialectical theology. Cf. James C. Livingston and Francis Schüssler Fiorenza, *Modern Christian Thought*, vol. 2 (Minneapolis: Fortress Press, 2006) 140.

[115] Marsden notes: "The portent of a new theonomous socialism where the empty and destructive features of bourgeois society were replaced by a more genuine and fulfilled human community clearly captivated" Tillich. John Marsden, "Paul Tillich and the Theology of German Religious Socialism," in *Political Theology* 10:1 (2009) 37.

[116] PE, 66.

notion of *Kairos*,[117] "an outstanding moment in the temporal process, a moment in which the eternal breaks into the temporal, shaking and transforming it...."[118] Theonomy is less prevalent in Tillich's Weimar writings, and it is notably absent from 1933's *The Socialist Decision*. The language of theonomy virtually disappears until Tillich's American period.

As the explicit language of theonomy wanes, it is taken up in *The Socialist Decision* by language of ethical actualization vis-à-vis the unconditional. Tillich writes: "This is human freedom, not that one has a so-called 'free will,' but that as a human being one is not bound to what one finds in existence, [but rather] that one is subject to a demand that something unconditionally new should be realized through oneself."[119] Such freedom is not a given and does not refer to the capacity or perception of choice, but rather the kind of freedom described here is simultaneously compelling and freeing; one is given an opportunity to actualize oneself ethically vis-à-vis the external demand for justice which arises from connection to the unconditional. What is important is not merely what humanity *is*, but what it *can be* and *can do*; what is crucial to Tillich, both existentially and ethically, is not so much essence but rather transformative possibility.

The demand of the 'whither' of existence breaks the cycle of bondage to myths of origin which characterize political romanticism and nationalism in particular; the question of 'whence' in fact orients all meaning-making schema.[120] Tillich's idea is that humanity is confronted by an external demand, an ethical decision, and in order to answer this demand, the finite and conditioned

[117] See especially Tillich's essay "*Kairos*" (1922) in *Protestant Era*, 44 ff.

[118] "Kairos," in *Protestant Era*, 45. "...'Kairos' [ist] ein herausgehobener Moment im zeitlichen Prozess, betrachtet werden, als ein Moment, in dem das Ewige in das Zeitliche einbricht, dieses erschüttert und umwendet und ein Krisis schafft im tiefstem Grunde der menschlichen Existenz." *GW* 6, 22.

[119] *SD*, 5. *GW* 2, 228.

[120] This is important in Tillich's *Socialist Decision*. "[H]uman beings not only find themselves in existence; they not only know themselves to be posited and withdrawn in the cycle of birth and death, like all living things. They experience a demand that frees them from being simply bound to what is given, and which compels them to add to the question 'Whence?' [*Woher*] the question 'Whither?' [*Wozu*]. With this question the cycle is broken in principle and human kind is elevated beyond the sphere of merely living things. For the demand calls for something that does not yet exist but should exist, should come to fulfillment. A being that experiences a demand is no longer simply bound to the origin.... Through the demand, humanity is directed to what ought to be." *SD*, 4. *GW* 2, 228.

subject must encounter the unconditional ground of being.[121] This ethical decision addresses the 'whither' of human existence, and its ground is something dynamic and unconditional. Here, it is sufficient to note that reason, when properly grounded (by bringing an awareness of the 'depth dimension,' of the ground of being, into all rational inquiry) in its metaphysical[122] origin, properly orients ethical action for Tillich.[123] Nevertheless, he recognized that actualizing even properly-grounded reason is by no means a given, and is not limited to or by any specific religious structure. Horkheimer and Adorno would challenge Tillich to explain how one could know that one's ultimate concern and ground of being was not, in fact, another myth.

III. The Challenge of 'Ultimacy': Identifying Norms of Critique

One of Horkheimer's early articulations of freedom in and through socialism in a 1930s entry from *Dawn and Decline* begins: "In socialism, freedom is to become a reality."[124] He notes the common misconception of the absence of freedom among the bourgeois, particularly those impressed by the 'laws' of capitalism which "fetishiz[e] the social process."[125] As was noted in the previous chapter on anthropology, true subjectivity leads to the genuine possibility of free agency. Under the conditions of modernity, Horkheimer believes that the precondition of authentic social change is undermining rigid notions of subjectivity. In order to change the status quo, one must realize that "the subject does not exist," according to Horkheimer. "Everything therefore depends on creating the free subject that consciously shapes social life. And this subject is nothing other than the rationally organized socialist society which regulates its own existence."[126] Such realization is held back in modern society by the claim of "religion and metaphysics that a [coherent] ground exists. In so doing, they try to keep

[121] "The profoundest demand of all is that we learn to speak of God in such a way that he appears not as an object above all other objects, nor as a mere symbol, but as the really real in everything that claims reality." *Protestant Era*, 217-8.

[122] Here, metaphysical and ontological are synonymous for Tillich.

[123] "*Protestant formative power is at work wherever reality is interpreted with respect to its ground and ultimate meaning.*" "Formative Power of Protestantism," in *Protestant Era*, 218; emphasis in original.

[124] DD, 50. *Dämmerung*, 97.

[125] DD, 50. *Dämmerung*, 98.

[126] DD, 51. *Dämmerung*, 99-100.

men from creating it through their own efforts."[127] Nevertheless, Horkheimer thinks that by employing "the Marxist categories of class, exploitation," etc., like-minded individuals can move beyond "preservation of contemporary society" through critique and using the Marxist categories and principles of critical theory, work toward "transformation into the right kind of society."[128] This is but one example of a norm guiding Horkheimer's social critique.

Justice is the central concept for Horkheimer, and the existence (or necessity) of a transcendent order or religion, as will be seen, is the conviction that the present order is fundamentally unjust. What is in danger of being lost with the idea of the transcendent is the crucial ideal of justice, which in any perfect form can only be guaranteed by a transcendent or metaphysical realm. This fatalism concerning the decline of religious transcendence is not regarded as reason's triumph, but rather as a portent of its doom. Horkheimer writes: "Religion is concerned with man's goals and destiny, science with truth alone. It is this division between the search for knowledge, on the one hand, and the evaluation of norms, on the other, which threatens to destroy all meaning."[129] This impasse, he suggests, is a symptom of something far more pernicious facing modern society.[130]

If one rejects the hypothesis of God (as the repository of the memory of suffering), on what basis can one ascribe meaning? Can one still hope for ultimate justice apart from a metaphysical system with a secure foundation? Horkheimer's answer seems to rest, in large part, on posited transcendence and a defiant rejection of the logic of immanence. It seems an unavoidable conclusion that some of Horkheimer's thought does ultimately rest on an unacknowledged normative principle of hope.[131] One central element of this normative hope is the

---

[127] DD, 51. *Dämmerung*, 100.

[128] *CT*, 218. "Die Marxschen Kategorien Klasse, Ausbedeutung...Zusammenbruch sind Momente eines begrifflichen Ganzen, dessen Sinn nicht in der Reproduktion der gegenwärtigen Gesellschaft, sondern in ihrer Veränderung zum Richtigen zu suchen ist." *KT* II, 167.

[129] Horkheimer, "Reason Against Itself: Some Remarks on Enlightenment," in *What is Enlightenment? Eighteenth Century Answers and Twentieth Century Questions*, ed. James Schmidt (Berkeley: University of California Press, 1996) 360. This essay was presented in English at the American Philosophical Association in Eugene, Oregon, on December 28, 1946.

[130] Recall the 'positivism debate' between Horkheimer and members of the Vienna School explored in the previous chapter.

[131] Eduardo Mendieta suggests: "What is significant...about [critical theory]...is precisely this attempt to rescue the Enlightenment, and with it reason, by means of a

consistent privileging of concepts like justice and freedom. A posited transcendence, without a transcendent foundation—"*transcending without any heavenly transcendence*"[132] as Ernst Bloch put it—is ultimately Horkheimer's (and arguably Adorno's) non-scientific, normative, and possibly even metaphysical hope.

Contra Horkheimer's one-dimensional characterization of metaphysicians above, Tillich argues that the religious grounding of metaphysics as the source and force behind social critique requires people to strive to create a better society with greater freedoms, and that this is at least potentially possible through Christian humanism and religious socialism. Tillich's early and enduring emphasis on culture as the vital theological lens seeks to challenge the presumed opposition between secular and sacred. In one of his earliest definitions of religion, offered in the 1919 lecture "On the Idea of a Theology of Culture," Tillich notes that religion pervades culture and is manifest as "directedness to the Unconditional."[133]

In his *Entwurf contra Paulum*, explored in detail in the previous chapter, Adorno criticizes and challenges Tillich's metaphysical assumptions, as seen in Tillich's 1943 essay "Man and Society in Religious Socialism." In that essay, Tillich proposed the thesis: "that without the acceptance of a religious foundation and the symbols expressing it no system of a planned society can escape a speedy self-destruction."[134] In the form of an extended letter, Adorno responds to Tillich's thesis: "The third article of faith [in Tillich's essay] is theoretically most precarious. Because the thesis...shows that precisely the direction which

---

refusal to grant immanence the last word." Mendieta, *The Frankfurt School and Religion,* 6.

[132] Ernst Bloch, *The Principle of Hope*, trans. Neville Plaice, et. al. (Cambridge: MIT Press, 1996) vol. 3, 1288; emphasis in original. "...*das Transzendieren ohne alle himmlische Transzendenz.....*" Ernst Bloch, *Gesamtausgabe* 5:2, 1522.

[133] Tillich, "On the Idea of a Theology of Culture," in *What is Religion?,* ed. James Luther Adams, 161. "Religion ist Erfahrung des Unbedingten und das heißt Erfahrung schlechthinniger Realität auf Grund der Erfahrung schlechthinniger Nichtigkeit...." MW/HW 2, 74. The editor of the *Main Works/Haupte Werke* notes that Tillich changed the phrase "Religion ist Erfahrung des Unbedingten," as it appears here, in the original 1919 version of the essay, to religion as "der Richtung auf das Unbedingte" in the 1921 revision of the same essay. Bloch, *The Principle of Hope*, 70. The shift from religion as an *experience of* the Unconditioned, to religion as *relatedness to* the Unconditioned is subtle.

[134] *MSRS*, 489.

pretends to deepen socialism is in truth decayed pragmatism."[135] Despite his personal knowledge of Tillich's thought and their lengthy friendship, Adorno understandably recoils from assertions of the *necessity* of metaphysical or religious foundations and symbols in 1943, particularly given the quasi-religious mythology and propagandistic symbology fueling the Nazi war maelstrom. Nevertheless, it is not immediately clear why Adorno understood Tillich's theoretical claim to be 'decayed pragmatism.' Within the context of the latter's writings, including the essay in question, his political affiliations at the time, his active work in the U.S. against the Nazi régime, it was certainly clear to Adorno that Tillich's theoretical claim dealt specifically with Judeo-Christian religious foundations and the system of symbols supporting such a foundation. It is reasonable to conclude that Adorno's concern was not with Tillich, but rather with how his remarks could be misused.

Characterizing Tillich's understanding of metaphysics (and implicitly ontology) as an insufficient and 'decayed pragmatism' which can only 'pretend' to advance socialism, Adorno hyperbolically cuts to the heart of the difference in perspectives and starting points of these two thinkers. He goes on to claim in the very next sentence, "Neither religion nor philosophy can be constituted by claiming that without it something would break."[136] It would seem that Adorno meant this as a direct critique of Tillich, but it is far from clear that Tillich would have disagreed with the claim, much less accepted it as a critique of his own ideas. That the letter was not sent, likely at the urging of Horkheimer, tells us nothing definitively, but suggests that Adorno's letter may have been composed rashly and possibly that it challenged Horkheimer's own views.

Tillich implicitly suggests that by claiming autonomy as the standard, thinkers like Adorno operate with a tacit, unacknowledged, and possibly mythological metaphysic, which, without a foundation in concepts like 'transcendence' and 'ultimacy,' finally has no critical backbone. He suggests that despite Adorno's profound awareness of the aesthetic realm as at least a subjective grounding, the normative hope of critical theory is vacuous. Tillich's review of Marcuse's *Reason and Revolution* in the *Institut's* journal in 1941 is incisive on this point: "Even a critical social theory cannot avoid an 'ultimate' in which its criticism is

---

[135] "Theoretisch am bedenklichsten ist der dritte Glaubensartikel.... [Das] zeigt, dass eben die Richtung, die den Sozialismus zu vertiefen prätendiert, in Wahrheit dem Pragmatismus verfallen ist." *Entwurf*, 280-1.

[136] "Weder eine Religion noch eine Philosophie lässt sich damit begründen, dass ohne sie etwas in die Brüche gehe." *Entwurf*, 281.

rooted because reason itself is rooted therein."[137] Without such a foundation, Tillich argues that "criticism itself becomes positivistic and contingent."[138] Gary Simpson understands Tillich's critique to refer to the 'reactionary' (what Tillich labels 'positivistic') nature of a weak foundation, which is "without convincing argument for the error and evil of a particular set of social and historical conditions."[139] Likewise, by 'contingent,' Simpson argues that "Tillich means a critical engagement dependent on mere happenstance and thus lacking an obligatory edge and an ontologically enduring impulse of staying power....Only an ultimate ground can empower critical revolutionaries beyond critical fatigue."[140] Although Tillich's 1941 comments were immediately directed as constructive criticism of Marcuse's book, the claim cuts to the heart of the challenge of articulating norms for a critical social theory. Adorno's early occlusion of metaphysics and Horkheimer's somewhat myopic and ambivalent views on metaphysics leave both with a significantly greater challenge in justifying both diagnoses and prognoses for society. In denying first principles, their challenge is persuading the reader that their critique, or their view of human flourishing for example, is superior to any other point of view except as a subjective aesthetic moment.

Tillich had noted this same challenge in *The Socialist Decision*, cited in the previous chapter, where he wrote:

> [I]t is certainly not necessary to posit an eternal human nature; but it is necessary to understand humanity living in encounter and in history, as a unity, since otherwise nothing at all could be asserted, even about the most concrete historical phenomenon. Most significantly, every norm would thereby be invalidated. The passion with which representatives of this professedly radical historical form of thinking make value judgments— for example about capitalism— shows that they are by no means lacking in awareness of the normative dimension. On the contrary, they have a vision of human society in which the human being will find a better fulfillment than it does at present.[141]

---

[137] Paul Tillich, "Review of Herbert Marcuse, *Reason and Revolution*," in *Studies in Philosophy and Social Science (Zeitschrift für Sozialforschung)* 9 (1941) 478.

[138] Tillich, "Review of Herbert Marcuse, *Reason and Revolution*," 478.

[139] Gary M. Simpson, *Critical Social Theory: Prophetic Reason, Civil Society and Christian Imagination* (Minneapolis: Fortress Press, 2002) 34.

[140] Simpson, 34.

[141] *SD*, 165, n. 7. *GW* 2, 231, n. 7.

Critical and normative judgments are central to the project of critical theory, and Tillich challenges his friends and colleagues to acknowledge and embrace these norms. He seems to suggest that this might even sharpen their critiques, but most importantly, the implication seems to be that although they have rejected any explicit metaphysical grounding for their claims, the critiques themselves risk self-referentiality and ineffectuality. Tillich notes, "representatives of this professedly radical historical form of thinking make judgments" and have a clear conception of not only the maladies of the present, but means by which humanity can reach a better future.[142] It is impossible to know precisely what or whom Tillich had in mind in this comment, but the specific referent is irrelevant.

To differing extents, Adorno and Horkheimer recognized the truth of Tillich's assertion concerning ultimacy and the necessary grounding of social critique, but neither could accept his explicitly religious solution to the grounding of reason. Nevertheless, one might say that their orientation to emancipatory justice functions as its 'ultimate concern,' to use Tillich's term, or its grounding.

IV. Conclusions

Tillich's Christian commitments lead him to suggest the necessity of a metaphysical ground for critique and a program for social action against forces of domination. By contrast, the early Adorno largely rejects any metaphysical assumptions or program, while Horkheimer attempts to walk a middle position between the two. An important similarity to be noted is that Tillich challenges traditional metaphysics, and in so doing, moves beyond traditional theism. Horkheimer and Adorno each, to differing extents, seek to retain the category of transcendence as a means of critique, while also going well beyond a theistic understanding of transcendence. Some of Horkheimer's early essays deal with metaphysics and religion in an ambiguous manner, but he is increasingly critical and has limited patience for metaphysics or religion as a positive or contributing social factor, for understandable reasons in the 1930s.

Tillich's metaphysical assumptions are rooted in his conception of theonomy. It is ontological at heart and ethical in scope. Theonomy seeks to (re)unite critical reason with its ground, and it serves as the source of metaphysical norms and the ideal against which the status quo can be judged. The problem of meta-

---

[142] Herbert Marcuse's 1932 work, *Hegel's Ontology and the Theory of Historicity*, seems to agree with Tillich's position on foundational norms and metaphysics.

physics for Horkheimer and Adorno mirrors the more general problem of articulating a basis of and criteria for critique. They maintain that critique does not require a metaphysical foundation, but they are not entirely consistent or convincing in this argument.

Horkheimer somewhat equivocally rejects metaphysics with a broad brush, but is highly imprecise in what he means by the term. It seems that what he is rejecting should be understood against the background of the logical positivism of the Vienna School—empiricism. Although he shared with members of the Vienna School an initial drive to unify the sciences and philosophy, Horkheimer came to recognize the necessity of philosophy's independence by 1937. Significant for the purposes of this chapter, Horkheimer's critique of Vienna School positivism is that it focuses on observation more than transformation. Yet on what basis did Horkheimer think society could, or should, be transformed? Only an independent philosophy could adequately critique the findings of science and explore the critical social relevance of such findings. Although the early Horkheimer clearly rejected some forms of metaphysical speculation, when faced with the alternative of logical empiricism, he retreated to another, more limited form of metaphysics, in an effort to preserve room for difference. Horkheimer continues to employ and engage two crucial metaphysical assumptions in his early essays, however: the need for transcendence of the given via critique and the importance of utopian hope as a critical counterpart to prevailing social scientific theories and methodologies, including logical positivism. These twin metaphysical concerns, although unacknowledged, arise from the central concerns for justice and the mitigation of suffering. The problem of the absence of a guarantor of absolute justice without a metaphysical basis is a central force behind the intense refusal to accept any intra-historical solution to societal ills.

Philosophy, for Adorno, was always independent of the sciences, unlike for Horkheimer. It is an independent philosophy which both criticizes the status quo and points—only in fleeting gestures—toward a different and perhaps better society. In his critique of the Vienna School, Adorno argues that philosophy must go beyond scientific research to responsible interpretation, even rearrangement of social constellations. This requires 'imaginative interpretation,' as one sees in "The Actuality of Philosophy," as well as the necessary experience of 'shock' and the movement beyond synthesis to a "change of perspective" one witnesses in "The Idea of Natural History." While it remains implicit, Adorno operates with a prioritization of transcendence, a form of critique which points obliquely to how things 'otherwise could be.' One can see this early on in the language of the "transcendence of longing" in his *Habilitation* on Kierkegaard and in his late formulation of 'emphatic concepts.'

The rejection of traditional metaphysics by Adorno and Horkheimer is clear, yet neither could escape a series of implicit metaphysical assumptions and norms which they use to fund their philosophical and social critiques. Both held clearly normative positions and made crucial value judgments throughout their careers—*Dialectic of Enlightenment* is a resounding critique of modern western society, and the vision of critical theory articulated therein presupposes certain norms against which modern society can and should be judged and potentially changed. However, Adorno and Horkheimer rarely acknowledge the presupposition of value within critique itself. Although obliquely denying it, much of their work rests upon normative, if not metaphysical assumptions. It is arguably the case that critique itself is, in an important sense, metaphysical for both because it alone is capable of preserving room for transcendence and operating with a persistent utopian longing for things as they 'otherwise could be.'

5.

Religion and Critical Theory

> Even we knowing ones of to-day, the godless and anti-metaphysical, still take *our* fire from the conflagration kindled by a belief a millennium old, the Christian belief, which was also the belief of Plato, that God is truth, that the truth is divine. —Friedrich Nietzsche, *The Gay Science*[1]

Introduction

The 'secularization hypothesis' assumed that the stringent critiques of religion arising from 19th century scientific, historical, and literary criticism and late 19th and early 20th century philosophical critiques marked the death-knell of religion.[2] Beyond evolution, it was thought that by explaining the philosophical and psychological roots of religious belief, along with the historical and cultural roots of 'sacred' scriptures, religion would gradually fade away in an increasingly rational and technological society. The secularization hypothesis essentially announced that religion had finally outlived its purpose. While the underlying idea was important for Adorno and Horkheimer, the secularization hypothesis was not uncritically accepted by either; both maintain some room for religious expression and see a limited role for religion in social critique.

Defining religion is notoriously challenging, and there is little agreement among scholars as to a singular definition; many deny the possibility of such a definition. Religion, for the purposes of this chapter, does not refer to specific beliefs, dogmas, practices, or sacred texts. These are clearly features of many religions, but the focus here is on religion more generally: a system of symbols relating to the transcendent serving to create and reflect meaning for human individuals and communities. The word 'religion' likely derives from the Latin *religo*, meaning 'to bind or tie.' In one sense, religion reflects what Tillich calls 'ultimate concern'—that to which one willingly binds oneself or by which one

---

[1] Friedrich Nietzsche, *The Gay Science*, trans. Thomas Common (Digireads: 2009) 132.

[2] Marx, Nietzsche, Freud, Weber, and others are associated with the umbrella term 'secularization hypothesis,' so it would perhaps be more accurate to say 'secularization hypotheses.' Weber in particular, is meant here.

experiences oneself to be bound in a broad framework of personal and communal meaning about the world and human purposes. Viewing religion in this way helps to illuminate Adorno and Horkheimer's contributions to an understanding of the perdurance of hope for a more just order in which suffering and oppression could be eradicated. While this is a deliberately vague working definition, a central question is whether 'religion,' as a content-free symbolic framework of emancipatory longing is sufficient to address, if not overcome, modern alienation and reification. The question should equally be posed of Tillich's more explicitly religious solution—in the modern era, can religious socialism, including theonomy, address and overcome modern alienation? Does Tillich's proposal sufficiently speak to those of other religions and of no religion? Adorno and Horkheimer issue the challenge of re-conceiving religion without ideology or traditional doctrinal content, suggesting religion as a cultural repository for hopes and the memory of suffering. As Nietzsche notes in the epigraph, even the rejection of religion is profoundly and necessarily rooted in vestiges of religion.

Traditional religion is, for Horkheimer and Adorno, a double-edged sword. On the one hand, it has been the vehicle of oppression and violence, and its conservative tendencies reinforce existing power structures. Other manifestations of the status quo have rendered religion, in many cases, the enemy of progress and liberation. Similarly, if counter-intuitively, religion is equally ambivalent and as problematic as it is beneficial for Tillich. On the other hand, however, both Horkheimer and Adorno recognize that religion retains a uniquely emancipatory voice, and in some forms, a 'religious' critique against the status quo can uniquely sustain the demand and hope for a future in which emancipation and justice are both possible and necessary.

Drawing upon the insights of the previous chapter on metaphysics and norms, here I demonstrate how each thinker understood and used religion both implicitly and explicitly; one important goal is to show how each thinker defined and sought to re-define religion. Tillich, while re-defining religion as that with which one is 'ultimately concerned' is still working within the traditional boundaries of Christianity in many senses. Drawing upon the resources of the Jewish tradition, with which they were loosely affiliated, Horkheimer and Adorno suggest the importance of Judaism in three areas: the determinate negation of religion through the prohibition against images, an 'inverse theology,' and a largely secular conception of messianism.

In the opening sentence of the Introduction to his "Towards a Critique of Hegel's *Philosophy of Right*," Marx proclaimed: "As far as Germany is concerned, the criticism of religion is essentially complete, and the criticism of religion is the presupposition of all criticism."[3] While criticism of religion may be the prerequisite of all criticism, the failure of the secularization hypothesis and resurgence of religion has shown that the criticism of religion is not yet complete. Tillich, Adorno, and Horkheimer agree and each seeks to further the critique of religion, albeit for distinct purposes. For Tillich, particularly as a Protestant philosopher and theologian, Christianity must be *semper reformanda*, constantly self-critiquing and reforming. Adorno to an extent, but particularly Horkheimer, seeks to critique religious structures by identifying oppressive manifestations and recalling emancipatory possibilities within religion. Operating on the premise that the critique of religion is not, and perhaps never will be complete, contra Marx, this chapter engages the critiques of Tillich, Horkheimer, and Adorno. The ongoing need for critique of religion is a place where critical theory and religion today can profitably engage one another in conversation.

After examining the views of each thinker on 'positive' or traditional religion, I engage and analyze the creative reappropriations of religion made by all three. The posited and abstracted 'transcendence' amenable to Adorno and Horkheimer is finally insufficient for funding emancipatory praxis. Furthermore, I argue that they not only recognized this inadequacy, but sought to reclaim this structural space for transcendence through the re-imagination of religion as a content-less, secular expression of longing for something better, for a more perfect justice and the cessation of oppression and suffering. As a result, both adamantly rejected any conception of theodicy. I finally argue that the resources of critical religion are compatible with and a productive companion to critical theory.

I. Religion and Critical Theory in Contemporary Scholarship

Many scholars of critical theory have avoided religion as a relevant locus of inquiry, much less as a potential conversation partner in the furthering of critical social thought in the present and future. Yet in his Introduction to *The Frankfurt School on Religion,* Eduardo Mendieta claims that "[r]eligion was neither

[3] Marx, "Towards A Critique of Hegel's *Philosophy of Right*: Introduction," in *Selected Writings*, 63. *Marx-Engels Gesamtausgabe*, 1:2 (1) 170. Emphasis in original.

reductively nor simplistically analyzed"[4] in the works of Frankfurt School theorists; this is clearly a debatable claim. Mendieta then goes on to make the striking, if not hyperbolic, claim that religion is near the core of critical theory:

> At the heart of the Frankfurt School critical theory we find not just an incidental or ancillary attention to religion, but a central, deliberate, and explicit confrontation with both religion and theology....[L]ike art and the products of mass culture, religion also becomes the site for the negotiation of critique, remembrance, and emancipatory projections.[5]

Yet religion, when it is mentioned in much of Horkheimer and Adorno's work, is most often explicitly construed as a problem, rather than as a solution or even a conversation partner for critical theory. This bias is particularly true of critical theory scholarship,[6] and to the detriment of critical theory. Perhaps *most* scholars of critical theory neglect or minimize religion altogether in their work,[7] and it must be acknowledged that many do so with at least superficial justification given the relatively rare occasions on which Adorno and Horkheimer directly address religion in their writings.

Mendieta insightfully suggests that for Adorno, following Walter Benjamin, religion functions in a complex fashion "as a language that antecedes meta-

---

[4] Eduardo Mendieta, "Introduction: Religion as Critique," in *The Frankfurt School on Religion*, 8.

[5] Mendieta, 8. Mendieta's edited volume deals with other Frankfurt School thinkers in addition to Adorno and Horkheimer, and depending how the Frankfurt School is defined and who is included, one can find more religious themes in other thinkers.

[6] Many of the major scholarly treatments of the Frankfurt School and critical theory make scant mention of religion, if it appears at all, in their discussions. Although undoubtedly viewing theology as a problem, Horkheimer curiously lists "enlightenment and theology" among the "main topics" of the first chapter of what would become *Dialectic of Enlightenment*, during its composition, in a February 1942 letter to Lowenthal. Horkheimer to Lowenthal, 23 May 1942. Cited in Wiggershaus, 314. This may have been Horkheimer's intention, but it is hard to discern this among the central topics of the manuscript as it exists today. Horkheimer does not further clarify what he meant, though he could have been using 'theology' as a generic term for the juxtaposition one sees between "enlightenment and myth" in *Dialectic of Enlightenment*.

[7] David Held's *Introduction to Critical Theory: Horkheimer to Habermas*, for example, has three, superficial references to religion and theology combined. Tillich is not mentioned. Rolf Wiggershaus' *The Frankfurt School: Its History, Theories, and Political Significance* mentions Tillich where appropriate but has a mere two references to religion. Martin Jay's *The Dialectical Imagination* is similar to Wiggershaus in its references to Tillich and virtual silence on religion, save claims about the group's 'Jewishness.' Peter E. Gordon's recent work has begun to correct this trend.

physics and ontology, but which nonetheless instigated the very demise and relativization of all metaphysical and ontological vocabularies."[8] Yet Michael Ott expresses a much more common opinion among scholars of religion, lamenting the dearth of attention paid to the intersection of religious studies and critical theory.[9] In this vein, David Kaufman notes "Anglophone Adorno criticism has wanted to side-step what is perhaps the most scandalous part of Adorno's philosophy; that is, the theology."[10] Some recent religion scholars like Pritchard, Simpson, and Brittain, inter al., have sought to explicate and engage the ambiguous function of religion in critical theory. By contrast, few critical theory scholars have treated religion as an important theme, and the majority of the scholarship engaging both disciplines continues to come from religious studies scholars. Yet early on, at the foundations of Frankfurt School critical theory, Tillich actively worked to engage critical theory as it evolved with Christian theology and religious socialism, questioning the presumed antagonisms between them. With a few notable exceptions, scholars have largely overlooked this engagement between Tillich and critical theory. This chapter, and this study more generally, reflect an attempt to redress this lacuna in scholarship.

II. Judaism in Adorno and Horkheimer

The assessment of Martin Jay and Zoltán Tar that the 'Jewishness' of the Frankfurt School members is among the few unifying features of their thought seems essentially correct, if misleading.[11] Given the diversity of this interdisciplinary group, it is nearly impossible to identify points of unity among all of the so-called members of the *Institut*, but a Jewish heritage is among the few common characteristics. Indeed, as was noted in the first chapter, even the label 'Frankfurt School' is a convenient fiction, suggesting more uniformity than any of its members ever experienced or wanted. Although almost all of the Frankfurt

---

[8] Mendieta, "Introduction," 9.

[9] Ott writes: "The exclusion of religion from the discourse on and development of the critical theory can be understood within the context of the modern antagonism between enlightenment and religion, science and metaphysics, reason and revelation...." Michael Ott, *Max Horkheimer's Critical Theory of Religion: The Meaning of Religion in the Struggle for Human Emancipation* (Lanham: University Press of America, 2001) 2.

[10] David Kaufman, "Correlations, Constellations and the Truth: Adorno's Ontology of Redemption," in *Philosophy and Social Criticism* 26:5 (2000) 62.

[11] Jay, *The Dialectical Imagination*, 31-35. See also, Martin Jay, "The Jews and the Frankfurt School," in *New German Critique* (1980) 137-49. Zoltán Tar, "Introduction" to *Foundations of the Frankfurt School of Social Research.*

School associates were of Jewish origin, most were rather, if not completely, secular in outlook. At the same time, each retained certain aspects of their Jewish identities; for Adorno to a limited extent, and Horkheimer more centrally, this resurfaced in more explicit and pronounced ways later in life.[12] Indeed, Tar notes Gershom Scholem's "cryptic remark...that the Institute for Social Research...was one of the most remarkable 'Jewish Sects' that German Jewry produced."[13] While the Jewish element of their thought may have been largely latent, most came from Jewish families and the Jewish elements discussed here (*Bilderverbot*, messianism, etc.) are common to most. Equally important, however, is the early *denial* of Jewish influence or cohesion by associates of the Frankfurt School, including Leo Löwenthal.[14]

It is readily acknowledged that there are exceedingly few references to positive religion or to the concrete practice of Judaism in the early writings of Horkheimer or Adorno. Their Jewish heritage is arguably implicit throughout, however. Perhaps the central Jewish narrative, the Exodus, is the story of movement from slavery to emancipation, and this is centrally echoed in the work of both. The critique of the Hebrew prophets, thematized by Tillich as prophetic critique and prophetic expectation, is found in Adorno and Horkheimer's striving to reveal sources of oppression and mitigate suffering.

One of the most explicitly Jewish elements implicit in the thought of Adorno and Horkheimer is the *Bilderverbot*, the Hebrew Bible's prohibition against images representing G-d arising from the second commandment.[15] In some of the Frankfurt School thinkers, one sees this applied not only to visual images, but expanded to verbal 'images' and representations as well; there is a quintessentially Jewish desire to avoid speaking of G-d or making claims about the divine in any way. In *Dialectic of Enlightenment*, Adorno and Horkheimer write:

---

[12] Agnes Heller suggests: "In Germany they were Jews, in America they became Germans." Heller, 217.

[13] Tar, 3, referring to Scholem's *Von Berlin nach Jerusalem*, 167.

[14] Zvi Rosen, "Max Horkheimer: über die gesellschaftliche Rolle des Judaismus," in *Kritische Theorie und Religion*, hrsg. Matthias Lutz-Bachmann (Würzburg: Echter, 1997) 23. Rosen does note that late in life, Löwenthal acknowledged that the "untergründige Einfluss der jüdischen Tradition mitbestimmend gewesen ist." Löwenthal, *Schriften*, bd. 4: Judaica, cited in Rosen, 23.

[15] Exodus 20:4-5. Adorno does not explicitly reference the *Bilderverbot* until later in his career; in *Quasi una Fantasia* and *Negative Dialectics*, for example.

> In the Jewish religion...the link between name and essence is still acknowledged in the prohibition on uttering the name of God.... The Jewish religion...places all hope in the prohibition on invoking falsity as God, the finite as the infinite, the lie as truth. The pledge of salvation lies in the rejection of any faith which claims to depict it, knowledge in the denunciation of illusion.[16]

In a traditional 'negative theology,' one can only speak of G-d in terms of negation—at the limits of language, one can say that G-d is not finite, but cannot say that G-d is infinite. Horkheimer and Adorno each illustrate this position, while complicating it, insisting that language is never adequate to represent the infinite (the logical claim behind the *Bilderverbot*). Ott explicitly links the *Bilderverbot* to the process of determinate negation when he claims:

> Horkheimer and Adorno focused on the radicalization of the second and third commandment of the Jewish Decalogue and secularized its prohibition against making names or images of the Absolute into the driving methodological force of their theory: the dialectic of determinate negation.[17]

Of course, this is not determinate negation in a strict Hegelian sense, where negation can disclose something positive through an *Aufhebung*.[18] For Adorno and Horkheimer, the negation of religious concepts may preserve a type of conceptual space for transcendence and justice, but the goal is not to reach a positive assertion about religion.[19]

---

[16] *DE*, 17. *DA*, 29-30.

[17] Ott, 10. Elsewhere, Ott argues that Horkheimer's critique of religion "*illustrates the dialectical process of determinate negation* as the obsolete and repressive form of religion is negated so as to allow the dynamic, emancipatory content of religion to migrate into the modern struggle for human enlightenment and emancipation." Ott, 31.

[18] Pritchard, in distinguishing Adorno from Hegel, argues that "Adorno insists that Judaism's deployment of the *Bilderverbot* entails determinate negation." Elizabeth Ann Pritchard, *Renouncing Knowledge for the Sake of Ethics: Negative Theology and Enlightenment in Theodor W. Adorno* (Ph.D. dissertation: Harvard University, 1999) 301. C.f. *Dialectic of Enlightenment,* 17, cited above.

[19] Wiggershaus summarizes this well, noting that the goal of determinate negation for Horkheimer and Adorno was to 'unleash enlightenment' and expose myth, not to return to myth. He writes: "In their joint publication, *Dialectic of Enlightenment*, Horkheimer and Adorno placed the concept of determinate negation in the foreground—a form of negation which referred to the effects of unleashing enlightenment, not to the continuation of myths." Wiggershaus, 322.

Secondly, the emphasis upon messianism is an important feature of Adorno and Horkheimer's thought, as well as the thought of Marcuse and other Frankfurt thinkers.[20] Some scholars have described this as a secular or atheistic Jewish messianism.[21] The hope for the advent of a more just order remained a largely secular and utopic hope, yet Horkheimer identified it as a Jewish hope. In a late entry in *Dawn and Decline*, he wrote that to be Jewish entails "hope for justice at the end of the world."[22] Of their own religious heritage, Adorno and Horkheimer write in *Dialectic of Enlightenment*: "Reconciliation is Judaism's highest concept, and expectation its whole meaning."[23] Since the messiah is thought to enter from outside of time, outside of the history of oppression, it is the expectation of the messiah's coming which orients all claims to justice and a future otherwise than the present order.[24] As Benjamin wrote in "Theses on the Philosophy of History:" "For every second of time was the straight gate through which the Messiah might enter."[25] The messianic hope is essentially a negative hope for Adorno and Horkheimer: it is a space or marker to preserve the possibility of a non-instrumental and more just reality. Seyla Benhabib connects utopian or messianic hope to the *Bilderverbot*: "Like the God of the Jewish tradition that must not be named but evoked, the utopian transcendence of the history of reason cannot be named but only reinvoked in the memory of men."[26] The challenge of understanding a secular Jewish messianism will resurface below in the discussion of Adorno's 'inverse theology.'

---

[20] George Freidman provocatively suggests that the "search for the revolutionary subject [following Marx and Lukács] is metaphorically the search for the Jewish Messiah." George Friedman, *The Political Philosophy of the Frankfurt School* (Ithaca: Cornell University Press, 1981) 99.

[21] Eduardo Mendieta goes further than Jay and Tar, claiming more specifically that "atheistic Jewish Messianism is an essential unifying feature." Mendieta, 5-6.

[22] Horkheimer, "The State of Israel," 1961-2, in *DD*, 206.

[23] DE, 165. *DA*, 209. George Friedman also writes, "For the Jew, the problematic nature of the Messianic intrusion deepens the possibilities that redemption holds out." Friedman, 92.

[24] "If the task of the Messiah and those who would invoke him is to move the world to the sacred from the profane, then the task of philosophy, of Critical Theory, in a profane age is to view the world through the prisms of the Messianic redemption: to view the world through the scraps of the divine that have been left behind in the world…." Friedman, 101.

[25] Walter Benjamin, *Illuminations: Essays and Reflections*, ed. Hannah Arendt, trans. Harry Zohn (New York: Schocken, 1985) 264. *Illuminationen*, 279.

[26] Seyla Benhabib, *Critique, Norm and Utopia: A Study of the Foundations of Critical Theory* (New York: Columbia University Press, 1986) 170.

For German Jewish thinkers, exiled from their home country and persecuted because of a religious heritage with which they only very loosely identified and allied themselves, Adorno and Horkheimer, like nearly all of the Frankfurt School members, were curiously dispassionate about this identification.[27] Considering the context in which many of the writings of the 1930s and 40s took form, even with limited knowledge of the extent of the horrors of the concentration camps, it is noteworthy that these thinkers remained so objective, even in their denunciation of anti-Semitism.[28] Horkheimer's essay, "The German Jews," ends with an admirable condemnation of injustice and persecution in general, rather than focusing on the particular exigencies of Jewish persecution at the time. He writes: "Men should become sensitive not to the injustice against the Jews, but to injustice as such, not to the persecution of the Jews but to any and all persecution."[29] His 1939 essay, "The Jews and Europe," concludes with the ominous textual note: "Completed in the first days of September 1939,"[30] just as Hitler's armies invaded Poland. Horkheimer's advice to Jews at the end of the essay is perhaps an exception to the apparent dispassion one—arguably—sees elsewhere. Here, he encourages Jews to recall abstract monotheism, reject idolatry, and refuse to treat anything finite as infinite.[31] Yet their general detachment remains instructive. Even Adorno's later emphasis on the rupture caused by Auschwitz and the incomprehensible evil perpetrated in the Final Solution remains seemingly detached from his Jewish ancestry and identity.

Qualifying such a reading slightly, letters exchanged between Horkheimer and Adorno in 1940 and 1941, when discussing the plans for what would become *Dialectic of Enlightenment*, put anti-Semitism at the core of their combined

---

[27] In "Thoughts on Freedom," written much later in 1967, Horkheimer was explicit, describing "Judaism [as] the religion I myself profess." Horkheimer, in *Critique of Instrumental Reason*, trans. Matthew O'Connell, et. al. (New York: Seabury Press, 1974) 150.

[28] Brett Wheeler writes: "Strikingly, antisemitism loses its group-specificity [in Adorno]. It becomes another name for the culture industry, merely identical with reified consciousness." "Antisemitism as Distorted Politics: Adorno on the Public Sphere," by Brett R. Wheeler, in *Jewish Social Studies*, NS 7:2 (2001) 118.

[29] Horkheimer, "The German Jews," in *Critique of Instrumental Reason*, 118. "Über die deutschen Juden," in *Zur Kritik der instrumentellen Vernunft*, 315-6.

[30] "Abgeschlossen erste Septembertage 1939." "Die Juden und Europa," *ZfS* 8 (1939) 136.

[31] Horkheimer, "The Jews and Europe," trans. Mark Ritter, in *Critical Theory and Society: A Reader*, 94. Original: "Die Juden und Europa," *ZfS* 8 (1939) 115-36.

project. In an August 1940 letter to Horkheimer, Adorno noted the following, in light of 'recent news from Germany:'

> It often seems to me as if all that we were used to seeing under the aspect of the proletariat has today passed into terrible focus on the Jews. I wonder if we, regardless of how it is going with the project, should say the things we really want to say in connection with the Jews who represent the counterpoint to the concentration of power.[32]

In a 1941 letter to Horkheimer, Adorno asked, "How would it be if we allowed our book to crystallize…around anti-Semitism?"[33] Horkheimer agrees in a letter a few days later: "I really think the idea of centering our work on anti-Semitism is worth considering."[34] Horkheimer also writes to Adorno in August 1941, concerning the place of theology in their (future) collaborative work: "That leads directly to the theological discussion, which we are approaching. Our work will depend, in large measure, on the fact that here we arrive at common formulations."[35] Precisely why Adorno and Horkheimer, despite this early discussion of focusing on Judaism, anti-Semitism, and the theological, decided to structure the final project in a different way is not entirely clear. There are, of course, numerous references to Judaism in the original text, but the penultimate section of *Dialectic of Enlightenment*, which focuses specifically on anti-Semitism, was only added several years after the original *Philosophical Fragments* were composed. The existing section clearly does not match the original plans described in the letter exchange.

---

[32] Letter, Adorno to Horkheimer, 5 August 1940. *Adorno-Horkheimer Briefwechsel*, bd. 2, 84. Author's translation, "Oftmals kommt es mir vor, als wäre all das, was wir unterm Aspekt des Proletariats zu sehen gewohnt waren, heute in furchtbarer Konzentration auf die Juden übergegangen. Ich frage mich, ob wir nicht, ganz gleich wie es mit dem Projekt wird, die Dinge, die wir eigentlich sagen wollen, im Zusammenhang mit den Juden sagen sollten, die den Gegenpunkt zur Konzentration der Macht darstellen."

[33] Letter, Horkheimer to Adorno, 2 October 1941. *Adorno-Horkheimer Briefwechsel*, bd. 2, 255. Author's translation, "Wie wäre es, wenn wir unser Buch…um den Antisemitismus sich kristallisieren ließen?"

[34] Letter, Horkheimer to Adorno, 4 October 1941. *Adorno-Horkheimer Briefwechsel*, bd. 2, 259. Author's translation, "Den Gedanken, unsere Arbeit um die Antisemitismus zu zentrieren, halte ich wirklich für recht erwägenswert."

[35] Letter, Horkheimer to Adorno, 28 August 1941. *Adorno-Horkheimer Briefwechsel*, bd. 2, 217. Author's translation, "Das führt unmittelbar auf die theologische Diskussion, die uns bevorsteht. Unsere Arbeit wird in weitem Maß davon abhängen, dass wir hier zu gemeinsamen Formulierungen kommen."

III. 'Religion' in the Thought of Horkheimer in the 1930s and 1940s

It is vital to consider the unique perspectives on the social uses and abuses of religion held by Adorno, Horkheimer, and Tillich during the 1930s and 1940s, in the service of connecting metaphysics and exploring remaining issues concerning transcendence, particularly those which blur the lines between metaphysics and religion. Horkheimer's reflections on religion are commonplace in his early writings, notably in *Dawn and Decline*, and relatively common in his essays throughout the 1930s. Most notable is the ambiguity with which Horkheimer treats religion in this early period. In one entry in *Dawn and Decline*, he describes Christianity as a possible source of "transfiguration of existing conditions,"[36] while a few entries later, he seemingly dismisses religion altogether as a "fetish."[37] According to Horkheimer, it is the "horrors of life and death which prepare the soil of the soul for positive religions...,"[38] but this is paradoxically positive because it resists the instrumental thinking of modernity and it preserves space for longing for transformation. Reflecting this paradox, he writes: "In its symbols, religion places an apparatus at the disposal of tortured men through which they express their suffering and their hope. *This is one of [religion's] most important functions.*"[39] Horkheimer is sincere, and this function of preserving hope is perhaps the central reason he wishes to *retain* religion in a modified form in the future.

The early Horkheimer understands religion to be capable of otherworldly escapism but also able to act decisively and constructively within its own social order, which it uniquely can judge to be unjust and oppressive. When religion

[36] DD, 59. "...als grobe Verklärung der bestehenden Verhältnisse gebraucht." *Dämmerung*, 117. In the full context here, Horkheimer is critiquing Christianity, while simultaneously noting its transformative capacities.

[37] DD, 66. "Soweit die Menschen sich nicht selbst helfen können, bedürfen sie der Fetische, und wären es die ihrer Not und Verlassenheit." *Dämmerung*, 131.

[38] DD, 65. "Solange die Schrecken des Lebens und des Todes, die den Boden der Seele für die positiven Religionen fruchtbar machen, durch die Arbeit einer gerechten Gesellschaft nicht klein geworden sind, wird sich auch der von Aberglauben freie Geist vor der Not in eine Stimmung flüchten, die etwas von der bergenden Ruhe des Tempels hat, mag auch der Tempel den Göttern zum Trotze erreicht sein." *Dämmerung*, 131.

[39] DD, 58; emphasis added. The English translation continues, "A respectable psychology of religion would have to distinguish between its positive and negative aspects, it would have to separate proper human feelings and ideas from an ideological form which falsifies them but which it is also partly their product." *Dämmerung*, 116.

rises to this task, it can serve as a powerful critique of oppression and vested interests and he acknowledges the potential for religion to incite transformative action seeking the very things he longs for: justice, freedom, and truth. I quote from Horkheimer at length:

> Historically, the religious machinery did not always serve to distract from earthly practice; in part, it itself developed the energies which today unmask these distractions. The idea of a justice which is absolutely impartial toward the things of this world is contained in the belief in the resurrection of the dead and the last judgment. If those ideas were to be discarded along with the myth, mankind would be deprived of a propulsive concept which, though certainly not as a belief, might today be applied as a criterion to judge the powers that be, and the church in particular. The criticism of religion as mere ideology is justified if it reveals that what were previously impulses in religious disguise, such as dissatisfaction with the order on earth, may become effective today in a different form.... But criticism of religion by a bourgeois usually contains none.[40]

The detail to which he goes in discerning the positive potential in religion, including the specific Christian doctrines of the resurrection and last judgment, is remarkable. While this is an early reflection from an aphoristic text published under a pseudonym, Horkheimer's positive assessment of the power of religion to participate in the common quest for justice and truth should not lightly be dismissed.

Religion is also clearly a significant social problem for Horkheimer, and his critique is extensive; much more so than Adorno. Horkheimer understands religion to be capable of transformative and emancipatory theory and praxis, but he shows historically how the church became almost inextricably entwined with capitalist structures in the origins of modernity. Noting the possibility the church had and failed to act upon, Horkheimer writes: "The alliance between the church and the ruling clique...is a fact, and that fact is all the more revolting because it is directed against the one element which might serve the church as an excuse: suffering men."[41] Instead of emphasizing conscience and religious freedom, the church became complicit in deeply irreligious social and political power structures that gradually eroded the relevance of the church and its ability to effectively critique society.

---

[40] DD, 58. *Dämmerung*, 116-7.

[41] DD, 60. *Dämmerung*, 119.

In his 1930 *Habilitation*, "Beginnings of the Bourgeois Philosophy of History," explored in the third chapter, Horkheimer explores the bourgeois history of religion, notably the roles that fear and power played in the development of religion and how that power was wielded against the public. His voice, much like the voice of Adorno in his own *Habilitation*, is difficult to locate at times. I have therefore chosen to err on the side of treating Horkheimer's remarks there as a judicious summary of others' views (Hobbes, Machiavelli, Vico, etc.), rather than analyzing them as expressions of his own views on religion. The critique there is similar to the critique in several of Horkheimer's historical essays in the mid- and late 1930s.

Biographer Zvi Rosen suggests that the mid-1930s were crucial for Horkheimer's evolving understanding of religion as an ambiguous social force, identifying in particular Horkheimer's 1935 "Thoughts on Religion" and his 1936 review of Theodor Haecker's 'The Christian and History.'[42] It has been argued throughout that one of Horkheimer's most consistent and central concerns was injustice. As was demonstrated in the previous chapter, he was particularly troubled by the challenges faced when trying to articulate norms for justice apart from a metaphysical ground. I agree with Siebert and others who understand this theme of justice and concern about oppressive conditions to be definitive of Horkheimer's early interest in religion.

The early Horkheimer did not retreat to traditional religion in order to ground his longing for justice (as he arguably did quite late in life), but an acute awareness of the challenge of religion for critical theory orients much of Horkheimer's thought.[43] Nevertheless, his articulation of the need for transcendence

---

[42] Zvi Rosen, *Max Horkheimer* (München: Beck, 1995).

[43] The question of a supposed 'conversion' late in Horkheimer's life is outside the scope of this study. While it is clear that Horkheimer took religion increasingly seriously, culminating in several interviews in the early 1970s concerning a profound "longing for the wholly other," it is my view that this does not reflect any 'conversion,' but rather a logical conclusion to what is implicit throughout Horkheimer's work and his insatiable commitment to justice and overcoming oppression. How are readers to interpret Horkheimer's later 'positive' concern with the religious, which is exemplified in a late letter written to Martin Jay in 1971 and became the 'Foreword' to Jay's *The Dialectical Imagination*? There, Horkheimer acknowledged a shift in his own thought concerning metaphysics, its limits, and the religious—his own 'ultimate concern.' Horkheimer writes: "The appeal to an entirely other (*ein ganz Anderes*) than this world has primarily a social-philosophical impetus. It led finally to a more positive evaluation of certain metaphysical trends, because the empirical 'whole is the untrue' (Adorno). The hope that earthly horror does not possess the last word is, to be sure, a non-scientific wish." 'Foreword," by

in the quest to preserve justice at points blurs the lines between philosophical metaphysics (even if it is purely implicit in his work) and a transcendent realm more closely related to a type of religious or utopian hope for ultimate justice. Although Horkheimer diagnosed modernity's barbarity in terms of the loss of the possibility of a metaphysical ground for reason, it represents for him an equivocal victory at best, if not a curse.

In "Thoughts on Religion" (1935), Horkheimer writes:

> The concept of God was for a long time the place where the idea was kept alive that there are other norms besides those to which nature and society give expression in their operation. Dissatisfaction with earthly destiny is the strongest motive for acceptance of a transcendental being. If justice resides with God, then it is not to be found in the same measure in the world. *Religion is the record of the wishes, desires and accusations of countless generations.*[44]

This concluding insight echoes Horkheimer's understanding of the central function of religion in *Dawn and Decline*, referenced above.[45] These insights will help elucidate Horkheimer's conception of the future use of religion. In the citation immediately above, it is not entirely clear whether Horkheimer is echoing a Freudian critique of religious transcendence as 'wish fulfillment,' or whether he is *lamenting* the loss of the norms and claims of justice which traditionally came

---

Max Horkheimer in Martin Jay, *The Dialectical Imagination: A History of the Frankfurt School and the Institute of Social Research 1923-1959* (Berkeley: University of California Press, 1996) xxvi. Is this merely the idealistic repudiation of such pleasure as hope in "an entirely other," penned in youth, only to be tempered by age, and perhaps mortality? Certainly even at their most 'metaphysical' or 'religious,' neither Adorno nor Horkheimer ever advocated anything like self-abandonment, but they both appear to retreat slightly to the hope in some kind of 'wholly Other.' Jay understands Horkheimer's later turn to religious themes to be fully consistent with Horkheimer's earlier thought, and consistent with the principles of critical theory in general, and I largely agree. Yet the reference and import of what Horkheimer describes as a "non-scientific wish" remains opaque and requires further examination, although it falls outside of the scope of this work. Horkheimer's reflections in 1969 and 1970, while insightful, do not provide sufficient warrant to retrospectively make any claims about critical theory's genesis. Habermas notes that for the later Horkheimer, "religion now appears as the only agency that—if it only could command assent—would permit distinguishing between truth and falsity, morality and immorality. [Religion] alone could still grant life a meaning that transcends mere self-preservation." Jürgen Habermas, "Remarks on the Development of Horkheimer's Work," in *On Max Horkheimer*, 60.

[44] *CT*, 129; emphasis added. *KT* I, 374.

[45] DD, 58. *Dämmerung*, 116.

with religion; both are plausible. Furthermore, the greatest reason for the acceptance of a transcendent order, according to Horkheimer, is the conviction that the present order is fundamentally unjust.

The *Sehnsucht nach dem ganz Anderen*—longing for the wholly Other—to which Horkheimer alluded late in life, and implicitly espoused throughout his work in his quest to expose suffering and injustice, is meant to reject 'identity thinking' and to preserve space for the possibility of a more just order preserving genuine difference—rejecting what Adorno called identity thinking. Yet this perspective is already present in Horkheimer's early work and consistent at least through the mid-1940s. Siebert's suggestion that many of his later, seemingly more 'religious' works "are merely variations of this theme,"[46] seems correct. In his 1936 review of Haecker's *Der Christ und die Geschichte*, Horkheimer identifies parallels between the pursuit of the just and the good in critical theory and in religion. He somberly writes:

> All these wishes for eternity and for the onset of universal justice and goodness are shared by materialist [i.e. early critical theory] and religious thinkers, in contrast to the impassivity of the positivist attitude. But if the latter is assuaged by the thought that desires will be fulfilled anyway, then the former are permeated by a feeling of the boundless forsakenness of humanity, which is the only true answer to an impossible hope.[47]

This critical insight discloses parallels between critical theory and religion; that Horkheimer acknowledges such parallels in 1936 is striking. While religion can take consolation in the belief in universal justice ultimately triumphing over injustice, Horkheimer notes that materialist thinkers recognize the impossibility of such belief, which leads to "a feeling of the boundless forsakenness of humanity;" solidarity with and the preservation of the memory of suffering is "the only true answer to an impossible hope" for Horkheimer. Yet the hope itself remains, in spite of all rational calculations.[48]

---

[46] Rudolf J. Siebert, *Horkheimer's Critical Sociology of Religion: The Relative and the Transcendent* (Washington: University Press of America, 1979) 45.

[47] I have used the translation by Kenneth Baynes and John McCole in J. Habermas, "Remarks on the Development of Horkheimer's Work," in *On Max Horkheimer*, 60. *KT* I, 372.

[48] Adorno's later *Negative Dialectics* (1966) mirrors this orientation: "For the sake of utopia, identification is reflected in the linguistic use of the word outside of logic, in which we speak, not of identifying an object, but of identifying with people and things." *Negative Dialectic*, 150. "Utopie wäre über der Identität und über dem Widerspruch, ein

In his 1938 essay "Montaigne and the Function of Skepticism," Horkheimer continues his critique of religions' complicity with power and abnegation of responsibility to address and overcome injustice. He writes:

> Among the dominant classes...religion became the uninterrupted affirmation of social forms. Its moral teaching coincides with the praxis of the decent businessman, and its pedagogy with socialization into frugality and profit making. The distinction is eradicated between the ways of God and the capitalist mechanism for distributing wealth.[49]

One of Horkheimer's most consistent critiques of religion is its propensity in the modern era to reinforce power relations rather than striving to undermine them. Religion is clearly connected not only with capitalism, but also with class, and different classes experience it differently. "It may be a consolation to those who must carry the burdens of society—a consolation which is supposed to keep them from despair as well as from revolution." For those in power, however, and in line with Weber and Troeltsch, Horkheimer argues that religion often "sanctions...personal relations and those of the bourgeois organization of society as a whole."[50] Horkheimer recognizes clearly that throughout early modernity, religion had both pacifying and revolutionary potentialities.

From "the mendicant orders" to the "early nineteenth century," the "Gospel had not simply a mystifying but a revolutionary significance as well." In addition, "oppositional religious leaders from Münzer to Tolstoy have held [the Gospel] up to the status quo."[51] Horkheimer even goes so far as to say that the

Miteinander des Verschiedenen. Um ihretwillen reflektiert Identifikation sich derart, wie die Sprache das Wort außerhalb der Logik gebraucht, die von Identifikation nicht eines Objekts sondern von einer mit Menschen und Dingen redet." *GS* 6, 153. This type of 'identification' is of a more benign sort—solidarity with the victims of Auschwitz, for example, one which rejects a culture of forgetfulness. It is analogous to Horkheimer's longing that 'injustice not have the final word.'

[49] BPSS, 285-6. *ZfS* 7 (1938) 24.

[50] BPSS, 286. *ZfS* 7 (1938) 25.

[51] BPSS, 284. "In der gesamten Periode des Frühkapitalismus, von der Entstehung der Bettelorden bis in die Anfänge des 19. Jahrhunderts hinein, besaß jedoch das Evangelium nicht bloß verklärende, sondern auch revolutionäre Bedeutung. Die Reformatoren haben es wenigstens nicht unmittelbar mit der irdischen Ordnung identifiziert, und die oppositionellen religiösen Geister von Müntzer bis Tolstoi haben es als 'Gesetz, wie es im Herzen geschrieben ist,' den bestehenden Verhältnissen entgegengehalten." *ZfS* 7 (1938) 22-3.

"Gospel is thus the negation of skepticism,"[52] but "with the transition from the absolutist to the liberal period, the progressive aspects of religion were obscured."[53] Based on his study of the history of bourgeois conscience and the development of religion in (European) history, Horkheimer sees a fundamental breach in the early 20th century. He has some extremely harsh words for some forms of liberal theology, which he sees as (in at least some cases) complicit with capitalist structures and even fascism. He writes that:

> Liberal theology...[like that of] D. F. Strauss had already shown how the transition could be made from theology into a naked, authoritarian attitude, hostile to workers. This vulgar materialist theologian virtually anticipated fascism. The Ritschl school...reached the apotheosis of the reconciliation of capitalism and Protestantism with its skeptical agnosticism.[54]

Horkheimer makes a significant and unwarranted generalization about 'liberal theology' here, which I will unpack. While not quite sounding the death-knell of religion altogether, Horkheimer thinks that in the wake of 'liberal theology' and "[w]ithin the limits of positive religion...faith can only continue to exist in a distorted way."[55] Yet he retains some, limited space for the positive functions of religion—a distorted faith of "paradoxical Christians,"[56] perhaps. In addition to the few, "isolated Catholic circles, retrieval of the progressive elements of religion—of the Gospel as a tribunal that can also come into opposition to the status quo—can be found in various orthodox tendencies in Protestantism."[57] What (and whom) Horkheimer might mean by 'orthodox tendencies in Protestantism' is also enigmatic—as is where Tillich might stand in this assessment—but it is important to note that Horkheimer still sees fleeting hints and glimmers of hope in the power of religion, even in the midst of this critique.

---

[52] BPSS, 284. *ZfS* 7 (1938) 24. Throughout this essay, 'skepticism' refers to "a pathological form of intellectual independence; it is immune to truth as well as to untruth." BPSS, 307.

[53] BPSS, 285. *ZfS* 7 (1938) 24.

[54] BPSS, 303. *ZfS* 7 (1938) 45.

[55] BPSS, 305. *ZfS* 7 (1938) 46.

[56] Horkheimer and Adorno use this curious phrase positively in *Dialectic of Enlightenment* in reference to Barth, Pascal and Kierkegaard. DE, 147.

[57] BPSS, 305. "Die Erinnerung an vorwärtstreibende Elemente der Religion, an das Evangelium als eine Instanz, die zum Bestehenden auch in Gegensatz geraten kann, findet sich außer in vereinzelten katholischen Kreisen bei verschiedenen orthodoxen Richtungen des Protestantismus." *ZfS* 7 (1938) 46.

III.1 Horkheimer Contra Tillich?

When exploring philosophical anthropology in the third chapter, Adorno lodges direct and often harsh criticisms of Tillich. While it is unlikely Horkheimer is doing anything as drastic, I suggest Horkheimer's omission of engagement with Tillich in his essays on religion merits closer investigation. It is *possible* that the omission was deliberate and reflects, as such, a critique of Tillich's conception of religion as ontological and theonomous, but perhaps it also hints at a rivalry of sorts between critical theory and religious socialism. Note that I am *not* making the stronger claim that Horkheimer is either explicitly or implicitly critiquing Tillich; I am merely probing the fact of the absence of engagement with Tillich in print.[58] Emboldened by the fact that many of Tillich's contemporaneous writings address similar issues, and in a few cases challenge Horkheimer's critiques and assertions, cautious inquiry is warranted here.[59]

Why did Horkheimer choose not to engage religious socialism, or Tillich in particular? Why did he choose to review Haecker's book rather than one by Tillich, for example?[60] Why would Horkheimer suggest that there was not an effective critical theory of religion, or that there was not an effective critical psychology of religion,[61] etc.? Tillich clearly does not provide a cohesive critical theory or psychology, but religious socialism, with which Horkheimer was familiar through Tillich and Heimann,[62] had already provided for what Horkheimer

---

[58] The absence of references to Horkheimer or Adorno in Tillich's work is granted; Tillich could also have engaged Horkheimer more directly in his own writing. Why Tillich did not make any comparison between religious socialism and the critical theory of his friends is an equally valid question, though likely equally unknowable.

[59] It is readily acknowledged that the absence of reference to the writings of both Horkheimer and Adorno in the published works of Tillich is equally enigmatic and could be profitably probed. The reason for the present line of inquiry is Horkheimer's suggestion of the absence of the type of religious critique that Horkheimer knew Tillich was producing.

[60] Although Horkheimer could have been asked to review Haecker's book by an editor, there is no reference to this in Horkheimer's letters.

[61] Apparently presuming such a thing did not already exist, Horkheimer suggests the need for deeper critical engagement with religion. "A respectable psychology of religion would have to distinguish between [religion's] positive and negative aspects, [and] it would have to separate proper human feelings and ideas from an ideological form which falsifies them but which is also partly their product." DD, 58. *Dämmerung*, 116.

[62] In January 1942, Tillich and Heimann participated in a series of discussions on Christianity and Marxism with which Horkheimer (and Adorno) were almost certainly familiar. See MW/HW 3, 475-6.

meant by "a respectable psychology of religion." That is, religious socialism had already articulated a means and system of critique which could distinguish between religion as a vehicle of the capitalist system and religion as a vehicle of longing for emancipation. Tillich certainly provided more content to religion as a vehicle of longing for emancipation than Horkheimer wanted, but this alone does not explain the curious silence. Why would Horkheimer not mention religious socialism as a step in the right (or even wrong) direction, for example? The critique of religion offered by Tillich cannot fairly be characterized as 'bourgeois,' and Tillich both readily and consistently notes the rampant ideology in religious disguise, almost certainly more than Horkheimer.

Michael Ott correctly notes that for Horkheimer, "the religious, mythical form of humanity's cry against the world's injustice has to be transformed into a this-worldly, revolutionary praxis to overcome the causes of this injustice."[63] Yet this is essentially what Tillich sought to do, undergirded by a religio-metaphysical foundation, so why does Horkheimer apparently not consider religious socialism or Tillich as a conversation partner in this quest? The easiest answer in reference to the texts considered above may lie in the aphoristic nature of the comments in *Dawn and Decline*; Horkheimer rarely refers to specific people or movements in the text except in passing—these are not systematic or constructive philosophical arguments. Furthermore, the first half of *Dawn and Decline* includes aphoristic notes between 1926 and 1931; Horkheimer would have known Tillich reasonably well only in the latter period.[64] Why Horkheimer did not engage Tillich in his writings elsewhere (before Tillich's death)[65]—as indeed

---

[63] Ott, 31.

[64] As the "Translator's Preface" to *DD* notes, "the author did not take the time to polish them" and "they do not constitute an orderly sequence." *DD*, 13. It is entirely possible that these particular aphorisms cited above were written before Horkheimer became acquainted with Tillich's writings and the principles of religious socialism.

[65] With very few exceptions beyond *Festschriften* and works after Tillich's death, Tillich is not mentioned in Horkheimer's published works. The earliest exceptions are a 1961 essay written for Tillich's 75th birthday; the second is a 1963 essay, two years before Tillich's death, entitled "Theismus—Atheismus," Horkheimer, *GS*, bd. 7. In this essay, Tillich is mentioned superficially and only in passing. In Horkheimer's *Nachgelassene Schriften*, Tillich appears numerous times, and in all of the writings after Tillich's death, Horkheimer largely—and unsurprisingly—praises Tillich. See *Werk und Wirken Paul Tillichs: Ein Gedenkbuch*, which includes an interview in 1966 with Horkheimer concerning Tillich and a memorial essay by Horkheimer for Tillich.

why Tillich avoided engaging Horkheimer in his own writings[66]—remains an open question. That deep friendship, ongoing intellectual debates, and personal respect reflect the primary connection between Tillich and Horkheimer was established in the first chapter and is obvious in extant letters and *Nachgelassene Schriften*.

Critical engagement—or even just critique—of religious socialism(s) would seem to naturally fit in Horkheimer's assessment of oppositional movement within progressive religion in "Montaigne and the Function of Skepticism." Why would Horkheimer there describe "orthodox tendencies in Protestantism"[67] as progressive and resisting the status quo, while ignoring the more familiar liberal Protestantism of Tillich and religious socialism?[68] It is inconceivable that Horkheimer would have grouped Tillich with Ritschl, and more so with Strauss, and by 1938, Horkheimer and Tillich had been in close contact, both in Frankfurt and in New York, for nearly a decade. Horkheimer knew what Tillich was working on as a liberal theologian, and Tillich almost certainly was familiar with Horkheimer's work. On the other hand, it seems that Horkheimer did find Tillich too 'liberal' in some sense. In a protocol discussion with Adorno on November 8, 1939, Horkheimer said Paulus "no longer believes in God with his various commandments. In place of God, he takes the question, 'what exists?'"[69] This was intended as a private conversation and may simply reflect an offhand critique of theological existentialism, but it may reflect Horkheimer's deeper concerns and opinions about Tillich's onto-theological project.

Given the accounts of extensive discussion groups, of which Horkheimer and Tillich were both part, would Tillich have been familiar with Horkheimer's critiques before the publication of "Montaigne and the Function of Skepticism,"

---

[66] Horkheimer's *Eclipse of Reason* is cited in Tillich's *Systematic Theology*, vol. 1, 72, but the thought of Horkheimer per se is not engaged.

[67] It is conceivable, though impossible to know with any certainty, that Horkheimer had thinkers like Karl Barth and other signers of the Barmen Declaration in mind, perhaps even Dietrich Bonhoeffer. Horkheimer and Adorno cite Barth positively as a "paradoxical Christian" in *Dialectic of Enlightenment*. DE, 147. It is also possible that Horkheimer is referring to an older period, or could have intended to include Tillich as an 'orthodox' thinker. Here in "Montaigne and the Function of Skepticism," Horkheimer notes that "In contrast to the total nihilism of the liberals…the courage of the orthodox reveals a higher truth." BPSS, 303.

[68] In comments in a memorial for Tillich in 1966, Horkheimer praised Tillich as a progressive and the most exemplary Christian he ever knew. *Werk und Wirken*, 125.

[69] Horkheimer, *GS* 12, 517. Author's translation, "'glaubt nicht mehr an Gott mit seinen verschiedenen Geboten. An die Stelle Gottes tritt die Frage 'was ist?"

or did he first read it in print? While the former is more likely given their frequent interactions in those years in New York, the more interesting—and unanswerable—question is how Tillich received and reacted to such critique, if he saw it as critique at all. Did he see Horkheimer attacking him in print, perhaps even siding with Tillich's 'rival,'[70] Karl Barth? Perhaps the best explanation, in the immediate context, is simply that a counter-example of a positive movement with similar presuppositions and goals in liberal Protestant theology did not fit with Horkheimer's argument.

Was there perhaps tension between Horkheimer and Tillich? Horkheimer had expected to assume Hans Cornelius' chair in philosophy in Frankfurt, and it must have been a disappointment to Horkheimer to have a Protestant philosopher of religion appointed to the position, particularly one so interested in ontology. Yet the two claimed to be and seemed to have been friends. It was only with Tillich's help that Horkheimer received an academic position at all, in conjunction with his assumption of the directorship of the *Institut*. It is unlikely that Horkheimer could have recognized religious socialism as an alternative, perhaps even competing movement to critical theory. He does argue that an independent and critical religious conscience—the freedom of a Christian[71]—dating back to the Reformation's quarrel with skepticism, has been subsumed and sublated by critical theory. He writes:

> What set the Reformation and skepticism against one another in the sixteenth century...has been released from these forms and transformed into a theory and praxis which, as active humanism, overcomes and retains the contradictions. It is critical theory, and the historical effort to which this belongs.[72]

Here one gets a clearer sense of a *possible* tension between critical theory and Tillich's religious socialism which, as was seen in the third chapter on anthropology, was transformed into the theory and praxis of 'Christian humanism.' Religious socialism, as a manifestation of 'Christian humanism,' sought to dialectically overcome the perceived contradictions between reason and faith, and between socialism and religion, in much the same manner that critical theory

[70] The word 'rival' is used with intentional 'scare quotes;' Barth was not a rival in any traditional sense, much less an adversary like Hirsch and others became, but the theologies of Barth and Tillich are, while arguably ultimately complementary, quite distinct.

[71] A combined emancipatory conscience and religious freedom is the subject of the previous two pages of Horkheimer's essay.

[72] BPSS, 307. *ZfS* 7 (1938) 47.

sought to overcome the irrationality and barbarism of modernity. While there may have been some implicit rivalry between these two thinkers and schools of thought, extant evidence leaves this as an open question. Nevertheless, there are numerous parallels between religious socialism and critical theory, and at some level, each must have recognized the overlaps in their respective programs, despite significant differences such as ontology. The friendship between the two thinkers, at least on the surface, mitigates against the conclusion of rivalry, but the absence of engagement with one another's work remains perplexing. In a private 1947 response to what may have been a critique, Tillich thanks Horkheimer for his book (likely *Dialectic of Enlightenment*)[73] and notes: "I look forward to each new paragraph and only wish the book was longer."[74] Even if Horkheimer was criticizing Tillich, indirectly or directly here, Tillich himself did not seem to interpret it in this way.

III.2 The Future of Religion for Horkheimer

In *Dawn and Decline*, Horkheimer linked religion and his own 'transcendent' ideals of justice and truth, as was noted in the previous chapter. He writes: "It is not part of life in this civilization to take religion seriously. Non-religious values such as justice, freedom or truth are not taken seriously either."[75] Given his understanding of the intertwining of religion and capitalist social structures, it is not surprising that on a superficial level, he saw a limited future for religion. For Horkheimer, only 'distorted faith' and 'paradoxical Christians' seem to be able—fleetingly—to interrupt the steady encroachment of instrumentality upon reason.

After arguing that it is not necessary to believe in a transcendent order, Horkheimer acknowledges that this absence creates new challenges. Returning to the epigraph of this chapter, taken from Nietzsche, metaphysics is not so easily overcome. In Horkheimer's words, "it is enormously difficult to avoid making a new religion out of this very absence.... [E]ven the spirit free of superstition will seek refuge from its distress in a mood which has something of the reassuring quiet of the temple, though that temple be built in defiance of the gods."[76]

[73] The editor notes on p. 875, fn. 3, that it is unclear exactly what manuscript is in question here, though some version of *Dialectic of Enlightenment* sees most likely.

[74] Letter, Tillich to Horkheimer, 14 August, 1947. Horkheimer, *GS* 17, 874. Author's translation, "Ich freue mich auf jeden neuen Paragraphen und wünschte nur, das Buch wäre länger."

[75] DD, 91. *Dämmerung*, 197.

[76] DD, 65. *Dämmerung*, 131.

He is not suggesting that atheism is the correct response, or even a viable response. What he does suggest initially is that most 'irreligious' persons are 'too weak' to go without some form of religion,[77] although he himself sought to retain a religious structure, albeit one voided of positive content, doctrine, and belief. In the end, does Horkheimer seek to 'make a new religion out of this very absence,' or to 'create a religion out of irreligion,' in order to preserve space for longing and emancipation? This conclusion is by no means foregone, but it seems difficult to escape. Whether this content-less repository of hope and longing can or should still be called 'religion' is not a simple question, but its structural presence is necessary for Horkheimer, who insists on retaining the language as well. In a modified form, emphasizing the structural capacity for longing for justice, something like religion remains necessary in Horkheimer's thought, even if only to preserve the memory of suffering and the silenced.[78]

IV. Religion in the Thought of Adorno in the 1930s and 1940s

Adorno's understanding of transcendence, like that of Horkheimer, is deeply intertwined with the challenge of differentiating metaphysics from religion. Similarly, Adorno's understanding of religion rests even more explicitly than that of Horkheimer within a larger philosophical, and superficially anti-metaphysical, framework.[79] Adorno asserts that concepts can never reach the objects or ideas they purport to represent; there is always an epistemic gulf. Religion, understood as a particular tradition's concept of a 'god,' inevitably faces such a gulf. Following Tillich's lead, one might legitimately understand Adorno's fierce methodological adherence to negativity and non-identity as his 'ultimate concern,' without trying to identify this drive or its object with any traditional sense of religiousness or doctrine, etc.[80] Adorno consistently rejected

[77] DD, 66. *Dämmerung*, 131.

[78] In the 1960s and 1970s, as has been hinted at elsewhere, Horkheimer became more explicitly interested in religion and the 'theological.' This is outside the scope of this work, but it offers a fascinating appendix to Horkheimer's evolving thought on metaphysics and religion.

[79] In later works such as "Subject and Object" (1969) and in *Negative Dialectics* (1966) Adorno wrestles with the notion that both the objects of sensory and intellective perception are always already bound up with the constitution of the subject's experiencing or perceiving.

[80] "Essentially, Adorno's thought testifies to a fundamental dissatisfaction with the 'present' state of things, viewed from the perspective of a kind of dialectical hermeneutics

social domination and what he later referred to as the "wounds which this order has and which...it inflicts on us."[81] Some aspects of theological discourse and motifs, albeit voided of any specific doctrinal content, appear to be a useful tool for Adorno in the struggle against suffering and for a better world, as will be seen below.[82]

Adorno's biography offers a certain degree of insight into his early relationship with religion. As noted in the first chapter, his father was a Jewish convert to Protestantism, and both his mother and beloved aunt were Catholics. During the 1920s, he took Catholicism very seriously and even considered converting.[83] In a 1934 letter to Benjamin, Adorno relates his theological interest, similar to that of Benjamin, going back to an unknown essay on Kafka in 1923. While the original essay is not extant, Adorno writes to Benjamin that he "claimed [Kafka] represents a photograph of our earthly life from the perspective of a redeemed life...."[84] This 1923 essay, Adorno claims, resonates with Benjamin's position on

that is utopian—although utopian in an apophatic and basically negative way. He reflects from the viewpoint of a possible state of peace, justice and reconciliation *without* turning this utopian dream into theory." Mattias Martinson, *Perseverance without Doctrine: Adorno, Self-Critique, and the Ends of Academic Theology* (Frankfurt: Peter Lang, 2000) 54; emphasis in original.

[81] *Negative Dialectics*, 18.

[82] According to Brittain, "Theological discourse is an important object of study for Adorno because the understands it to be an expression of these wounds and sufferings. Furthermore, he argues that theology illuminates how thought and experience constantly reach beyond the limits of the given moment. That is to say that, in theological discourse, Adorno observes experiences and expressions that challenge the dominance of the current social *actuality*, as religion both testifies to, and gives expression to, a concern for alternative social *possibilities*." Christopher Craig Brittain, *Adorno and Theology* (New York: T & T Clark, 2010) 7-8.

[83] *Theodor W. Adorno und Ernst Krenek: Briefwechsel*, hrsg. Wolfgang Rogge (Frankfurt am Main: Suhrkamp Verlag, 1974) 46.

[84] Letter, 17 December 1934, Theodor W. Adorno to Walter Benjamin, *The Complete Correspondence 1928-1940*, ed. Henri Lonitz, trans. Nicholas Walker (Cambridge: Harvard University Press, 1999) 66. "Führe ich Ihnen meinen ältesten, 9 Jahre zurückliegenden Deutungsversuch zu Kafka an: er sei ein Photographie des irdischen Lebens aus der Perspektive des erlösten...." Adorno-Benjamin *Briefwechsel*, 90. The editor of the translated Adorno-Benjamin correspondence notes that "nothing more is known about this earliest attempt," but there are possible resonances in the beginning of Adorno's essay "Remarks on Kafka" in *GS* 10, 254 ff. *Adorno und Ernst Krenek*, 71.

'theology.'[85] Like Kafka, Adorno seeks to expose and protest conditions of dehumanization in his philosophy.[86]

Adorno does not centrally address religion in his published writings in the 1930s, with the exception of his *Habilitation* on Kierkegaard, in which it can be extremely difficult to locate the author's own voice. Indeed, Anson Rabinbach notes that "the text [*Kierkegaard*] remains indecipherable, however open to interpretation it might be...."[87] The book ends with the concept of 'longing,' but throughout, Adorno's close reading and exhaustive citation muddles his own view in relation to his interpretation of Kierkegaard. Kierkegaard's concept of the 'leap of faith' struck Adorno as too undialectical to be seriously considered. He suggests that the religious and aesthetic moment is "deprecatorily transformed...into simple creaturely immediacy" by Kierkegaard. This is a central problem for Adorno who argues that "it is precisely this immediacy that should be broken by paradox...."[88] One sees this theme of 'breaking immediacy' develop into his more mature position of the philosophical pursuit of non-identity as critique. In a 1934 letter to Benjamin, Adorno acknowledges that 'theology' is central to his project in *Kierkegaard*, much as Benjamin does in his *Arcades* project. Adorno suggests that his "Kierkegaard study was concerned with nothing else"[89] than a type of theology which he describes in the same letter as *inverse*, the details of which will be explored.

---

[85] Adorno leaves 'theology' in quotation marks, going on to describe his "inverse theology" discussed below.

[86] Elizabeth Pritchard argues: "According to Adorno's reading of Kafka, the standpoint of a resolute negativity is indistinguishable from the perspective of salvation—both reveal the world as hell. But because the vision of resolute negativity is at the same time the perspective of salvation, it is a source of hope." Pritchard, 308.

[87] "'Why Were the Jews Sacrificed?' The Place of Antisemitism in Adorno and Horkheimer's *Dialectic of Enlightenment*," by Anson Rabinbach, in *Adorno: A Critical Reader*, 138.

[88] Adorno, *Kierkegaard*, 15. "Angesichts des 'Sprunges' zum Glauben wird das Ästhetische au seiner Stufe im dialektischen Prozess, nämlich der des sich Nicht-Entscheidens, deprekativ verwandelt in kreatürliche Unmittelbarkeit schlechthin. Denn sie eben soll durchs Paradox gebrochen werden und macht dessen absolutes Widerspiel aus." Adorno, *GS* 2, 25. 'Paradox,' on Adorno's reading of Kierkegaard, is "the idea...that should overcome philosophy and the context of mere nature" or the "unity of time and eternity." E.g. Rabinbach, *Adorno: A Critical Reader*, 108, 117.

[89] Letter, Adorno to Benjamin, 17 December 1934, *Complete Correspondence*, 67. "...ja meinem Kierkegaard war es um nichts anderes zu tun als inverse Theologie." *TWA-WB Briefwechsel*, 90.

The ambiguity of Adorno's text notwithstanding, Robert Hullot-Kentor, the translator and editor of *Kierkegaard*, claims in his 'Foreword' that "theology is always moving right under the surface of all Adorno's writings," and that "theology penetrates every word...."[90] Hullot-Kentor makes a case that Adorno's later writings on religion reflect a theological undercurrent latent in his study of Kierkegaard, his *Habilitation* approved by Tillich. While this theological undercurrent is not immediately obvious (and seems to be limited in large part to letters rather than published works by the 1940s), interestingly Horkheimer shares this view in his review of Adorno's *Habilitation* in 1931. As noted in the first chapter, Horkheimer remarked that the philosophical interests and method of Adorno therein:

> are not related to my own philosophical aspirations. If Wiesengrund considers that he has recovered hope and reconciliation, of all things, from Kierkegaard's thought, he has thereby expressed a basic theological conviction which points to philosophical intentions radically different from my own, and this is noticeable in every single sentence.[91]

Also telling in this regard is Adorno's early admission to Kracauer, in a letter dated August 6, 1930, concerning his Kierkegaard study: "...I went more deeply into theological categories than I had hoped, and I worry I have whinnied too much in rescue, and of course, above all, in reconciliation."[92] It is true that Adorno acknowledges the importance of theology—perhaps an "inverse theology"—in his *Habilitation*, in a letter to Benjamin. Where this "secret coded character of...theology"[93] goes in Adorno's later work, if it is not dissolved entirely, is highly debatable.

Adorno is highly critical of Kierkegaard's theology, particularly the latter's concept of hope. He writes: "The twilight of Kierkegaardian hope is the sallow light of the twilight of the gods that proclaims the vain end of an age or the aim-

---

[90] Robert Hullot-Kentor, "Forward," in Theodor W. Adorno, *Kierkegaard: Construction of the Aesthetic*, xi.

[91] Max Horkheimer, "Bemerkungen in Sachen der Habilitation Dr. Wiesengrund," February 1931, in the Theodor Adorno file of the philosophy faculty of the University of Frankfurt am Main. Cited in Wiggershaus, 93. This does not appear in Horkheimer's *Gesammelte Schriften*.

[92] *Adorno-Kracauer Briefwechsel*, bd. 7, 244. Author's translation, "...ich bin tiefer in theologische Kategorien gekommen, als ich gewünscht hatte und habe Angst, dass ich bei Rettung und vor allem natürlich Versöhnung zu viel gewiehert habe."

[93] Letter, Adorno-Benjamin, 17 December 1934, 67. Adorno-Benjamin *Briefwechsel*, 91.

less beginning of a new one, but not salvation."[94] Kierkegaard's theology often falls victim to a "mythical dialectic," according to Adorno.[95] Although Adorno does not offer a positive view of his own, he lays out against Kierkegaard central facets of critique which continue throughout most of his writings: systematic negation, a cancellation of transcendence, adherence to a dialectical method and perspective, and a concern with suffering.

Adorno's early relationship with philosophy of religion and theology is intimately tied to Benjamin, who also engaged theology in this period.[96] The erratic contact between these two exiled friends continued through the 1930s, finalized by the untimely death of Benjamin in 1940. His correspondence with Benjamin provides valuable insight, and perhaps the primary lens, into his thoughts on religion in the 1930s.[97] A letter Adorno wrote to Benjamin from Oxford in 1934 expresses much the same sentiment, wherein Adorno challenges Benjamin to avoid 'Brechtian atheism,' which he regards as a false 'inverse theology.' Instead, Adorno encouraged Benjamin to continue through his work on the *Arcades* project "to realize every part of the theological content and all the literalness of its most extreme claims." He continues:

> For it really seems to me that here, where the most absolutely decisive and fundamental issues are concerned, one has to speak out loudly and clearly, and thereby *reveal the undiminished categorical depth of the question, without neglecting theology here*; and then, at this decisive level, I believe that we can all the more easily avail ourselves of the Marxian theory precisely because we have not been forced to appropriate it externally in a subservient fashion....[98]

---

[94] Adorno, *Kierkegaard*, 110. Adorno, *GS* 2, 156.

[95] *Kierkegaard*,113. "Mythische Dialektik." Adorno, *GS* 2, 161.

[96] To a lesser degree, Benjamin shaped Horkheimer's thinking on religion as well. Wiggershaus notes that the publication of Horkheimer and Adorno's essays in a memorial volume published by the *Institut* in exile, dedicated to Benjamin, was widely misunderstood as having been written by Benjamin himself. "This may be seen as an indication of the extent to which both Horkheimer and Adorno had assimilated the theological basis for the critique of progress...." Wiggershaus, 312.

[97] Rabinbach writes: "there are innumerable indications of Adorno's interest in Jewish theological motifs in his writings during the 1930s, many of which self-consciously suggest Benjamin's notion of redemption...." "'Why Were the Jews Sacrificed?' The Place of Antisemitism in Adorno and Horkheimer's *Dialectic of Enlightenment*," by Anson Rabinbach, in *Adorno: A Critical Reader*, 137.

[98] Letter, 6 November 1934, Adorno-Benjamin, *The Complete Correspondence*, 53-4; emphasis added. Adorno-Benjamin *Briefwechsel*, 74. Emphasis in original.

What, precisely, Adorno means by 'theology' remains unclear. A similar letter from Adorno to Benjamin in 1935 expresses Adorno's hope that Benjamin's work would provide a "restoration of theology, or better still, a radicalization of dialectic introduced into the glowing heart of theology, [that] would simultaneously require the utmost intensification of the social-dialectical, and indeed economic, motifs."[99] The concept of 'theology' for the early Adorno, even within the immediate context of his correspondence, remains perplexing, though it is almost certainly linked to the "undiminished categorical depth" he describes as questions resisting facile resolution. For this reason and others, there is little univocal opinion in Adorno scholarship concerning how to interpret these comments and what significance they had for his work after the mid-1930s. Thus, according to Brittain, "Adorno is interested in theology because he thinks it reveals important insights into existing social conditions. His use of theological concepts is intended to help realize the ideals of Enlightenment reason, not overcome them."[100] On the other hand, Albrecht Wellmer identifies a "materialistic appropriation of theology" which results in "an insoluble conflict between materialist and metaphysical (i.e. theological) motifs" in Adorno.[101]

In letters Adorno wrote to Horkheimer as late as 1941, shortly before he moved from New York to Los Angeles, Adorno cryptically articulates what Wiggershaus terms the "fundamental significance of theological motifs"[102] in his thinking, which he hoped to include in their joint work. In the midst of conversation about anti-Semitism, Adorno describes his ongoing concern with the 'theological' in a letter dated September 4, 1941, drawing upon the conviction of both Spinoza and Hegel that truth is its own criterion. Adorno writes:

> I have a weak, infinitely faint feeling that this was once possible in whatever form, but I am honestly unable to formulate that any longer

---

[99] Letter, Adorno-Benjamin, 2 August 1935, 108. Adorno-Benjamin *Briefwechsel*, 143. Concerning this particular correspondence, Siebert writes: "Adorno hoped that Benjamin would deliver in his *Passage Work* a restitution of theology or better still a radicalization of the materialistic dialectic into its 'inner theological glowing fire.'" Rudolf J. Siebert, *The Critical Theory of Religion: The Frankfurt School, From Universal Pragmatic to Political Theology* (Amsterdam: Mouton Publishers, 1985) 23.

[100] Brittain, 2.

[101] Albrecht Wellmer, *Endgames: The Irreconcilable Nature of Modernity, Essays and Lectures*, trans. David Midgley (Cambridge: MIT Press, 1998) 191. Wellmer's comments take later texts of Adorno, such as *Negative Dialectics*, which lies outside the scope of this work, into consideration.

[102] Wiggershaus, 503.

> today. The adoption of a smaller and less visible theology is subject to another conviction, that in one of the most central points, the distinction between negatives and positives, theology says nothing.... But above all, I believe that in all this, what we experience to be true and not false [blind], rather in the movement of the concept, lessens what does not really present itself to us as knowledge of itself and its opposite, and it carries this light only as a reflection of another light.[103]

What this 'secret' is remains obscure, as is the assertion that "there is no difference between" the "positives" and the "negatives," but both likely reflect Adorno's 'inverse theology.' The 'light' Adorno refers to in the last sentence is almost certainly that of redemption, which, regardless of its specific referent, remains an ineliminably theological motif. If Adorno was advocating 'theological motifs' to a skeptical Horkheimer as late as 1941, this opens up new possibilities for interpreting the role of religion and the theological in his work, and a lens into the pre-history of *Dialectic of Enlightenment.*

In the mid-1940s, particularly in *Dialectic of Enlightenment*, one can see elements of religion brought into Adorno's philosophical discussion, but the 'theological motifs' which remained in 'secret' in 1941 are buried, if not absent. It was not until 1957's "Reason and Revelation"[104] that Adorno directly engaged with 'positive' religion in his published writings in any detail.[105] While his writings in the 1960s engage both metaphysics and religion more than do his early

---

[103] Letter, Adorno to Horkheimer, 4 September 1941, *Adorno-Horkheimer Briefwechsel*, bd. 2, 222. Author's translation, "Ich habe ein schwaches, unendlich schwaches Gefühl, dass das möglich sei und auf welche Art, bin aber ehrlich außerstande, das heute schon zu formulieren. Die Annahme vom Kleiner- und Unsichtbarwerden der Theologie ist ein Motiv dazu, ein anderes die Überzeugung, dass von einem zentralsten Standpunkt aus der Unterschied des Negativen und des Positiven zur Theologie nichts besagt.... Vor allem aber glaube ich, dass all das, was wir als wahr erfahren, und zwar nicht blind, sondern in der Bewegung des Begriffs, und was sich uns wirklich als Index sui et falsi zu lessen gibt, dies Licht nur als Widerschein jenes anderen trägt." Adorno appears to be citing Spinoza's dictum that 'the true is the index of itself and the false.'

[104] Adorno, "Reason and Revelation," in *Critical Models: Interventions and Catchwords*, trans. Henry W. Pickford (New York: Columbia University Press, 1998) 135-42.

[105] Here, Adorno writes: "I see no other possibility than that of extreme asceticism toward any faith in revelation, and extreme allegiance to the *Bilderverbot*." Translation from Elizabeth Pritchard, "*Bilderverbot* Meets Body in Adorno's Inverse Theology." "Darum sehe ich keine andere Möglichkeit als äußerste Askese jeglichem Offenbarungsglauben gegenüber, äußerste Treue zum Bilderverbot, weit über das hinaus, was es einmal an Ort und Stelle meinte." Adorno, *GS*, bd. 10.2, 616.

writings,[106] one does not see anything like the extent to which the (re)turn to religious themes can be seen in Horkheimer's late writings.

IV.1 'Negative' Theology?

One of the central challenges faced by Horkheimer and Adorno vis-à-vis both metaphysics and religion (understood in a more traditional sense of propositional belief and dogma) was simply that while they continued to draw riches from the wells of Kant and Hegel, they could no longer assent to the metaphysical worldviews from which these resources had been mined. The Kantian postulates and transcendentals, like the Hegelian dialectic of the particular and the universal consummated in the self-awareness of *Geist,* lost their metaphysical moorings, particularly in the 'left' branch of Hegelianism almost immediately after Hegel's death in the work of Feuerbach and Marx, inter al. Yet the dialectical structure so central to the Frankfurt School, to Marxism, and to some of the burgeoning theological movements in the early twentieth century all rely, to greater or lesser extents, upon Hegel and his dialectic. Hegel was not, however, the progenitor of the dialectic.[107] That is to say, Hegel's dialectic is enmeshed in traditional religious structures from which many of Hegel's intellectual progeny recoiled but could not entirely escape, and the origins of the dialectic are arguably oriented toward a negative theology.

If the dialectical structure used by Hegel and adapted by Horkheimer and Adorno has its roots in medieval Christian mysticism, then the claim that critical theory reflects a 'negative theology' merits consideration. Following the mystical writings of Dionysius the Aeropagite, medieval mystics sought to preserve divine alterity by speaking of God only in terms of negation. For Meister Eckhart, Nicholas Cusanus and others, the existence of God was not strictly questioned, but positivistic accounts of divine attributes were eschewed. Their conviction was that language is incapable of reaching or describing God and scripture should thus be interpreted allegorically, especially where it appears to anthropomorphize God. Hegel's adaptation of the dialectic, like Kant's use of the antinomies, argued for a mediating ground between extremes. 'Negative

---

[106] Adorno's lectures and book on metaphysics and notably *Negative Dialectics* offer far more material for analysis of Adorno's understanding of religion.

[107] "Hegel's dialectic," according to Rudolf Siebert, "originate[s] from the mystical theological writings of Master [sic] Eckhart, maybe of Nicholas of Cusa, certainly of Boheme and through him possible also from the works of the Kabbalists and the Hassidim." Siebert, *The Critical Theory of Religion*, 51.

theology,' on the other hand, sought to preserve God's otherness by negating any attribute ascribed to God. The parallel to Adorno's mature method of negative dialectics, negating instrumental reason while seeking to preserve the possibility of hope in a more just society, is instructive, but by no means conclusive.

Several scholars have argued that a 'negative theology' of sorts is at work, particularly in Adorno; some have linked this with the *Bilderverbot*, the Jewish prohibition of images, allegedly seeking to preserve room for divine alterity or the possibility of reconciliation.[108] Mendieta writes: "Negative, qua redemptive, theology is...reason in quest of its possibility, hope, and truth."[109] While the scholarship pursuing this argument is not entirely convincing, the question of a negative theology in Adorno (and to an extent Horkheimer as well) should not be lightly dismissed. To deny the possibility of a negative theology in his work, on either semantical or more substantive grounds, leaves the challenge of accounting for the possible lacuna between Adorno's emancipatory ethic and his epistemology.

Accepting the presence of a negative theology as a guiding rubric for one aspect of critical theory raises the challenge of adequately accounting for the emancipatory longing which cannot be fulfilled in time, and the ethical force which names and seeks to rectify injustice. If there is a negative theology at work in Horkheimer and Adorno's engagement with religious themes, I agree with

---

[108] Susan Buck-Morss is one of the first to link negative theology to Adorno in her book *The Origins of Negative Dialectics*. Similarly, Siebert claims "There are elements of negative theology and even mystical atheism...in Horkheimer's, Adorno's, Benjamin's and Fromm's social philosophy and sociology... tendencies to leave God for the sake of God, to let go of God for God's sake, toward an atheism in God." Siebert, *The Critical Theory of Religion,* 23. Eduardo Mendieta is convinced that there is a negative theology in the work of not only Adorno, but Horkheimer and Benjamin as well. He writes: "Critical theory's theology can only be a form of 'negative theology'—a theology that begins with the absence of God, or of a God that has been exiled from creation by the disaster that history has turned." Mendieta, 10. Other scholars who claim to find a negative theology in the Frankfurt School include Joseph Colombo, in *An Essay on Theology and History* (Atlanta: Scholars Press, 1990) and Hauke Brunkhorst, in "Irreconcilable Modernity: Adorno's Aesthetic Experimentalism and the Transgression Theorem," in *The Actuality of Adorno: Critical Essays on Adorno and the Postmodern,* ed. Max Pensky (Albany: State University of New York, 1997). Albrecht Wellmer also accuses Adorno of creating a default "negative theology" given the "aporia" of reason in his philosophy. Wellmer suggests Adorno understands the conditions of human experience "in ecstatic terms rather than as a real utopia; the happiness that it promises is not of this world." Albrecht Wellmer, *The Persistence of Modernity*, trans. David Midgley (Cambridge; MIT Press, 1991) 7, 12.

[109] Mendieta, 11.

Steunebrink that it is an *ethical negativity*; "the absence of a God who should have been there,"[110] in Auschwitz, and the preservation of messianic longing that somehow injustice can yet be overcome. This should not suggest any type of theodicy, however. Both Adorno and Horkheimer vehemently reject any attempts to justify suffering in the name of an otherworldly justice.

Another thesis related to negative theology is that Adorno and Horkheimer, far from seeking 'salvation' in a re-enlightened reason—c.f. the proposed *Rettung der Aufklärung—Rescue of Enlightenment*—sought to reclaim the secular content of the Judeo-Christian concept of the messiah. Benjamin attempted to rescue the secular content of the Jewish idea of the messiah in his "Theses on the Philosophy of History;" a messiah who would come from beyond time and redeem time.[111] Since the messiah to which Benjamin referred, and toward which Adorno and Horkheimer occasionally allude, is a distinctly 'secular messiah,' one is again faced with what might be called a 'negative messianism,' salvific precisely because it lies beyond of the confines of this world.[112] Richard Wolin argues that although it remained latent in *Dialectic of Enlightenment*, secular messianism was of great importance to Adorno, particularly later in his life, and he explicitly links messianism to negative theology. Wolin notes: "in Adorno's work the messianic strategy of negative theology remains prominent."[113] Scholars who claim to find a negative theology, or weak messianism, explicitly in the work of Adorno often turn to the infamous final passage of *Minima Moralia,* which will be discussed subsequently. Ultimately, I find the idea of an 'inverse' theology more useful and evocative for interpreting Adorno (and Horkheimer to a lesser extent) than that of negative theology.

---

[110] Gerrit Steunebrink, "Is Adorno's Philosophy a Negative Theology?" in *Flight of the Gods: Philosophical Perspectives on Negative Theology*, ed. Ilse N. Bulhof and Laurens Ten Kate (New York: Fordham University Press, 2000) 294.

[111] Benjamin's close friend Gershom Scholem writes that the messianic idea "was better able to stand a reinterpretation into the secular realm than the other ideas." Gershom Scholem, "Reflections on Jewish Theology," in *On Jews and Judaism in Crisis* (New York: Schocken, 1976) 284.

[112] Wolin notes, "Via the influence of Benjamin, the standpoint of secular messianism came to play an important role in the critical theory of the Frankfurt School." Wolin, 52.

[113] Wolin, 52-3.

IV.2 'Inverse' Theology

While several scholars have argued that there is a negative theology in the work of Adorno and Horkheimer, its presence or absence, particularly early on, may ultimately depend upon semantics, though there are good reasons to question the validity of this as an adequate label.[114] Significantly, shortly after Adorno's death, Horkheimer himself accepted the label of negative theology for their work.[115] Nevertheless, other scholars have found Adorno's conception of 'inverse theology' to be more insightful as a description of how theology is functioning in the writings of Adorno in particular.[116] With Pritchard, Brittain, and others, I argue the language of 'inverse theology'[117] and 'hopeful negativity' best encapsulates the way the religion is manifest throughout the thought of Adorno. These terms exemplify Adorno's adamant negation of reifying social structures which contribute to modern damaged life, while simultaneously holding out the possibility of and longing for a transformation of this unjust world.

The cryptic phrase 'inverse theology' is Adorno's own, coined in a 1934 letter to Benjamin. Adorno writes:

> It seems to me doubly important that the image of theology, into which I would gladly see our thoughts dissolve, is none other than the very one which sustains your thought here—it could indeed be called an 'inverse theology.' The position, directed against natural and supernatural interpretation alike...strikes me as utterly identical with my own.[118]

---

[114] Mendieta argues that the negative theology in the work of Adorno and Horkheimer "turns into a redemptive and hopeful theology, for which the two central theologemes are memory and hope, remembrance and utopia. The goal...is not faith, but truth and reason." Mendieta, 11.

[115] It is important to note that Horkheimer himself in a late interview quite explicitly draws the connection to negative theology shortly after Adorno's death which Horkheimer gave to the periodical *Der Spiegel.* This article appeared on August 19, 1969, under the title "Himmel, Ewigkeit und Schönheit."

[116] Elizabeth Pritchard, Anson Rabinbach, David Kaufmann, Christopher Brittain, René Buchholz, et. al.

[117] Some scholars, including Buck-Morss and Mendieta seem to equate the terms negative theology and 'inverse theology.' This conflation is not entirely convincing, as will be seen below.

[118] Letter, Adorno to Benjamin, December 17, 1934. Adorno and Benjamin, *The Complete Correspondence,* 66-7. The immediate context includes Kierkegaard and Kafka. Part of this letter was cited above. Adorno-Benjamin *Briefwechsel*, 90.

The word 'inverse' has both musical and mathematical connotations, both referring to a type of reversal or transformation.[119] Inverse theology is fundamentally related to Adorno's philosophy of non-identity;[120] it is the adamant insistence that that which is hoped for, the potential of redemption, is in no way continuous with the current order of injustice and suffering, while—importantly—not lying outside of time or history. Any hypothetical redemption cannot be contiguous with the status quo. In this vein, Pritchard argues:

> Adorno can find no bridge from damaged life to redemption that does not lead straight into history's cavities of death, suffering, and oppression. Adorno...is convinced that it is only by abiding with those who unjustly suffer that one might catch a glimpse of the light of redemption.[121]

Inverse theology is neither positive nor negative; it is directed, according to Adorno, against both natural and supernatural interpretations of theology.[122] It is neither a positive theology, accepting an *Aufhebung* arising from the negation of negativity, nor is it most accurately described as a negative theology which often contained a mystical element. Adorno is insistent that the critical theorist has no special knowledge or access to truth, and that any response to injustice and suffering must begin from the suffering subject in history. Inverse theology, according to Brittain's reading of Adorno, reflects "a negative and dialectical analysis of the contradictions within social existence...." Inverse theology focuses "on the brokenness of present life, and prevent[s one] from escaping to the con-

---

[119] Pritchard notes the interesting insight that Marx tried to invert Hegel and Adorno may be trying to invert Marx theologically. Adorno "proclaims a convergence between materialism and theology where Marx sees contradiction." Pritchard, 309-10.

[120] Anson Rabinbach agrees; he understands 'inverse theology' to refer largely to "non-identity" and a "social and philosophical challenge to homogeneity and domination." Rabinbach, 138-9. Rabinbach also notes that although it was implicit in *Dialectic of Enlightenment*, Adorno's concept of 'inverse theology' underwent a transformation in light of anti-Semitism.

[121] Pritchard, 311.

[122] David Kaufmann suggests that Adorno's distancing from both 'natural' and 'supernatural' interpretations illustrates the "twin perils of uncritical piety and materialist reduction. Adorno's criticism is aimed at all thought based on scarcity (economics) or phenomenology (Heideggerian finitude)." Kaufmann, 169. Kaufmann further argues that for Adorno, 'theology' connotes "the dialectical overcoming of a mythic sense of subjection to alien (and in truth merely alienated) powers." David Kaufmann, "Beyond Use, Within Reason: Adorno, Benjamin, and the Question of Theology," *New German Critique* 83 (2001) 171.

solations of sentimentality or ideology."[123] Structurally, Adorno's inverse theology inverts the traditional model of positive revelation as theology's starting point; it offers no knowledge about the divine, but rather about the human and the world of suffering and injustice. Similarly, Pritchard argues inverse theology "entails not the concealment of the divine, but the revelation of our fallen reality."[124] Starting from the end, so to speak—(hypothetical) redemption—rather than from the 'beginning,' which traditionally is positive knowledge of the divine, Adorno's inverse theology seeks to preserve hope for the 'light' of redemption and the hope that injustice itself can somehow be inverted.

In one sense, inverse theology should be seen in the light of determinate negation, though clearly without the Hegelian assumption of the necessity of a positive outcome. Adorno's engagement with religion and the theological, however opaque at times, seeks, like the rest of his philosophy to negate the negative without presuming a positive. Pritchard insightfully ties Adorno's use of the *Bilderverbot* to his concept of inverse theology, thereby disclosing a hint of the possibility of redemption. She writes:

> To negate the negativity that is damaged life is not to thereby posit redemption; nonetheless, the unblinking, uncompromising vision of damaged life is a kind of photographic negative of the messianic light.... The perspective of negativity is the inverted image projected by the light of redemption.[125]

Like Adorno's image of Kafka, in his letter to Benjamin cited above, the possibility of redemption is "a kind of photographic negative of the messianic light," as Pritchard eloquently puts it. Within Adorno's inverse theology, Pritchard argues that the *Bilderverbot* should not be seen as:

> Creat[ing] and maintain[ing] a chasm between this world and that of the divine or redemption, but rather...investigat[ing] the specific causes of this perceived chasm. In order to do this, Adorno inverts our gaze; he does not simply prohibit pictures of the absolute, but would have us assemble pictures of this fallen world from the *imagined* perspective of the absolute.[126]

---

[123] Brittain, 83.
[124] Pritchard, 295.
[125] Pritchard, 306.
[126] Pritchard, 295; emphasis added.

This "*imagined* perspective of the absolute" is evocative of the image of an 'imaginary witness' in *Dialectic of Enlightenment*.[127] Concerning the perils and pitfalls of modernity, instrumental rationality and the encroachment of barbarism, Adorno and Horkheimer write:

> What is suspect is not, of course, the depiction of reality as hell but the routine invitation to break out of it. If that invitation can be addressed to anyone today, it is neither to the so-called masses nor to the individual, who is powerless, but rather to *an imaginary witness* [*ein eingebildeter Zeuge*], to whom we bequeath it so that it is not entirely lost with us.[128]

The invitation to break out of the hellish reality of injustice and suffering is offered not to the proletariat or the individual subject, but to an 'imaginary witness.' No one can escape history, and any thought system claiming access to a non-historical perspective is an ideology for Adorno.

Following Pritchard, I maintain that Adorno's 'inverse theology,' seen in light of the *Bilderverbot*, unveils the possibility of redemption from the "*imagined* perspective of the absolute," or perhaps to a hypothetical 'imaginary witness' of the barbarity of history. Benjamin's image of Klee's 'Angelus Novus,' being pushed backward into the future, is helpfully evocative in this regard. The possibility of redemption ultimately necessitates thinking *as if* there is a divine perspective, but does not necessitate a divine being for Adorno. As such, inverse theology also illustrates the enigmatic conclusion to Adorno's *Minima Moralia* where Adorno writes the following concerning redemption:

> The only philosophy which can be responsibly practiced in the face of despair is *the attempt to contemplate all things as they would present themselves from the standpoint of redemption*. Knowledge has no light but that shed on the world by redemption: all else is reconstruction, mere technique. Perspectives must be fashioned that displace and estrange the world, reveal it to be, with its rifts and crevices, as indigent and distorted as it will appear one day in the messianic light.[129]

---

[127] Joan Alway writes: "Horkheimer and Adorno's imaginary witness stands outside of action, and with disrespect for what is and infinite patience and tenderness, preserves the emancipatory hopes and possibilities that history threatens to extinguish." Alway, 47.

[128] DE, 213, emphasis added; *DA*, 273.

[129] *Minima Moralia*, #153: *Finale*, 247; emphasis added. *GS* 4, 283.

An inverse theology is rooted in the quest to expose injustice and identity thinking, while hoping for the possibility of redemption. The hypothetical standpoint of redemption is the source of light, the source of potential hope for Adorno. Mentioned in the previous chapter and seen more clearly now in light of Adorno's 'inverse theology,' Adorno and Horkheimer end up with hope in what Bloch described as the act of "*transcending without any heavenly transcendence*...."[130] One cannot consistently, rationally, or responsibly posit transcendence, and any transcending remains ephemeral, breaks in interpretation and constellations. There is a familiar ethical push, however, toward transcending, even without transcendence, in both Adorno and Horkheimer.

V. Religion in the Thought of Tillich in the 1930s and 1940s

As defined in Tillich's early essay "On the Idea of a Theology of Culture," religion is the "experience of" or relatedness to" the "Unconditioned."[131] Tillich's understanding—and critique—of religion has been explored ad hoc throughout this work. Thus, central religious issues and concerns including religious socialism and the Protestant Principle will be sidestepped here, and Tillich's engagement with Judaism will be treated separately below. Tillich's understanding of the Enlightenment and its philosophical legacy decisively shaped his formulations of reason, revelation, and knowledge of God. Beyond the ideals of rationality, liberty, and equality, Tillich understood the "belief in harmony...[to be] the most profound principle of the Western Enlightenment.... It is the principle that has given the Enlightenment its optimism and has given bourgeois society

---

[130] Ernst Bloch, *The Principle of Hope*, vol. 3, 1288; emphasis in original. "...*das Transzendieren ohne alle himmlische Transzendenz*....." Ernst Bloch, *Gesamtausgabe* 5:2, 1522.

[131] This was cited and addressed in chapter 4 as well. "Religion ist Erfahrung des Unbedingten und das heißt Erfahrung schlechthinniger Realität auf Grund der Erfahrung schlechthinniger Nichtigkeit...." "Über die Idee einer Theologie der Kultur," MW/HW 2, 74. The editor of the *Main Works/Haupte Werke* notes that Tillich changed the phrase "Religion ist Erfahrung des Unbedingten," as it appears here, in the original 1919 version of the essay, to religion as "der Richtung auf das Unbedingte" in the 1921 revision of the same essay. "Über die Idee einer Theologie der Kultur," 70. The shift from religion as an *experience of* the Unconditioned, to religion as *relatedness to* the Unconditioned is subtle. Tillich would later describe God, as the goal of religion, as the 'ground of Being.'

its world historical power."[132] Tillich is well aware of the Enlightenment critiques of religion and metaphysics, and he accepts many of these critiques. Insofar as the traditional conceptions of God before the Enlightenment regarded God as a (supreme) being which could be described by human categories and explored as the subject of human knowledge (however limited), Tillich largely accepts this Enlightenment critique of religion. On the other hand, his theology is decidedly apologetic, through his dialectical method of mediation,[133] or what he came to refer to as correlation.[134] Tillich seeks to revive and revitalize the role of religion in the modern world in full awareness of the metaphysical critique of the Enlightenment. The apologetic method employed by Tillich does not seek to recover pre-Enlightenment religion or metaphysics, but rather to supplement its critique with a type of ontology by reclaiming the 'Unconditioned.'[135]

---

[132] *SD*, 51. *GW* II, 268. This conception of harmony is also central in Tillich's essay "Storms of our Times," delivered as a lecture in 1942, a decade after *Socialist Decision* was written.

[133] For Tillich, "*the task of theology is mediation*...between the eternal criterion of truth as it is manifest in the picture of Jesus as the Christ and the changing experiences of individuals and groups, their varying questions and their categories of perceiving reality." Tillich, "Author's Introduction," in *The Protestant Era*, xiii; emphasis in original. Tillich seeks to reclaim 'dialectical theology;' dialectics is one of the means of mediation. Dialectics for Tillich is fundamentally Hegelian: it "is the way of seeking for truth by talking with others from different points of view, through 'Yes' and 'No,' until a 'Yes' has been reached which is hardened in the fire of many 'No's' and which unites the elements of truth promoted in the discussion." Tillich, "Author's Introduction," in *The Protestant Era*, xiii.

[134] Very briefly, Tillich thought that Christian theology should be more proactively involved in interacting with and interpreting 'secular' culture. In his later *Systematic Theology* in particular, Tillich sought to correlate specific social questions with answers from the Christian tradition.

[135] This is specifically in relation to Tillich's ontological philosophy of religion, which will be explored in the following pages. *Theology of Culture*, 43. In this essay, "Aspects of a Religious Analysis of Culture," written in English in the 1950s, Tillich argues that in the modern world, the human subject experiences displacement and the "consequent loss of the dimension of depth in [one's] encounter with reality." Tillich locates the temporal source of this estrangement in the Enlightenment: "[s]ince the beginning of the 18th century God has been removed from the power field of [human] activities.... As the universe replaces God, as [humanity] in the center of the universe replaces the Christ, so the expectation of peace and justice in history replaces the expectation of the Kingdom of God." *Theology of Culture*, 43-44. While Tillich locates the origins of modern estrangement in the Enlightenment, Adorno and Horkheimer emphasize enlightenment as an ongoing process. Nevertheless, Tillich would agree with Adorno and Horkheimer that the alienating process of which the 18th C. Enlightenment is a paragon, is but a reflection

Drawing upon the insights from the third chapter on anthropology, estrangement from self and from the unconditional is the problem to which religion addresses its answer, according to Tillich. There are two ways religion addresses estrangement: the ontological and cosmological. In a 1946 essay, Tillich wrote:

> One can distinguish two ways of approaching God: the way of overcoming estrangement and the way of meeting a stranger. In the first way man discovers *himself* when he discovers God; he discovers something that is identical with himself although it transcends him infinitely, something from which he is estranged, but from which he never has been and never can be separated. In the second way man meets a *stranger* when he meets God. The meeting is accidental. Essentially they do not belong to each other. They may become friends on a tentative and conjectural basis. But there is no certainty about the stranger man has met. He may disappear, and only *probable* statements can be made about his nature. The two ways symbolize the two possible types of philosophy of religion: the ontological type and the cosmological type.[136]

The ontological way religion addresses and seeks to overcome estrangement is analogous to an encounter with an authentic other, through which one paradoxically encounters oneself. In an ontological encounter with God, one simultaneously encounters oneself. The cosmological way of approaching God, by contrast, is analogous to approaching a stranger: it is unintentional and this lack of intention is manifest in the subject's unwillingness to disclose oneself fully to this other. A cosmological philosophy of religion cannot overcome estrangement, according to Tillich. He clearly prefers the ontological, rooted in idealism, which he argues best addresses human needs, and which alone can overcome estrangement and dehumanization.

Knowledge of God is possible for Tillich, but it is a *participatory* knowledge, not an epistemic certainty; such knowledge is accessible primarily in the realm of symbolism. Religious knowledge is different from other types of

---

of a process, rooted in sin, which goes back to the very foundations of humanity. The reference here is to inner-historical utopian belief and movements, of which Tillich was deeply critical, as were both Adorno and Horkheimer.

[136] Paul Tillich, "The Two Types of Philosophy of Religion," in *Theology of Culture*, ed. Robert C. Kimball (New York: Oxford University Press, 1959) 10; emphasis in original.

knowledge, and while Tillich emphasizes faith, he is insistent that faith must be more than passive cognitive assent; it requires grace. Tillich writes:

> You cannot reach God by the work of right thinking or by a sacrifice of the intellect or by a submission to strange authorities, such as the doctrines of the church and the Bible.... Neither works of piety nor works of morality nor works of the intellect establish unity with God.[137]

He insists that religious knowledge, like religious language, is symbolic by its very nature—a point many Enlightenment and post-Enlightenment theologians overlooked. Symbols function expressively, and questions of religious truth are comprehensible primarily in the symbolic realm.

Arguably the central insight of Martin Luther, in whose tradition Tillich understood himself, was the idea of 'justification by faith alone.' For Luther, based on a reading of Paul's *Epistle to the Romans,* this amounted to a critique of medieval Catholic[138] emphasis on and over-reliance upon 'works,' such as indulgences, as opposed to faith in the salvific power of God's action in the Christ event alone. Tillich takes the idea of justification and extends it to the intellect and the quest for truth and justice. In homage to his teacher Martin Kaehler, and in the spirit of Luther, Tillich reflects on his own theological journey in his Introduction to *The Protestant Era.*[139] He cites as decisive the

> insight that the principle of justification through faith refers not only to the religious-ethical *but also to the religious-intellectual life.* Not only he who is in sin but also he who is in doubt is justified through faith. The situation of doubt, even of doubt about God, need not separate us from God. *There is faith in every serious doubt, namely, the faith in the truth as such, even if the only truth we can express is our lack of truth.* But if this is experienced in its depth and as an ultimate concern, the divine is present; and he who doubts in such an attitude is 'justified' in his thinking.[140]

---

[137] *The Protestant Era*, xv.

[138] Luther understood himself as a faithful Catholic seeking to reform the Roman Church at the time of this insight.

[139] The "Author's Introduction" by Tillich is not dated, but the book, which is a collection of Tillich's early essays translated into English, was published in 1948; this Introduction was most likely written in the mid-1940s.

[140] *Protestant Era*, xiv; emphasis added.

From this, he identifies the paradox that "he who seriously denies God, affirms him."[141] Tillich identifies this type of 'faith,' being justified by one's quest for truth and justice, as one's 'ultimate concern.' Without realizing this paradox, Tillich admits that he

> could not have remained a theologian… [because] there is…no place *beside* the divine, there is no possible atheism, there is no wall between the religious and the nonreligious. The holy embraces both itself and the secular. Being religious is being unconditionally concerned, whether this concern expresses itself in secular or (in the narrower sense) religious forms.[142]

Tillich almost certainly understood his Frankfurt School friends and colleagues[143]—and indeed himself at times—in this light of justification by doubt and intellect, where one's ultimate concern is sometimes manifest in the denial of untruth and injustice.

As has been demonstrated, Tillich is in agreement with critical theorists that the 'paradox of enlightenment' lies in the fact that the promise of enlightenment—liberation from suffering and anxiety and domination over external reality—is incapable of coming to fruition and maturation. Enlightenment rationality functions as an explanatory (and thereby demythologizing) principle for everything else, but cannot explain or critique itself. A critical theory of society relies on the insights of religion for Tillich, and the glaring absence or refusal to engage religion as a constructive conversation partner characteristic of the critical theory of Horkheimer and particularly Adorno, is problematic.

V.1 Tillich and Judaism

In the years following the First World War, Berlin was a focal point of creative and intellectual angst and galvanization. Many intellectuals saw this moment

---

[141] *Protestant Era*, xv.

[142] *Protestant Era*, xv; emphasis in original. He continues: "The radical and universal interpretation of the idea of justification through faith had important theological consequences beyond the personal. If it is valid, no realm of life can exist without relation to something unconditional, to an ultimate concern. Religion, like God, is omnipresent; its presence, like that of God, can be forgotten, neglected, denied. But it is always effective, giving inexhaustible depth to life and an inexhaustible meaning to every cultural creation." *Protestant Era*, xv-xvi.

[143] Horkheimer cites Tillich's broader understanding of justification and ultimate concern approvingly in his memorial address in 1966. See *Werk und Wirken*, 128, *inter al.*

after the 'Great War' as a decisive turning point, not only for Germany, but also for western civilization as a whole. In the early 1920s in Berlin, discussions of the concept of *Kairos*—or the fullness of time—led to the formation of an interdisciplinary group known as the 'Kairos Circle,' a group sympathetic to religious socialism which formed around Tillich and Mennicke. Two Jewish economists were core members of the Kairos Circle—Eduard Heimann[144] and Adolf Löwe. The Kairos Circle saw reformed theologian Karl Barth's distancing of himself from religious socialism as an attempt to escape from the challenges facing church and world through an emphasis on the utter transcendence of God.[145] Tillich, on the other hand, emphasized the immanence of the transcendent with the concept of prophetic expectation, rooted in the protest of the Jewish prophets. The Kairos Circle saw themselves and their understanding of religious socialism to be reclaiming the prophetic strain of the Hebrew prophets in contemporary society.[146]

During the Frankfurt years, described in the first chapter, Tillich was proud to be referred to as 'Paulus among the Jews.' Hannah Tillich, Paul's wife, notes that their time in Frankfurt was marked by both intense political conversation and lavish dinner parties.[147] The majority of their friends were Jewish intellectuals and colleagues from the university. *The Socialist Decision*, written in 1932 and published in 1933 as the Nazis came to power, is Tillich's most important political work; Löwe described it as his 'most Jewish book.' The book was dedicated to Heimann[148] and Löwe, who were Jewish economists and members of both the Kairos Circle and the Frankfurt School.[149] Tillich returned to the He-

---

[144] As has been noted, Heimann was also interested in religious socialism. See MW/HW 3, 475-6.

[145] This is a debatable point since Barth was centrally involved in the Barmen Declaration, a 1935 treatise written on behalf of German Protestants against the National Socialist government. This document is far more theological then political; far more so than Tillich's "10 Theses Against the Nazis."

[146] Pauck and Pauck, 72-3.

[147] See chapter one, the Paucks' biography, and Hannah Tillich's memoir, *From Time to Time*.

[148] Heimann was born a Jew but identified strongly with Christianity later in life.

[149] John Stumme's "Introduction" to *The Socialist Decision* notes: "Tillich's later remark...that of all of his books, he was most proud of *The Socialist Decision*. And because of its timely 'prophetic word' as well as its stress on the attitude of expectation, many readers will also agree with Adolf Loewe that this writing is Tillich's 'most prophetic book' as well as his 'most Jewish book.'" *SD*, xxv; Stumme quotes Löwe from an interview 4 May 1972.

brew prophets as one of the central sources of his critique of modernity and instrumental rationality, suggesting the necessity of a 'prophetic criticism,' inspired by the prophets and going beyond rational criticism. In *The Socialist Decision*, Tillich wrote:

> Prophetic expectation is transcendent; rational expectation is immanent.... Prophetic expectation acknowledges factors in human life that are in principle incomprehensible; rational expectation, only factors that have not as yet been comprehended.... Both prophetic and socialist expectations are a witness of life to its fundamental openness. They are a protest of life against false concepts of transcendence that inevitably call forth, in opposition, false concepts of immanence.[150]

In 1933, shortly before Hitler came to power in Germany, the University of Frankfurt asked Tillich to deliver the Founder's Day Lecture. In this lecture, rather than placating the authorities and seeking to retain his position, Tillich boldly spoke about prophetic Jewish contributions to German culture from Spinoza to Marx.[151] The Frankfurt years were not a brief and discontinuous interlude in Tillich's life, but rather these formative years capture a crucial part of the very fabric of Tillich's intellectual and personal life, through his interactions with Jews and Judaism. Hitler's ascension to power in 1933 prematurely cut this period of collaboration between these scholars.

Tillich's genuine openness to and willingness to freely dialogue with Judaism remains the *sine qua non* for his interaction at anything more than a professional level with his Jewish friends and colleagues. It also positively distinguishes him from the vast majority of his fellow Christian theologians in the 1920s-40s. Tillich's support and respect for Jews was a major source of his separation from his long-time friend and fellow Lutheran theologian, Emmanuel Hirsch. Following what was by then (early to mid-1930s) a common interpretation of Luther's two kingdoms doctrine (one vehemently rejected by Tillich), Hirsch supported the so-called 'Aryan Paragraph' by arguing that it was primarily a political, not a theological matter of separation. Hirsch's argument is that "Germans and Jews are two distinct peoples," who have little in common with each other because of distinct racial and historical origins, but also in terms of 'natural' make-up. Hirsch continues: "We are more strongly distinguished from the

---

150 *SD*, 110-1; emphasis in original. *GW* 2, 318-9.

151 Paul Tillich, "The Jewish Question: Christian and German Problem," in *Jewish Social Studies* 33:4 (1971) 261.

Jews than from any other of our national neighbors in Europe."[152] Tillich strongly disagreed and engaged in a heated epistolary debate with Hirsch before finally breaking off the friendship. After his final dismissal from Frankfurt in 1934, Tillich also cut his ties with his beloved Wingolf fraternity to protest their exclusion of Jews.[153]

Soon after arriving in New York, in 1936 Tillich helped found a 'Self-Help for Émigrés from Central Europe' group, of whom a great many were Jewish immigrants. He was also instrumental in finding teaching positions in the New York area for a number of his Jewish friends from Germany. Quoting the Paucks, during the 1930s, Tillich "identified himself with the fate of the Jews to such an extent that they were everlastingly grateful to him."[154] Although Tillich had been very involved politically in Germany, following his arrival in New York in 1933, he rarely spoke out politically[155] until after the *Kristallnacht* in November 1938. Two days thereafter, Tillich wrote and subsequently delivered a lecture at Madison Square Garden entitled "The Meaning of Anti-Semitism" wherein he attacked Nazi ideology and anti-Semitism in all forms.[156] He repeatedly emphasized, not only in this particular lecture, but throughout his career, that Christians cannot surrender their Jewish heritage without simultaneously giving up their Christian identity. While this idea is unobjectionable, if not commonplace among theologians today, this was an extremely strong claim, perhaps particularly made by a German theologian, amidst very few similar theological voices.

Tillich's political advocacy on behalf of German Jewish people during the Second World War is somewhat better known, and the U.S. Department of

---

[152] Hirsch opined that if Jews had been, or were ever allowed to assimilate fully into German culture, not only would the German race be threatened, but German Christianity itself. Tillich vehemently disagreed. Although he was not as radically anti-Semitic as other theologians of his day, Hirsch continues: "The category into which Jews ought to be placed is not that of those who are inferior, unworthy, depraved, but simply the category of those who are foreign, not suited to us, and with whom we cannot mix without suffering damage." Cited in A. James Reimer, *The Emmanuel Hirsch and Paul Tillich Debate: A Study in the Political Ramifications of Theology* (Lewiston: Edwin Mellen Press, 1989) 85. Originally published as "Theologisches Gutachten in der Nichtarierfrage."

[153] Pauck and Pauck, 151.

[154] Pauck and Pauck, 157.

[155] This was in part because Tillich spoke no English when he arrived in New York in 1933, and in part because it took Tillich a long time to understand the American political system.

[156] Pauck and Pauck, 196-7; *GW* 13: 219.

War was quick to pick up on it. Tillich's first radio broadcast into occupied Europe for 'Voice of America' on March 31, 1942 directly confronted anti-Semitism.[157] As Stone and Weaver note in the Introduction to *Against the Third Reich: Paul Tillich's Wartime Radio Broadcasts into Nazi Germany*, Tillich began his radio addresses with anti-Semitism "because the Jewish Question was central to his thought."[158] He began by addressing German Protestants, reminding them that "their religion was prepared in the womb of Jewish history," that Jesus was Jewish, and that "as long as we want to remain Christians, we cannot renounce that we live out of the same religious roots from which the religious Jew lives."[159] The Jewish question, Tillich claims, "is a question of the religious understanding of universal history." Despite horrific persecution, Jews not only will, but *must* survive:

> because they have a vocation without which the vocation of the human race cannot be fulfilled: the Jewish people are called to bear witness to the God of justice and to the oneness of all people and to the God who is God alone, beyond the gods of nations, beyond all national values and ideals.[160]

By the end of 1942, Tillich's radio addresses explicitly described the death-trains, concentration camps, and machine-gun executions of Jews, which he predicted would leave blood on future generations. He told his German audience that "crime[s] against humankind such as occurs only once in millennia"[161] were happening in central Europe on a daily basis and the Jews were being singled out. In these addresses and elsewhere, Tillich regularly argued that crimes against Judaism were not only crimes against humanity, but also against Christianity.

Theologically, Tillich often refers to Judaism and Jews as a religion and people of 'time,' rather than a people of space. Nazism, on the other hand, privileges space, blood, and race. By breaking the 'myth of origin,' Tillich wrote that

---

[157] "The Question of the Jewish People," in *Against the Third Reich: Paul Tillich's Wartime Radio Broadcasts into Nazi Germany*, ed. Ronald H. Stone and Matthew Lon Weaver, trans. Matthew Lon Weaver (Louisville: Westminster John Knox, 1998).

[158] ATR, 7.

[159] ATR, 13.

[160] ATR, 14.

[161] ATR, 88.

Judaism elevates time over space.[162] Prophetic critique and messianic expectation are central to Judaism, and the Jewish emphasis on temporality over locality leads Tillich to write that Judaism is "the community that serves as the bearer of history."[163] He insisted on the necessity of preserving the prophetic Jewish spirit in Christianity and, significantly for the time, rejected any talk of seeking to convert Jews.

Tillich's mediating soteriology already includes God's eternal covenant with the Jewish people. This is clearly in line with his consistent argument against Christian mission to Jews and his life-long insistence on reclaiming the prophetic Jewish tradition into the heart of Christian theology. As early as his 1924 essay "Justification and Doubt,"[164] Tillich is exploring the salvific particularity of grace, and he sketches a unique mediating position between traditional Lutheran soteriology and a more universalistic position.[165] Tillich refers to the central insight of this important early essay as a 'breakthrough principle,' and he argues for a nuanced unification of justification and doubt in the event of salvation in a manner which is implicitly Christocentric, but which refuses to articulate a limit to God's salvific grace. There is what Tillich describes as a 'foundational revelation,' which is distinct from what one might term 'natural revelation.' This foundational revelation (*Grundoffenbarung)* is held in dialectical tension with the particularity of sacred revelation (*Heilsoffenbarung)*, and this 'foundational revelation' is uniquely oriented toward Judaism.

VI. Reason and Religion

Scholars of critical theory and those who have written extensively on both Adorno and Horkheimer have proffered a wide array of interpretations of the function of metaphysics and religion (or their absence) in their respective writings. Certainly in *Dialectic of Enlightenment*, 'religion' in general is derided in its stereotypical form via Feuerbach and Marx; Horkheimer and Adorno largely agree with the disclosure of religion's function as a human construct. They see it broadly as yet another myth maintaining social cohesion and reinforcing a status quo which gradually loses meaning through the inevitable processes of disen-

[162] This was discussed briefly in the third chapter and comes from Tillich's analysis of 'myths of origin' in *The Socialist Decision*. The political romanticism of National Socialism elevated soil, blood, race and Fatherland in its 'myth of origin.'

[163] *SD*, 21. *GW* 2, 242.

[164] Paul Tillich, "*Rechtfertigung und Zweifel*," in *GW* 8; MH/HW 6.

[165] See also Tillich's *Dialektik* of 1925.

chantment and secularization. Yet they nuance 'religion' in a slightly different manner than Marx had done. For example, Odysseus escapes myth (religion) through repression and internalization, but the means of his resistance mirrors that which he resists, and Odysseus' ultimate 'enlightenment' is undermined by becoming myth (religion) again.

Via Hegel, Adorno and Horkheimer understood the 'terror' of enlightenment as the gradual elimination of metaphysics and religion through Weberian disenchantment, which both leads to and is a symptom of instrumental rationality, since it is thought that reason can ostensibly no longer be grounded in metaphysics. Thus enlightenment returns to terror in the form of instrumental rationality, mass culture, domination, and anti-Semitic barbarism. Yet in *Dialectic of Enlightenment*, and particularly in many of their later works, both Adorno and Horkheimer broach the topic of religion in more positive terms.

Critical reason functioned as a lynchpin for much of Horkheimer and Adorno's work in the absence of acknowledged metaphysical norms. The May 1944 preface to *Dialectic of Enlightenment* portends the critique of reason being answered by a renewed reason itself. The critique of reason's servitude to instrumentality in *Dialectic of Enlightenment* was not meant to transcend, but rather to return and reorient reason against the forces of domination: the critique "is intended to prepare a positive concept of enlightenment which liberates it from its entanglement in blind domination."[166] Adorno and Horkheimer's starting point for their 'philosophical fragments' avows: "We have no doubt—and herein lies our *petitio principii*—that freedom in society is inseparable from enlightenment thinking."[167] Although they clearly recognized that "myth is already enlightenment, and enlightenment reverts to mythology,"[168] Adorno and Horkheimer sought to 're-enlighten' the enlightenment. If anything, they were *too* successful in their critique, and many interpreters have rightly questioned what possibilities for freedom or enlightenment remain in the wake of *Dialectic of Enlightenment*.[169] There was the intention to produce a companion volume, *Rettung*

---

[166] *DE*, xviii. *DA*, 6.

[167] *DE*, xvi. *DA*, 3.

[168] *DE*, xviii. *DA*, 6.

[169] Lambert Zuidervaart makes the important point that "A fundamental mistake in many interpretations of *Dialectic of Enlightenment* occurs when readers take such theses [concerning myth and enlightenment] to be *theoretical definitions of unchanging categories rather than critical judgments about historical tendencies*." "Theodor W. Adorno," by Lambert Zuidervaart, in *The Stanford Encyclopedia of Philosophy (Summer 2011 Edition)* ed.

der Aufklärung, but this never materialized for reasons which have been noted elsewhere.[170]

Both critical theory and some contemporaneous religious currents of the early and mid-twentieth century focused on solidarity with victims through anamnestic remembrance. Horkheimer's assertion that "Past injustice will never be made up; the suffering of past generations receives no compensation,"[171] is clearly echoed in Adorno's later works.[172] It is important to note that Horkheimer and Adorno unwaveringly reject any theodicy on precisely this basis. The unique contributions of critical theory to religious discourse lie in the realm of epistemology rather than ontology. Critical theory, as opposed to traditional theory in the terms of Horkheimer's early essay "Traditional and Critical Theory," recognizes its situatedness and abjures any claims to neutrality. This central tenet of critical theory is in some important ways echoed in the work of Tillich.

In *Dialectic of Enlightenment*, Adorno and Horkheimer even praise a few theologians whom they label "paradoxical Christians," including Pascal, Kierkegaard, and their contemporary, Karl Barth.[173] What Adorno and Horkheimer saw in those thinkers was likely a confluence of purposes, across ideological or confessional boundaries, wherein those theologians challenged religion's abuses from within. These thinkers also spoke, with the Frankfurt School, against the historical forces of domination, historical forgetting, reification, self-aggrandizement, and intolerance. These theologians who embraced the paradox of their faith were likewise seeking the liberation of humanity from the forces of domination, calling upon critical resources they understood to be internal to religion, seeking justice for today and tomorrow, while maintaining the memory of the abuses of yesterday.

Edward N. Zalta; emphasis added. URL: <http://plato.stanford.edu/archives/sum2011/entries/adorno/>. Accessed 9/12/2011.

[170] The most detailed account comes from four *Diskussionsprotokollen* during October 1946, as recorded under the title "Rettung der Aufklärung. Diskussionen über eine geplante Schrift zur Dialektik," in Horkheimer, *GS* 12, 593-605. As has been noted, Horkheimer's letters to Tillich and Lowe, inter al., in 1947 also discuss aspects of the planned sequel to *Dialectic of Enlightenment.*

[171] *CT*, 26. *ZfS* 2 (1933) 16.

[172] In a fragment within *Negative Dialectics* (1966) entitled 'After Auschwitz,' Adorno writes:' "Our metaphysical faculty is paralyzed because actual events have shattered the basis on which speculative metaphysical thought could be reconciled with experience." *Negative Dialectics*, 362.

[173] DE, 147.

Tillich's conception of religion as 'ultimate concern' and his idea of 'justification by intellect' in the quest for truth and justice are helpful aids in the explication of the Frankfurt School's thought on religion, but are ultimately insufficient. The two crucial distinctions between Adorno and Horkheimer's understanding of religion and that of Tillich offered above (the 'Unconditioned,' or source of 'ultimate concern') are: firstly, for Tillich, 'ultimate concern' implies ontology, while the Frankfurt School, and Adorno in particular, vehemently rejected ontology outright.[174] Adorno and Horkheimer both abjured ontological statements to the end, contra Tillich, although all three shared a powerful indictment of any religious views resting on claims of certainty and secure epistemic access to the divine as an instrument of the forces of domination, which they often saw reflecting a barbarous anti-Semitism. Secondly, while Horkheimer and Adorno tended to regard religion as another conceptual placeholder, Tillich understood religion in terms of symbolic systems of meaning and significance. This is crucial and serves as a qualification of his ontology: Tillich understands religion to be a system of symbols which relate by means of analogy to ultimate reality, or to that which is one's 'ultimate concern.'

God is understood to be the unconditioned 'ground of being' for Tillich, yet Being transcends categories and cannot be reduced to them; thus God cannot be said to 'exist,' since 'existence' is a category and implies a causal relationship of predication. Likewise, God is not 'transcendent,' nor even 'transcendence' itself. Instead, he understands God analogously as the ground of all Being. Although it is well within the realm of positive ontology to say, as Tillich later did, that 'God is Being Itself,'[175] the early Tillich often stands closer to Adorno and Horkheimer's adamant rejection of ontology, insofar as humanity's epistemic access to God *qua* Being is only in proleptic participation. This is an apophatic, or negative, theological move unparalleled in any of Tillich's contemporaries, yet perhaps strangely echoed in the negative dialectical utopia hinted at in the late writings of Adorno and Horkheimer, beyond the scope of this study.

Like both Horkheimer and Adorno, Tillich rejects any utopia tied to myths of origin or thought to be actualizable within a historical place. For Tillich, 'utopia' draws its power from its roots in prophetic Jewish messianic expec-

---

[174] Indeed, the entirety of Part I of Adorno's *Negative Dialectics* is dedicated to a trenchant critique of Heideggerian ontology.

[175] Tillich makes this claim in vol. 1 of his *Systematic Theology*, but he almost immediately retracts and qualifies it in the beginning to vol. 2. This is beyond the time period on which this work focuses and has been explored thoroughly in Tillich scholarship.

tation. It is that force which animates the present by constantly emphasizing the tension between past injustices and future justice, and by critiquing the present. It is not to be confused with the Kingdom of God, however. Tillich says that utopia, properly understood as a critical concept, is fruitful—it "opens up possibilities" for "human fulfillment" through "anticipatory inventiveness," possibilities which otherwise "would remain hidden."[176] Utopia has the power to transform the given, Tillich writes in "The Political Meaning of Utopia," and he regards it as a fundamentally Jewish movement. "Judaism is perhaps the most momentous utopian movement of human history, for directly and indirectly it has elevated all mankind to another sphere of existence on the basis of its utopia of the coming reign of God,"[177] according to Tillich.

Although the concept of utopia is temporal, it is axiomatically '*ou topos*'—without place. "The root of its power," Tillich notes, "is the essential or ontological discontent of man in all directions of his being."[178] The Marxian 'utopias' that Tillich and others wrestled with in the 1920s made the mistake of reducing their power to one (or a few dimensions) of human existence, e.g. the economic dimension in the Leninist state. The Nazi dystopia emphasized race, blood, and land. Emphasizing the necessity for any 'utopia' to address every dimension of human existence, Tillich rejects any hypothetical utopia whose anticipatory power is reducible solely to the religious dimension. He continues to insist upon an orientation to the Kingdom of God—distinct from utopia—and he emphasizes the Jewish principles of prophetic anticipation, ethical responsibility, and justice as criteria. Tillich believed that the demand for a more just society would best be exemplified by socialism as he understood it in the 1930s, supplemented by Christian humanism in the form of religious socialism. There remains, nevertheless, a certain degree of ambiguity insofar as utopia appears to function largely as an unrealizable critique and the Kingdom of God is purely other-worldly, functioning primarily as hope.

VII. Conclusions

Just as the central task of critical theory has been and remains to challenge the forces of domination, so too are there resources within religion which share the same goal, even if the reasons for so doing remain distinct. Tillich is insistent

[176] *PE,* 169. "The Political Meaning of Utopia" was a series of four lectures Tillich delivered in Berlin in 1951. MW/HW 3, 568.

[177] *PE,* 169. MW/HW 3, 569.

[178] *PE,* 169. MW/HW 3, 569.

upon an ongoing critique of religion; his Lutheran heritage and training emphasized the principle of *semper reformanda*, and his mediating (later correlating) methodology sought to update Christian and biblical answers in conversation with contemporary questions. At this point, I return to the reminder by Tillich, that "critical social theory cannot avoid an 'ultimate' in which its criticism is rooted because reason itself is rooted therein."[179] It is arguable that both Adorno and Horkheimer recognize this, yet they constantly struggle in all of their writings, particularly after the horrors of the Holocaust were more widely known, with how to speak of this 'ultimate,'[180] if at all. It is incredibly difficult to compare the views on religion held by each thinker, and its final utility is questionable given the distinct aims. I *do not* wish to suggest that Tillich's philosophy of religion was somehow 'better' in an evaluative sense, but by providing a conception of an ultimate ground, Tillich's critique of religion and of society has a greater depth and resonance, with political and emancipatory potentialities more ready-to-hand than does that of either Adorno or Horkheimer.

In both Horkheimer and Adorno's work, including their joint work, one can see several traditional Jewish features presented in a non-traditionally Jewish fashion. In addition to the critique of anti-Semitism, the emphasis on the *Bilderverbot* applying not only to images, but to words and ideas about G-d as well, is central to their reflections on religion. The liberative narrative of *Exodus* is clearly echoed in their pursuit of emancipatory theory and praxis to challenge and undermine instrumental rationality, structural oppression, and individual and social alienation. A modified messianic hope, with the emphasis on a this-worldly longing for justice, is another structurally Jewish feature of their thought.

Horkheimer envisions a future for religion, voided of any positive, doctrinal content. Nevertheless, religion is an important structural placeholder for him, entailing the repository of the memory of suffering and the hope for the possibility of justice and transcending, with or without transcendence. In 1935,

---

[179] Cited above. *ZfS*, 9 (1941) 478.

[180] On the occasion of Tillich's death in 1965, Horkheimer wrote in a *Festschrift* for Tillich: "I believe that there is no philosophy to which I could consent which did not contain a theological moment, for it relates indeed to the recognition of how much the world in which we live is to be interpreted as relative." Horkheimer, *GS* 7, 276, as cited by Eduardo Mendieta, "Introduction," in *Religion and Rationality: Essays on Reason, God, and Modernity*, by Jürgen Habermas, ed. Eduardo Mendieta (Cambridge: MIT Press, 2002) 7.

Horkheimer wrote: *"Religion is the record of the wishes, desires and accusations of countless generations."*[181] Religion has an important ongoing (although altered) role to play in Horkheimer's critical theory. This chapter has also called into question Horkheimer's reticence to engage Tillich publically in his writings while Tillich was still alive. Horkheimer's critiques are relevant and incisive, but it is curious that he overlooks resources readily available to him from his knowledge of and friendship with Tillich.

Adorno's concept of 'inverse theology' is obscure, but it is clearly neither a return to positive religion nor is it a reflection of negative theology in a classical sense, in which negation leads to a type of affirmation through other sources of knowledge. He insists that any hypothetical redemption must be within history and must take as its starting point the realities of human suffering and structural injustice without reverting to ideology in the attempt to overcome it. The enigmatic reference to an "imaginary witness" in *Dialectic of Enlightenment*, as well as the knowledge of which Adorno speaks in *Minima Moralia*, in the messianic light of redemption, offer unique conceptions of facing injustice and oppression head-on and refusing to be distracted by ideology or apocalyptic solutions.

[181] *CT*, 129. *KT* I, 374.

Conclusion

This work has focused on several key moments of parallel thought and some direct points of intersection among Adorno, Horkheimer, and Tillich, along with similar crucial points at which their thought makes fundamentally incompatible moves. Going beyond previous scholarly attempts to prove or disprove 'mutual influence,' I have argued that 'influence' is moot and cannot be shown given the limited interactions in published texts among the three. Instead, I have focused on the contextual and personal parallels and differences among them. Placing them in conversation has revealed numerous specific ways in which the thinkers engage one another personally and (albeit often obliquely) professionally. The analysis of this consonance and dissonance has taken shape under the following four rubrics (represented in chapters two through five): rationality with an emancipatory goal, critical anthropology, metaphysics, and religion. In so doing, I have analyzed critical conversations with the texts of the other two thinkers, based on texts within similar periods. Thereby, it has been shown that starting with similar resources yet different emphases, Tillich, Horkheimer, and Adorno effectively structure complementary critical interpretations of a diseased modernity which they each hoped to overcome, to prophetically interrupt, and possibly to redeem, in largely compatible ways.

Some of the most striking similarities that have been revealed common to Tillich, Adorno, and Horkheimer include a mutual early orientation to Hegelian dialectical structure, Marxian emancipatory rationality, and Lukács' analysis of reification. As a result of this, coupled with the influence of Nietzsche and Weber, all three thinkers were centrally concerned with alienation and estrangement. An awareness of the insidious logic of instrumental rationality and the attempt to utilize it as a critical philosophical tool against instrumental logic itself is crucial for all three thinkers. Drawing upon the economic and cultural analyses of Marx and Weber, all three came to understand bourgeois capitalism as a central social evil, and actively sought, at least for some time, to overcome capitalism through theoretical critique, and to varying extents, through socialism and social action. A common emphasis on the centrality of justice and a shared desire not only to eliminate suffering, but also to account for past injustice and ongoing injustices further unifies these three. As such, Adorno, Horkheimer, and Tillich each utilize these shared concerns in their respective attempts to articulate an emancipatory critical social theory. While there is a common desire and a longing for transcendence beyond present injustice, this is where their paths begin to part in substantial ways.

Although it is admittedly an oversimplification to say that Adorno, Horkheimer, and Tillich shared a common diagnosis of the ills of modernity, they held far more in common with regard to diagnoses of social ills than in terms of prognoses for or solutions to the problems faced. Adorno and Horkheimer came to understand the extent and pervasiveness of both instrumental reason and reification as far more entrenched than Tillich was willing to allow. While the latter arguably remained within the sphere of Marxian thought well into his American years, Adorno and Horkheimer made definitive moves away from Marxism by the 1940s. The differences between the two editions of *Dialectic of Enlightenment* in 1944 and 1947 demonstrate this clearly enough. The respective conceptualization and application of the idea of 'determinate negation' arising from Hegel reflects another distinct difference between Tillich on the one hand, who was willing to accept the possibility of an *Aufhebung* of sorts, even if only through divine grace, and Adorno and Horkheimer, who insisted simultaneously that Hegelian determinate negation was absolutely critical to their common project, but that no reconciliation was possible or conceivable. This leads to the final key differences among Tillich, Adorno, and Horkheimer: metaphysics and religion. These have been explored in chapters four and five, but Tillich's transcendence toward God as ground of Being, or as one's 'ultimate concern,' is profoundly distinct from the messianic longing characteristic of Adorno and Horkheimer, which has been summarized by reference to Ernst Bloch's notion of a "*transcending without any heavenly transcendence.*"[1] Indeed, Tillich's notion of God as the ground of Being, even in the 1930s and 40s, is inescapably ontological at a certain core level, and is an idea completely rejected by both Adorno and Horkheimer.

In the context of life-long personal and professional friendships among the three, examined in this work during the Frankfurt period and the U.S. exile, their respective philosophies were worked out in ways which substantially overlap, both historically and intellectually, despite some profound differences which arose among them. Working from many of the same sources and largely similar presuppositions, there are important complementarities to their ideas in many

[1] Ernst Bloch, *The Principle of Hope*, vol. 3, 1288, emphasis in original.

areas, some of which serve to illumine the others' thought in heretofore-unseen ways. The critical social theory represented by Horkheimer and Adorno, and the religious socialism represented by Tillich, are two complementary emancipatory solutions to a common problematic in light of the alienation of modern subjectivity (and perhaps democracy) through instrumental rationality, identity thinking, and the reification of modernity's 'steel-hard casing.'

Emancipatory social critique is *not* inherently secular, as Tillich tirelessly argues. In fact, I argue that critical social theory can be profoundly strengthened and challenged to refine some of its core assumptions and values through conversation with religion. The religious dimension of human existence—however it is manifest—is fundamentally social. Despite the history of and potential for abuse of religion's power, the transformative power of religious traditions can be profitably used in pursuit of emancipatory praxis, as Horkheimer acknowledges. Critical theory and emancipation are *both* secular *and* religious, embodying a prophetic interruption of the status quo.

. . . . . .

The project of the early 'critical theory' of the Frankfurt School as it moved from a materialist-base to a theoretical critique is programmatically articulated in Horkheimer's 1937 essay "Traditional and Critical Theory." This essay set the tone and scope of the research of the *Institut* for the following decade, and it is justifiably celebrated. Complementary to this program of critical theory articulated in 1937 is Tillich's interpretation of the socio-religious *Kairos* and his similar critical and social program articulated in religious socialism. The parallels between religious socialism, developed collaboratively nearly a decade before Horkheimer's most succinct articulation of critical theory, and the critical theory exemplified by Horkheimer and Adorno in particular, are striking. The obvious and profound difference of Tillich's assumption of a metaphysical ground of being in religious socialism, which is entirely absent from critical theory, should not minimize the substantial similarities between the two critical social agendas. What does it mean for emancipatory social critique, typically associated with a rejection of metaphysics and religion, that a Protestant philosopher and theologian was actively involved in a similar constructive pursuit at the same time, and in conversation with the progenitors of allegedly secular critical theory?

Tillich presciently wrote in 1933 in *The Socialist Decision*, if "political romanticism and, with it, militant nationalism proves victorious, a self-annihilating struggle of the European peoples is inevitable. *The salvation of European society from a return to barbarism lies in the hands of socialism.*"[2] For Tillich, religion was an equal partner with socialism, not its opposite. It was Tillich's great disappointment and regret that 'secular' socialists were not willing to engage or work with other religious socialists in any sustained manner. While one may view Tillich as somewhat naïve in this regard, as Adorno seems to have, at least in private correspondence, it would be a serious mistake to doubt his sincerity and commitment to the ideal and cause of social transformation through communal, social, and collective action, standing up to forces of barbarism. Indeed, in hindsight, it was naïve of Tillich to think that his 1932 "Ten Theses" against National Socialism could have had any significant impact on German churches, on galvanizing the fledgling religious socialist movement, or in encouraging secular socialists to join forces to stand up to National Socialism.

Tillich's understanding of the legacy of the Enlightenment, and the means-ends calculus of instrumental rationality in particular, should be viewed in tandem with the insights of critical theory as parallel prophetic interruptions of sameness. One central tenet of critical theory is that knowledge should be expansive and emancipatory; the legacy of enlightenment in general, and the Enlightenment itself in particular, has actually produced the *opposite* and reason has become largely subservient to instrumental rationality. Instrumental rationality and 'identity thinking,' to use Adorno's term, not only pervades, but literally *infects* thought. Reification likewise infects all social and cultural forms, and encroaches even upon interpersonal relationships. For Adorno and Horkheimer, by their mid-1940s collaborative work, reification ominously applies not only to objects, but also to subjects, to people who are used as objects—as means—rather than as ends in themselves. In line with Lukács, however, Tillich disagrees with Adorno and Horkheimer's assumption that reification affects the human person fundamentally. As a result, one can discern a profound difference in terms of agency here, with Tillich joining Adorno and Horkheimer in decrying the insidious encroachment of reification in social relations and cultural forms, while at the same time, Tillich denies that subjects fundamentally become objects, as Adorno and Horkheimer, in their bleakest formulations, will assert. Horkheimer's thought evinces more of a progression in this regard: in the 1930s, Horkheimer maintained a degree of cautious hope for the possibilities of individual and social transformation, and in so doing, he acknowledged, at least

[2] *SD*, 161.

implicitly, the importance of a working understanding of the 'nature of humanity' foundational to transformative social praxis.

Structures and technological innovations that were initially heralded as liberative came to be used as instruments of domination. In the process of dominating nature, humanity has lost an important degree of agency. Adorno and Horkheimer grow increasingly skeptical of the emancipatory capacities of the subject, individual and collective, and of reason itself, as they see increasing social domination and the encroachment of instrumental rationality into all areas of life, from the inter-personal to the cultural. The shift in the 1940s away from emancipatory rationality to instrumentality and domination is evident even in the stylistic changes made by Adorno and Horkheimer, including the gradual excision of Marx and can be seen in the shift away from systematic philosophical and social analysis to aphoristic prose.

It is overly simplistic to analyze either Adorno or Horkheimer's development as a move from a cautious optimism to a resigned pessimism. Rather, one sees a dialectical tension between emancipation and domination playing out throughout their thought. Yet in the final analysis, as Richard Wolin notes, "Despite its manifest brilliance, Adorno's philosophy prematurely abandoned the idea that reason could adequately think through or conceptualize domination."[3] By the time of the composition of *Dialectic of Enlightenment*, the differences between Adorno and Horkheimer concerning the emancipatory capacities of reason can be summarized as follows, according to Seyla Benhabib: "Adorno...views reason to be inherently an instrument of domination," while Horkheimer "acknowledges that reason had an emancipatory force which it has since lost under current conditions...."[4] With every move toward emancipation, innovative forms of domination arise to squelch liberative possibilities.

While some scholars see a definitively pessimistic progression in Horkheimer's thought in the 1940s, others see a consistent negativity throughout his corpus.[5] Horkheimer is in fact largely consistent throughout his life, and particularly so within the period on which this study focuses, despite some obvious changes in method. Horkheimer's own view, and perhaps that of Adorno, can be illuminated by a quote from their contemporary, the Italian communist Antonio Gramsci. In a December 19, 1929 letter from prison, Gramsci makes the

[3] Richard Wolin, *The Frankfurt School Revisited*, 7.
[4] Benhabib, 164.
[5] See, for example, Shaw, 161-2.

assertion, "I'm a pessimist because of intelligence, but an optimist because of will."[6] This captures the essence of both Adorno and Horkheimer's consistent outlook concerning not only critical emancipatory reason, but anthropology, metaphysics, and religion as well. While not a perfect analogy, particularly concerning the role of the will, Gramsci's view elucidates the increasing tension seen particularly in Horkheimer's work through the 1930s and 1940s. While the locus of optimism for Adorno and Horkheimer was not political praxis as it was for Gramsci, an 'optimism of the will' is manifest in their implicit anthropological and metaphysical assumptions concerning possibilities for resistance within the individual, prophetically interrupting the encroachment of instrumentality. While they had every reason to surrender to a type of pessimism, they retained something like an 'optimism of the will' in their belief, contrary to evidence, in the potential of emancipatory reason, in the potential of non-instrumental human subjectivity and interaction, and in the potential of transcendence holding off the logic of immanence. Adorno and Horkheimer each seek to imagine society as it could otherwise be. In the conclusion to his 1938 essay "Montaigne and the Function of Skepticism," Horkheimer writes:

> [T]he critical theory which we espouse, in contrast to skepticism, does not make an antitheoretical absolutism of the insight into the inadequacy of things as they are and the transitoriness of cognition. Instead, even in the face of pessimistic assessments, critical theory is guided by the unswerving interest in a better future.[7]

Reason with an emancipatory goal serves as the critical core of rationality for the early Horkheimer, and functions to a lesser extent, although still centrally, in Adorno's early essays. Horkheimer's concept of reason with an emancipatory goal changes slightly as he insists more on the autonomy of philosophy, particularly following the positivism dispute with Neurath. His 1941 "Reason and Self-Preservation" argues that self-preservation comes at the cost of reason. In this vein, *Dialectic of Enlightenment* is clearly a transitional text. By 1944, Horkheimer and Adorno no longer see much emancipatory capacity remaining in reason itself. Adorno's student and successor, Jürgen Habermas found the

---

[6] Antonio Gramsci, *Letters from Prison*, vol. 1, ed. Frank Rosengarten, trans. Raymond Rosenthal (New York: Columbia University Press, 1994); letter of December 19, 1929, to 'Carlo,' 299. Gramsci may have borrowed this phrase from the French writer Romain Rolland. See Gramsci's *Letters from Prison*, vol. 1, 300, n. 1. See also Gramsci's *Prison Notebooks*, vol. 3, 429 n. 2.

[7] BPSS, 311. *ZfS* 7 (1938) 52.

critique in *Dialectic of Enlightenment* to be so all-encompassing that Adorno and Horkheimer could not extricate themselves from the pernicious jaws of instrumental rationality.[8] Habermas argues that *Dialectic of Enlightenment* reflects a "performative contradiction,"[9] criticizing reason based solely on reason, which led Adorno and Horkheimer into an intellectual cul-de-sac. For Tillich, prophetic criticism retains emancipatory potential, but the role of rational criticism is arguably diminished, and it is not entirely clear whether reason remains inherently emancipatory for Tillich by the 1940s.

Throughout this text, particularly in the anthropology chapter—the central and longest—I have argued that a rough, structural conception of a hypothetical 'nature of humanity' seems necessary for any robust emancipatory theory and praxis to gain any critical traction, despite the prescient reservations expressed by Adorno. He consistently—and consciously—refuses to engage anything like a 'nature of humanity.' As such, it would not immediately seem that his work could lead to viable emancipatory praxis, and Adorno had given up on Marxian ideas and ideals of revolution relatively early on. At the same time, revolutionary transformation of the social was not his goal, and his admirable adherence to critical negation of hegemonic power structures and narratives is one of his enduring contributions to critical social theory, and to philosophy more generally. Adorno's insistence on radical questioning, if not negation of that which was often perceived as a 'given' reflects his desire to preserve room for alterity, and perhaps even for a hypothetical moment of future, albeit inner-historical, transformation, even if such could only be seen in momentary constellations, or in the reflection of (messianic) light.

Horkheimer's work in the 1930s up to and including *Eclipse of Reason* cautiously utilizes language and metaphors evocative of a 'nature of humanity' as a way of situating his understanding of the subject of emancipation and hypothetical social transformation. Tillich is even more explicit in this, following his intuition concerning the centrality of subjectivity in the early Marx's understanding of transformative social praxis, insisting on reintroducing the repressed religious dimensions of the earliest Marxian anthropology. Tillich consistently thematizes the human subject in an attempt to diagnose the challenges faced in modernity and to articulate the conditions of the possibility of the emancipation

---

[8] Jürgen Habermas, "The Entwinement of Myth and Enlightenment: Re-Reading *Dialectic of Enlightenment*," in *New German Critique* 26 (1982) 18.

[9] Habermas, *The Philosophical Discourse of Modernity*, 119.

of the subject, and one's capacity to claim and make meaning in light of one's 'ultimate concern.' This does not make Tillich's anthropological conception 'better' than that of Horkheimer or of Adorno, but his theory does more easily allow for the praxis potential within social transformation, both personally and collectively.

The similarities between Horkheimer's anthropological views and presuppositions up to the mid-1940s and Tillich's views on the 'nature of humanity' are striking. Even more significant is the light shed on this commonality in the early Horkheimer and Tillich by Adorno's trenchant critique of Tillich's anthropology in his *Entwurf contra Paulum*. Adorno critiques Tillich's assertion in a 1943 essay that humanity can be understood as "finite and creative freedom." Written in the first person plural, Adorno intended this *Entwurf* as a joint effort with Horkheimer, but the latter had nothing to do with its composition and almost certainly could not assent to its content after reading it, which is likely why the 26-page letter was never sent to Tillich. I have suggested that Horkheimer may have recognized some of his own views on philosophical anthropology in Adorno's critique of Tillich. That Adorno may not have realized that his critique of Tillich had implications with respect to Horkheimer's position is not surprising, and it makes the *Entwurf* all the more fascinating. Adorno never openly critiqued Horkheimer's views on anthropology, which lends further credence to Agnes Heller's characterization of Adorno as Horkheimer's "faithful knight," unwilling to critique, or perhaps even to acknowledge an important difference between himself and Horkheimer at the height of their collaborative interaction when they claimed to be thinking with one mind.[10]

Adorno's adamant rejection of any language concerning the 'nature of humanity' as laden with inherently oppressive potentialities is an impressive and largely compelling critique of Tillich, and perhaps of Horkheimer, and by extension any positive philosophical anthropology or attempt to positively ground subjectivity. Adorno as such simply cannot—and will not—account for the authentic possibility of the social transformation of subjects. To be clear, he was not interested in immediate, much less intermediate, transformation. He totally rejects the possibility of complete transformation within history and consistently rejects any focus on the otherworldly or utopian ideals.

While Adorno sharply critiques Tillich for 'essentializing humanity' and his utilization of ontological categories, it is important to note that in the early

[10] Heller, 216.

1930s, Adorno himself engages ontology and somewhat freely uses the Heideggerian term *Dasein*, referring to human-being-in-the-world, as does Horkheimer up to at least 1938.[11] Tillich's use of the term *Dasein* in *The Socialist Decision* (1933) should not be surprising, nor can it be legitimately used to suggest a profound distinction from Adorno and Horkheimer, at least in the early and mid-1930s; most philosophers of that era engaged with Heidegger in one way or another. It is nevertheless true that Tillich continued to utilize Heideggerian terminology long after Adorno and Horkheimer had abandoned it. The influence of Heidegger on Tillich's own ontology can be seen in later works, while such concerns and language essentially disappear from the writings of Adorno and Horkheimer by the mid-1930s.

In concluding the examination of anthropology and subjectivity, it is instructive to briefly recall that in a discussion with Horkheimer in October 1946 concerning the possible sequel to *Dialectic of Enlightenment*, Adorno curiously mentions 'social and anthropological realism' as a factor in articulating a critical yet positive starting point for a potential response to their trenchant critique of modernity. For Horkheimer and Adorno, there is an increasing loss of agency and subjectivity as the effects of domination and the 'administered society' become more evident and seemingly inescapable in *Dialectic of Enlightenment.* As noted toward the end of chapter three, in the final recorded discussion with Horkheimer concerning the possibility of a sequel to their *magnum opus*, which might redeem enlightenment and reason from domination and instrumentality, Adorno suggested that the 'illness' of reason [*die Vernunft erkrankt ist*] could itself function as a 'foundation' [*Leitfaden*] in their attempt to articulate a 'cure' for enlightenment's inability to realize its own promises and goals. Challenging Horkheimer's fear that no such 'guide' [*Leitfaden*] remained for them, Adorno says:

> We must bring together the thought of the disease of reason and the possibility of its recovery by means of the sickness with the demand to bring the forms of consciousness themselves and their social or

[11] Horkheimer, z.B., "Materialismus und Metaphysik" (1933) von Max Horkheimer, in *ZfS* 2 (1933) 9; "Der neueste Angriff auf die Metaphysik" (1937) in *KT* II, 82, 113, usw.; "Traditionelle und kritische Theorie" (1937) in *KT* II, 159; "Montaigne" (1938). For Adorno's use of *Dasein*, see *Kierkegaard: Konstruktion des Ästhetischen*, and see "The Actuality of Philosophy" (1932) 131. Adorno again uses the term *Dasein*, albeit highly critically, in *Negative Dialectics.*

anthropological reality that are simultaneously their own meaning and the ground for the inadequacy of each form of consciousness.[12]

Of course the *Rettung der Aufklärung* was never attempted, with Adorno and Horkheimer privately and implicitly acknowledging that their original critique was too trenchant to offer a positive corrective, at least at that point in time. One should not take Adorno's off-hand comment in a private meeting with Horkheimer too far, but his suggestion of a *demand* to bring forms of consciousness to bear on 'social and anthropological realities' is striking, particularly in the context of a final attempt to articulate a foundation for a sequel meant to 'rescue' enlightenment itself. It is, of course, impossible to know what Adorno had in mind here, and it is not implied in any way that he suddenly had a change of heart or saw anthropology as suddenly important to a philosophical program of critique, even a hypothetical positive program. On the other hand, this glimpse into the final discussion which sealed off the possibility of a sequel to *Dialectic of Enlightenment* arguably contains at least a hint that Adorno recognized the importance of theorizing subjectivity more fully in order to articulate the conditions for the possibility of any hypothetical social transformation. Yet this remains pure speculation. Adorno and Horkheimer acknowledge the depth of their critique leaves them without a 'guide' or 'manual' for any attempt to 'rescue' enlightenment.

We now return to the heart of Tillich's critique of critical theory as practiced by Adorno and Horkheimer: without a source of 'ultimacy,' without some *Leitfaden* guiding critical theory, critique itself is in danger of becoming positive and contingent. Tillich's review of Marcuse's *Reason and Revolution* in the *Institut's* journal in 1941 claimed: "Even a critical social theory cannot avoid an 'ultimate' in which its criticism is rooted because reason itself is rooted therein."[13] Without such a foundation, "criticism itself becomes positivistic and contingent."[14] Without some type of grounding for their critical project, the critical theory of Adorno and Horkheimer by the late 1940s increasingly runs the risk of developing into something like the 'decayed pragmatism' which Adorno accused Tillich of espousing in his anthropology.

---

[12] Adorno, cited above, in the final *Diskussionsprotokol* concerning a possible sequel to *Dialectic of Enlightenment*, in Horkheimer, *GS* 12, 604. Emphasis mine.

[13] Paul Tillich, "Review of Herbert Marcuse," *ZfS* (1941) 478.

[14] Tillich, "Review of Herbert Marcuse,", 478.

It has neither been suggested nor implied that Adorno was in some sense uninterested in subjectivity, or incapable of theorizing it. While his theorization may ultimately leave him at odds with the praxis of emancipatory subjectivity, it is important to again acknowledge the nuance of his thought. Emancipation in some sense *precedes* subjectivity—which is always a damaged subjectivity—for Adorno. He seeks to embrace subjectivity paradoxically by rejecting any attempt to *utilize* the subject, even in the name or service of its purported liberation. The 'emancipatory moment' is almost as elusive as the messianic moment; it can be accessed only in 'constellations,' which offer momentary breaks in perception. Adorno's 'constellations' in "The Actuality of Philosophy" seek momentary insight to break identity thinking, not sustained transformation like early Horkheimer and Tillich consistently seeks. Likened to dissolution rather than solution, constellations represent momentary flashes of insight into an otherwise mechanized world. Adorno writes: "Philosophy has to bring its elements, which it received from the sciences, into changing constellations…into changing trial combinations, until they fall into a figure which can be read as an answer, while at the same time the question disappears."[15] In his 1932 lecture, "The Idea of Natural History," Adorno argues that interpretation requires the experience of 'shock' and involves not merely synthesis, but a "change of perspective."[16]

……

The twin goals of minimizing suffering and an epistemic emancipation from the constraints of antiquated forms of thought and belief were thought to be able to fund a type of liberation from false enchantment with the world of homogeneity and concomitant domination. Yet given the unyielding focus on instrumentality and identity-thinking perpetuating structures of oppression, Adorno and Horkheimer came to despair of the ability of theory to reveal possibilities of things 'as they otherwise could be.' As such, Benjamin Snow insightfully and succinctly characterizes Adorno as a "metaphysician with no faith in metaphysics," and Horkheimer as a "moralist with no belief in Divine Providence."[17]

In *Dialectic of Enlightenment*, the reader quickly ascertains the quasi-normative premise that '*whatever seeks to uncover and expose myth, becomes itself a*

[15] AP, 127.

[16] INH, 118.

[17] Benjamin Snow, "Introduction to Adorno's 'The Actuality of Philosophy,' in *Telos* (1977) 117.

myth.' Despite their apparent rejection of metaphysics, the primary concern for Adorno and Horkheimer is not, as has been emphasized, metaphysics itself, but rather critical and normative functions assumed by metaphysics. Even in the absence of metaphysics, the power vacuum which the displacement of metaphysics creates something equally, if not more, insidious. This type of displacement is, in the end, also true for Adorno and Horkheimer's attempt through *Dialectic of Enlightenment* to uncover the mythology animating western civilization. They acknowledge that "every definite theoretical view is subjected to the annihilating criticism that it is only a belief."[18] Of course the goal was not to undermine enlightenment, but rather to re-enlighten both enlightenment and 'the Enlightenment,' to provide a new way forward in the anticipated second volume of collaboration between Adorno and Horkheimer, which never materialized.

Central normative (and quasi-metaphysical) assumptions of Horkheimer and Adorno revolve around the emancipatory capacities of reason and the need to minimize (if not eradicate) suffering and maximize justice wherever and whenever possible. Even though they do not believe true justice is possible in this world, and there is no future world which will—much less could—justify the suffering of this world, they each retain a hint of hope for another way of being in the world and for fleeting possibilities for insight and the potential for change. The transcendent realm, in religion and philosophy, must be retained in some guise as a manifestation of the hope for things as they 'otherwise could be.' Unable to ground the norms of justice and emancipatory rationality in their own critical philosophy, Adorno and Horkheimer each return to 'myth' of sorts in placing their hopes in a religious realm voided of all positive content. Both, altogether too blithely, shrug off the non-hegemonic resources of their Jewish heritage via an uncritical Weberian sentiment that 'we cannot go back.'[19]

In Horkheimer's work, a defiant clarion call against the rationalization of suffering and the erasure of the memory of suffering leads him to the one remaining emancipatory social form capable of retaining such memories and hopes: a neutered form of religion. While Horkheimer critiques religion throughout the period of this study, he consistently sees emancipatory potentialities inherent to religion, which he correctly lambastes organized religion for failing to act upon. Although he is by no means suggesting a return to previous

---

[18] DE, 7. *DA,* 17.

[19] Although they make an obscure suggestion which may suggest the resources of Judaism can be a positive force in the resistance of encroaching instrumental rationality.

forms of religion, and in fact has in mind a 'religion' voided of all doctrinal content, Horkheimer wishes to retain the structure of religious hope and longing for not only a better future (even if only as a hypothetical) but also for a redeemed—or at least remembered—legacy of unanswered suffering. This comes through a prophetic interruption of suffering for Max Horkheimer.

For Adorno, one sees this clearly in his theoretical return to the *Bilderverbot* and his 'inverse theology.' While Horkheimer insists on the necessity of religion as the repository of suffering and the shattered hopes of the dispossessed and slaughtered, Adorno's curiously evocative and elusive phrase 'inverse theology,' coined in a 1934 letter to Benjamin, suggests an inversion of thinking about otherness. It evokes thinking from the hypothetical standpoint of the divine, or more properly, from the standpoint of redemption, about humanity as 'other' and the responsibilities one has to others because of suffering and injustice. This hypothetical standpoint of an 'imaginary witness' to the barbarity of modernity reflects a prophetic interruption of insipid sameness for Theodor Adorno.

Is there any hope in-spite-of-hope for Adorno and Horkheimer? Given the exigencies and circumstances under which *Dialectic of Enlightenment* and other texts were written and published, there would appear to be quite little hope, if any. One of the fragments from 'Notes and Sketches' claims that "what threatens the prevailing praxis and its inescapable alternatives is not nature, with which that praxis coincided, but the remembrance of nature."[20] Memories of nature and memories of suffering implicitly challenge any totalizing system, recasting temporality as discontinuity rather than seamless progress. As repression is always a defense mechanism, it can clearly be seen as a necessary defense against a glib nihilism in the face of the absurdity of enlightenment rationality, much like a 'run-away train with no conductor.' The memory of moments of non-identity, whether experienced as oppression or as human suffering, at least potentially stands as a defiant critique against hegemony.

......

While there is some continued interest in the later, ethical works of Tillich within liberal religious circles today, such as *Love, Power and Justice* and *The New Being*, etc., his works have, for better or worse, been eclipsed in many senses. Likewise, except as a figurehead of the Frankfurt School, interest in Horkheimer

[20] DE, 212.

is largely limited to a narrow subset of scholars. Why is there a perduring interest in the work of Adorno in particular? In no small part, the fascination is rooted in the opacity of Adorno's brilliance and the cryptic implications of his aesthetic theories. His work retains an almost poetic, elegiac quality—not of nostalgia for that which has gone, but of melancholic lament for reason's incapacity to liberate itself, for the inability of enlightenment to reach the noble goals it set out. Many readers of Adorno are attracted to or identify with a yearning without a distinct object, a longing for the preservation of alterity that eludes succinct categorization or application.

Of what relevance is the interaction among these three thinkers today? The 'third generation' of critical theory continues to engage in scholarly reflection in conversation with 'first generation' thinkers like Adorno and Horkheimer and 'second generation' thinkers like Habermas and Honneth, but there has not been any sustained engagement with religion. Habermas, perhaps more than other critical theorists, has engaged religion and theology,[21] and his engagement with Catholic theologian Johannes Baptist Metz[22] is a substantial moment in this collaborative discourse not seen since the days of Adorno, Horkheimer, and Tillich. Yet what role could critical theory play in conversation with religious discourse in today's pluralistic society?

In one sense, while many things have changed, the central issues which Adorno, Horkheimer, and Tillich agreed upon as problems, namely alienation and domination, have not fundamentally changed. The central concerns for justice, the cessation of suffering, the memory and hope for redemption of past injustices and suffering, etc., remain as relevant as they were in a different context in the 1930s and 40s. These concerns still animate critical social theory and many religious discourses; the problem is that although some religious groups are increasingly engaging one another in ecumenical dialogue, there is little dialogue between persons and groups who share the goals of critical social theory and scholars of critical theory who are often dubious of engaging the religious 'other.' Just as human rights discourse continues to struggle with articulating a distinctive grounding for rights, so too critical theory continues to struggle with

[21] See, inter al., *Habermas, Modernity, and Public Theology*, ed. Don S. Browning and Francis Schüssler Fiorenza (New York: Crossroad, 1992) and *Habermas and Theology*, Nicholas Adams (Cambridge: Cambridge University Press, 2006).

[22] See Habermas, "Israel or Athens: Where does Anamnestic Reason Belong? Johannes Baptist Metz on Unity Amidst Multicultural Diversity," in *Religion and Rationality*, 129-38.

articulating a ground or norm by which critical theory can not only judge social injustices but seek to affect change. Admittedly, many theorists today, much like Adorno, are not explicitly interested in transformative social action as a direct goal of their critical philosophies. For those who are, however, there are dialogue partners who understand 'God,' in some sense as a critical foundation for justice and social norms, and most are highly nuanced in their understanding of the limitations and emancipatory potentialities of their respective beliefs. The question of how to promote a dialogue between these groups is an open one, but one which Adorno, Horkheimer, and Tillich would likely encourage us to pursue with passion, despite the numerous challenges to such discourse and dialogue. Indeed, Jürgen Habermas came to a similar conclusion:

> Among the modern societies only those that are able to introduce into the secular domain the essential contents of their religious traditions which point beyond the merely human realm will also be able to rescue the substance of the human.[23]

Contemporary anthropologist David Harvey suggests the possibility of collaboration between secular humanism and religious progressives, something this work has advocated throughout. Harvey writes:

> There is, I believe, a crying need to articulate a secular *revolutionary* humanism that can ally with those religious-based humanisms (most clearly articulated in both Protestant and Catholic versions of the theology of liberation as well as in cognate movements within Hindu, Islamic, Jewish and indigenous religious cultures) to counter alienation in its many forms and to radically change the world from its capitalist ways. There is a strong and powerful—albeit problematic—tradition of secular revolutionary humanism both with respect to both theory and political practice. This is a form of humanism that...has a powerful and articulate expression in the Marxist and radical traditions as well as beyond. It is very different from bourgeois liberal humanism. It refuses the idea that there is an unchanging or pre-given 'essence' of what it means to be human and forces us to think about how to become a new kind of human.[24]

Harvey's suggestion of creating an *alliance* between "secular *revolutionary* humanism" and "with those religious-based humanisms...to counter alienation"

---

[23] Jürgen Habermas, quoted in Michael Reder and Josef Schmidt, SJ, "Habermas and Religion," in Jürgen Habermas, et. al., *An Awareness of What Is Missing: Faith and Reason in a Post-Secular Age* (Cambridge: Polity Press, 2010) 5.

[24] David Harvey, *Seventeen Contradictions and the End of Capitalism* (Oxford: Oxford University Press, 2014) 287.

is precisely what Tillich was trying to offer, and what Horkheimer and Adorno desired. With Adorno's insistence that there can be no given human nature, Harvey reminds us that the social project of the present should "force us to think about how to become a new kind of human," something with which both Adorno and Tillich would have strongly concurred. While Adorno and Horkheimer remained skeptical about the role of religion, Harvey's insight that there can be collaboration between revolutionary secular and religious humanisms reflects the hope of Tillich and a minor but resurgent trend in social theory. It is toward such collaboration with the shared goal of critically-engaged, emancipatory possibilities of prophetic interruption that this study points in hope.

Appendix

Translation of Adorno's *Entwurf contra Paulum* (1944)

(277): Dear Paulus,

It has been our intention for a long time to continue our philosophical exchange that has been interrupted for years. Your programmatic essay "Man and Society in Religious Socialism" is a welcomed trigger. We do well know that the form of talk as well as the restriction of speech [...] urged you to simplify, which is reflected in the primitivism of our answer. Therefore, I would like to ask you beforehand to forgive the element of 'unfairness,' which is given through the literary situation. On the other hand, it seems to us as if the drastic thesis and counterarguments could help to get our discussion going, which could not possibly have started with subtle distinctions. Like you do in your essay, we too do without explicitly discussing theological questions and hang on to politics and philosophy, however, without avoiding touching theological background at some points.

(278): You start with contrasting followers of Religious Socialism, which, in your opinion, is political and not only a pure 'idea,' with parties. It is worrying to deny the party character of a political group right from the beginning. It should make us factually suspicious that the fascist's slogan was the fight against parties. The particular which confesses, marks off and—due to social theory—limits itself may well represent the common good; the interest of a society freed from rackets. The question of a party is dialectical: only the particular, which resists the negative whole, is able to neutralize the particular, that is to say the particular acts as principal of the negative whole. But if a group denies its particular character and abruptly presents itself as overcoming the differences, it falls back on exactly that particular principle which it claimed to have neutralized by wrongly believing in harmony. It then sounds like Gundolf's assurance that the *Georgkreis* is not a clique. There is no more reliable sign for a clique than that of pretending not to be one. There has never in the world's history, since the Platonic Republic, been a repressive group which did not justify itself in its reflection of not being a party but acting in the name of a higher good. The empathic term 'party' that Marxism introduced serves to unmask this invariant of all ideologies. It means to fall behind that if a socialist speaks and claims not to know parties. The criticism of the state of the Marxist party should not be used as an excuse for slipping in a party overlapping belief in reforms—a belief in the 'new-construction of the world' by the *homes de bonne volonté*—which, by denying the differences, hands itself over to the system that keeps itself alive through these differences. By open-heartedly admitting young conservatives into 'Religious Socialism,' they paid for the proven spiritualization and internalization of socialism by tolerating people who were closer to fascism than the old conservatives.

(279): But that is due to its nature. A party naming itself a movement because it does not want anything to do with the constraints of party programs is not more but less than a party. It is a unit of integration making a deal with leadership by generously ignoring it. Things may look bad for the proletarian party but in contrast to the dynamic front of unity, from the young conservatives up to De Man, the term 'party' is still substantial enough. The only thing that today's party could be accused of is of not being party enough but too much movement and people's front and not vice versa.

The neutralization of the political education of the will, which is due to the inclusion of heterogeneity, can be seen in the articles of faith you put first. The first one stresses the terms of the bourgeoise and the catastrophe. However, it does not become clear what bourgeoise means when the term is stripped off its meaning of class. According to later remarks you mean something like an individualistic conviction. The opposite, collectivism as such, without transparent relations to collectivization of means of production and its political expression, would cover an institution of states asset as well as a socialistic one—and that one would be 'bourgeoise,' wouldn't it. The term catastrophe, however, belongs to the fixtures of the new form of rule if we consider it as a fixed quantity. In our studies about fascist propaganda we did not accidentally work out a 'Last Hour Device' as a core piece with its abstract vision of revolution combined with its glorification, the believe in the twilight of the gods, the destruction. At the end of your essay (21) the affirmation of the catastrophe (along that scheme) as price for the suffering is brought to light.

(280): If there is something bourgeoise and unsuitable of being the antonym to bourgeoise, it is the idea of catastrophe. Its prerequisite is a 'normal' working bourgeoise order, to which the catastrophe should put an end. However, exactly that notion is the illusion which is held by bourgeoise society itself. The criticism of political economy countered that, although reproducing life, the form of reproduction itself is a permanent catastrophe and what we nowadays experience as the fate of market economy is not its breaking off through external powers but the execution of its own principles, even the revelation of those. It has always included the threat of catastrophe for all those thrown into it. Revolution is not the catastrophe which is followed by renewal but which stops the permanent catastrophe. The apparent radicalism wishing for a catastrophe is (if earnestly wished and not only deluded by pure inwardness) the consent with what has always been and of which that radicalism deeply wants to finally show its uncovered face. In the age of concentration camps it is not radical to want the catastrophe but to stop the horror that toady is confessed as catastrophe.

Commenting on the second article, which describes the term socialism as out of fashion (however, not the word 'religious') and wants to substitute it by collectivism, there is little more to do than referring to a passage, where we anticipated this term before the breakout of the Third Reich. The following words are put into the mouth of an academic sympathizing with socialism: "The term of humanity was dishonored and emptied by the worst capitalistic practice, which used it as disguise over centuries. Decent people could no longer earnestly use that term so they stopped using it.... Some weeks later a book about the reality of Christianity was published by that academic. First I was surprised, then I discovered: he did not reject/condemn the word, but the thing as such.

The third article of faith is theoretically most precarious. Because the thesis: "that without the acceptance of a religious foundation and the symbols expressing it no system of a planned society can escape a speedy self-destruction" shows that precisely the direction which pretends to deepen socialism is in truth decayed pragmatism.

(281): Neither religion nor philosophy can be constituted by claiming that without it something would break. The maneuver becomes striking when looking at the term 'symbol.' It arises with clear associations of mass psychological convenience, yet without being asked for the substantial religious symbolic, its relation to magic [5], or its factual possibility. The Cross becomes the successor of the Three Arrows, which were introduced as an antidote against the swastika. This recommendation not only wrongs religion but is as powerless against reality as the try of setting up post-war Europe as holy Alliance. The enacted symbolic fits only too well with the coming social reconstruction, which simulates a solitary society (as constructor).

Concerning the doctrine of humanity, we do not want to take up our old ontology debate again today, but rather restrict ourselves to the connection between religion and the doctrine of humanity which exists beyond question. It is however precisely on the basis of this connection that organized religion has positioned itself in the service of repression. The logical control of the individual through its subsumption under the form of human nature involves societal control. The nullity before God which is ascribed to (human nature) in such subsumption virtually makes (human nature) into an object of discipline and manipulation. Every sentence which takes the form of "the human is ..." implies that content is already written through just this form: the human person is filth [*der Mensch ist Dreck*]. Bringing the idea of the person back to the existence of being is a gesture of authority which is to be greeted with contempt in the convenient pre-decision which dissects the human. To sharpen the point: the human is not actually human, whereby the human is determined as human, but rather the possible difference of humans from this concept. There also exists the authoritarian gesture whereby one attests that the human is good, but perhaps there particularly maliciously. The institution that controls the human to such an extent - the church - adjusts the individual by virtue of the power of the doctrine of humanity as an administrative object, and grasps it. The pathos with which the church always knows better what the human is than the person him/herself knows recommends and entitles the church at the same time to the administration of the human.

(282): Your expressed antipathy (11) of religious socialists towards their own cause cannot compulsively account for the necessity to newly present such a doctrine [6]. This antipathy does not express something as substantial. You could simply think of the unease of a concept in which every radical question is inevitably followed by a moderate answer, or of the reluctance to end up on the losing side with a nationalized Christianity in the age of fascism, as you yourself quote. Apparently you would see this as a falsification, similar to your explanation that the Greek philosophers could only sacrifice their term of political freedom when they themselves became Roman slaves. It seems to us that the "thought of *kairos*" is slightly overdone in this case.

Ad chapter I: The argument against Nietzsche is formalistic and makes the factual question of (the) possibility of philosophical anthropology into pure nomenclature. If we really only call 'human' the one existing in class society, it is easy to design an anthropology that excludes everything else that would be different. Yet you use a static, naive logic that ridicules the factual history of humankind. You argue as if the terms were fixed forever per definition—like our teacher Cornelius—and as if there was no motion of the term, only movement within the defined terms. You own a belief in definitions (less from modern ontology and more from the homiletic tradition) that goes along much better with the common sense demand for clear and identically conserved terms than with philosophy. To put definitions at the beginning and argue and deduce norms from them is critical: the whole power of modern philosophy, even Descartes, Kant and Hegel stand against that. That your method forgets that is more telling about the restorative character of the whole concept than all theses. The defining-exegetical method that deals with a dogma, translates it into different words and interprets as one would do for a sermon. [7]

A thinking that like yours, prerequisites to discursively deduce the doctrine out of itself and which is proud of the radicalism in the question, cannot answer the question of the possibility of philosophical anthropology 'by a merely logical operation,' namely, through the choice of definition.

(283): It is not a matter of Marxist counter-position against ontology but it is a matter of knowledge that bourgeoise idealism at its height had already won. According to Hegel "concrete as well as spiritual/intellectual things are subjects of definitions"—and "human nature" surely belongs to that—"things with many features/characteristics." (*Logik*, ed. Glöckner II, 292 ff.). To know which of those characteristics is the essential one "it is necessary to realize in which relation they stand to each other, if one is already said by the other. To do this there does not exist another criterion except *being* itself.... The attestation that the identification of a thought or a singular of the immediate characteristics can make out the simple and defined nature of a thing can only be a *deduction* of such an identification out of the concrete nature" (292-293). It is exactly that "deduction," the actual work with the term, that you save yourself from by putting your definitions, like verses of the Bible, before the exegesis. Therefore, you lapse, despite the stress of the apparently fundamental of your declaration, into the criticism that Hegel had already passed on the definitory method: "defining abandons itself with definitions that would be the main principles of things, and satisfies itself with attributes, i.e. characteristics, that aim at being an *indication* for the external reflection and are indifferent to the substantiality of the thing. Such a singular and external determination is too inappropriate to the concrete totality and the nature of the notion, as that a concrete whole could find its real expression and designation in this determination on its own." (293-94). The definition of humanity as "finite freedom" (and you explicitly define the human like that because according to your understanding of the doctrine of humanity it is not allowed to superordinate a substrate from which it is defined is, methodically seen, as arbitrary and 'superficial' as the definition of the human by the specific characteristic of the tip of the ear that distinguishes him/her from all other animals and of which Hegel says that it "could be used as distinctive character in the definition of the physical human being" (294) not only to make fun of this scientific observance but also the empathic definitions in philosophy.

(284): The 'finite freedom' would only be an attribute, a specific difference and not even that for the sake of a non-binding generality: it is absolutely unsuitable to give an image of humanity's nature and that the doctrine of nature has to lapse into such acts of violence shows its own philosophical insufficiency: in the arbitrariness of the definition the arbitrariness of those 'plans' that phenomenology concocted comes to light. Hegel has anticipated the whole criticism of Husserl and Heidegger: "The content of the definition is taken from the immediate existence, and because it (the content) is immediate, it has no justification; ... by naming the term as immediate one abandons to comprehend it (the term).... However, since immediacy only emerges out of mediation, it therefore must return to mediation." (296). Yet, you make the mediated into a pure matter of immediacy. This is a form of action that is not too different of what politically happens if fascists claim the highly mediated society of late capitalism as the immediacy of the 'people.'

Nietzsche's doctrine of the superman is no *metabasis eis allo genos*, but a purely dialectical effort to simultaneously think the term of humanity in his/her identity and nonidentity. His doctrine was not as biological and naturalistic as the German university philosophy [*Universitätsphilosophie*] accused it of [9]. Basically he wanted to express that the reduction of humanity to its definition and its suppression is the same thing. However, in the sense of Hegel it would be as abstract to positively anticipate the image of the freed humanity within the definition. It is this double-impossibility, not the obstinate hatred towards metaphysics that excludes the possibility of a philosophical, positive anthropology.

It is surprising, how near your method takes you to the prevalent positivism, similar to the neo-Thomists, although we agree in the criticism of them. Every pragmatist would enthusiastically sign the phrase "It is the matter of logical decision of which characteristics we assert that they constitute a new genus" (12). You are much too shrewd to overlook the dubiousness of the definitory method. Yet you take a back seat by suspending the demand of truth at a central passage and make knowledge into a matter of expediency. By that your form of metaphysics becomes a compliment to the normal, 'natural' view of the world.

Your form of metaphysics crowns and glorifies the view of the world but does not dissolve it.

(285): One word to your distinction of humanity between up and down, angel and animal. It seems that this classification in the world of creatures comes to one conclusion: the principle that binds humanity as original sinner to that determination for one and all time is the same (principle) that lifts humanity out of nature. It is that unlimited repression that captures humanity by being practiced by him/her. Human dignity and disrespect fall together. That could already be shown with Kant but especially emerges in your writing through the transformation of Protestantism into an ontological 'plan.' If men would learn not to insist on the difference between themselves and animals, they would probably not need to humiliate themselves so much in front of angels.

To Marx: foremost is the sentence that humanity has to reproduce him/herself through material action, a statement about factual things which has nothing to do with the question of philosophical anthropology, [...] no Marxist axiom. The question of anthropology inhibits material activity or stands in no reasonable, theoretical relation to that sentence. In any case the argument is that ontology inhibits men, as such no statement about truth and possibility of ontology. The pragmatic problem of how to act on the basis of a given theory is neither decisive for Marx nor for philosophy. The question *cui bono*, which you—by the phrase "they state..."—put into the Marxists' mouths is rather distinct for the vulgar relativists of the group around Mannheim. However, this does not change the fact that established power benefits from the doctrine of the radically corrupted nature of humanity. If we socially/corporately said something against the term ontology, without entering the relation of the dialectic logic we discussed in reference to Hegel, we likely would represent the opinion that it is untrue to justify the knowledge of the world through the knowledge of humanity because this world is not the one of mankind, but an alienated, mediated, objective one and because every attempt to directly hear the human voice within the fossilized relations certifies society what it lacks.

(286): The Marxist criticism of ontology is the deduction of capitalistic society from the exchange in which men are only abstractly present as 'negativity,' as producers of goods or as wares. To reduce the world to anthropology means to look at it as if it was not a society of universal exchange, a society of wares.

The thought that ontology would be possible after a change of the social system—which Lukács sometimes represented—is also incompatible with the spirit of the theory. If there is something bourgeoise and anti-dialectical, it is the belief in an only-afterwards-relation in essential matters. The banal thought comes to one's mind that humanity "is not yet mature for socialism." You cannot reflect on humanity if finally in the future there is peace and harmony. But this rather denies the contemplative question of the nature of humanity. The thinking of the classless [11] society has to shake off the logic of this only-afterwards, the embodiment of sanity and reason and human's notion of time, or it remains in a bad sense traditionalistic.

Our distinct philosophical difference lies in the sentences: "And Marx could not talk permanently about the dehumanization in early capitalism without a vague picture of a really human society. They all have a doctrine of humanity." According to that, you need something 'positive' to be able to articulate the negation. But the only positive thing you 'have' is the given in its depravity beyond that our knowledge/realization cannot go other than by identifying the depravity through its immanent contradiction to the given. The positive is the negative and only the negative, the defined negation, is actually positive. What humanity is can only be said by what they are not. To presume a necessary positive means to deify the world. In the sense of dialectical logic dehumanization precedes the term of humanity. This term can only be won by the ongoing deeper insight into dehumanization, not by subtracting all 'dehumanized' from the static sum of qualities and carrying home the beggarly rest, 'the human being,' as eternal possession. The Barthians, as really paradoxical and dialectical Christians, seem to be nearer to truth than religious socialists and their 'fanaticism' is as little an argument against this as is the objection against Marxists of being "ignorant about the human beings with whom they had to work."

(287): Was that not exactly that De Man's objection against socialism? Is not a psychology which uncovers the objective insight into society and therefore the objective determination of the nature of men (they oppose to) the necessary complement to religious socialism's doctrine of invariance? [12] By putting the term far too idealistically your theory falls into the empirical state of humanity, created by the system on which you direct your main criticism.

You try to avoid those indicated difficulties by making humanity's history to the core piece of your anthropology. But that is [objectively seen] a trick. The nature of the human then would be that s/he changes. That means either to assume something distinct and static on which those changes are taking place and that is not named out of bashfulness. Or this nature is in its substance historical: then it dissolves (as nature). The source of error is not the particular way of defining the human and how you want to tie that up by dynamic sampling, but rather the philosophical method that always looks for the 'first,' no matter what is chosen as this first. "Having a history" is also no ontological quality of the human; there is nothing that belongs to the person "as such," and that is prescribed to the world. Having a history means to be involved in dialectics, into the subject-object relation. In other words, history is constituted, not by life as pure life of humanity, but by extra-humanization and alienation. To put it more simply, one could say that history is not a characteristic quality of the human but is rather the embodiment of suffering. Of course the human is aware of history, like you say on the bottom of page 12, and it would be foolish to deny the included distinctions. But one can neither 'cocoon' humanity out of knowledge nor out of "having a history." To know history and to have (a) history is not the same and on the bottom line of history, the suffering, knowledge has changed very little. On the other hand, having a history reaches far beyond consciousness and every part of nature, as a suffering one, has an eternal part in it. The phrase, by the means of knowledge the human simultaneously is within and above history, is in that [13] form, an illusion. The claim "humanity is free … from history in so far as he knows history" cannot be kept up, at least not unmediated.

(288): There are political groups that have a very distinct notion of the world's history and their own situation and they nevertheless, or particularly because of that, are doomed. You could not allege that they are 'free' from history if you wanted to say more than only something about their awareness, which would be, as we act on that assumption, tautological. Schopenhauer thought that animals were better off (in an ironic sense 'above history') because they do not know. The comfort that the knowledge about the negativity equals its neutralization, is the century-lasting assurance of philosophy, in which the critical dialectics do no longer trust. However, we only want to remind you of a phrase from a dialectical Christian, Pascal: "We, who are restricted in everything—why are we so little (restricted) in matters of suffering?" In that more is said about the relation between knowledge and history than in the formula above history, which now, exceptionally, seems to us too unbrokenly Hegel-like. The phrase "genuine history is recorded history" is exactly what separates us from Hegel. It concedes the given: what more is codified and in a certain sense 'known' history than the one approbated by all prevailing classes throughout centuries? We would say: genuine history is unrecorded history and by that would not, as Hegel countered, mean the arbitrary and the singular but the law that the unmeasured suffering under rule adds neglect/oblivion. Forgotten is the adaption of suffering by the rule(r).

The finally won definition, humanity was free, is however, objectively seen, a clever move to idealize and simultaneously keep anthropology free-floating. Then it is a metaphorical term, [14] which prerequisites the biological existence of humanity to make any sense but which is too noble to admit that and additionally believes to escape by that the reification of singular scientific regulations. The 'is' is only a pathetic circumscription without factually changing anything. So detached from existence, [*die ihm gerade als solche verfällt*], the overstrained determination becomes too weak to accomplish what it should. One has to think of Diogenes who threw a plucked cock into the Platonic academy because it fit the Platonic definition.

(289): 'Finite freedom' does not, or only implicitly, include everything possible which would lead to precisely that moment of existence that the ontological demand wants to exclude, because these empirical moments, in your opinion, presuppose the definition of humanity. Simultaneously, however, the definition tells too much: freedom cannot define humanity as being if that freedom, like in our society, does not exist. All that shows the impossibility of the method. In the thought of the 'description' of the structure of humanity, *i.e.* when unfolding the term, this is secretly admitted—however, the whole building would start to stagger if the work on such a 'description' started.

If you say (13) that humanity's nature is a criterion for our future society you put exactly the restricting function to your concept, which you denied (page 12) as a pure Marxist remark. Nietzsche, whom you basically accuse of logical 'squalidness,' did at least say that humanity was something that has to be overcome. In your case your insistence on the singular and somehow self-contained definition prohibits that qualitative transfer. Scheler's destiny is repeated, however, methodically smarter but with regard to content, due to caution/wariness, poorer. [15]

Ad chapter II: First of all, we revolt against the church entitled as 'vertically oriented,' it is, rather, 'horizontal business.' You were and are willing to accept the given. That you, due to your office, talk of truth, hope, and redemption does not prove that the theoretical and practical actions of church have anything to do with living these ideas. That religious socialism has to bridge the breakage between workers and church does not only insinuate a substantiality that church has lost long ago but grotesquely misjudges social weights. There is neither a higher theoretical and political concern to reconcile workers with church, nor can workers render the authority more than as a late and barely tolerated service within the games of power in our society.

(290): Behind the illusion of having to bring workers and church together stand gloomy images like the one of the 'materialistic desolation' of the working class. We have to think these images over, not to adopt them. The deformation, as far as it is true, derives from the order with which church holds together and not from the revolt against it. To ask the church for help is like putting the fox in charge of the henhouse. The church's interest in the working class is objectively seen (despite all personal good will) to neutralize them by 'absorption.' If philosophy's vital principle is to relate ideas and reality then the rule, not to look for relations where reality claims ideas as its property, becomes valid. If one identifies churches with the vertical orientation und the paradox term of history, one lapses into the particular glorification of existence, you put up a fight against it. (The political utopia does not coincide with the theological, the theocracy).

The term tragedy is a new motif in your thinking that you urge in your criticism of a utopia. Yet tragedy does not in vain belong to aesthetics. It is bound to the restriction of singular experiences and notions but does not cover the whole of history—this is worse but also [16] less distinct than tragic. Your construction completely agrees, maybe without your realization, with Hebbel's (and consequently with German *Neukantianismus*). But this was directed at drama. It belongs to the era of bourgeoise thinking when Hegel's philosophy, the definition of reality, has lost its power and only lived on in an as-if; Hegel, who renounced the concept of the whole (with reason) and brought the dialectic down to a kaleidoscope of historical images which only inherited the 'tragedy' of dialectic. However, Hebbel's drama failed: with such resignation history itself, which was a core piece of all his works, slipped through his fingers. Everyone becomes an illustration of the same, the 'tragic conflict' between finitude and infinity, always represented by two antagonistic epochs, no matter if one dealt with the breakup of the ancient world, the pagan-Germanic pre-world or, restricted by tradition, the middle class. The history of the world becomes what it looks like in the theatre, a pure costume. We are afraid that your theory of history will not do any better. The abstraction of all historical dialectic onto the tension between finiteness and endlessness makes history, against all insistence on humanity's historicity, to an eternal same, to a Danaids' work.

(291): In the terminology of one of our last works we would say: your notion of history has fallen back into mythology. The main blame takes the word-pair finite-infinite. They had their righteous place within the big speculation, as moments of the process in which they were concretized and neutralized. You, like Hebbel—and surely led by very earnest motives—fall back into the abstract, by being mistaken by the possibility to define reality as identical with intellect, against which the whole pathos of Hegel's system was directed. As a simple statement of facts it is arbitrary and empty to say of men hath he/she is finite or infinite or both. A transfer from such a philosophical residue to a political program is only possible over hill and dale. Politics is badly constituted by the doctrine [17] of humanity being finite and simultaneously infinite. A Lutheran old conservative would agree as well as an idealistic social democrat à la Natorp. You could almost argue that a concrete political determination only starts after dismissing the philosophical popular front. Terms like creative activity have always agreed with the doctrine of 'pantragismus' as well as Protestantism has united the call for infinite effort with the doctrine of futility. We would be responsible to raise awareness for that false method, but not to artificially hold (by transposition) an even more diluted and undogmatic word-pair alive. Even Hebbel was socially radical enough to pass the principle of tragedy, in its "un-reconciliation of finiteness and infiniteness," into the absolute, into the ground of the world: by that he has something from Schopenhauer. You, however, put the whole speculation about infinity into a spotless agreement with Christianity, suggesting that one should sublate with the idealists. By your process of dilution, you drove pantheism out of idealism as well as the set of believers out of religion and now it is without substance so that in the end it can be united with the bulkiest dogma. But sure enough it would go against the grain of every Protestant to name the divine curse that followed the fall of humanity as 'tragic.' Then on the one hand, one cheats the contemplative shaking of the head seeing the tragedy—'it's just too bad'—of which you speak, of the earnest;

(292): on the other hand is the positive religion, as far as it is order of salvation and promise of redemption, in its demand more than tragic. The fact of being unable to unite the tragic and the Christian point of view is another index for the impossibility to reconstruct/reconstitute Christianity.

Instead the doctrine of finite freedom goes along even better with the political reaction. You attack the utopia "because finite freedom in[18]cludes tragedy." That is exactly what you isolate yourself from at a different point: the barrier becomes the norm. Marx surely fought against utopias—maybe even more than was good. But he was against the utopia because he wanted it to become true and he had the evil eye for the powerlessness of setting the absolute aim, because the aim as such should be reached. You use the anti-utopian realism as instrument to cover up for class society. You say: "Christians and Marxists agree in the idea of an intermediary period between now and the ultimate fulfillment."

Now here, where you once rely on Marx, lies probably a weakness of Marxism that is related to the already shortly mentioned only-afterwards-problem. At least one can say that in today's objective situation the thought of a necessary transitional period to absolute-socialism contradicts the status of the substantial productive power so much that it almost sounds like an excuse for the constituted authority. After all, due to fairness, one has to say that even the most thoughtful of all Marxists, those who in fact were non, imagined the first phase much shorter than the Christians the time between the birth of Jesus and the *Parousia*, a period of time which covers the whole of temporality. If you, in regard to the Marxists, continue "but actually the transition soon becomes fixed and prevented from change by interests vested in it," that is worse than vertical patience. It cannot be accounted for to look with deep regret at the turn in Russia to then derive the denunciation from what once happened there. Obviously, the rehabilitation of priests is a proof for the freedom of humanity. If the world's history is, like the New Kantians say, an endless series of transitions and if we should work for another such transition but simultaneously defame the aim of that transition, one can only ask what the word socialism has to do in a world view like that. Socialism seems to belong to the [19] 'symbols' a culture cannot miss.

(293): One cannot earnestly assume that the 'feeling' of the endless significance of finite and hopeless acts can overcome the capitulation of the existent, as your theory claims. "To realize the infinite meaning a finite act may have" is a pure encouragement you hear at a funeral. Every relation to a qualitative content of history is erased. The only thing left of socialism is the word under which it is hastily buried like primitive cultures did with their victims who were slaughtered and then glorified.

It becomes frivolous when pastoral care takes possession of the political, which leaves its life. Because he does not die for an infinite relevance/meaning but for a finite aim. (If it does make any sense to talk of infiniteness in that context, this sense would have to be searched here). One should not abuse that absolutely most earnest thing, death without hope, which really sees through the *principium individationis*, as a means for an Advertising Christ Child [*Reklamechristkindchen*]. What would the author of the *Akkumulationsbuch* have said if he/she was engrossed as martyr for the same religious socialism of which delegates represented the opposite (to her/him) in every singular political question and of which ministers and bourgeoise servants of the *Nosketradition* arose? Would religious socialism really have the courage to tell the person he/she did not understand him/herself, that he/she was much more radical than he/she assumed and therefore much deeper? And what about that depth? Is depth not mutilated in the same moment as it struts? You only have to apply the term of risk to that person and to religious socialism to detect the perversion.

Ad chapter III: Like the universalists you oppositely hypostasize the category of the individual. It (the category) is through and through historical and especially in these days changes invasively. As true as your objection against personified collectivity is, the less it is "always the indivi[20]dual person who decides and acts." However, although you tend to give the idea of the individual too much, in reality you give it too less, as if it (the individual) has to be content with an installment for eternity. At first one should hardly be in command yet "politics can be one of the realms in which individual actualize creative freedom."

(294): Politics is either a resort of the culture business, namely as the institutional fight over power/authority, or its façade. If something fading, its politics like that. We are in charge to critically meet that whole resort, not to see it within the neutralized culture as another such part in which we, similar to erotic or sports, enjoy our lives. That would suit the racket of professional politicians. Or you understand politics as the effort to put an end to politics and the business it belongs to. Then, however, it (politics) is not a 'realm' in which you fulfill your creativity, but the embodiment of a fight for objective freedom. The term realm itself belongs to the organization of society against which true politics should be directed. As soon as politics are made to an area, it becomes the individual's enemy, although defined as a playground for them. The private question "Is political freedom in the sense of participation in political creativity necessary for everybody?" assumes politics as a 'job,' which is inextricably linked to a society not in charge of itself. Once you have defined politics as such it is easy to expound the problems of giving entrance to that resort to everyone and consistently leaving a backdoor ajar for the restriction of democratic rights. That such rights under a monopoly turn into the opposite has always been a reason for the monopoly to fully abolish them.

Repeatedly in your essay you take up critical moments against liberalism from the left and convert them until they function for the opposite as well. Page 17 includes particularly [21] many of them. You criticize the democratic procedure and call it attempt … to institutionalize the genuine demand for political self-determination, implied in humanity's essential freedom. Who is subject of such attempts? The world spirit? That would contradict your notion of transcendence. In reality democratic procedures are results of historical fights, which then, the more they became independent from the supporting power-relations, took on a more and more ideological character. To call them 'attempts' without saying who tried and discussing the success or failure dislocates the stress. By assessing the attempts and adding the questionable term of creative activity it becomes possible to oppose 'forms' to the democratic procedures, which differ from them in terms of immediacy. Behind that stands an intention of the real historical dialectic and its compulsion.

(295): The immediacy of the craftsman's place, the guild and the village's administration is not better but worse than the anonymity of social democracy. Surprisingly you find on the same level with those examples of that good immediacy the 'cell' next to the clan and the extended family. You give too much to formal sociology if you put the revolutionist to creativeness. The sentence that the overemphasis on a special democratic procedure may spell the doom of democracy is in the abstract right, connected with the praise of immediacy and the whole constellation in which it occurs in your context it sounds like a prelude of a new theory of elites. We cannot fight fascism by meeting it in core pieces of theory.

We see the same danger in your criticism of the term of equality. The definition of freedom by creative freedom is twisted: you only have to call it "*schöpferische Freiheit*" in German to get the inappropriateness. Terms from the intellectual environment of youthfully driven girls doing gymnastics [22], trying to express themselves because they have nothing to express, are used to formulate the term of equality, although it could be much more vividly experienced in the southern states. A critical motif is perverted into an apologetical one. We have said so many possible things against equality and meant by that the repressiveness of conformism; you turn this into a disguised tolerance of the existing inequality: the criticism of egalitarianism and equality "does not demand the chance for everybody to get everywhere." This is naively biased towards social categories. Because the term of chance, of which already Mannheim made a lot, cannot be separated from a competitive society and 'career.' Socialism does not want to inappropriately expand this but to abolish it. However, therefore it firstly needed to be, like a nonreligious socialist wrote in a today unpopular book, that the remaining functions of a state could be directed by a cleaning woman. Only if that becomes unmistakably clear the criticism on equality can be allowed. To restrict equality due to the finitude of human nature is obscurantism.

Substantially speaking: our criticism on the ideal of equality is directed at a state of richness, in which it would be repressive, to count beefsteaks

(296): of which everyone eats because everybody can anyway eat as much as they want, whereas others would not eat meat in such a situation. As long as the time has not come the vulgar-materialistic phrase of sharing is right. To demand an equality of chances exhausts socialism in the abolishment of school fees and the raising of the legacy tax. The monopoly feels well.

The hatred of security, which you join on page 18, is one basic part of the delusive outlawry of the bourgeois by the later bourgeoisie. This hatred is highly related to the belief in a catastrophe. The discovery of security in the world, that is better characterized by aircraft bombs than the Beveridge plan, uncovers the secret fear of the urgently near [23] possibility of socialism. In the past it was said that there was not enough caviar in the world for everyone; now that there is virtually enough they reassure that there is too much, so that they do not get him for eating. As if not in socialism too, as long as people get ill, have to die and exploit other creatures, existed barely enough insecurity.

You refer to Huxley's *Brave New World*. It has been our intention for a while to write something on that book and Jasper's *Geistige Situation der Zeit* (the philosophical commentary on it). Huxley is a clever man and has expanded, like hardly anyone else, the lines of the contemporary situation until they meet in the image of a negative utopia. Nevertheless, the basic tendency is wrong. He, like Nietzsche in his doctrine of the last person, in fact shouts: Catch the thief: he puts those traits on to socialism or the vague future society that are owed to the complete authority. At least he allows them to exist—therefore differentiates his image from socialism—by leaving the power of decree in the hands of the elite which conditions the people. It is the image of state's capitalism and it shows Huxley's insight when he leaves state's capitalism to swallow communism as 'ideology' and naming the sexual executive Lenina.

(297): On the other hand, Huxley's criticism of monopolism is, in a hidden sense, the individualistic one that embraces monopolism too easily. One is forced often enough to defend the monopole against the implicit laudation *temporis acti*—like in that main scene where Lenina tries to seduce the 'savage,' who should be a 'real' human being, whereby she unwillingly appears more likeable and he as a puritan Methodist. The bad thing about brave new world is not security but the authority that migrated into men themselves and created a fantasy of security because they apparently do not need the power structure any longer (however, in realty and in Huxley's world this structure forms the background).

That's the innermost meaning of Nietzsche's "No shepherd [24] and a herd." The animals of the herd come off, not because they no longer have a shepherd, but because they fully succeeded in internalizing the shepherd, the universal priesthood. Their finite freedom is actually 'broken.'

However security is dealt with, it is impossible to separate (not even by idea) the good existential fear from the bad purely capitalistic one. It is due to such arbitrary cuts—according to the trivial model eternal and only perishable—that we think of anthropology as misconduct. The so-called existential fear in Heidegger's sense is something highly modern. One could show that it is hardly earlier attested than in Poe, Kierkegaard, and Baudelaire. It likely reflects the absolute socialization which captures men so there is no other way out. Fear becomes *a priori* because within the closed system, fear is put before every single situation. This results in the feeling of the absolute 'thrownness.' The merely empirical fear of war and unemployment is in its nature identical with the alleged existential one und can only be separated by scholastic classification. The phrase "levels of anxiety" testifies against itself. Should one have 'sophisticated fear?'

You become radical in your criticism of social individualism. At that point you lead us into temptation of becoming conservative. Exactly these traits of a social individual, which you accuse of being contorted, are those, by which the individual within the individualistic society, however in vain, puts up a fight against it (the individualistic society). The collective ideal that is opposed to the "metaphysical loneliness or the aristocratic detachment from the concrete demands of the community" is exactly that brave new world you do not want to have anything to do with.

(298): What you scold about represents that which does not take part in the universal malevolence, the opposite to the universal shoulder slapping. It has more to do with truth [25] than all activity in the present forms of community. To us it is highly questionable if socialism should bring along a collectivistic "form of life." Today one produces individualistically and lives collectively. In socialism one produces collectively so that there is no more necessity for that indispensable repressive collectivism. We are not apt, like you, to sign "the destruction of many great traditions," in other words, dehumanization itself, out of being obsessively bound to socialism, in which by itself lies the willingness to deny it. But we are bourgeoise enough to expect from socialism to put exactly that tradition into reality and abolish today's collective humanity as well as the specific form 'mass.' By doing so we do not misjudge that the individual you condemn was created by the pressure of society. But within society, one stands in for the better.

Consequently, we cannot join in the half-praise of common sense conformism that you have adopted from Löwe. In that we see one of the most worrying signs: National Socialism did only somewhat quickly and insistently establish such conformism because time has not yet come on the continent. That is what you admit in the following. But then you should not attest that spirit anti-individualistic gains while it (the spirit), in the name of society, deliberately breaks the individual, what you would call, the thing that goes beyond the given situation. In other words, the relation between individual and society is dialectical through and through. You withdraw yourself from this dialectic by the means of synthesis that brings together opposites in their middle instead of defining one by the other. So that individualism is created that should be integrated within a collectivistic society. *Vestiga terrent.* May your *Deus absconditus* save us from every form of integration.

(299): It does not depend on the reconciliation between individual and society but on the question if along with society's emancipation every single [26] member of [that society] is emancipated. It makes us shiver that the "working individual" was the real human being of the future. Socialism has to reduce the social necessary work to a minimum. To make labor to the measurement of humanity is the principle of capitalism.

Los Angeles, February 16th, 1944

Bibliography

Primary Sources

Adorno, Theodor W. *The Adorno Reader*. Edited by Brian O'Connor. Oxford: Blackwell, 2000.

_____. *The Authoritarian Personality*. New York: Harper, 1950.

_____. *Can One Live After Auschwitz? A Philosophical Reader*. Edited by Rolf Tiedemann. Translated by Rodney Livingstone, et. al. Stanford: Stanford University Press, 2003.

_____. *Critical Models: Interventions and Catchwords*. Translated by Henry W. Pickford. New York: Columbia University Press, 2005.

_____. *The Culture Industry: Selected Essays in Mass Culture*. Edited by J. M. Bernstein. London: Routledge, 1991.

_____. *Gesammelte Schriften*. Herausgegeben von Rolf Tiedemann. Frankfurt a.M.: Suhrkamp Verlag, 1970-. In 23 Bände.

_____. *Hegel: Three Studies*. Translated by S. Nicholsen. Cambridge, MA: MIT Press, 1993.

_____. "Husserl and the Problem of Idealism." *The Journal of Philosophy* 37:1 (1940): 5-18.

_____. *Kierkegaard: Construction of the Aesthetic*. Translated and edited by Robert Hullot-Kentor. Minneapolis: University of Minnesota Press, 1989.

_____. *Lectures on Negative Dialectics: Fragments of a Lecture Course 1965-1966*. Edited by Rolf Tiedemann. Translated by Rodney Livingstone. Cambridge: Polity Press, 2008.

_____. *Minima Moralia: Reflections from Damaged Life*. Translated by E.F.N. Jephcott. New York: Verso, 2002.

_____. *Negative Dialectics*. Translated by E. B. Ashton. London: Routledge, 1973.

_____. "On Kierkegaard's Doctrine of Love." *Studies in Philosophy and Social Science* 8 (1939-40): 413-29.

_____. *Problems of Moral Philosophy*. Translated by Rodney Livingstone. Cambridge: Polity, 2000.

_____. *Quasi una Fantasia: Essays on Modern Music*. Translated by Rodney Livingstone. New York: Verso, 1992.

_____. "Theodor W. Adorno contra Paul Tillich: eine bisher unveröffentlichte Tillich-Kritik Adornos aus dem Jahre 1944," hrsg. von Erdmann Sturm. *Zeitschrift für neuere Theologiegeschichte* 3:2 (1996): 251-99.

_____. *Vorlesung über Negative Dialektik: Fragmente zur Vorlesung 1965-66*. Herausgegeben von Rolf Tiedemann. Frankfurt am Main: Suhrkamp Verlag, 2003.

Adorno, Theodor W. and Benjamin, Walter. *The Complete Correspondence 1928-1940.* Edited by Henri Lonitz. Translated by Nicholas Walker. Cambridge: Harvard University Press, 1999.

Adorno, Theodor W. und Benjamin, Walter. *Briefwechsel 1928-1940.* Herausgegeben von Henri Lonitz. Frankfurt am Main: Suhrkamp Verlag, 1994.

Adorno, Theodor W. und Kracauer, Siegfried. *Briefwechsel 1923-1966.* Herausgegeben von Wolfgang Schopf. Auch als *Adorno Briefe und Briefwechsel,* Band 7. Frankfurt am Main: Suhrkamp Verlag, 2008.

Benjamin, Walter. *Briefe, in zwei Bände.* Herausgegeben von Gershom Scholem und Theodor Adorno. Frankfurt am Main: Suhrkamp, 1978.

_____. *Illuminationen: Ausgewählte Schriften.* Frankfurt a.M.: Suhrkamp Verlag, 1961.

_____. *Illuminations: Essays and Reflections.* Edited by Hannah Arendt. Translated by Harry Zohn. New York: Schocken, 1985.

_____. *Zur Kritik der Gewalt und andere Aufsätze.* Frankfurt a.M.: Suhrkamp Verlag, 1971.

Heimann, Eduard. *Freedom and Order: Lessons from the War.* New York: Charles Scribner's Sons, 1947.

_____. *Reason and Faith in Modern Society: Liberalism, Marxism and Democracy.* Middletown: Wesleyan University Press, 1961.

_____. *Theologie der Geschichte: Ein Versuch.* Stuttgart: Kreuz-Verlag, 1966.

Horkheimer, Max. *Anfänge der Bürgerlichen Geschichtsphilosophie.* Stuttgart: W. Kohlhammer Verlag, 1930.

_____. *Between Philosophy and Social Science: Selected Early Writings.* Translated by G. Frederick Hunter, et. al. Cambridge: MIT Press, 1993.

_____. *Critical Theory: Selected Essays.* Translated by Matthew O'Connell, et. al. New York: Herder and Herder, 1968.

_____. *Critique of Instrumental Reason.* Translated by Matthew O'Connell, et. al. New York: Seabury Press, 1974.

_____. *Dawn and Decline: Notes 1926-1931 and 1950-1969.* Translated by Michael Shaw. New York: Seabury Press, 1978.

_____. *Dämmerung: Notizen in Deutschland.* Von Heinrich Regius. Zürich: Verlag Oprecht & Helbling, 1934.

_____. *Eclipse of Reason.* New York: Continuum, 1974.

_____. *Gesammelte Schriften.* Herausgegeben von Alfred Smith und Gunzelin Schmid Noerr. Frankfurt a.M.: S. Fischer Verlag, 1985-1996. In 19 Bände.

_____. "Die Juden und Europa." *Zeitschrift für Sozialforschung/Studies in Philosophy and Social Science* 8 (1941): 115-36.

_____. *Kritische Theorie: Eine Dokumentation.* Herausgegeben von Alfred Schmidt. Frankfurt am Main: S. Fischer, 1968. In 2 Bände.

_____. *A Life in Letters: Selected Correspondence.* Edited, translated and introduced by Manfred R. Jacobson and Evelyn M. Jacobson. Lincoln: University of Nebraska Press, 2007.

_____. *Die Sehnsucht nach dem ganz Anderen: ein Interview mit Kommentar von Helmut Gumnior.* Hamburg: Furche-Verlag, 1970.

_____. *Sozialphilosophische Studien; Aufsätze, Reden und Vorträge 1930-1972.* Herausgegeben von Werner Brede. Frankfurt am Main: Fischer Verlag, 1972.

_____. *Traditionelle und kritische Theorie: Vier Aufsätze.* Frankfurt am Main: Fischer Taschenbuch Verlag, 1970.

_____. "Vernunft und Selbsterhaltung." In *Walter Benjamin zum Gedächtnis*, hrsg. von Max Horkheimer und Theodor W. Adorno, 17-59. New York: Institute for Social Research, 1942.

_____. *Zur Kritik der Instrumentellen Vernunft: aus den Vorträgen und Aufzeichnungen seit Kriegsende.* Frankfurt am Main: Athenäum Fischer Taschenbuch Verlag, 1974.

Horkheimer, Max and Adorno, Theodor W. *Dialectic of Enlightenment: Philosophical Fragments.* Edited by Gunzelin Schmid Noerr. Translated by Edmund Jephcott. Stanford: Stanford University Press, 2002.

_____. Dialektik *der Aufklärung: Philosophische Fragmente.* Nachwort von Jürgen Habermas. Kelkheim: G. Schneider & Söhne, 1986.

_____. *Briefwechsel, 1927-1969. Theodor W. Adorno/Max Horkheimer.* Herausgegeben von Christoph Gödde und Henri Lonitz. Frankfurt am Main: Suhrkamp, 2003. In 4 Bände.

Horkheimer, Max, et. al. *Wirtschaft, Recht und Staat im Nationalsozialismus: Analysen des Instituts für Sozialforschung, 1939-1942.* Herausgegeben von Helmut Dubiel und Alfons Söllner. Frankfurt am Main: Suhrkamp, 1984.

Löwe, Adolf. *The Price of Liberty: A German on Contemporary Britain.* London: Hogarth Press, 1937.

Max Horkheimer in Selbstzeugnissen und Bilddokumenten. Dargestellt von Helmut Gumnior und Rudolf Ringguth. Reinbek bei Hamburg: Rowohlt Taschenbuch Verlag, 1973.

"Paul Tillich und Max Horkheimer im Dialog: drei bisher unveröffentlichte Texte (1942/45)," hrsg. von Erdmann Sturm. *Zeitschrift für neuere Theologiegeschichte* 1:2 (1994): 275-304.

Tillich, Paul. *Against the Third Reich: Paul Tillich's Wartime Radio Broadcasts into Nazi Germany.* Edited by Ronald H. Stone and Matthew Lon Weaver. Translated by Matthew Lon Weaver. Louisville: Westminster John Knox Press, 1998.

_____. *An meine deutschen Freunde: Politische Reden.* Stuttgart: Evangelisches Verlagswerk, 1973.

_____. *Biblical Religion and the Search for Ultimate Reality.* Chicago: University of Chicago Press, 1955.

_____. "The Christian and the Marxist View of Man." December 1935. Harvard University, Paul Tillich Archives.

_____. *Dynamics of Faith.* New York: Harper & Row, 1957.

_____. *Ergänzungs-und Nachlassbände zu den Gesammelten Werken von Paul Tillich.* Herausgegeben von Erdmann Sturm. Berlin: Walter de Gruyter, Stuttgart: Evangelisches Verlagswerk, 1971-. In 17 Bände.

_____. "Existential Philosophy." *Journal of the History of Ideas* 5:1 (1944): 44-70.

_____. *Frankfurter Vorlesungen 1930-1933.* Herausgegeben von Erdmann Sturm. Berlin: Walter de Gruyter, 2013.

_____. *Gesammelte Werke.* Herausgegeben von Renate Albrecht. Stuttgart: Evangelisches Verlagswerk, 1959-1975. In 14 Bände.

_____. *The Interpretation of History.* New York: Charles Scribner's Sons, 1936.

_____. "The Jewish Question: Christian and German Problem." *Jewish Social Studies* 33:4 (1971).

_____. *Love, Power, and Justice: Ontological Analyses and Ethical Applications.* New York: Oxford University Press, 1960.

_____. *Main Works/Haupt Werke.* Edited by Carl Heinz Ratschow. Berlin: De Gruyter, 1987-1998. In 6 volumes.

_____. *My Search for Absolutes.* New York: Simon & Schuster, 1984.

_____. *The New Being.* London: SCM Press, 1956.

_____. "Nietzsche and the Bourgeoise Sprit." *Journal of the History of Ideas* 6:3 (June 1945): 307-9.

_____. *On The Boundary: An Autobiographical Sketch.* New York: Charles Scribner's Sons, 1966.

_____. *Political Expectation.* Translated by Victor Nuovo. New York: Harper & Row, 1971.

_____. *The Protestant Era.* Edited and translated by James Luther Adams. Introduction by R.H. Daubney. London: Nisbet & Co., 1951.

_____. *Protestantisches Prinzip und proletarische Situation.* Bonn: Friedrich Cohen, 1931.

_____. "Religion and Secular Culture." *The Journal of Religion* 26:2 (April 1946): 79-86.

_____. *Religiöse Verwirklichung.* Berlin: Furche Verlag, 1930.

_____. *The Religious Situation.* Translated by H. Richard Niebuhr. New York: Henry Holt and Company, 1932.

_____. *Die religiöse Lage der Gegenwart.* Berlin: Ullstein, 1926.

_____. "The Right to Hope." *Neue Zeitschrift für Systematische Theologie* 7 (1965): 371-77.

_____. *The Shaking of the Foundations.* New York: Charles Scribner's Sons, 1948.

_____. *Die sozialistische Entscheidung.* Potsdam: A. Protte, 1933.

_____. *The Socialist Decision.* Translated by Franklin Sherman. New York: Harper & Row, 1977.

_____. *Systematic Theology in Three Volumes.* Chicago: University of Chicago Press, 1951-63.

_____. *Theology of Culture.* Edited by Robert C. Kimball. New York: Oxford University Press, 1964.

_____. *My Travel Diary: 1936, Between Two Worlds*. Edited by Jerald C. Brauer. Translated by Maria Pelikan. New York: Harper & Row, 1970.
_____. "Victory in Defeat: The Meaning of History in the Light of Christian Prophetism." *Interpretation* 6 (1952): 26.
_____. "What Is Wrong with the 'Dialectic' Theology?" *The Journal of Religion* 15:2 (April 1935): 127-45.
Zeitschrift für Sozialforschung / Studies in Philosophy and Social Science. Institute of Social Research. bd. 1-9 (1932-1941).

Secondary Sources

Abbott, Daniel Phillips. *Divine Participation and Eschatology in the Theodicies of Paul Tillich and Jürgen Moltmann*. Ph.D. dissertation: University of Virginia, 1987.
Abromeit, John. *Max Horkheimer and the Foundations of the Frankfurt School.* Cambridge: Cambridge University Press, 2011.
_____. *The Actuality of Adorno: Critical Essays on Adorno and the Postmodern*. Edited by Max Pensky. Albany: SUNY Press, 1997.
Adams, James Luther. *Paul Tillich's Philosophy of Culture, Science, and Religion.* New York: Schocken Books, 1970.
Adams, Nicholas. *Habermas and Theology.* Cambridge: Cambridge University Press, 2006.
Adorno: A Critical Reader. Edited by Nigel Gibson, et. al. Malden: Blackwell Publishers, 2002.
Agger, Ben. *The Discourse of Domination: From the Frankfurt School to Postmodernism.* Evanston: Northwestern University Press, 1992.
Albrecht, Renate Und Schüssler, Werner. *Schlüssel zum Werke von Paul Tillich: Textgeschichte und Bibliographie sowie Register zu den Gesammelten Werken, Gesammelte Werke, bd. 14*, zweite neubearb. und erweiterte Aufl. Berlin: W. de Gruyter, 1990.
_____. *Paul Tillich: sein Leben.* Frankfurt am Main: Peter Lang, 1993.
Alway, Joan. *Critical Theory and Political Possibilities: Conceptions of Emancipatory Politics in the Works of Adorno, Horkheimer, Marcuse and Habermas.* Westport: Greenwood Press, 1995.
Les Ambiguïtés de la Vie Selon Paul Tillich: Trovaux Issus du XXe Colloque International de L'association Paul Tillich D'expression Française. Ed. Marc Dumas, Jean Richard, and Bryan Wagoner. Berlin: de Gruyter, 2017.
Anderson, Ben. "'Transcending Without Transcendence:' Utopianism and an Ethos of Hope." *Antipode* 38:4 (2006): 691-710.
Asbach, Olaf. *Kritische Gesellschaftstheorie und historische Praxis: Entwicklungen der Kritischen Theorie bei Max Horkheimer 1930-1942/3.* Frankfurt am Main: Peter Lang, 1997.

Baehr, Peter. "The 'Iron Cage' and the 'Shell as Hard as Steel:' Parsons, Weber and the *stahlhartes Gehäuse* Metaphor in *The Protestant Ethic and the Spirit of Capitalism.*" *History and Theory* 40 (2001): 153-69.

The Barbarism of Reason: Max Weber and the Twilight of Enlightenment. Edited by Asher Horowitz and Terry Maley. Toronto: University of Toronto Press, 1994.

Baum, Gregory. "Paul Tillich on Socialism and Nationalism." *Studies in World Christianity* 2:1 (1996): 97-112.

Bauschulte, Manfred und Krech, Volkhard. "Saulus-Situationen: zum Verhältnis von Kritischer Theorie und Religiösem Sozialismus." In *Das Feld der Frankfurter Kultur und Sozialwissenschaften vor 1945.* Herausgegeben von Richard Faber und Eva-Maria Ziege, 49-62. Würzburg: Königshausen & Neumann, 2007.

Benhabib, Seyla. *Critique, Norm and Utopia: A Study of the Foundations of Critical Theory.* New York: Columbia University Press, 1986.

_____. *On Max Horkheimer: New Perspectives.* Edited by Seyla Benhabib, et. al. Cambridge: MIT Press, 1993.

Bernstein, J. M. *Adorno: Disenchantment and Ethics.* New York: Cambridge University Press, 2001.

Bloch, Ernst. *The Principle of Hope.* Translated by Neville Plaice, et. al. Cambridge: MIT Press, 1996. In 3 volumes.

_____. *Das Prinzip Hoffnung: in fünf Teilen.* Auch als Bloch *Gesamtausgabe* 5:1-5:2. Frankfurt am Main: Suhrkamp Verlag, 1959.

_____. *The Utopian Function of Art and Literature: Selected Essays.* Translated by Jack Zipes, et. al. Cambridge: MIT Press, 1988.

Brittain, Christopher Craig. *Adorno and Theology.* New York: T & T Clark, 2010.

Buchholz, René. *Zwischen Mythos und Bilderverbot: Die Philosophie Adornos als Anstoß zu einer kritischen Fundamental Theologie in Kontext der späten Moderne.* Frankfurt am Main: Peter Lang, 1991.

Buchwalter, Andrew. "Hegel, Adorno and the Concept of Transcendent Critique." In *The Frankfurt School: Critical Assessments*, vol. 3. Edited by Jay Bernstein, 173-97. New York: Routledge, 1994.

Buck-Morss, Susan. *The Origin of Negative Dialectics: Theodor W. Adorno, Walter Benjamin and the Frankfurt Institute.* Hassocks: Harvester Press, 1977.

Bush, Randall B. *Recent Ideas of Divine Conflict: The Influences of Psychological and Sociological Theories of Conflict upon the Trinitarian Theology of Paul Tillich and Jürgen Moltmann.* San Francisco: Mellen Research University Press, 1991.

The Cambridge Companion to Adorno. Edited by Tom Huhn. Cambridge: Cambridge University Press, 2004.

The Cambridge Companion to Critical Theory. Edited by Fred Rush. Cambridge: Cambridge University Press, 2004.

Carey, John J. *Paulus Then and Now: A Study of Paul Tillich's Theological World and the Continuing Relevance of his Work.* Macon: Mercer University Press, 2002.

Champion, James W. "Tillich and the Frankfurt School: Parallels and Differences in Prophetic Criticism." *Soundings* 69:4 (1986).

Christen und Nationalsozialisten: Darstellung und Dokumente. Herausgegeben von Georg Denzler und Volker Fabricus. Frankfurt am Main: Fischer Taschenbuch Verlag, 1993.

Christophersen, Alf. *Kairos: Protestantische Zeitdeutungskämpfe in der Weimarer Republik.* Tübingen: Mohr Siebeck, 2008.

Clary, Betsy Jane. "Lowe and Tillich on the Church and the Economic Order." In *Political Economics in Retrospect: Essays in Memory of Adolph Lowe*, 257-82. Edited by Harald Hegemann and Heinz D. Kurz. Northampton: Edward Elgar, 1998.

Claussen, Detlev. *Theodor W. Adorno: One Last Genius.* Translated by Rodney Livingstone. Cambridge: Harvard University Press, 2008.

Cohen, G. A. *Karl Marx's Theory of History: A Defense.* Princeton: Princeton University Press, 2001.

Colombo, Joseph. *An Essay on Theology and History.* Atlanta: Scholars Press, 1990.

The Essential Frankfurt School Reader. Edited by Andrew Arrato and Eike Gebhardt. New York: Continuum, 1982.

Connerton, Paul. *The Tragedy of Enlightenment: An Essay on the Frankfurt School.*New York: Cambridge University Press, 1980.

Cook, Deborah. "Adorno's Critical Materialism." *Philosophy & Social Criticism* 32:6 (2006): 719-37.

_____. "Adorno, Ideology and Ideology Critique." *Philosophy & Social Criticism* 27:1 (2001): 1-20.

Critical Theory and Society: A Reader. Edited by Stephen Eric Bronner and Douglas MacKay Kellner. New York: Routledge, 1989.

Dahms, Hans-Joachim. *Positivismusstreit: die Auseinandersetzungen der Frankfurter Schule mit dem logischen Positivismus, dem amerikanischen Pragmitismus und dem kritischen Rationalismus.* Frankfurt: Suhrkamp, 1994.

Davis, John Jefferson. *Paul Tillich and Religious Socialism: The Significance of the Early Socialist Writings for the Interpretation of his Late Thought.* Ph.D. dissertation: Duke University, 1975.

Deneen, Patrick J. *The Odyssey of Political Theory: The Politics of Departure and Return.* Lanham: Rowman & Littlefield, 2003.

DeVries, HENT. *Minimal Theologies: Critiques of Secular Reason in Adorno & Levinas.* Translated by Geoffrey Hale. Baltimore: Johns Hopkins University Press, 2005.

Dews, Peter. *The Limits of Disenchantment: Essays on Contemporary European Philosophy.* New York: Verso, 1995.

Dienstagsgespräche mit Zeitgenossen. Herausgegeben von Gerhard Rein. Stuttgart: Kreuz Verlag, 1976.

Donnelly, Brian. *The Socialist Émigré: Marxism and the Later Tillich.* Macon: Mercer University Press, 2003.

Dubiel, Helmut. *Theory and Politics: Studies in the Development of Critical Theory.* Translated by Benjamin Gregg. Cambridge: MIT Press, 1985.

Earley, Glenn David. *An 'Everlasting Conversation:' Judaism in the Life and Thought of Paul Tillich.* Ph.D. dissertation: Temple University, 1987.
The Early Frankfurt School and Religion. Edited by Margarete Kohlenbach and Raymond Geuss. New York: Palgrave Macmillan, 2005.
Enlightenment and Genocide: Contradictions in Modernity. Edited by James Kaye and Bo Strath. New York: Peter Lang, 2000.
Eriksen, Robert P. *Theologians Under Hitler: Gerhard Kittel, Paul Althaus and Emmanuel Hirsch.* New Haven: Yale University Press, 1985.
"Exilrufe nach Deutschland: Die Rundfunkreden von Thomas Mann, Paul Tillich und Johannes R. Becher 1940-1945," hrsg. von Winfried Halder. *Tillich-Studien, Beihefte* Nr. 3 (2002): 15ff.
Feenberg, Andrew. *The Philosophy of Praxis: Marx, Lukács and the Frankfurt School.* London: Verso, 2014.
Feige, Franz G. M. *The Varieties of Protestantism in Nazi Germany: Five Theopolitical Positions.* Lewiston : E. Mellen Press, 1990.
Ferreira, M. Jamie. *Love's Grateful Striving: A Commentary on Kierkegaard's* 'Works of Love.' New York: Oxford University Press, 2001.
Figal, Günter. "Selbsterhaltung und Selbstverzicht. Zur Kritik der neuzeitlichen Subjektivität bei Max Horkheimer und Walter Benjamin." *Zeitschrift für philosophische Forschung* 37:2 (1983): 161-79.
Finlayson, James Gordon. "Adorno on the Ethical and the Ineffable." *European Journal of Philosophy* 10:1 (2002): 1-25.
Flight of the Gods: Philosophical Perspectives on Negative Theology. Edited by Ilse N. Bulhof and Laurens Ten Kate. New York: Fordham University Press, 2000.
Foundations of the Frankfurt School of Social Research. Edited by Judith Marcus and Zoltán Tar. New Brunswick: Transaction Books, 1984.
The Frankfurt School: Critical Assessments. Edited by Jay Bernstein. New York: Routledge, 1994. In 5 volumes.
The Frankfurt School and Religion: Key Writings by the Major Figures. Edited by Eduardo Mendieta. New York: Routledge, 2005.
Friedman, George. *The Political Philosophy of the Frankfurt School.* Ithaca: CornellUniversity Press, 1981.
Gane, Nicholas. *Max Weber and Postmodern Theory: Rationalization Versus Re-Enchantment.* New York: Palgrave, 2002.
Gay, Peter. *Weimar Culture: The Outsider as Insider.* New York: Harper & Row, 1970.
Geertz, Clifford. *The Interpretation of Cultures.* New York: Basic Books, 1973.
Geras, Norman. *Marx and Human Nature: Refutation of a Legend.* New York: Verso, 1983.
Glöckner, Konrad. *Personsein als Telos der Schöpfung: Eine Darstellung der Theologie Paul Tillichs aus der Perspektive seines Verständnisses des Menschen als Person.* Münster: LIT Verlag, 2004.
Grabner-Haider, Anton und Strasser, Peter. *Hitlers mythische Religion: theologische Denklinien und NS-Ideologie.* Wien: Böhlau Verlag, 2007.

Grand Hotel Abgrund: Eine Photobiographie der Kritischen Theorie. Herausgegeben von Gunzelin Schmid Noerr und Willem van Reijen. Hamburg: Junius Verlag, 1988.

Habermas, Jürgen. *The Philosophical Discourse of Modernity*. Translated by Frederick G. Lawrence. Cambridge: MIT Press, 1991.

_____. *Religion and Rationality: Essays on Reason, God, and Modernity*. Edited by Eduardo Mendieta. Cambridge: MIT Press, 2002.

_____. *Theory of Communicative Action*, vol. 1. Translated by Thomas McCarthy. Cambridge: Polity Press, 1991.

Habermas, Jürgen, et.al. *An Awareness of What Is Missing: Faith and Reason in a Post-Secular Age*. Cambridge: Polity Press, 2010.

Habermas, Modernity, and Public Theology. Edited by Don S. Browning and Francis Schüssler Fiorenza. New York: Crossroad, 1992.

Hammond, Guyton B. *Conscience and its Recovery: from the Frankfurt School to Feminism*. Charlottesville: University of Virginia Press, 1993.

_____. *Man in Estrangement: A Comparison of the Thought of Paul Tillich and Erich Fromm*. Nashville: Vanderbilt University Press, 1965.

_____. "Patriarchy and the Protestant Conscience: A Critique." *Journal of Religious Ethics* 9:1 (1981): 84-102.

_____. "Tillich, Adorno, and the Debate about Existentialism." *Laval théologique et philosophique* 47:3 (1991): 343-55.

Handbook of Critical Theory. Edited by David Rasmussen. Oxford: Blackwell, 1996.

Harvey, David. Seventeen Contradictions and the End of Capitalism. Oxford: Oxford University Press, 2014.

Hegel, Georg Wilhelm Friedrich. *Lectures on the Philosophy of Religion, One Volume Edition. The Lectures of 1827*. Edited by Peter C. Hodgson. Berkeley: University of California Press, 1988.

_____. *Lectures on the Philosophy of World History: Introduction*. Translated by H. B. Nisbet. New York: Cambridge University Press, 1975.

_____. *Phänomenologie des Geistes*. Stuttgart: Philipp Reclam, 1987.

_____. *Phenomenology of Spirit*. Translated by A. V. Miller. New York: Oxford University Press, 1977.

_____. *Science of Logic*. Translated by A. V. Miller. Atlantic Highlands: Humanities Press International, 1989.

Held, David. *Introduction to Critical Theory: Horkheimer to Habermas*. Berkeley: University of California Press, 1980.

Herf, Jeffrey. *Reactionary Modernism: Technology, Culture, and Politics in Weimar and the Third Reich*. New York: Cambridge University Press, 1984.

Hesse, Heidrun. *Vernunft und Selbstbehauptung: Kritische Theorie als Kritik der neuzeitlichen Rationalität*. Frankfurt a. M.: Fischer Taschenbuch Verlag, 1984.

Hohendahl, Peter U. "The Dialectic of Enlightenment Revisited: Habermas' Critique of the Frankfurt School." *New German Critique* 35 (1985): 3-26.

Hohendahl, Peter Uwe. *Prismatic Thought: Theodor W. Adorno*. Lincoln: University of Nebraska Press, 1995.

Honneth, Axel. *The Critique of Power: Reflective Stages in a Critical Social Theory.* Translated by Kenneth Baynes. Cambridge: MIT Press, 1991.

_____. *The Fragmented World of the Social: Essays in Social and Political Philosophy.* Edited by Charles W. Wright. Albany: SUNY Press, 1995.

Hughes, John. "Unspeakable Utopia: Art and the Return to the Theological in the Marxism of Adorno and Horkheimer." *Cross Currents* 53:4 (2004): 475-92.

Hullot-Kentor, Robert. *Things Beyond Resemblance: Collected Essays on Theodor W. Adorno.* New York: Columbia University Press, 2006.

The Influence of the Frankfurt School on Contemporary Theology: Critical Theory and the Future of Religion. Edited by A. James Reimer. Lewiston: Edwin Mellen Press, 1992.

Jäger, Lorenz. *Adorno: A Political Biography.* Translated by Stewart Spencer. New Haven: Yale University Press, 2004.

Jay, Martin. *Adorno.* Cambridge: Harvard University Press, 1984.

_____. *The Dialectical Imagination: A History of the Frankfurt School and the Institute of Social Research 1923-1950.* Berkeley: University of California Press, 1996.

_____. "The Jews and the Frankfurt School," in *New German Critique* (1980), 137-49.

Joseph, Jonathan. *Social Theory: An Introduction.* New York: NYU Press, 2004.

_____. *Marxism and Social Theory.* New York: Palgrave MacMillan, 2006.

Kaufmann, David. "Beyond Use, Within Reason: Adorno, Benjamin and the Question of Theology." *New German Critique* 83 (2001): 151-73.

_____. "Correlations, Constellations and the Truth: Adorno's Ontology of Redemption." *Philosophy and Social Criticism* 26:5 (2000): 62-81.

Kellner, Douglas. *Critical Theory, Marxism and Modernity.* Cambridge: Polity Press, 1989.

Kelsey, David H. *The Fabric of Paul Tillich's Theology.* New Haven: Yale University Press, 1967.

Die Kirche und das dritte Reich: Fragen und Forderungen deutscher Theologen. Herausgegeben von Leopold Klotz. Gotha: Leopold Klotz Verlag, 1932.

Kolakowski, Leszek. *Main Currents of Marxism.* Oxford: Oxford University Press, 1978.

Kritische Theorie und Religion. Herausgegeben von Matthias Lutz-Bachmann. Würzburg: Echter, 1997.

Lau, Stephen Shek Lam. *Faith and the Human Condition: Paul Tillich's Politicization of Theology.* Ph.D. dissertation: Louvain, 1982.

Lee, Raymond L. M. "Weber, Re-Enchantment and Social Futures." *Time and Society* 19 (2010): 180-92.

Lewis, Pericles. "The 'True' Homer: Myth and Enlightenment in Vico, Horkheimer, and Adorno." *New Vico Studies* 10 (1992): 24-35.

Lewis, Thomas A. *Freedom and Tradition in Hegel: Reconsidering Anthropology, Ethics and Religion.* Notre Dame: University of Notre Dame Press, 2005.

Livingston, James C. and Fiorenza, Francis Schüssler. *Modern Christian Thought,* vol. 2. Minneapolis: Fortress Press, 2006.

Logical Positivism. Edited by A. J. Ayer. Glencoe: Free Press, 1959.

Löwith, Karl. *Max Weber and Karl Marx*. Edited by Tom Bottomore and William Outhwaite. London: Routledge, 1993.

Lukács, Georg. *History and Class Consciousness*. Cambridge: MIT Press, 1972.

_____. *Geschichte und Klassenbewusstsein: Studien über marxistische Dialektik*. Darmstadt: Hermann Luchterhand Verlag, 1981.

Lunn, Eugene. *Marxism and Modernism: An Historical Study of Lukács, Brecht, Benjamin, and Adorno*. Berkeley: University of California Press, 1982.

Macht und Gewalt: Annäherungen im Horizont des Denkens von Paul Tillich. Herausgegeben von Werner Schüssler und Erdmann Sturm. Münster: Lit Verlag, 2005.

Mali, Joseph. *The Rehabilitation of Myth: Vico's 'New Science.'* New York: Cambridge University Press, 1992.

Manent, Pierre. *The City of Man*. Translated by Marc A. Le Pain. Princeton: Princeton University Press, 1998.

Marck, Siegfried. *Die Dialektik in der Philosophie der Gegenwart, erster Halbband*.Tübingen: Mohr Siebeck, 1929.

Marsden, John. "Paul Tillich and the Theology of German Religious Socialism." *Political Theology* 10:1 (2009).

Martin, Bernard. *The Existentialist Theology of Paul Tillich*. New York: Bookman Associates, 1963.

_____. *Paul Tillich's Doctrine of Man*. Welwyn: James Nisbet and Co., 1966.

Martinson, Mattias. *Perseverance Without Doctrine: Adorno, Self-Critique, and the Ends of Academic Theology*. Frankfurt am Main: Peter Lang, 2000.

Marx, Karl. *Early Writings*. Translated by Rodney Livingston and Gregor Benton. New York: Vintage Books, 1975.

_____. *Selected Writings*. Edited by David McLellan. New York: Oxford University Press, 1977.

_____. *Das Kapital: Kritik der politischen Ökonomie*. Berlin: Gustav Kiepenheuer Verlag, 1932.

_____. *Das kommunistische Manifest* von 1848. Frankfurt/Main: Heinrich Reinhardt, 1946.

Marx, Karl with Friedrich Engels. *Collected Works*. Translated by Richard Dixon, et. al. New York: International Publishers, 1975-2004. In 50 volumes.

Marx, Karl und Friedrich Engels. *Gesamtausgabe*. Berlin: Dietz Verlag, 1982.

---------------- Werke. Berlin: Dietz Verlag, 1961.

Max Horkheimer Heute: Werk und Wirkung. Herausgegeben von Alfred Schmidt und Norbert Altwicker. Frankfurt a.M.: Fischer, 1986.

Mayer, J. P. *Max Weber and German Politics*. London: Faber & Faber, 1962.

McBride, Eugene James. *Messianic Time and German Politics Between the Wars (1919-1940): A Comparative Analysis of the Writings of Paul Tillich and Walter Benjamin*. Ph.D. Dissertation: Graduate Theological Union, 1985.

Meier, Kurt. *Der Evangelische Kirchenkampf in drei Bänden*. Göttingen: Vandenhoeck & Ruprecht, 1984.

_____. *Theologischen Fakultäten im dritten Reich.* Berlin: Walter de Gruyter, 1996.

Migdal, Ulrike. *Die Frühgeschichte des Frankfurter Instituts für Sozialforschung.* Frankfurt a. M.: Campus, 1981.

Milbank, John. *The Religious Dimension in the Thought of Giambattista Vico.* Lewiston: E. Mellen Press, 1992. In 2 volumes.

Miller, Jared A. "Phenomenology's Negative Dialectic: Adorno's Critique of Husserl's Epistemological Foundationalism." *Philosophical Forum* 40:1 (2009): 99-125.

Mosse, George L. *The Crisis of German Ideology: Intellectual Origins of the Third Reich* New York: Schocken Books, 1981.

Müller-Doohm, Stefan. *Adorno: A Biography.* Translated by Rodney Livingston. Cambridge: Polity Press, 2005.

Murphy, John W. "Paul Tillich and Western Marxism." *American Journal of Theology and Philosophy* 5:1 (1984): 13-24.

Negativity and Revolution: Adorno and Political Activism. Edited by John Holloway, et. al. London: Pluto Press, 2009.

New Critical Theory: Essays on Liberation. Edited by William S. Wilkerson and Jeffrey Paris. Lanham: Rowman & Littlefield, 2001.

New Essays on the Frankfurt School of Critical Theory. Edited by Alfred J. Drake. Newcastle upon Tyne: Cambridge Scholars Publishing, 2009.

Nietzsche, Friedrich. *The Gay Science.* Translated by Thomas Common. Digireads, 2009.

_____. *The Gay Science: With a Prelude in German Rhymes and an Appendix of Songs.* Translated by Josefine Nauckhoff. Cambridge University Press, 2003.

O'Keefe, Terrence. "Tillich and the Frankfurt School." In *Theonomy and Autonomy: Studies in Paul Tillich's Engagement with Modern Culture*, ed. by John J. Carey, 67-88. Macon: Mercer University Press, 1984.

_____. "Paul Tillich's Marxism." *Social Research* 48:3 (1981).

O'Neill, John and Uebel, Thomas. "Horkheimer and Neurath: Restarting a Disrupted Debate." *European Journal of Philosophy* 12:1 (2004): 75-105.

On Critical Theory. Edited by John O'Neill. Lanham: University Press of America, 1989.

Ott, Michael R. *Max Horkheimer's Critical Theory of Religion: The Meaning of Religion in the Struggle from Human Emancipation.* Lanham: University Press of America, 2001.

Papastephanou, Marianna. "Ulysses' Reason, Nobody's Fault: Reason, Subjectivity and the Critique of Enlightenment." *Philosophy and Social Criticism* 26:6 (2000): 47-59.

Paris, Jeffrey. "Obstinate Critique and the Possibility of the Future." In *New Critical Theory: Essays on Liberation.* Edited by William S. Wilkerson and Jeffrey Paris, 15-36. Lanham: Rowman & Littlefield, 2001.

Pauck, Wilhelm and Pauck, Marion. *Paul Tillich: His Life and Thought,* vol. 1: Life. New York: Harper & Row, 1976.

Paul Tillich: A New Catholic Assessment. Edited by Raymond F. Bulman and Frederick J. Parrella. Collegeville: Liturgical Press, 1994.

Paul Tillich im Exil. Herausgegeben von Christian Danz und Werner Schüßler. Berlin: De Gruyter, 2017.

Paul Tillich: Theologian of the Boundaries. Edited by Mark K. Taylor. San Francisco: Collins, 1987.

Peccora, Vincent P. "Nietzsche, Genealogy, Critical Theory." *New German Critique* 53 (1991) : 104-30.

Pellicani, Luciano. *The Genesis of Capitalism and the Origins of Modernity*. Translatedby James G. Colbert. New York: Telos, 1994.

Pensky, Max. "Natural History: The Life and Afterlife of a Concept in Adorno." *Critical Horizons* 5:1 (2004): 227-58.

Pritchard, Elizabeth. "*Bilderverbot* Meets Body in Theodor W. Adorno's Inverse Theology." *Harvard Theological Review* 95:3 (2002): 291-318.

Pinkard, Terry. *Hegel's Phenomenology: The Sociality of Reason*. New York: Cambridge University Press, 1996.

_____. *Hegel: A Biography*. New York: Cambridge University Press, 2000.

Pippin, Robert. *Hegel's Idealism: The Satisfaction of Self-Consciousness*. Cambridge: Cambridge University Press, 1989.

_____. *Idealism as Modernism: Hegelian Variations*. Cambridge: Cambridge University Press, 1997.

Plamenatz, John. *Karl Marx's Philosophy of Man*. Oxford: Clarendon, 1975.

Pritchard, Elizabeth Ann. *Renouncing Knowledge for the Sake of Ethics: Negative Theology and Enlightenment in Theodor W. Adorno*. Ph.D. dissertation: Harvard University, 1999.

The Problems of Modernity: Adorno and Benjamin. Edited by Andrew Benjamin. New York: Routledge, 1989.

Rabinbach, Anson. *In the Shadow of Catastrophe: German Intellectuals Between Apocalypse and Enlightenment*. Berkeley: University of California Press, 1997.

Recki, Birgit. "The Metaphysics of Critique: On the Relationship Between Metaphysics and Experience in Max Horkheimer and Theodor W. Adorno." Translated by Nicholas Walker. In *Theodor W. Adorno: Critical Evaluations in Cultural Theory*. Edited by Simon Jarvis. New York: Routledge, 2007.

Reed, Esther D. *A Theological Reading of Hegel's Phenomenology of Spirit, with Particular Reference to its Themes of Identity, Alienation and Community: Salvation in a Social Context*. Lewiston, NY: Mellen University Press, 1996.

Reichmann, Eva G. "Max Horkheimer the Jew: Critical Theory and Beyond." *The Leo Baeck Institute Yearbook* 19:1 (1974): 181-95.

Reimer, A. James. *The Emmanuel Hirsch and Paul Tillich Debate: A Study in the Political Ramifications of Theology*. Lewiston: Edwin Mellen Press, 1989.

_____. *Paul Tillich: Theologian of Nature, Culture and Politics*. Münster: LIT Verlag, 2004.

Rethinking the Frankfurt School: Alternative Legacies of Cultural Critique. Edited by Jeffrey T. Nealon and Caren Irr. Albany: SUNY Press, 2002.

Rosen, Zvi. *Max Horkheimer.* München: C. H. Beck, 1995.
_____. "Max Horkheimer: über die gesellschaftliche Rolle des Judaismus." In *Kritische Theorie und Religion.* Herausgegeben von Matthias Lutz-Bachmann. Würzburg: Echter, 1997.
Sayer, Derek. *Capitalism and Modernity: An Excursus on Marx and Weber.* London: Routledge, 1991.
Scharf, Uwe Carsten. *The Paradoxical Breakthrough of Revelation: Interpreting the Divine-Human Interplay in Paul Tillich's Work, 1913-1964.* New York: De Gruyter, 1999.
Scharlemann, Robert P. *Religion and Reflection: Essays on Paul Tillich's Theology.* Edited by Erdmann Sturm. Münster: LIT Verlag, 2004.
_____. "Totality: A Philosophical and Theological Problem Between Tillich and the Frankfurt School." *Laval théologique et philosophique* 47:3 (1991): 329-41.
Schecter, Darrow. *The Critique of Instrumental Reason from Weber to Habermas.* New York: Continuum, 2010.
Scheuerman, William E. *Frankfurt School Perspectives on Globalization, Democracy and the Law.* New York: Routledge, 2008.
Schmidt, Amos. *Materialismus zwischen Metaphysik und Positivismus: Max Horkheimers Frühwerk, Darstellung und Kritik.* Opladen: Westdeutscher Verlag, 1993.
Schmidt, James. "Language, Mythology, and Enlightenment: Historical Notes on Horkheimer and Adorno's *Dialectic of Enlightenment.*" *Social Research* 65:4 (1998): 807-38.
_____. "Genocide and the Limits of Enlightenment: Adorno and Horkheimer Reconsidered." In *Enlightenment and Genocide: Contradictions in Modernity.* Edited by James Kaye and Bo Strath. New York: Peter Lang, 2000.
Scholem, Gershom. *On Jews and Judaism in Crisis.* New York: Schocken, 1976.
Schultz, Karla L. *Mimesis on the Move: Theodor W. Adorno's Concept of Imitation.* New York: Peter Lang, 1990.
Schweppenhäuser, Gerhard. *Ethik nach Auschwitz: Adornos negativ Moralphilosophie.* Hamburg: Argument, 1993.
Schoolman, Morton. "Avoiding 'Embarrassment:' Aesthetic Reason and Aporetic Critique in *Dialectic of Enlightenment.*" *Polity* 37:3 (2005): 335-64.
Scharlemann, Robert P. "Totality: A Philosophical and Theological Problem Between Tillich and the Frankfurt School." *Laval théologique et philosophique* 47:3 (1991): 329-41.
The Semblance of Subjectivity: Essays in Adorno's Aesthetic Theory. Edited by Tom Huhn and Lambert Zuidervaart. Cambridge: MIT Press, 1997.
Shaw, Brian J. "Reason, Nostalgia, and Eschatology in the Critical Theory of Max Horkheimer." *The Journal of Politics* 47:1 (1985): 160-81.
Sherman, David. "Adorno's Kierkegaardian Debt." In *Theodor W. Adorno,* vol. 1: 51-80. London: SAGE Publications, 2004).
Sherratt, Yvonne. *Adorno's Positive Dialectic.* New York: Cambridge University Press, 2002.

Siebert, Rudolf J. *The Critical Theory of Religion: The Frankfurt School, From Universal Pragmatic to Political Theology.* Amsterdam: Mouton Publishers, 1985.

_____. *From Critical Theory to Critical Political Theology: Personal Autonomy and Universal Solidarity.* New York: Peter Lang, 1994.

_____. *Horkheimer's Critical Sociology of Religion: The Relative and the Transcendent.* Washington: University Press of America, 1979.

Simmel, Georg. *The Problems of the Philosophy of History: An Epistemological Essay.* Translated and edited by Guy Oakes. New York: Free Press, 1977.

Simpson, Gary M. *Critical Social Theory: Prophetic Reason, Civil Society, and Christian Imagination.* Minneapolis: Fortress Press, 2002.

Singer, Peter. *Hegel.* New York: Oxford University Press, 1983.

Sombart, Werner. *Deutsche Sozialismus.* Charlottenburg: Bucholz und Weisswange, 1934.

_____. *The Jews and Modern Capitalism.* Translated by M. Epstein. New Brunswick: Transaction Books, 1982.

Der Spannungsboden: Festgabe für Paul Tillich zum 75. Geburtstag. Herausgegeben von Karl Hennig. Stuttgart: Evangelisches Verlagswerk, 1961.

Spurensuche: Lebens- und Denkwege Paul Tillichs. Herausgegeben von Ilona Yord und Yorick Spiegel. Münster: LIT Verlag, 1999.

Stein, Eva. *Subjektive Vernunft und Antisemitismus bei Horkheimer und Adorno.* Oldenburg: Universität Oldenburg, 2002.

Stenger, Mary Ann and Stone, Ronald H. *Dialogues of Paul Tillich.* Macon: Mercer University Press, 2002.

Stirk, Peter M. R. *Max Horkheimer: A New Interpretation.* Lanham: Barnes & Noble Books, 1992.

Stone, Ronald. "Tillich: Radical Political Theologian." *Religion in Life* 46 (1977); 44-53.

_____. "Tillich's Critical Use of Marx and Freud in the Social Context of the Frankfort School." *Union Seminary Quarterly Review* 33 (1977).

Stone, Ronald H. *Paul Tillich's Radical Social Thought.* Atlanta: John Knox, 1980.

Stroup, John. "Political Theology and Secularization Theory in Germany, 1918-1939: Emmanuel Hirsch as a Phenomenon of his Time." *Harvard Theological Review* 80:3 (1987): 321-68.

Stumme, John R. *Socialism in Theological Perspective: a Study of Paul Tillich, 1918-1933.* Missoula: Scholars Press, 1978.

Sünker, Heinz. "Foundations of Critical Theory: On the History of the Frankfurt School." *International Sociology* 22:2 (2007): 129-37.

Tassone, Giuseppe. "The Politics of Metaphysics: Adorno and Bloch on Utopia and Immortality." *European Legacy* (2004): 357-67.

Taylor, Charles. *Hegel.* New York: Cambridge University Press, 1977.

Theodor Adorno. Edited by James Schmidt. Burlington: Ashgate, 2007.

Theodor W. Adorno. Edited by Gerard Delanty. London: SAGE Publications, 2004. In 4 volumes.

Theodor W. Adorno: Critical Evaluations in Cultural Theory. Edited by Simon Jarvis. New York: Routledge, 2007. In 4 volumes.

Theologie als Religionsphilosophie: Studien zu den problemgeschichtlichen und systematischen Voraussetzungen der Theologie Paul Tillichs. Herausgegeben von Christian Danz. Wien: LIT Verlag, 2004.

The Theological Paradox/Das theologische Paradox: Interdisciplinary Reflections on the Centre of Paul Tillich's Thought/Interdisziplinäre Reflexionen zur Mitte von Paul Tillichs Denken. Edited by Gert Hummel. Berlin: Walter de Gruyter, 1995.

The Theology of Paul Tillich. Edited by Charles W. Kegley. New York: Pilgrim Press, 1982.

Theonomy and Autonomy: Studies in Paul Tillich's Engagement with Modern Culture. Edited by John J. Carey. Macon: Mercer University Press, 1984.

Tillar, Elizabeth K. "*The Influence of Social Critical Theory on Edward Schillebeeckx's Theology of Suffering for Others*." *The Heythrop Journal* 42 (2001): 148-72.

Varon, Jeremy. "The Dreadful Concatenation: Modernity and Massacre in Todorov, Adorno and Horkheimer." *New German Critique* 59 (1993): 155-92.

Vico, Giambattista. *The New Science of Giambattista Vico*. Translated by Thomas Goddard Bergin and Max Harold Fisch. Ithaca: Cornell University Press, 1948.

Vogt, Stefan. *Nationaler Sozialismus und soziale Demokratie: die sozialdemokratische Junge Recht 1918—1945*. Bonn: Dietz, 2006.

"Von der Gerechtigkeit der Wahrheit: der ontologische Gottesbeweis bei T. W. Adorno mit einem Blick auf die Theologie Karl Barths." *Neue Zeitschrift für Systematische Theologie und Religionsphilosophie* 37:2 (1995): 144-64.

Weber, Max. *The Protestant Ethic and the Spirit of Capitalism*. Translated by Talcott Parsons. New York: Scribner, 1958.

_____. *The Protestant Ethic and the 'Spirit' of Capitalism and Other Writings*. Translated by Peter Baehr and Gordon C. Wells. New York: Penguin Books, 2002.

_____. *Die protestantische Ethik: Eine Aufsatzsammlung*. München: Siebenstern Taschenbuch Verlag, 1965.

The Weimar Republic Sourcebook. Edited by Anton Kaes, Martin Jay and Edward Dimendberg. Berkeley: University of California Press, 1994.

Wellmer, Albrecht. *Endgames: The Irreconcilable Nature of Modernity, Essays and Lectures*. Translated by David Midgley. Cambridge: MIT Press, 1998.

_____. *The Persistence of Modernity*. Translated by David Midgley. Cambridge; MIT Press, 1991.

Werk und Wirken Paul Tillichs: Ein Gedenkbuch. Stuttgart: Evangelisches Verlagswerk, 1967.

What is Enlightenment? Eighteenth Century Answers and Twentieth Century Questions. Edited by James Schmidt. Berkeley: University of California Press, 1996.

Wheatland, Thomas. *The Frankfurt School in Exile*. Minneapolis: University of Minnesota Press, 2009.

Wheeler, Brett R. "Antisemitism as Distorted Politics: Adorno on the Public Sphere." *Jewish Social Studies* NS 7:2 (2001): 114-48.

White, Stephen K. *Sustaining Affirmation: The Strengths of Weak Ontology in Political Theory.* Princeton: Princeton University Press, 2000.

Whitebook, Joel. "Fantasy and Critique: Some Thoughts on Freud and the Frankfurt School." In *Handbook of Critical Theory.* Edited by David Rasmussen, 287-304. Oxford: Blackwell, 1996.

Wiggershaus, Rolf. *The Frankfurt School: Its History, Theories, and Political Significance.* Cambridge: MIT Press, 1994.

_____. *Max Horkheimer zur Einführung.* Hamburg: Junius Verlag, 1998.

Wirtschaft, Recht und Staat im Nationalsozialismus: Analysen des Instituts für Sozialforschung 1939-1942. Herausgegeben von Helmut Dubiel und Alfons Söllner. Frankfurt am Main: Europäische Verlagsanstalt, 1981.

Wolin, Richard. *Labyrinths: Explorations in the Critical History of Ideas.* Amherst: University of Massachusetts Press, 1995.

_____. *The Frankfurt School Revisited: and Other Essays on Politics and Society.* New York, Routledge, 2006.

_____. *The Seduction of Unreason: The Intellectual Romance with Fascism from Nietzsche to Postmodernism.* Princeton: Princeton University Press, 2004.

_____. *The Terms of Cultural Criticism: The Frankfurt School, Existentialism, Poststructuralism.* New York: Columbia University Press, 1992.

Wood, Allen W. *Karl Marx.* New York: Routledge, 2004.

Wright, J. R. C. *'Above Parties': The Political Attitudes of the German Protestant Church Leadership 1918-1933.* New York: Oxford University Press, 1974.

Zahrnt, Heinz. *The Question of God; Protestant Theology in the Twentieth Century.* Translated by R. A. Wilson. New York: Harcourt, Brace & World, 1969.

Zeige, Eva-Maria. *Antisemitismus und Gesellschoftstherorie: die Frankfurter Schule im amerikanischen Exil.* Frankfurt am Main: Suhrkamp, 2009.

Zuidervaart, Lambert. *Adorno's Aesthetic Theory: The Redemption of Illusion.* Cambridge: MIT Press, 1991.

_____. *Social Philosophy After Adorno.* New York: Cambridge University Press, 2007.

_____. "Theodor W. Adorno." *The Stanford Encyclopedia of Philosophy (Summer 2011 Edition).* Edited by Edward N. Zalta. URL: <http://plato.stanford.edu/archives/sum2011/entries/adorno/>.

Index